THE SACRED BOOKS OF THE EAST

F. MAX MULLER (ED.)

LIST OF THE 50 VOLUMES

1. Upanishads.
2. Sacred Laws of Aryas.
3. Texts of Confucianism.
4. Zend-Avesta.
5. Pahlavi Texts.
6. Qur'an.
7. Institutes of Vishnu.
8. Bhagavadgita, & c.
9. Qur'an.
10. (i) Dhammapada.
10. (ii) Sutta-Nipata.
11. Buddhist Suttas.
12. Satapatha-Brahmana.
13. Vinaya Texts.
14. Sacred Laws of Aryas.
15. Upanishads.
16. Texts of Confucianism.
17. Vinaya Texts.
18. Pahlavi Texts.
19. Fo-sho-hing-tsanking.
20. Vinaya Texts.
21. Saddharma Pundarika.
22. Gaina-Sutras.
23. Zend-Avesta.
24. Pahlavi Texts.
25. Laws of Manu.
26. Satapatha-Brahmana.
27. Texts of Confucianism (Li Ki).
28. Texts of Confucianism (Li Ki).
29. Grihya-Sutras.
30 Grihya-Sutras.
31. Zend-Avesta.
32. Vedic Hymns.
33. Minor Law-Books.
34. Vedanta-Sutras.
35. Milinda.
36. Milinda.
37. Pahlavi Texts.
38. Vedanta-Sutras.
39. Texts of Taoism
40. Texts of Taoism
41. Satapatha-Brahmana
42. Atharva-veda.
43. Satapatha-Brahmana.
44. Satapatha-Brahmana.
45. Gaina-Sutras.
46. Vedic Hymns.
47. Pahlavi Texts.
48. Vedanta-Sutras.
49. (i) Buddhakarita.
49. (ii) Mahayana Texts.
50. A General Index

The Sacred Books of the East, Vol. 14

THE SACRED LAWS OF THE ARYAS

AS TAUGHT IN THE SCHOOLS OF APASTAMBA, GAUTAMA, VASISHTHA, AND BAUDHAYANA

Edited by

F. MAX MULLER

Translated by

GEORG BUHLER

PART II

VASISHTHA AND BAUDHAYANA

GYAN

Published by

Gyan Publishing House
5, Ansari Road
Daryaganj, New Delhi-110002
Phone: 011-47034999, 9811692060
E-mail: books@gyanbooks.com

Distribution Network
gyanbooks.com
India, USA, Canada, UK, Australia, France

ISBN : 978-81-212-2937-1 (Set)
ISBN : 978-81-212-2876-3 (PB)
First Published, 1882

2nd Impression 2021

Printed at: Gyan Press, Delhi.

The Sacred Books of the East, Vol. 14

The Sacred Laws of the Aryas, Part-II
Edited by: F. Max Muller, Translated by: Georg Buhler

THE

SACRED LAWS OF THE ÂRYAS

AS TAUGHT IN THE SCHOOLS OF

ÂPASTAMBA, GAUTAMA, VÂSISH*TH*A, AND BAUDHÂYANA

TRANSLATED BY

GEORG BÜHLER

PART II

VASISH*TH*A AND BAUDHÂYANA

Oxford

AT THE CLARENDON PRESS

1882

CONTENTS.

BAUDHÂYANA DHARMAŚÂSTRA.

INTRODUCTION

TO

VASISH*TH*A.

THE Vâsish*th*a Dharma*s*âstra is, like that of Gautama, the last remnant of the Sûtras of a Vedic school, which, as far as our knowledge goes at present, has perished, together with the greater part of its writings. We owe the preservation of its Dharma-sûtra probably to the special law schools of India, which, attracted as it would seem by its title and the legend connecting it with Vasish*th*a Maitrâvaru*n*i, one of the most famous *Ri*shis of the Rig-veda and a redoubtable champion of Brâhmanism, made it one of their standard authorities. The early existence of a legend according to which the Vâsish*th*a Dharma-sûtra was considered either to be a work composed by the *Ri*shi Vasish*th*a, or at least to contain the sum of his teaching on the duty of man, is indicated by several passages of the work itself. For the Dharma-sûtra names Vasish*th*a, or appeals to his authority on no less than three occasions. First, we find a rule on lawful interest, which is emphatically ascribed to Vasish*th*a[1]. 'Learn the interest for a money lender,' the Sûtra says, 'declared by the word of Vasish*th*a; five mâshas (may be taken) for twenty (kârshâpa*n*as every month).' Again, at the end of a long string of rules[2] which contain the observances to be kept by sinners who undergo K*rikkh*ra penances, Vasish*th*a's name is brought forward as the authority for them, and the last words are, 'Thus speaks the divine Vasish*th*a.' Finally, the concluding Sûtra of the whole work[3] gives

---

[1] Vâsish*th*a Dharma*s*âstra II, 51.

[2] Vâsish*th*a Dharma*s*âstra XXIV, 5.

[3] Vâsish*th*a Dharma*s*âstra XXX, 11. Similar invocations of teachers at the end of Sûtras occur frequently, e.g. Â*s*valâyana *S*rauta-sûtra XII, 15, 14; Rig-vidhâna V, 3, 4; Yâska, Nirukta, Roth, p. 216.

expression to the devotion felt by the author for the *Ri*shi, 'Adoration to Vasish*th*a, *S*atayâtu, the son of Mitra and Varu*n*a and of Urva*s*î.' The epithets used in this last passage conclusively show that the Vasish*th*a after whom the Dharma-sûtra is named, is the individual who, according to the Brâhmanical tradition, is the *Ri*shi of a large portion of the seventh Ma*nd*ala of the Rig-veda and the progenitor of the Vâsish*th*a clan of Brâhmans, and who in some hymns of the Rig-veda appears as the purohita or domestic priest of king Sudâs and the rival of Vi*s*vâmitra, and in other Sûktas as a half mythical being. For the verses Rig-veda VII, 33, 11–14 trace the origin of this Vasish*th*a to the two sons of Aditi, Mitra and Varu*n*a, and to the Apsaras Urva*s*î, and contain the outline of the curious, but disgusting story of his marvellous birth, which Sâya*n*a narrates more circumstantially in the commentary on verse 11. Moreover, the word *S*atayâtu, which in the Dharma-sûtra is used as an epithet of Vasish*th*a, occurs Rig-veda VII, 18, 21 in close connexion with the *Ri*shi's name. Sâya*n*a explains it in his commentary on the latter passage as 'the destroyer of many demons,' or, 'he whom many demons seek to destroy,' and takes it as an epithet of the sage Parâ*s*ara, who is named together with Vasish*th*a. It would, however, seem that, if the verse is construed on strictly philological principles, neither Sâya*n*a's interpretation, nor that suggested by the Dharma-sûtra can be accepted, and that *S*atayâtu has to be taken as a proper name[1]. But, however that may be, it is not doubtful that we may safely infer from the expressions used in the last sentence of the Dharma-sûtra, that the Vasish*th*a to whom the invocation is addressed and the composition of the work is ascribed, either immediately or through the medium of pupils, is the individual named in the Rig-veda. The connexion of the Dharma-sûtra with one of the *Ri*shis of the Rig-veda which is thus established, possesses a particular interest and importance, because it corroborates the statement of Govindasvâmin, the commentator of Baudhâyana, that the Institutes of Vasish*th*a were

[1] See Petersburg Dictionary, s. v. satayâtu.

originally studied by and authoritative for the Bahv*rik*as, the *Rig*vedins alone, and afterwards became an authority for all Brâhmans[1]. In the introduction to Gautama it has been shown that a similar assertion which Govinda makes with regard to the Gautama Dharma-sûtra can be corroborated by a considerable amount of external and internal evidence. It has been pointed out that not only the fact that the spiritual pedigrees of the *Kh*andoga schools enumerate several Gautamas, but also the partiality for texts of the Sâma-veda, which the Institutes of Gautama show on several occasions, strongly support the tradition that the Gautamîya Dharma*s*âstra originally was the exclusive property of a school of Sâmavedins. In the case of the Vâsish*th*a Dharma*s*âstra indications of the latter kind are, if not entirely wanting, at least very faint. The number of Vedic passages quoted is, no doubt, large; but few among them belong to the class of Mantras which are recited during the performance of g*ri*hya rites, and must be taken from the particular recension of the Veda to which the performer belongs. Besides, the texts of this description which actually occur, do not bear the mark of a particular Veda or *S*âkhâ. The numerous texts, on the other hand, which are quoted in support or explanation of the rules, are taken impartially from all the three ancient Vedas. For this reason it would be dangerous to use the references to a dozen *Rik*as in chapters XVII and XXVI, as well as to the legend of *S*una*h*sepa, which is told only in works belonging to the Rig-

[1] See Sacred Books of the East, vol. ii, p. xlix, note 2. As Govindasvâmin's statements possess a considerable importance, I give here the whole commentary on Baudhâyana I, 1, 2, 6, according to my two MSS., C. I. and C. T.: ननु किमिति व्यवस्था यावता मूलश्रुतिरेपामविशेषेण कल्प्यते यथा होलिकादीनां यथा वा बोधायनीयं धर्मशास्त्रं कैश्चिदेव पठ्यमानं सर्वाधिकारं भवति तथा गोतमीयगोभिलीये छन्दोगैरेव पठ्येते [पठ्यंते C. I.; पठ्यते C. T.] वासिष्ठं तु बह्वृचैः [।] सथ च सर्वाधिकाराणि [।] यथा वा गृह्यशास्त्राणि सर्वाधिकाराणि तद्वदनुपनीतेन सह भोजनादीन्यपि समानानि [असमानि C. I.; असानि C. T.] भवन्तीत्याशङ्क्याह ॥ तत्र तत्र देशप्रामाण्यमेव स्यात् ॥६॥ एवं व्यवस्थितविषयैव मूलश्रुतिः । किं त्विमामनुपपत्तिं न कल्पयतीत्यभिप्रायः । तस्माद् व्यवस्थितविषयमेवानुष्ठानं तद्वर्जनं च ॥

veda, as a proof that the Vâsish*th*a Dharma*s*âstra is the work of a *Ri*gvedin. Under these circumstances the three passages, mentioning Vasish*th*a's name, and especially the last which identifies him with the *Ri*shi of the Rig-veda, have a particularly great importance, as they are the only pieces of internal evidence which can be brought forward in favour of Govindasvâmin's valuable statement. But the latter is, even without any further corroboration, credible enough, because no reason is apparent why Govinda should have invented such a story, and because his assertion fully agrees with the well-established facts known about the other existing Dharma-sûtras, which all were composed not for the benefit of the Âryans in general, but in order to regulate the conduct of particular sections of the Brâhmanical community.

There is, however, one point in Govindasvâmin's statement which requires further elucidation. He says that the Bahv*rik*as, i.e. the *Ri*gvedins in general, formerly studied the Vâsish*th*a Dharma*s*âstra. It might, therefore, be inferred that the work possessed equal authority among the Â*s*valâyanîyas, the *S*âṅkhâyanîyas, the Mâ*nd*ûkâyanas, and all the other schools of the Rig-veda, and that it belonged to the most ancient heirlooms of its adherents. That is, however, improbable for several reasons. For, first, neither the Â*s*valâyanîyas nor the *S*âṅkhâyanîyas of the present day study or attach any special importance to the Vâsish*th*a Dharma*s*âstra. Secondly, if the Vâsish*th*a Dharma*s*âstra had ever been the common authority on Dharma in all the different schools of the Rig-veda, it would be necessary to ascribe to it an antiquity which it clearly does not possess. All Sûtras were originally composed for a single school only. Where we find that the same Sûtra is adopted by several *K*ara*n*as, as is the case with the Dharma-sûtra, which both the Âpastambîyas and the Haira*n*yake*s*as study, and with the *K*ayana-sûtra, which the Bhâradvâ*g*as and the Haira*n*yake*s*as have in common, it is evident that the later school did not care to compose a treatise of its own on a certain subject, but preferred to take over the composition of an earlier teacher. If, now, a Sûtra on a certain subject were acknowledged by all the schools of one Veda, it would follow that it must belong to the most ancient books of that Veda, and must have been adopted successively by all its later schools. In such a case the Sûtra must certainly show signs of its great antiquity. But if we look for the latter in the Vâsish*th*a Dharma-sûtra, the trouble will be in vain. Though that work contains a good deal that is archaic, yet, as will be shown presently, its numerous quotations from Vedic writings and older Dharma-sûtras clearly prove that it does not belong to the oldest productions of its class, but takes even among the still existing Institutes of the Sacred Law only a secondary rank. Under these circumstances the correct interpretation of Govindasvâmin's words will be, that according to the Brâhmanical tradition, known to him, some school of *Ri*gvedins, the name of which he did not know, or did not care to give, originally possessed the Vâsish*th*a Dharma*s*âstra as its exclusive property, and that the work later, through the action of the special law schools, acquired general authority for all Brâhmans. It is a pity that no authentic information regarding the name of that school of *Ri*gvedins has been handed down. But, considering the fact that Vedic schools are frequently named after Vedic *Ri*shis, it seems not improbable that it was called after the Vasish*th*a whose authority the Dharma-sûtra invokes, and that we may assume the former existence of a Vâsish*th*a school, a Sûtra-*k*ara*n*a, of the Rig-veda [1], founded perhaps by a teacher of the Vâsish*th*a gotra. This conjecture, which, it must be confessed, is not supported by any corroborative evidence from the Brâhmanical tradition, will explain why the title-pages of this and of the first part speak of a school of Vâsish*th*a.

The position of the Vâsish*th*a Dharma-sûtra in Vedic literature can be defined, to a certain extent, by an analysis

[1] A school of Vâsish*th*as, belonging to the Sâma-veda, certainly existed in ancient times. I have formerly put forward a conjecture that the Vâsish*th*a Dharma*s*âstra might belong to that school (Digest of Hindu Law Cases, p. xxii, first edition). But Govindasvâmin's explicit statement makes it evident that it has to be abandoned.

of its numerous quotations from the Samhitâs, Brâhmanas, and the older Sûtras. By this means it will become evident that the work belongs to a period when the chief schools of the three ancient Vedas had been formed and some of the still existing Dharma-sûtras had been composed. Faint indications will be found which make it probable that the home of the school to which it belonged, lay in the northern half of India, north of the Narmadâ and of the Vindhyas. As regards the quotations from the Sruti, the revealed texts of the Hindus, they are chiefly taken from the Rig-veda and from three recensions of the Yagur-veda. Passages from the Rig-veda-samhitâ are quoted IV, 21; XVII, 3–4; and XXVI, 5–7. With respect to the quotations in the latter chapter it must, however, be noted that its genuineness is, as will be shown in the sequel, not above suspicion. A Brâhmana of the Rig-veda seems to be referred to in XVII, 2, 32, 35. But the extracts, given there, agree only in part with the text of the Aitareya, and it is probable that they are taken from some lost composition of the same class. A curious Sûtra, II, 35, shows a great resemblance to the explanations of Vedic passages given by Yâska in the Nirukta[1]. The passage points either to a connexion of the author with the school of the Nairuktas or, at least, to an acquaintance with its principles. Among the schools of the Yagur-veda, that of the Kathas is twice referred to by name, XII, 29; XXX, 5. But Professor Weber, who kindly looked for the quotations in the Berlin MS. of the Kâthaka, has not been able to find them. A third passage, I, 37, said to be taken from the Kâturmâsyas, i.e. the portion of a Samhitâ which treats of the Kâturmâsya sacrifices, actually occurs in the Kâthaka. But, as it is likewise found in the Kâturmâsya-kânda of the Maitrâyanîyas, it must remain uncertain from which of the two recensions of the Black Yagur-veda it has been quoted. The chapter on the duties of women, vers. 6–8, contains a

[1] This resemblance has not escaped Krishnapandita, who says in his commentary, निरुक्तमप्यस्य मन्त्रस्य दर्शयति ॥ लाङ्गलमित्यादि ॥ श्रुत्यनुक्तमपि निरुक्तकृत्संगृह्णाति ॥

long quotation which, in spite of some small discrepancies, seems to have been taken from the Taittirîya-samhitâ of the Black Yagur-veda. Passages of the Taittirîya Âranyaka are quoted or referred to X, 35 and XXIII, 23. The White Yagur-veda is mentioned several times as the Vâgasaneyi-sâkhâ or the Vâgasaneyaka. The former expression occurs III, 19 and XXIII, 13. The quotations, marked as taken from the Vâgasaneyaka, XII, 31, XIV, 46 are found in the Satapatha-brâhmana, and another passage of the same work is quoted I, 45, without a specification of the source. A very clear proof that the author of the Dharma-sûtra knew the Vâgasaneyi-samhitâ is furnished by the Mantra, given II, 34. The text, quoted there, occurs in three different Sâkhâs, that of the Vâgasaneyins, that of the Taittirîyas and the Atharva-veda, and in each shows a few variae lectiones. Its wording in the Vâgasaneyi-samhitâ literally agrees with the version, given in the Sûtra. The Sâma-veda is referred to III, 19, and particular Sâmans are mentioned in the borrowed chapter XXII, 9. A passage from the Nidâna, probably a work on Stomas and metres, which belonged to the Bhâllavins, an ancient school of Sâmavedins, occurs I, 14–16. An Upanishad, connected with the Atharva-veda, the Atharvasiras, is mentioned in the borrowed chapter XXII, 9, and the existence of the Atharva-veda is pre-supposed, also, by 'the vows called Siras,' which are alluded to in the suspicious chapter XXVI, 11, and are said to be peculiar to the Atharvavedins[1]. The chapters, which are undoubtedly genuine, contain no allusion to the fourth Veda.

As regards the older works on Dharma, the author of the Institutes of Vasishtha certainly knew and used a treatise, attributed to Yama, the Dharma-sûtras of Manu, Hârîta and Gautama, and perhaps that of Baudhâyana. With respect to two verses, which, as the Sûtra says, were proclaimed by Pragâpati, XIV, 24, 30, it is somewhat doubtful, if it is meant that they have been taken from a work, attributed to Pragâpati, or that they are merely utterances, supposed to have been made by that deity for the benefit

[1] See Baudhâyana Dharma-sûtra II, 8, 14, 2, note.

of mankind. The latter view seems, however, the more likely one, as it is customary in the Smritis to ascribe the revelation of social institutions, ceremonies, and penances to Pragâpati, who, in the older works, occupies much the same position as Brahmâ, the creator, in the later religious systems. It is not impossible that some of the references to Yama, e.g. XI, 20, have to be explained in the same manner. But other passages, attributed to Yama, e.g. XVIII, 13–16, seem to have been taken from a work which was considered the production of the Dharmarâga. Of course, none of the Yamasmritis, which exist in the present day, can be meant. The quotations from Manu are numerous [1]. They have all been taken from a book attributed to a Manu, and possess a very high interest for the history of the present metrical Manusmriti. For the prose passage from the Mânava, given IV, 5, furnishes the proof that the author of the Vâsishtha Dharmasâstra quotes from a Dharma-sûtra attributed to a Manu, while other quotations show that the Mânava Dharma-sûtra contained, also, verses, some of which, e.g. XIX, 37, were Trishtubhs, and that a large proportion of these verses has been embodied in Bhrigu's version of the Manusmriti. Fifteen years ago [2] I first called attention to Vasishtha's prose quotation from the Mânava, and pointed out that, if the MSS. of the Vâsishtha Dharmasâstra were to be trusted, a small piece of the lost Mânava Dharma-sûtra, on which the present Manusmriti is based, had been found. The incorrectness and the defective state of the materials which I then had at my disposal did not allow me to go further. Since that time several, comparatively speaking, good MSS. of the Institutes of Vasishtha and many inferior ones have been found, and all, at least all those which I have examined, give the quotation in prose exactly in the same form. The fact that Vasishtha gives, in IV, 5, a prose quotation from Manu may, therefore, be considered as certain [3]. Moreover several of the best MSS.

[1] They occur Vâsishtha Dharmasâstra I, 17; III, 2; IV, 5–8; XI, 23; XII, 16; XIII, 16; XIX, 37; XX, 18; XXIII, 43; XXVI, 8.

[2] Digest of Hindu Law Cases, p. xxxi, note, first edition.

[3] Such, I suppose, will be the opinion of all European scholars. Those Hindus

show, by adding the particle 'iti' at the end of Sûtra 8, that the quotation from the Mânava is not finished with Sûtra 5, but includes the two verses given in Sûtras 6 and 7 and the second prose passage in Sûtra 8. Among the verses the first is found entire in the metrical Manusm*ri*ti, and the second has likewise a representative in that work, though its concluding portion has been altered in such a manner that the permission to slaughter animals at sacrifices has been converted into an absolute prohibition to take animal life. Sûtra 8, which again is in prose, has no counterpart in the metrical Manusm*ri*ti, as might be expected from its allowing 'a full-grown ox' or 'a full-grown he-goat' to be killed in honour of a distinguished Brâhma*n*a or Kshatriya guest. A closely corresponding passage is found in the *S*atapatha-brâhma*n*a, and a verse expressing the same opinion in the Yâ*gñ*avalkya Sm*ri*ti, the versification of a Dharma-sûtra of the White Ya*g*ur-veda. As the last part of the quotation resembles the text of the Brâhma*n*a and its language is very archaic, it is quite possible that, though belonging to the passage from the Mânava-sûtra, it contains a Vedic text, taken from some hitherto unknown Brâhma*n*a which Manu adduced in support of his opinion. On this supposition the arrangement of the whole quotation would be as follows. Sûtra 5 would give the original rule of the author of the Mânava in an aphoristic form; Sûtras 6–7 would repeat the same opinion in verse, the latter being probably *S*lokas current among the Brâhmanical community; and Sûtra 8 would give the Vedic authority for the preceding sentences. This arrangement would be in strict conformity with the plan usually followed by the authors of Dharma-sûtras. But whether Sûtra 8 contains a second original aphorism of the Mânava Dharma-sûtra or a Vedic passage, it seems indisputable that the author of the Vâsish*th*a Dharma-sûtra knew a treatise attributed to a teacher called Manu, which, like all other Dharma-sûtras, was partly written in apho-

who allow their religious convictions to get the better of their reason, will perhaps prefer K*ri*sh*n*apa*nd*ita's ingenious, but unsound explanation of the words iti mânavam, by iti manumatam, 'such is the opinion of Manu.'

ristic prose and partly in verse. The passage furnishes, therefore, the proof for Professor Max Müller's conjecture that our metrical Manusm*ri*ti, like all the older works of the same class, is based on the Dharma-sûtra of a Vedic Sûtra-*k*ara*n*a. In connexion with this subject it may be mentioned that the Institutes of Vasish*th*a contain, besides the above-mentioned passages, no less than thirty-nine verses[1], which are not marked as quotations, but occur in Bh*ri*gu's metrical Manusa*m*hitâ. Some of them present more or less important variae lectiones. Moreover, there are four verses which, though Vasish*th*a attributes them to Hârîta and Yama[2], are included in our Manusm*ri*ti and treated as utterances of the father of mankind. The bearing of both these facts on the history of the Manusm*ri*ti is obvious. But the frequency of the references to or quotations from Manu which Vasish*th*a makes, teaches another important lesson. Like the fact that Manu is the only individual author to whom Gautama refers[3], it shows that in ancient times Manu's name had as great a charm for the Brâhman teachers as it has for those of the present day, and that the old Mânava Dharma-sûtra was one of the leading works on the subject, or, perhaps, even held that dominant position which the metrical Manusm*ri*ti actually occupied in the Middle Ages and theoretically occupies in our days. It is interesting to observe that precisely the same inference can be drawn from the early Sanskrit inscriptions. If these speak of individual authors of Sm*ri*tis, they invariably place Manu's name first[4].

Vasish*th*a gives only one quotation from Hârîta, II, 6. Hârîta was one of the ancient Sûtrakâras of the Black Yagur-veda, who is known also to Baudhâyana. From a passage which K*ri*sh*n*apa*nd*ita quotes in elucidation of

[1] Vâsish*th*a Dharmasâstra I, 22; II, 3, 10, 27, 48; III, 5, 11, 60; V, 2; VI, 6, 8, 11, 13, 19; VIII, 7, 15; X, 21–22; XI, 27–28, 32, 35; XIII, 48; XIV, 13, 16, 18; XVI, 18, 33-34; XVII, 5, 8; XVIII, 14, 15; XIX, 48; XX, 18; XXV, 4-5, 7; XXVII, 3.

[2] Vâsish*th*a Dharmasâstra II, 6; XVIII, 14-15; XIX, 48.

[3] Sacred Books of the East, vol. ii, p. lvii.

[4] See e.g. the grant of Dhruvasena I, dated Sa*m*vat, i.e. Guptasa*m*vat 207, Pl. i, l. 7; Ind. Ant., vol. iv, p. 105.

Vasish*th*a XXIV, 6, I conclude that Hârîta was a Maitrâya*n*îya[1]. The relation of the Vâsish*th*a Dharma-sûtra to Gautama and Baudhâyana has already been discussed in the introduction to the translation of the former work[2]. To the remarks on its connexion with Baudhâyana it must be added that the third Pra*s*na of the Baudhâyana Dharma-sûtra, from which Vasish*th*a's twenty-second chapter seems to have been borrowed, perhaps does not belong to the original work, but is a later, though presumably a very ancient, addition to the composition of the founder of the Baudhâyana school. The reasons for this opinion will be given below. If Baudhâyana's third Pra*s*na is not genuine, but has been added by a later teacher of that school, the interval between Baudhâyana and the author of the Vâsish*th*a Dharma-*s*âstra must be a very considerable one. I have, however, to point out that the inference regarding the priority of Baudhâyana to Vasish*th*a is permissible only on the supposition that Vasish*th*a's twenty-second chapter is not a later addition to the latter work, and that, though it is found in all our MSS., this fact is not sufficient to silence all doubts which might be raised with respect to its genuineness; for we shall see presently that other chapters in the section on penances have been tampered with by a later hand. It will, therefore, be advisable not to insist too strongly on the certainty of the conclusion that Vasish*th*a knew and used Baudhâyana's work.

In the introduction to his translation of the Vish*n*usm*ri*ti[3], Professor Jolly has pointed out two passages of Vasish*th*a which, as he thinks, have been borrowed from Vish*n*u, and prove the posteriority of the Vâsish*th*a Dharma*s*âstra, if not to the Vish*n*usm*ri*ti, at least to its original, the Kâ*th*aka Dharma-sûtra. He contends that the passage Vasish*th*a XXVIII, 10–15 is a versification of the Sûtras of Vish*n*u LVI, which, besides being clumsy, shows a number of

[1] He says: तथा च हारीतः। तदेतद्ब्राह्मणः पुत्राय [°णो नापुत्राय?] नाशिष्याय नासमाम्निकाय नासंवत्सरोषिताय नाविदितकुलशीलाचाराय दद्यादित्याह भगवानयोनिजो रश्मिसंभवो मित्रयुतो [?] मैत्रायणिरिति ॥

[2] Sacred Books of the East, vol. ii, pp. liii-lv.

[3] Sacred Books of the East, vol. vii, p. xviii.

corruptions and grammatical mistakes, and that Vasishtha XXVIII, 18–22 has been borrowed from Vishnu LXXXVII. Professor Jolly's assertion regarding the second passage involves, however, a little mistake. For the first two Slokas, Vasishtha XXVIII, 18–19, describe not the gift of the skin of a black antelope, which is mentioned in the first six Sûtras of Vishnu LXXXVII, but the rite of feeding Brâhmans with honey and sesamum grains, which occurs Vishnu XC, 10. The three verses, Vasishtha XXVIII, 20–22, on the other hand, really are the same as those given by Vishnu LXXXVII, 8–10. It is, however, expressly stated in the Vishnusmriti that they contain a quotation, and are not the original composition of the author of the Dharma-sûtra. Hence no inference can be drawn from the recurrence of the same stanzas in the Vâsishtha Dharma-sûtra. As regards the other passage, Vasishtha XXVIII, 10–15, Professor Jolly is quite right in saying that it is a clumsy versification of Vishnu's Sûtras, and it is not at all improbable that Vasishtha's verses may have been immediately derived from the Kâthaka. The further inference as to the priority of the ancient Kâthaka-sûtra to Vasishtha, which Professor Jolly draws from the comparison of the two passages, would also be unimpeachable, if the genuineness of Vasishtha's twenty-eighth chapter were certain. But that is unfortunately not the case. Not only that chapter, but the preceding ones, XXV–XXVII, in fact the whole section on secret penances, are, in my opinion, not only suspicious, but certainly betray the hand of a later restorer and corrector. Everybody who carefully reads the Sanskrit text of the Dharma-sûtra will be struck by the change of the style and the difference in the language which the four chapters on secret penances show, as compared with the preceding and following sections. Throughout the whole of the first twenty-four chapters and in the last two chapters we find a mixture of prose and verse. With one exception in the sixth chapter, where thirty-one verses form the beginning of the section on the rule of conduct, the author follows always one and the same plan in arranging his materials. His own rules are given first in the form of aphorisms, and after these follow the authorities for his doctrines, which consist either of Vedic passages or of verses, the latter being partly quotations taken from individual authors or works, partly specimens of the versified maxims current among the Brâhmans, and sometimes memorial verses composed by the author himself. But chapters XXV–XXVIII contain not a single Sûtra. They are made up entirely of Anush*t*ubh *S*lokas, and the phrases[1] 'I will now declare,' 'Listen to my words,' which are so characteristic of the style of the later metrical Sm*ri*tis and of the Purâ*n*as, occur more frequently than is absolutely necessary. Again, in the first twenty-four and the last two chapters the language is archaic Sanskrit, interspersed here and there with Vedic anomalous forms. But in the four chapters on secret penances we have the common Sanskrit of the metrical Sm*ri*tis and Purâ*n*as, with its incorrect forms, adopted in order to fit inconvenient words into the metre. Nor is this all. The contents of a portion of this suspicious section are merely useless repetitions of matters dealt with already in the preceding chapters, while some verses contain fragmentary rules on a subject which is treated more fully further on. Thus the description of the K*rikkh*ra and *K*ândrâya*n*a penances, which has been given XXI, 20 and XXIV, 45, is repeated XXVII, 16, 21. Further, the enumeration of the purificatory texts XXVIII, 10–15 is merely an enlargement of XXII, 9. Finally, the verses XXVIII, 16–22 contain detached rules on gifts, and in the next chapter, XXIX, the subject is begun once more and treated at considerable length. Though it would be unwise to assume that all genuine productions of the old Sûtrakâras must, throughout, show regularity and consistency, the differences between the four chapters and the remainder of the work, just pointed out, are, it seems to me, sufficient to warrant the conclusion that they do not belong to the author of the Institutes. Under these circumstances it might be assumed that the whole section is simply an interpolation. But that would be going too far. For, as other Dharma-sûtras show, one or even several chapters on secret penances belonged to such works.

[1] See XXV, 1; XXVII, 10; XXVIII, 10, 20.

Moreover, in the section on women, Vasish*th*a V, 3–4, the author makes a cross-reference to the rahasyas, the section on secret penances, and quotes by anticipation half a *S*loka which is actually found in chapter XXVIII. The inference to be drawn from these facts is, that the section on secret penances is not simply a later addition intended to supply an omission of the first writer, but that, for some reason or other, it has been remodelled. The answer to the question why this was done is suggested, it seems to me, partly by the state of the MSS. of the Vâsish*th*a Dharma*s*âstra, and partly by the facts connected with the treatment of ancient works by the Pa*nd*its, which my examination of the libraries of Northern India has brought to light[1]. MSS. of the Vâsish*th*a Dharma*s*âstra are very rare, and among those found only three are complete. Some stop with chapter X, others with chapter XXI, and a few in the middle of the thirtieth Adhyâya. Moreover, most of them are very corrupt, and even the best exhibit some Sûtras which are hopeless. These circumstances show clearly that after the extinction of the Vedic school, with which the work originated, the Sûtra was for some time neglected, and existed in a few copies only, perhaps even in a single MS. The materials on which the ancient Hindus wrote, the birch bark and the palm leaves, are so frail that especially the first and last leaves of a Pothî are easily lost or badly damaged. Instances of this kind are common enough in the *G*aina and Ka*s*mîr libraries, where the beginning and still more frequently the end of many works have been irretrievably lost. The fate of the Vâsish*th*a Dharma*s*âstra, it would seem, has been similar. The facts related above make it probable that the MS. or MSS. which came into the hands of the Pa*nd*its of the special law schools, who revived the study of the work, was defective. Pieces of the last leaves which remained, probably showed the extent of the damage done, and the Pa*nd*its set to work at the restoration of the lost portions, just as the Ka*s*mîrian Sâhebrâm Pa*nd*it restored the Nîlamata-purâ*n*a for Mahârâ*g*a Ra*n*avîra*s*i*m*ha. They,

[1] See Report on a Tour in Ka*s*mîr, Journal of the Bombay Branch of the Royal Asiatic Society, vol. xii, p. 33.

of course, used the verses which they still found on the fragments, and cleverly supplied the remainder from their knowledge of Manu and other Smritis, of the Mahâbhârata and the Purânas. This theory, I think, explains all the difficulties which the present state of the section on secret penances raises. Perhaps it may be used also to account for some incongruities observable in chapter XXX. The last two verses, XXX, 9–10, are common-places which are frequently quoted in the Mahâbhârata, the Harivamsa, the Pañkatantra, and modern anthologies. With their baldness of expression and sentiment they present a strong contrast to the preceding solemn passages from the Veda, and look very much like an unlucky attempt at filling up a break at the end of the MS. In connexion with this subject it ought, however, to be mentioned that this restoration of the last part of the Vâsishtha Dharmasâstra must have happened in early times, at least more than a thousand years ago. For the oldest commentators and compilers of digests on law, such as Vigñânesvara[1], who lived at the end of the eleventh century A. D., quote passages from the section on secret penances as the genuine utterances of Vasishtha. These details will suffice to show why I differ from Professor Jolly with respect to his conclusion from the agreement of the verses of Vasishtha XXVIII, 10–15 with the Sûtras of Vishnu LVI.

With the exception of the quotations, the Vâsishtha Dharmasâstra contains no data which could be used either to define its relative position in Sanskrit literature or to connect it with the historical period of India. The occurrence of the word Romaka, XVIII, 4, in some MSS., as the name of a degraded caste of mixed origin, proves nothing, as other MSS. read Râmaka, and tribes called Râma and Râmatha are mentioned in the Purânas. It would be wrong to assert on such evidence that the Sûtra belonged to the time when the Romans, or rather the Byzantines (Rômaioi), had political relations with India. Nor will it be advisable to adduce the fact that Vasishtha

[1] Thus Vasishtha XXVIII, 7 is quoted in the Mitâksharâ on Yâgñavalkya III, 298; XXVIII, 10–15 on Yâgñavalkya III, 309; and XXVIII, 18–19, 22 on Yâgñavalkya III, 310.

XVI, 10, 14, 15 mentions written documents as a means of legal proof, in order to establish the 'comparatively late' date of the Sûtra. For though the other Dharma-sûtras do not give any hint that the art of writing was known or in common use in their times, still the state of society which they describe is so advanced that people could not have got on without writing, and the proofs for the antiquity of the Indian alphabets are now much stronger than they were even a short time ago. The silence of Âpastamba and the other Sûtrakâras regarding written documents is probably due to their strict adherence to a general principle underlying the composition of the Dharma-sûtras. Those points only fall primarily within the scope of the Dharma-sûtras which have some immediate, close connexion with the Dharma, the acquisition of spiritual merit. Hence it sufficed for them to give some general maxims for the fulfilment of the gunadharma of kings, the impartial administration of justice, and to give fuller rules regarding the half-religious ceremony of the swearing in and the examination of witnesses. Judicial technicalities, like the determination of the legal value of written documents, had less importance in their eyes, and were left either to the desâkâra, the custom of the country, or to the Nîti and Artha-sâstras, the Institutes of Polity and of the Arts of common life. It would, also, be easy to rebut attempts at assigning the Vâsishtha Dharma-sûtra to what is usually 'a comparatively late period' by other pieces of so-called internal evidence tending to show that it is an ancient work. Some of the doctrines of the Sûtra undoubtedly belong to an ancient order of ideas. This is particularly observable in the rules regarding the subsidiary sons, which place the offspring even of illicit unions in the class of heirs and members of the family, while adopted sons are relegated to the division of members of the family excluded from inheritance. The same remark applies to the exclusion of all females, with the exception of putrikâs or appointed daughters, from the succession to the property of males, to the permission to re-marry infant widows, and to the law of the Niyoga or the appointment of adult widows, which Vasish*th*a allows without hesitation, and even extends to the wives of emigrants. But as most of these opinions occur also in some of the decidedly later metrical Sm*ri*tis, and disputes on these subjects seem to have existed among the various Brâhmanical schools down to a late period, it would be hazardous to use them as arguments for the antiquity of the Sûtra.

The following points bear on the question where the original home of the Vedic school, which produced the Dharma-sûtra, was situated. First, the author declares India north of the Vindhyas, and especially those portions now included in the North-western Provinces, to be the country where holy men and pure customs are to be found, I, 8–16. Secondly, he shows a predilection for those redactions of the Veda and those Sûtras which belong to the northern half of India, viz. for the Kâ*th*aka, the Vâ*g*asaneyi-*s*âkhâ, and the Sûtras of Manu and Hârîta. Faint as these indications are, I think, they permit us to conclude that the Sûtra belongs to a *K*ara*n*a settled in the north.

As regards the materials on which the subjoined translation is based, I have chiefly relied on the Benares edition of the text, with the commentary of K*ri*sh*n*a-pa*nd*ita Dharmâdhikârî, and on a rough edition with the varietas lectionum from the two MSS. of the Bombay Government Collection of 1874–75[1], B. no. 29 and Bh. no. 30, a MS. of the Elphinstone College Collection of 1867–68, E. no. 23 of Class VI, and an imperfect apograph F. in my own collection, which was made in 1864 at Bombay. The rough edition was prepared under my superintendence by Vâmanâ*k*ârya *Gh*alkîkar, now teacher of Sanskrit in the Dekhan College, Pu*n*a. When I wrote the translation, the Bombay Government MSS. were not accessible to me. I could only use my own MS. and, thanks to the kindness of Dr. Rost, Colebrooke's MS., I. O. no. 913, from which the now worthless Calcutta editions have been derived either immediately or mediately. These materials belong to two groups. The Bombay MS. B., which comes from Benares, closely agrees with K*ri*sh*n*apa*nd*ita's text; and E., though

[1] See Report on Sanskrit MSS. 1874–75, p. 11.

purchased at Puna, does not differ much from the two. Bh., which comes from Bhuj in Kakh, and my own MS. F. form a second group, towards which Colebrooke's MS., I. O. no. 913, also leans. Ultimately both groups are derived from one codex archetypus.

The first group of MSS. gives a fuller and in general a correcter text than the second. But it seems to me that the text of B., and still more Krishnapandita's, has in many places been conjecturally restored, and that the real difficulties have been rather veiled than solved. I have, therefore, frequently preferred the readings offered by the second group, or based on them my conjectural emendations, which have all been given in the notes. To give a translation without having recourse to conjectural emendations was impossible, as a European philologist is unable to avail himself of those wonderful tricks of interpretation which permit an Indian Pandit to extract some kind of meaning from the most desperate passages. In a few cases, where even the best MSS. contain nothing but a conglomerate of meaningless syllables or unconnected words, I have thought it advisable to refrain from all attempts at a restoration of the text, and at a translation. A critical edition of the Vâsishtha Dharmasâstra is very desirable, and I trust that Dr. A. Führer, of St. Xavier's College, Bombay, will soon supply this want. Krishnapandita's commentary, for which he had not the aid of older vrittis, shows considerable learning, and has been of great value to me. I have followed him mostly in the division of the Sûtras, and have frequently given his opinions in the notes, both in cases where I agree with him and in those where I differ from him, but think his opinion worthy of consideration.

In conclusion, I have to thank Professors R. von Roth, Weber, and Jolly, as well as Dr. L. von Schröder, for the verification of a number of Vedic quotations, which they kindly undertook for me, as I was unable to use my own books of reference during the translation of the work.

INTRODUCTION

TO

BAUDHÂYANA.

THE case of the Baudhâyana Dharma-sûtra is in many respects analogous to that of the Institutes of the Sacred Law, current in the schools of Âpastamba and Hiranyakesin. Like the latter, it is the work of a teacher of the Black Yagur-veda, who composed manuals on all the various subdivisions of the Kalpa, and founded a Sûtra-*k*ara*n*a, which is said to exist to the present day[1]. The Brâhmanical tradition, too, acknowledges these facts, and, instead of surrounding Baudhâyana's work with a halo of myths, simply states that it was originally studied by and authoritative for the followers of the Taittirîya-veda alone, and later only became one of the sources of the Sacred Law for all Brâhmans[2]. Moreover, the position of Baudhâyana among the teachers of the Yagur-veda is well defined, and his home, or at least the home of his school, is known. But here the resemblance stops. For while the Sûtras of Âpastamba and Hira*n*yake*s*in have been preserved in carefully and methodically arranged collections, where a certain place is assigned to each section of the Kalpa, no complete set of the Sûtras of Baudhâyana's school has, as yet, been found, and the original position of the detached portions which are obtainable is not quite certain. Again, while the works of Âpastamba and Hira*n*yake*s*in seem to have been kept free from extensive interpolations, several parts of

---

[1] I must here state that during my residence in India I have never met with a follower of Baudhâyana's school, and cannot personally vouch for its existence. But many Pa*n*dits have assured me that many Baudhâyanîyas are to be found among the Telingana and Kar*n*â*t*aka Brâhmans.

[2] See Govinda's statement, quoted above, p. xiii.

Baudhâyana's Sûtras have clearly received considerable additions from later hands.

According to the researches of Dr. A. Burnell[1], whose long residence in Southern India and intimate acquaintance with its Brâhmanical libraries have made him the first authority on the literature of the schools of the Taittirîya-veda, the Sûtras of Baudhâyana consist of six sections, viz. 1. the *S*rauta-sûtras, probably in nineteen Pra*s*nas; 2. The Karmânta-sûtra in twenty Adhyâyas; 3. The Dvaidha-sûtra in four Pra*s*nas; 4. The G*ri*hya-sûtra in four Pra*s*nas; 5. The Dharma-sûtra in four Pra*s*nas; 6. The *S*ulva-sûtra in three Adhyâyas. The results of the search for Sanskrit MSS. in other parts of India, and especially in Western India, do not differ materially from those obtained by Dr. Burnell. The G*ri*hya-sûtra, which in Western India occasionally bears the title Smârta-sûtra[2], contains, however, nine instead of four Pra*s*nas. The MSS. of the Baudhâyana-sûtras, which contain the text alone, are all incomplete, mostly very corrupt and in bad order, and rarely give more than a small number of Pra*s*nas on detached subjects. The copies in which the text is accompanied by a commentary are in a better condition. Thus the Kalpavivara*n*a of Bhavasvâmin[3] extends over the whole of the *S*rauta-sûtra, and over the Karmânta and the Dvaidha-sûtras. It shows the proper sequence of the Pra*s*nas on *S*rauta sacrifices, and that probably the Karmânta and the Dvaidha immediately followed the *S*rauta-sûtra. But there is no hint in the MSS. or in the commentaries how the G*ri*hya, Dharma, and *S*ulva-sûtras were originally placed. With respect to these sections, it is only possible to judge from the analogy of the other extant sets of Kalpa-sûtras

[1] See Burnell, Catalogue of a Collection of Sanskrit MS., pp. 24–26, 28, 34–35, and Tanjore Catalogue, pp. 18a–20b, and especially his remarks at pp. 18b and 20a.

[2] This title is found in the best copy known to me, Elphinstone College Collection of 1867–68, Class B. I, no. 5, which has been prepared from the MS. of Mr. Limaye at Ash*t*e. The other copies of the work, found in Western India, e.g. no. 4 of the same collection and my own copy, are in a bad state, as they are derived from a MS. the leaves of which were out of order.

[3] Burnell, Catalogue of a Collection of Sanskrit MSS., no. LXXXVIII, and Tanjore Catalogue, no. CXVII.

and from internal evidence. On these grounds it may be shown that the order, adopted by Dr. Burnell, is probably the correct one. For the beginning of the G*ri*hya-sûtra[1] shows by its wording that it was not a separate treatise, but was immediately connected with some preceding Pra*s*na. The analogy of the collections of the Âpastambîyas, the Hira*n*yake*s*as, the Ka*th*as, and other schools permits us to infer that it stood after the *S*rauta-sûtra. It is further clear that, in its turn, it was succeeded by the Dharma-sûtra. For two passages of the latter work, I, 2, 3, 15, and II, 8, 15, 9, clearly contain references to the G*ri*hya-sûtra. In the former, the author gives the rule regarding the length of the staff to be carried by a student, as well as the general principle that the staff must be cut from a tree fit for sacrificial purposes. With respect to the latter clause he adds that 'the details have been given above.' As the Dharma-sûtra contains nothing more on this subject, it follows that the expression 'above' must refer to G*ri*hya-sûtra II, 7, where the usual detailed rules regarding the employment of particular woods for the several var*n*as are given. In the second passage Baudhâyana says that the rules for the performance of funeral sacrifices have been fully explained in the section on the Ash*t*akâhoma, which occurs G*ri*hya-sûtra II, 17–18. It is, therefore, perfectly certain that Baudhâyana, just like Âpastamba, placed the Pra*s*nas on the Sacred Law after those on the domestic ceremonies, and that the Dharma-sûtra was not a separate work. Under these circumstances it becomes highly probable that the *S*ulva-sûtra formed, as is the case in other sets of Kalpa-sûtras, the conclusion of the whole. Thus the only treatise, whose position remains doubtful, is the Pravarakha*nd*a, the list of the Brâhmanical gotras and of their deified ancestors[2]. Possibly it may have stood at the end of the *S*rauta-sûtra.

[1] According to the Elph. Coll. MS., Cl. I, B. 5, and my copy, it runs thus: यथो एतद्धुतः प्रहुत ऽाहुतः शूलगवो बलिहरणं प्रत्यवरोहणमष्टकाहोम इति सप्त पाकयज्ञसँस्था इति ॥१॥ ता ऽनुव्याख्यास्यामः ॥२॥

[2] Burnell, Catalogue of a Collection of Sanskrit MSS., no. CXVIII.

The destruction of the continuity of Baudhâyana's Kalpa-sûtra has had the consequence which is commonly observable in other dismembered works, that several of its detached portions have received considerable additions from later and, as it would seem, from several hands. There can be no doubt that a small portion only of the nine Prasnas, found in the Western copies of the Grihya-sûtra, really belongs to Baudhâyana. For the description of the Grihya rites, which strictly follows the general plan laid down in the first Sûtra, is completed in two or three Prasnas[1]. Next follows a Prasna on the anukritis, rites resembling those comprised in the subdivisions treated before, and then a Prasna on prâyaskittas, or expiations of mistakes committed during, and of the neglect of, the performance of the Grihya-karmâni. The remaining Prasnas are filled with a medley of paribhâshâs, general rules, and of full descriptions of ceremonies, some of which have been given before, while others are added afresh. Many of the newly-added rites do not belong to the ancient Brâhmanical worship, but to the Paurânic religions, the service of Siva, Skanda, Nârâyana, and other deities, and some show an admixture of Tântric elements. In some of the later Prasnas, especially IV and V, the language closely resembles that of the first three, and shows the same stereotyped phrases and the same Vedic anomalous forms. But in other sections, particularly VI–IX, we find, instead of Sûtras, the common Anushtubh Sloka throughout, and expressions peculiar to the metrical Smritis and the Purânas. At the end of most Adhyâyas we read the phrase, ity âha Baudhâyanah, or bhagavân Baudhâyanah, 'thus speaks Baudhâyana, or the divine Baudhâyana.' Finally, while the first three Prasnas are divided into Kandikâs or Khandas, the following ones consist of Adhyâyas or chapters. These differences, as well as the fact that the most important Grihya rites, arranged according to a special plan, are done with in the

[1] Elphinstone College Collection, no. 5, according to which all quotations have been made, gives three Prasnas, my own MS. two Prasnas. The number of the Khandas is, however, the same.

first three Prasnas, necessarily lead to the conclusion that the whole remainder does not belong to Baudhâyana, but consists of so-called Parisish*t*as, which were composed by the adherents of his school. Further, the fact that the last six Prasnas do not show everywhere the same style and language, makes it probable that the additions were made at different times and by different persons.

The Dharma-sûtra seems to have undergone exactly the same fate as the G*ri*hya-sûtra. It will be obvious even to the readers of the translation that its fourth Prasna is a later addition. It consists of two parts. The first, which ends with the fourth Adhyâya, treats of penances, both public and secret ones. The second, Adhyâyas 5-8, describes the means of obtaining siddhi, the fulfilment of one's desires, and recommends for this purpose the offering of the Ga*n*ahomas after a previous sanctification of the worshipper by means of a course of austerities. The first part is perfectly superfluous, as the subject of penances has already been discussed in the first sections of the second Prasna, and again in chapters 4-10 of the third Prasna. Its rules sometimes contradict those given before, and in other cases, e.g. IV, 2, 10-12, are mere repetitions of previous statements. The introduction of the means of gaining siddhi, on the other hand, is without a parallel in other Dharma-sûtras, and the subject is entirely foreign to the scope of such works. Its treatment, too, shows that chapters 5-8 do not belong to the author of the bulk of the Dharma-sûtra. For the description of the preparatory 'restraints' or austerities contains somewhat more detailed rules for a number of penances, e.g. the K*rikkh*ras and the *K*ândrâya*n*a, which have already been described in the preceding Prasnas. Moreover, the style and the language of the whole fourth Prasna are very different from those of the three preceding ones, and the differences observable are exactly the same as those between the first five and the last four Prasnas of the G*ri*hya-sûtra. The epic *S*loka nearly throughout replaces the aphoristic prose, and the common slipshod Sanskrit of the Purâ*n*as appears instead of the archaic forms. Finally, the fourth Prasna is divided into

Adhyâyas, not into the Ka*nd*ikâs or Kha*nd*as and Adhyâyas which are found in the first two Prasnas.

This latter peculiarity is also observable in the third Prasna, and raises a suspicion against the genuineness of that part also. For, though the third Prasna in style and language resembles the first two, it is hard to believe that the author should, for no apparent reason, suddenly have changed the manner of dividing his work towards its end. This suspicion is further strengthened by two other circumstances. First, Prasnas I–II really exhaust the discussion of the whole Dharma, and the third offers supplementary information only on some points which have been touched upon previously. Secondly, several Adhyâyas of Prasna III seem to have been borrowed from other works, or to be abstracts from them. Thus the tenth chapter has certainly been taken from the Gautamîya Dharmasâstra, the sixth bears a very close and suspicious resemblance to Vish*n*u XLVIII[1], and the third looks very much like a short summary of the doctrine of Vikhanas, whose lost Sûtra contained the original rule of the order of the Vaikhânasas or hermits, living in the forest. These circumstances justify, it seems to me, the assumption that Baudhâyana's original Dharma-sûtra consisted, like Âpastamba's, of two Prasnas only, and that it received, through followers of his school, two separate additions, first in very ancient times Prasna III, where the style of the master is strictly followed, and later Prasna IV, where the language and phraseology of the metrical Sm*ri*tis are adopted. It ought to be noted that Govindasvâmin, too, does not take the whole of the four Prasnas for Baudhâyana's composition. With respect to several passages[2] where Baudhâyana's name is introduced in order to give weight to the rules, he says that the Sûtras may belong to 'a pupil.' I do not think that the criterion which he uses can be relied on in every case, because oriental authors without doubt occasionally speak of themselves as of third

[1] See also Jolly, Sacred Books of the East, vol. vii, p. xix.
[2] E. g. Dharma-sûtra III, 5, 7.

persons. But the fact that the commentator, though an orthodox Hindu, had misgivings as to the genuineness of portions of the work, is not without significance. It seems also that even the first two Prasnas are not quite free from interpolations. Thus the Kandikâs on the Tarpana[1] are certainly much enlarged by additions, the verse at I, 5, 11, 36, a repetition of I, 5, 9, 5, and some prose quotations which are introduced by the words athâpy udâharanti, 'now they quote also,' standing usually before verses only, are at least suspicious. That the genuineness of many single passages should be doubtful, is no more than might be expected, not only on account of the separation of the Dharma-sûtra from the other parts of the Kalpa, but also because the work, as we shall see further on, remained for a long time without the protection of a commentary. The practical conclusion to be drawn from this state of things is that the greatest caution must be observed in using the Baudhâyana Dharma-sûtra for historical purposes, and that it will be advisable to draw no inferences regarding Baudhâyana's relation to other teachers and schools from the last two Prasnas, and not to trust too much to historical inferences drawn from single passages of the first two.

The position which Baudhâyana occupies among the teachers of the Taittirîya-veda has already been discussed in the Introduction to Âpastamba. It has been shown that according to the Brâhmanical tradition preserved by Mahâdeva, the commentator of the Hiranyakesi-sûtras, he composed the first Sûtra for the followers of his Sâkhâ. Internal and external evidence has also been adduced, proving that he certainly was more ancient than Âpastamba and Hiranyakesin. It is now possible to bring forward some further facts bearing on these points. First, in the section on the Tarpana, the libations of water offered to various deities, Rishis, and the manes, II, 5, 9, 14, Kânva Baudhâyana receives his share immediately after the Rishis of the Veda and before Âpastamba, the Sûtrakâra, and

[1] Baudhâyana Dharma-sûtra II, 5, 8–9.

Satyâshâ*dh*a Hira*n*yake*s*in. The same order is observed in the distribution of the offerings at the Sarpabali, described in the G*ri*hya-sûtra[1], where the following teachers of the Ya*g*ur-veda are specially named, viz. Vai*s*ampâyana, Phulingu, Tittiri, Ukha, Aukhya, Âtreya the author of the Pada-text, Kau*nd*inya the author of the commentary, Kâ*n*va Baudhâyana the author of the Prava*k*ana, Âpastamba the author of the Sûtra, and Satyâshâ*dh*a Hira*n*yake*s*in. Neither of these two passages belongs to Baudhâyana. They are both clearly interpolations. But they show that Mahâdeva's statement, which makes Baudhâyana the first expounder of the Kalpa among the Taittirîyavedins, agrees with the tradition of the Baudhâyanîyas themselves. For not only the place allotted to Baudhâyana's name, but still more the title Prava*k*anakâra which he receives, show that the followers of his school placed him before and above all other teachers of the ritual. The term prava*k*ana, which literally means 'proclaiming or recitation,' has frequently the technical sense of 'oral instruction,' and is applied both to the traditional lore contained in the Brâhma*n*as, and to the more systematic teaching of the Angas[2]. If, therefore, a teacher is called the author of the Prava*k*ana of a *S*âkhâ, that can only mean that he is something more than a common Sûtrakâra, and is considered to be the originator of the whole system of instruction among its followers. The epithet Kâ*n*va, which Baudhâyana receives in both the passages quoted above, indicates that he belonged to the Vedic Gotra of the Ka*n*vas. It deserves to be noted that Govindasvâmin, too, on I, 3, 5, 13, explains the name Baudhâyana by Kâ*n*vâyana[3].

---

[1] Baudhâyana G*ri*hya-sûtra IV, 8 (fol. 29, B. 5, Elph. Coll. copy, no. 5). अथ दक्षिणतः प्राचीनावीती नो (?) वैशंपायनाय फुलिङ्गवे तित्तिरय उखायौख्यायात्रेयाय पदकाराय कौण्डिन्याय वृत्तिकाराय काण्वाय बौधायनाय प्रवचनकारायापस्तम्बाय सूत्रकाराय सत्याषाढाय हिरण्यकेशाय (?) आचार्येभ्य ऊर्ध्वरेतोभ्यो वैंशस्येभ्य एकपत्नीभ्यः कल्पयामीति ॥ See also Weber, Hist. Ind. Lit., p. 91 note; Max Müller, Hist. Anc. Sansk. Lit., p. 223; Burnell, Catalogue of a Collection of Sanskrit MSS., p. 14, no. LIII.

[2] See Max Müller, Hist. Anc. Sansk. Lit., p. 109.

[3] The discovery that Baudhâyana bore also the name Kâ*n*va makes it possible

The style of Baudhâyana's works furnishes, as Dr. Burnell has pointed out[1], another argument for their high antiquity. Compared with the Sûtras of Âpastamba and Hira*n*yake*s*in they are much simpler in their arrangement, and the complete absence of that anxiety to save 'half a vowel' which characterises the fully developed Sûtra-style is very remarkable. The last point has been noticed by Govindasvâmin also. In commenting on I, 2, 3, 17–18, where Baudhâyana first permits students to beg food of men of all castes, and afterwards explains that he means Âryans who follow their lawful occupations, he says[2], '(If anybody should ask), "Why give two Sûtras, while one Sûtra, ('A student shall ask) Âryans who follow their lawful occupations,' would have sufficed?" (his objection will be) correct. For this teacher is not particularly anxious to make his book short.' In other cases we find a certain awkwardness in the distribution of the subject matter, which probably finds its explanation through the fact that Baudhâyana first attempted to bring the teaching of the Taittirîyas on the Dharma into a systematic form. Thus the rules on the law of inheritance are given without any apparent necessity and against the custom of the other Sûtrakâras in two different chapters, I, 5, 11, 9–16 and II, 2, 3, 1–44. The section on purification, too, is divided into two separate portions, I, 4, 6–10 and I, 6, 13–15, and the second, which treats of the purification of the vessels at sacrifices, properly ought to have been placed into the *S*rauta-sûtra, not into the Dharma-sûtra. Again, the discussion of several topics is repeatedly interrupted by the introduction of rules belonging to different subjects, and Govindasvâmin's ingenuity is often taxed to the utmost in order to find the reason why certain Sûtras which appa-

to refer Âpastamba's quotation of an opinion of a Kâ*n*va, I, 6, 19, 7, to Baudhâyana, instead of to a teacher of the White Yagur-veda, Sacred Books of the East, vol. ii, p. xxvi.

[1] Tanjore Catalogue, p. 20 b.

[2] ननु द्विजातिषु स्वकर्मस्थेष्विति सूत्रयितव्ये किमिति सूत्रद्वयारम्भः। सत्यम्। अयं ह्याचार्यो नातीव ग्रन्थलाघवाभिप्रायो भवति॥

rently are unconnected with the main subject have been inserted. A third argument for the great antiquity of Baudhâyana's Sûtras, derived from the archaic character of some of his doctrines, has been discussed in the Introduction to Âpastamba[1]. The number of instances where Baudhâyana's rules are based on a more ancient order of ideas than Âpastamba's might be increased very considerably. But, as now the comparison of the two works is open to all students, I omit the cases contained in the two Dharma-sûtras, and content myself with adducing one more from the less accessible G*ri*hya-sûtras. It is a well-known fact that the ancient Vedic ritual in certain cases admitted *S*ûdras, and particularly the Rathakâra or carpenter, who, according to all accounts, has *S*ûdra blood in his veins, to a participation in the *S*rauta rites. The Taittirîya-brâhma*n*a even gives certain Mantras to be recited by the Rathakâra at the Agnyâdhâna sacrifice[2]. Now Baudhâyana, who, Dh. S. I, 9, 17, 6, derives the origin of the Rathakâras from a Vai*s*ya male and *S*ûdra female, apparently reckons him amongst the twice-born, and explicitly allows him to receive the sacrament of the initiation. He says, G*ri*hya-sûtra II, 5, 8-9, 'Let him initiate a Brâhma*n*a in spring, a Kshatriya in summer, a Vai*s*ya in autumn, a Rathakâra in the rainy season; or all of them in spring[3].' But Âpastamba, who shows great hostility against the mixed castes, and emphatically denies the right of *S*ûdras to be initiated, gives the same rule regarding the seasons for the initiation both in his G*ri*hya and Dharma-sûtras[4]. He, however, omits the Rathakâra in both cases. There can be no doubt that Âpastamba's exclusion of the carpenter, which agrees with the sentiments prevailing in modern Brâhmanical society, is an offshoot of a later doctrine, and as both he and Baudhâyana

[1] Sacred Books of the East, vol. ii, pp. xviii-xx.

[2] See Weber, Indische Studien X, 12.

[3] वसन्ते ब्राह्मणमुपनयीत ग्रीष्मे राजन्यं शरदि वैश्यं वर्षासु रथकारमिति ॥८॥ सर्वानेव वा वसन्ते ॥९॥

[4] G*ri*hya-sûtra II, 4, 10, 5; Dharma-sûtra I, 1, 1, 18.

belong to the same vidyâvamsa, or spiritual family, this difference may be used as an argument for his posteriority to Baudhâyana. In connexion with this rule of Baudhâyana's it ought to be mentioned that even in the present day certain subdivisions of the modern Sutârs or carpenters actually wear the Brâhmanical thread, and, in spite of the adverse teaching of the Sâstras, find Brâhmans willing to perform the ceremony of investiture for them.

While it thus appears not incredible that Baudhâyana really was the first Sûtrakâra of the Taittirîyas, the numerous quotations which his works contain, permit us to form an idea of the extent of the Vedic and profane literature known to him. Among the Vedic works which he adduces as authorities, or otherwise refers to, the three sections of the Taittirîya-veda, the Samhitâ, the Brâhmana, and the Âranyaka, naturally take the first place. For the Âranyaka he seems to have used the Ândhra version, as Dh. S. II, 10, 18, 7, 11 references to the seventy-first Anuvâka of the tenth Prapâthaka occur. Two long passages, Dh. S. I, 2, 4, 3–8; II, 6, 11, 1–8, which apparently have been taken from the Satapatha-brâhmana, testify to his acquaintance with the White Yagur-veda. Baudhâyana does not say expressly that he quotes from the Brâhmana of the Vâgasaneyins, but Govinda has no hesitation in pointing to the Satapatha as their source. It is remarkable that the fact noticeable in Âpastamba's quotation from the Satapatha reappears here, and that the wording of the two quotations does not fully agree with the printed text of the Brâhmana. The differences in the first passage are, no doubt, partly owing to corruptions and interpolations in Baudhâyana's text; but that cannot be said of the second[1]. References to the Sâma-veda and the Sâmans occur repeatedly, and the passage from the Nidâna of Bhâllavins regarding the geographical extent of true Brâh-

[1] Professor Eggeling has lately discussed the question of the discrepancies between Âpastamba's quotations from the Brâhmana of the Vâgasaneyins and the existing text. I can only agree with him that we must wait for a comparison of all those quoted, with both the recensions of the Satapatha, before we draw further inferences from the fact. See Sacred Books of the East, vol. xii, p. xl.

manical learning, which Vasishtha adduces, is given I, 1, 2, 11-12. From the Rig-veda a few expiatory hymns and verses, such as the Aghamarshana and the Taratsamandîs, are quoted. The Atharva-veda is not referred to by name, but the existence of Âtharvana schools may be inferred from the mention made of the vows called Siras, II, 8, 14, 2. Among the authorities on the Sacred Law, mentioned in the Dharma-sûtra, Kâtya I, 2, 3, 46, Maudgalya II, 2, 4, 8, and Aupagandhani II, 2, 3, 33, do not occur in other works of the same class[1]. Hârîta, who is mentioned II, 1, 2, 21, and who probably was a teacher of the Maitrâyanîya school, is named by Vasishtha and Âpastamba also. The Gautama who is quoted I, 1, 2, 7 and II, 2, 4, 17, is, as has been shown in the Introduction to Gautama, most probably the author of the still existing Institutes of Gautama. To the arguments for the latter view, adduced there, I may add that two other passages of the Dharma-sûtra, II, 6, 11, 15 and 26, point to a close connexion between Baudhâyana's and Gautama's works. The former of the two Sûtras contains, with the exception of one small clause in the beginning, exactly the same description of the duties of a hermit in the forest as that given by Gautama III, 26-35. The second Sûtra states, just as Gautama's rule III, 36, that the venerable teacher (âkâryâh) prescribes one order only, that of the householders. The reason given for this opinion differs, however, according to Baudhâyana, from that adduced in Gautama's text. The almost literal identity of the first long passage makes it not improbable that Baudhâyana borrowed in this instance also from Gautama without noting the source from which he drew. On the other hand, the argument drawn from the fact that the tenth Adhyâya of Prasna III has been taken from Gautama's Sûtra loses its force since, as I have shown above, it is improbable that the third Prasna formed part of Baudhâ-

[1] Possibly Kâsyapa, whose name occurs in a Sloka, I, 11, 21, 2, may also be an ancient teacher to whom Baudhâyana refers. In the Grihya-sûtra a teacher called Sâlîki is repeatedly quoted, and once, I, 11 (end), his opinion is contrasted with that of Baudhâyana and of Âkârya, i.e. Baudhâyana's teacher. The Grihya-sûtra refers also to Âtreya, Kâsakritsna, and Bâdari.

yana's original work. A metrical work on the Sacred Law seems to be quoted II, 2, 4, 14-15. For, as the second verse, adduced there, says that the penance for one who violated his Guru's bed has been declared above, it seems impossible to assume that the two *S*lokas belonged to the versified maxims of the Dharma current among the learned Brâhmans. If this quotation is not an interpolation, it proves that, side by side with the Dharma-sûtras, metrical treatises on the Sacred Law existed in very early times[1]. One quotation, finally, which gives a verse from the dialogue of the daughters of U*s*anas and V*ri*shaparvan seems to have been taken from an epic poem. The verse is actually found in the Mahâbhârata I, 78, 10, and again 34, where the altercation between *S*armish*th*â and Devayânî forms part of the Yayâtyupâkhyâna. Considering what has been said above regarding the state of the text of the Dharma-sûtra, and our imperfect knowledge of the history of the Mahâbhârata, it would be hazardous to assert that the verse proves Baudhâyana's acquaintance with Vyâsa's great epic. It will be safer to wait for further proofs that it was known to the Sûtrakâras, before one bases far-going speculations on this hitherto solitary quotation.

The arguments which may be brought forward to show that Baudhâyana's home lay in Southern India are not as strong as those which permit us to determine the native country of Âpastamba. The portions of the Sûtras, known to me, contain no direct mention of the south except in the de*s*a-nir*n*aya or disquisition on the countries, Dharma-sûtra I, 1, 2, where certain peculiar customs of the southern Brâhmans are enumerated, and some districts of Southern India, e.g. Kaliṅga, are referred to as barbarous countries which must not be visited by Âryans. These utterances show an acquaintance with the south, but by no means prove that Baudhâyana lived there. A more significant fact is that Baudhâyana declares, I, 1, 2, 4, 'going to sea' to be a custom prevailing among the northern Brâhmans, and afterwards, II, 1, 22, places that act at the head of the Pata-

[1] See also West and Bühler, Digest of Hindu Law Cases, p. xxvii, 2nd ed.

nîyas, the more serious offences causing loss of caste. It is probable that by the latter rule he wished to show his standpoint as a southerner. But the most conclusive argument in favour of the southern origin of the Baudhâyanîyas is that they, like the Âpastambîyas and all other adherents of the Taittirîya schools, are entirely confined to the Dekhan, and are not found among the indigenous subdivisions of the Brâhmans in Central and Northern India. This fact is, if not explicitly stated, at least implied by the passage of the Mahârnava quoted in the Introduction to Âpastamba[1]. It is proved by the present state of things, and by the evidence of the land grants of the southern dynasties, several of which have been made in favour of Baudhâyanîyas. Thus we find a grant of Bukkarâya, the well-known ruler of Vigayanagara[2], dated Sakasamvat 1276 or 1354-5 A.D., in which a Brâhmana, studying the Baudhâyanîya-sûtra, is mentioned as the donee of a village in Maisûr. Again, in an inscription of Nandivarman Pallavamalla, which its editor, the Rev. Mr. Foulkes, places in the ninth century A.D.[3], a considerable number of Brâhmanas of the Pravakana-sûtra are named as recipients of the royal bounty, together with some followers of the Âpastambha[4] school. As we have seen that Baudhâyana is called in the Grihya-sûtra the Pravakanakâra, it is not doubtful that the Pravakana-sûtra of this inscription is the Sûtra of his school. The villages which the grantees received from Nandivarman were situated on the Pâlâr river in the Kittûr districts of the Madras Presidency. Besides, the interesting tradition which asserts that Mâdhava-Sâyana, the great commentator of the Vedas, was a Baudhâyanîya[5] is another point which may be brought forward as evidence for the location of the school in Southern India. Further,

[1] Sacred Books of the East, vol. ii, p. xxx; see also L. von Schröder, Maitrâyanîya Samhitâ, p. xxvii.

[2] Journal of the Bombay Branch of the Royal Asiatic Society, XII, 349-351.

[3] Indian Antiquary, VIII, 273-284.

[4] As all the older inscriptions hitherto published give Âpastambha instead of Âpastamba, I am now inclined to consider the former as the original form of the name.

[5] Burnell, Tanjore Catalogue, p. 20 b, remarks on no. CCXXVI.

it must not be forgotten that most and the best MSS. of Baudhâyana's Sûtras are found in Southern India. There are also some faint indications that the Ândhra country is the particular district to which Baudhâyana belonged. For his repeated references to voyages by sea and his rule regarding the duty payable on goods imported by sea show that he must have lived in a coast district where sea-borne trade flourished, and the fact that he uses the Ândhra recension of the Taittirîya Âra*n*yaka makes it probable that he was an inhabitant of the eastern coast.

My estimate of the distance between Baudhâyana and Âpastamba and of that between the latter and the historical period of India has been given in the Introduction to Âpastamba, pp. xxii and xliii, and I have nothing further to add on that subject. The oldest witness for the existence of the *S*rauta-sûtra of Baudhâyana is its commentator Bhavasvâmin, whom Dr. Burnell places in the eighth century A. D. The Dharma-sûtra is first quoted by Vig*ñ*âne*s*vara, circiter 1080–1100 A.D. Several of the passages adduced by him are, however, not traceable in the MSS.

As regards the materials on which the translation is based, I had at my disposal six MSS. of the text and two copies of Govindasvâmin's commentary, the Bodhâyanîya-dharmavivara*n*a[1], one of which (C. I.) gives the text also. These MSS. belong to two chief groups, a northern and a southern one. The northern group contains two subdivisions. The first comprises (1) D., a MS. bought by me for the Government of Bombay at Ahmadâbâd (no. 6 of the Dekhan College collection of 1868–69), and about one hundred or one hundred and fifty years old; (2) P., an old MS. of my own collection, bought in 1865 at Pu*n*a; (3, 4) B. and Bh., two modern transcripts, made for me in Baroda and Bombay. Among these, D. alone is of real value, as P., B., and Bh. faithfully reproduce all its clerical errors and add a good many new ones. The second subdivision of the northern group is represented by K., a modern transcript, made for

[1] It ought to be noted that in the south of India the forms Bodhâyana and Bodhâyanîya are invariably used for Baudhâyana and Baudhâyanîya. But it seems to me that the southerners are in error, as the affix âyana requires v*ri*ddhi in the first syllable.

the Government of Bombay at Kolhâpur in the southern Marâ*th*a country (Elphinstone College collection of 1867–68, Class VI, no. 2). The MSS. of the northern group, which give the vulgata current since the times of Nîlaka*nth*a (1650 A.D.) and Mitramis*r*a (circiter 1700 A.D.) in Western and Central India, can be easily recognised by the omission of the third Adhyâya of Pras*n*a IV, and by their placing IV, 5, 1 b–25 after IV, 7, 7. One of the chief differences between K. and the other MSS. of the northern group is the omission of II, 5, 8, 4–II, 6, 11, 15 in the latter. The southern group of MSS. is formed by M., a slovenly Devanâgarî transcript of a Grantha MS., no. $\frac{610}{1929}$ of the Madras Government collection[1], and by the text of C. I., a Devanâgarî copy of the MS. of Govindasvâmin's commentary, presented by Dr. Burnell to the India Office library[2]. The second copy of the commentary, C. T., a Telugu paper MS. from Tanjore, I owe to the kindness of Dr. Burnell.

As might be expected, on account of the southern origin of the Baudhâyanîya school, M. gives on the whole the best form of the text. It also carefully marks the Ka*nd*ikâs[3] in the first two Pras*n*as, ignoring the Adhyâyas altogether, and contains at the end of each Pras*n*a the first words of each Ka*nd*ikâ, beginning with the last and ending with the first, after the fashion which prevails in the MSS. of the Taittirîya Sa*m*hitâ, Brâhma*n*a, and Âra*n*yaka. Very close to M. comes Govinda's copy, where, however, as in most northern MSS., the Adhyâyas alone are marked. It is, however, perfectly certain that in some very difficult passages, which are disfigured by ancient corruptions, he corrected the text conjecturally[4]. In a certain number of cases the northern MSS. present better and older readings than M. and C. I.[5] Under these

[1] Taylor, Catalogue Raisonnée (!), I, p. 190. The clerical errors in my transcript are exceedingly numerous, and mostly owing to the faulty rendering of the value of the Grantha characters, which seem not to have been familiar to the copyist. There are also some small lacunae, and the last leaf has been lost.

[2] See Burnell, Catalogue of a Collection of MSS., p. 35, no. CXVII.

[3] I alone am responsible for the title Ka*nd*ikâ, given to the small sections. M. marks only the figures. D. and the better northern MSS. show only breaks at the end of the Ka*nd*ikâs and their first words at the end of the Pras*n*as.

[4] See e.g. Dharma-sûtra I, 2, 3, 35, note.

[5] See e.g. Dharma-sûtra I, 5, 11, 35; II, 1, 2, 36; II, 2, 3, 3; II, 2, 4, 10; II, 3, 6, 3; II, 7, 12, 5; III, 9, 2.

circumstances it has not been possible to follow the commentary or M. throughout. Though they had to be made the basis, they had in many passages to be set aside in favour of readings of the northern group. In some cases I have also been obliged to make conjectural emendations, which have all been mentioned in the notes. Three Sûtras, I, 8, 16, 13–15, have been left untranslated, because the MSS. offer no safe basis for a conjectural restoration, and the commentary is defective.

Govinda, who, as Dr. Burnell informs me, is said to be a modern writer, seems to have composed his vivara*n*a without the aid of older *vri*ttis. Though he apparently was well acquainted with the writings belonging to the Taittirîya-veda, with the ritual and with the common law-books, he has not succeeded in explaining all the really difficult passages. Sometimes he is clearly mistaken, and frequently he passes by in silence words or whole Sûtras, the sense or the general bearing of which is by no means certain. Though it would be ungrateful on my part to underrate the importance of his work for my translation, I cannot place him in the same rank with Haradatta, the commentator of Âpastamba and Gautama, and can only regret that no older commentary based on the living tradition of the Baudhâyanîyas has been available. If such a work were found, better readings and better explanations of many difficult passages would probably come to light. With the materials at my disposal the translation has been a work of some difficulty, and in trying to settle the text I have often experienced the feeling of insecurity which comes over the decipherer of a difficult inscription when the facsimiles are bad. The short Adhyâya on adoption, given in the appendix to the Dharma-sûtra, has been taken from the Smârta or G*ri*hya-sûtra. It does not belong to Baudhâyana, but is frequently quoted by the writers on civil law, who wrote in the sixteenth and seventeenth centuries of our era.

VASISH*TH*A.

VASISH*TH*A.

Chapter I.

1. Now, therefore, the desire to know the sacred law for their welfare (should arise) in (initiated) men.

2. He who knows and follows the (sacred law is called) a righteous man.

3. He becomes most worthy of praise in this world and after death gains heaven.

4. The sacred law has been settled by the revealed texts and by the tradition (of the sages).

5. On failure of (rules given in) these (two sources) the practice of the *S*ish*t*as (has) authority.

6. But he whose heart is free from desire (is called) a *S*ish*t*a.

7. (Acts sanctioned by) the sacred law (are those) for which no (worldly) cause is perceptible.

I. 1. The word 'now' serves, in this as in analogous cases, various purposes. It marks the beginning of the book, serves as an auspicious invocation (maṅgala), and indicates that something else, the initiation, must precede the study of the sacred law. 'Therefore' means 'because, after initiation, the neophyte is to be taught the prescribed rules regarding personal purification.'—K*r*ish*n*apa*nd*ita. For the wording of the Sûtra compare the beginning of *G*aimini's Mîmâ*m*sâ-sûtras.

3–6. Gautama I, 1–4; XXVIII, 48.

7. The Sûtra contains a limitation of Sûtra 5. It indicates that the customs of the *S*ish*t*as, for which worldly motives are perceptible, have no authority, and are not to be followed. The principle enunciated is one inculcated by the Mîmâ*m*sakas (P. M. S.

8. The country of the Âryas (Âryâvarta) lies to the east of the region where (the river Sarasvatî) disappears, to the west of the Black-forest, to the north of the Pâripâtra (mountains), to the south of the Himâlaya.

9. (According to others it lies to the south of the Himâlaya) and to the north of the Vindhya range (being limited east and west by the two oceans).

10. Acts productive of spiritual merit, and customs which (are approved of) in that country, must be everywhere acknowledged (as authoritative);

11. But not different ones, (i.e. those) of (countries where) laws opposed (to those of Âryâvarta prevail).

I, 3, 3–4). See also Âpastamba I, 1, 4, 5–10; I, 4, 12, 8; and Introduction, p. xxvii. Krishnapandita has misunderstood the Sûtra. He reads, against the MSS., agrihyamânakârano 'dharmah, 'unlawful acts are those for which no motive, i.e. no sacred source such as the Vedas, is perceptible.'

8. The region where the river Sarasvatî disappears is the Pattiâlâ district in the Pañgâb. The Pâripâtra mountains belong to the great Vindhya range, and are probably the hills in Mâlvâ. The position of the Kâlakavana or Black-forest is not accurately known. But it must probably be sought in Bihâr. All the MSS. as well as Krishnapandita read in this Sûtra prâgâdarsanât instead of prâgadarsanât, 'to the east of the region where the river Sarasvatî disappears.' This circumstance gains some importance by the fact that the Mahâbhâshya on Pânini II, 4, 10, quotes the same definition of the Âryâvarta, giving, however, instead of adarsanât prâgâdarsât, 'to the east of Âdarsa, i.e. the Âdarsa mountains.' It seems to me not improbable that our Sûtra, too, had originally prâgâdarsât, and that some Pandit who knew nothing about the Âdarsa hills, but remembered Manu II, 21, and Baudhâyana I, 1, 25, where the word vinasanât, 'the disappearance of the Sarasvatî,' undoubtedly occurs, added the syllable na and forgot to correct the â, after prâg.

9. The translation follows Krishnapandita's commentary, which recommends itself on account of the analogous definition of Âryâvarta given by Manu II, 22.

11. My translation follows the text given by Krishnapandita and

12. Some (declare the country of the Âryas to be situated) between the (rivers) Gangâ and Yamunâ.

13. Others (state as) an alternative, that spiritual pre-eminence (is found) as far as the black antelope grazes.

14. Now the Bhâllavins quote also (the following) verse in the Nidâna:

15. 'In the west the boundary-river, in the east

B., and the explanation of the former, because it seems to me that the general sense which they give, is the correct one. I feel, however, not certain that the word pratilomakadharmâ*n*âm, 'of those countries where opposite laws prevail,' is more than a careless correction. The majority of the MSS. read pratilomakakshadharmâ*n*a*h* (kalpadharmâ*n*a*h*), which by itself is difficult of explanation. But, as the text of the next Sûtra contains an apparently superfluous phrase, I fear, we shall have to admit that the text is here disfigured by corruptions, which with our present MSS. it is impossible to remove with certainty.

12. K*ri*sh*n*apa*nd*ita reads this Sûtra 'etad âryâvartam ityâ*k*akshate gangâyamunayor antaretyeke,' and takes it as one sentence, the subject of which is 'eke.' I feel no doubt that this explanation is utterly untenable, and that the first four words have nothing to do with this Sûtra, the second part of which occurs also in the Baudhâyana Dharma-sûtra I, 1, 27. My opinion is that they originally belonged to Sûtra 11, though the state of the MSS. at my disposal does not allow me to say how Sûtra 11 has to be corrected. The general sense of Sûtra 12 is, however, perfectly certain.

13. Manu II, 23; Yâ*g*ñavalkya I, 2. It deserves to be noted that the black antelope (black-buck), Oryx cervicapra, selects for its home the well-cultivated, rich plains of India only, and is entirely wanting in the sandy, mountainous or forest districts, which are now, just as in ancient times, the portion of the aboriginal tribes.

14. Regarding the Bhâllavins, see Max Müller, History of Ancient Sanskrit Literature, pp. 193, 364. K*ri*sh*n*apa*nd*ita thinks that Nidâna means de*s*anir*n*aya, 'the disquisition on the countries,' which is the title of a section which occurs in most modern compilations on law. But it will be safer to take it as the name of a Vedic work, identical with or similar to that quoted in *S*aunaka's B*ri*haddevatâ, Weber, Hist. Ind. Lit., p. 81.

15. Sindhur vidhâra*n*î or vidhara*n*î, as B. reads, cannot be

B 2

the region where the sun rises,—as far as the black antelope wanders (between these two limits), so far spiritual pre-eminence (is found).'

16. 'Those religious acts which men, deeply versed in the knowledge of the three Vedas and acquainted with the sacred law, declare to be lawful, (are efficient) for purifying oneself and others.'

17. Manu has declared that the (peculiar) laws of countries, castes, and families (may be followed) in the absence of (rules of) the revealed texts.

18. Sinful men are, he who sleeps at sunrise or at sunset, he who has deformed nails or black teeth, he whose younger brother was married first, he who married before his elder brother, the husband of a younger sister married before the elder, the husband of an elder sister whose younger sister was married first, he who extinguishes the sacred fires, (and) he who forgets the Veda through neglect of the daily recitation.

---

taken with K*ri*shn*a*pan*d*ita, as 'the ocean,' because in the latter sense sindhu is a masculine. It must be a boundary-river, probably the Sarasvatî. By sûryasyodana, 'the region where the sun rises,' the udayagiri or 'mountain of the east' may possibly be meant.

16. This verse, too, is marked as a quotation by the concluding word iti, though it is not necessary that it should be taken as a quotation from the Nidâna. Here, and in the sequel verses ending in iti are marked as quotations by hyphens.

17. Manu VII, 203; VIII, 41; Gautama XI, 20. *G*âti, 'castes,' which sometimes, and perhaps as appropriately, has been translated by 'tribes,' denotes in my opinion those numerous subdivisions of the four great var*n*as, which we now find all over India, and which can be shown to have existed for a very long time. Usually the word 'caste' is also applied to them.

18. K*ri*shn*a*pan*d*ita explains vîrahâ, 'he who extinguishes the sacred fires,' by 'the destroyer of his sons or of his spiritual clients'

19. They state that there are five mortal sins (mahâpâtaka),

20. (Viz. violating) a Guru's bed, drinking (the spirituous liquor called) surâ, slaying a learned Brâhma*n*a, stealing the gold of a Brâhma*n*a, and associating with outcasts,

21. Either by (entering into) spiritual or matrimonial (connexion with them).

22. Now they quote also (the following verse): 'He who during a year associates with an outcast becomes (likewise) an outcast; not by sacrificing for him, by teaching him or by (forming) a matrimonial (alliance with him), but by using the same carriage or seat.'

23. A minor offence causing loss of caste (upapâtaka, is committed by him) who (after beginning an Agnihotra sacrifice) forsakes the sacred fires, and by him who offends a Guru, by an atheist, by him who takes his livelihood from atheists, and by him who sells the Soma (plant).

24. Three wives (are permitted) to a Brâhma*n*a according to the order of the castes, two to a Kshatriya, one to a Vai*s*ya and to a *S*ûdra.

(yagamâna); but the rules given below, XX, 11, and XXI, 27, in the section on penances, confirm the explanation given above.

20. Vish*n*u XXXV, 1–2. Guru means here the father, see below, XX, 15.

21. Vish*n*u XXXV, 3–5. Spiritual connexion, i.e. becoming the teacher or priest of an outcast, or his pupil or spiritual client (yagamâna).

22. Identical with Manu XI, 181. It must be understood that spiritual or matrimonial connexion with an outcast causes immediate degradation, as Vish*n*u states expressly.

23. Vish*n*u XXXVII, 6, 31; Gautama XXI, 11. Regarding the precise meaning of pratigahnuyât, 'offends,' see below, XXI, 27.

24–25. Manu III, 13; Yâg*ñ*avalkya I, 57; Pâraskara G*ri*hya-sûtra I, 4, 8–11.

25. Some declare (that twice-born men may marry) even a female of the *S*ûdra caste, like those (other wives), without (the recitation of) Vedic texts.

26. Let him not act thus.

27. For in consequence of such (a marriage) the degradation of the family certainly ensues, and after death the loss of heaven.

28. There are six marriage-rites,

29. (Viz.) that of Brahman (brâhma), that of the gods (daiva), that of the *Ri*shis (ârsha), that of the Gandharvas (gândharva), that of the Kshatriyas (kshâtra), and that of men (mânusha).

30. If the father, pouring out a libation of water, gives his (daughter) to a suitor, that (is called) the Brâhma-rite.

31. If (the father) gives his daughter, decking her with ornaments, to an officiating priest, whilst a sacrifice is being performed, that is called the Daiva-rite.

32. And (if the father gives his daughter) for a cow and a bull, (that is called) the Ârsha-rite.

33. If a lover takes a loving female of equal caste, that (is called) the Gândharva-rite.

34. If they forcibly abduct (a damsel), destroying (her relatives) by strength (of arms), that (is called) the Kshâtra-rite.

35. If, after making a bargain (with the father, a

26–27. Manu III, 14–19. 28. Âpastamba II, 5, 11, 17–20.
30. Vish*n*u XXIV, 19; Â*s*valâyana G*ri*hya-sûtra I, 6, 1.
31. Vish*n*u XXIV, 20; Â*s*valâyana G*ri*hya-sûtra I, 6, 2.
32. Vish*n*u XXIV, 21; Â*s*valâyana G*ri*hya-sûtra I, 6, 3.
33. Vish*n*u XXIV, 23; Â*s*valâyana G*ri*hya-sûtra I, 6, 5.
34. Vish*n*u XXIV, 25; Â*s*valâyana G*ri*hya-sûtra I, 6, 8.
35. Vish*n*u XXIV, 24; Â*s*valâyana G*ri*hya-sûtra I, 6, 6.

suitor) marries (a damsel) purchased for money, that (is called) the Mânusha-rite.

36. The purchase (of a wife) is mentioned in the following passage of the Veda, 'Therefore one hundred (cows) besides a chariot should be given to the father of the bride.'

37. (It is stated) in (the following passage of) the *K*âturmâsyas, 'She (forsooth) who has been bought by her husband (commits sin, as) afterwards she unites herself with strangers.'

38. Now they quote also (the following verse): 'Lost learning comes back; when the family is lost all is lost. Even a horse becomes estimable on account of its pedigree; therefore men marry wives descended from an (unblemished) family.

39. The three (lower) castes shall live according to the teaching of the Brâhma*n*a.

---

36. *S*ânkhâyana G*ri*hya-sûtra I, 14; Pâraskara G*ri*hya-sûtra I, 8, 18; Âpastamba II, 6, 13, 12. Though Vasish*th*a's quotation is less complete than Âpastamba's, still the following Sûtras show that he knew the conclusion of the passage, and does not take it as an authority for the sale of a daughter.

37. K*ri*sh*n*apa*nd*ita makes a mistake by connecting the word '*k*âturmâsyeshu' with the next Sûtra. He is right in saying that 'the *K*âturmâsyas' is the name of a book. It is, however, not a separate work, but the kâ*nd*a or section of a Vedic work treating of the *K*âturmâsya sacrifices (see Max Müller, Hist. Anc. Sansk. Lit., p. 355). The particular work from which our quotation has been taken, is either the Maitrâyâ*n*îya Sa*m*hitâ, or the Kâ*th*aka. For, as Dr. von Schroeder informs me, Maitrâyâ*n*îya Sa*m*hitâ I, 10, 11 reads 'an*ri*ta*m* vâ eshâ karoti yâ patyu*h* krîtâ satyathânyai*s* *k*arati,' and the title of the kâ*nd*a is *K*âturmâsyâni. Professor Weber, Ind. Stud. V, 407, has found the same words in the *K*âturmâsya section of the Kâ*th*aka XXXVI, 5. In the translation I have added the beginning of the passage which Vasish*th*a omits, according to the Maitrâyâ*n*îya Sa*m*hitâ.

39–41. Gautama XI, 25–27.

40. The Brâhmana shall declare their duties,

41. And the king shall govern them accordingly.

42. But a king who rules in accordance with the sacred law, may take the sixth part of the wealth (of his subjects),

43. Except from Brâhmanas.

44. It has been declared in the Veda, 'But he obtains the sixth part of (the merit which Brâhmanas gain by) sacrifices and charitable works.'

45. (It is further stated in the Veda), 'The Brâhmana makes the Veda rich; the Brâhmana saves from misfortune; therefore the Brâhmana shall not be made a source of subsistence. Soma is his king.'

46. Further (another passage says), 'After death bliss (awaits the king who does not oppress Brâhmanas).'

---

42. Vishnu III, 22-25. Though the ambiguous word dhana, 'wealth,' is used in the text, it seems not doubtful that Vasishtha alludes to the land-tax, which generally consists of one sixth of the produce.

43. Vishnu III, 26.

44. Vishnu III, 27-28. Pûrta, 'the merit gained by charitable works,' i. e. by planting trees, digging wells, and so forth. The words 'iti ha,' placed at the end of the Sûtra, indicate that it is a quotation, and that vigñâyate, 'it is declared in the Veda,' has to be understood from Sûtra 46. Gautama XI, 11, too, alleges that the rule is based on a Vedic passage.

45. Satapatha-brâhmana V, 4, 2, 3. Krishnapandita's division of the quotation into several Sûtras is unnecessary. His explanation of anâdya, which he takes to mean 'the first of all,' is wrong. He asserts that the Brâhmana is said 'to make the Veda rich,' because by sacrificing and so forth he fulfils its object and protects it. But the phrase is probably corrupt. If it is said that Soma is the king of the Brâhmanas, the object is to indicate that an earthly king is not their master, see Gautama XI, 1.

CHAPTER II.

1. There are four castes (var*n*a), Brâhma*n*as, Kshatriyas, Vai*s*yas, and *S*ûdras.

2. Three castes, Brâhma*n*as, Kshatriyas, and Vai*s*yas, (are called) twice-born.

3. Their first birth is from their mother; the second from the investiture with the sacred girdle. In that (second birth) the Sâvitrî is the mother, but the teacher is said to be the father.

4. They call the teacher father, because he gives instruction in the Veda.

5. They quote also (the following passage from the Veda) to the same (effect): 'Of two kinds, forsooth, is the virile energy of a man learned in the Vedas, that which (resides) above the navel and the other which below (the navel) descends downwards. Through that which (resides) above the navel, his offspring is produced, when he initiates Brâhma*n*as, when he teaches them, when he causes them to offer oblations, when he makes them holy. By that which resides below the navel the children of his body are produced. Therefore they never say to a *S*rotriya, who teaches the Veda, "Thou art destitute of offspring."'

II. 1–2. Vish*n*u II, 1–2; Manu X, 4.

3. Identical with Manu II, 169[a], 170[a], and Vish*n*u XXVIII, 37–38. The Sâvitrî or the verse addressed to Savit*ri* is found Rig-veda III, 62, 10.

4. Gautama I, 10; Manu II, 171.

5. The reading tathâpyudâharanti, which several of my MSS. give, seems to me preferable to K*ri*sh*n*apa*nd*ita's udâharati. K*ri*sh*n*apa*nd*ita explains sâdhu karoti, 'makes them holy,' by adhyâtmam upadi*s*ati, 'teaches them transcendental knowledge.'

6. Hârîta also quotes (the following verse): 'No religious rite can be performed by a (child) before he has been girt with the sacred girdle, since he is on a level with a Sûdra before his (new) birth from the Veda.'

7. (The above prohibition refers to all rites) except those connected with libations of water, (the exclamation) Svadhâ, and the manes.

8. Sacred learning approached a Brâhmana (and said to him), 'Preserve me, I am thy treasure, reveal me not to a scorner, nor to a wicked man, nor to one of uncontrolled passions: so (preserved) I shall become strong.'

9. 'Reveal me, O Brâhmana, as to the keeper of thy treasure, to him whom thou shalt know to be pure, attentive, intelligent, and chaste, who will not offend thee nor revile thee.'

10. '(That man) who fills his ears with truth, who frees him from pain and confers immortality upon him, (the pupil) shall consider as his father and mother; him he must never grieve nor revile.'

11. 'As those Brâhmanas who, after receiving instruction, do not honour their teacher by their speech, in their hearts or by their acts, will not be profitable to their teacher, even so that sacred learning (which they acquired) will not profit them.'

---

6. Vishnu XXVIII, 40. Instead of Krishnapandita's 'yâvadvedo na gâyate,' 'yâvadvede na gâyate,' which occurs in several MSS. and in the parallel passages of Manu II, 172 and other Smritis, must be read.

7. Gautama II, 5. The rites referred to are the funeral rites.

8–9. Vishnu XXIX, 9–10, and introduction, p. xxiii; Nirukta II, 4.

10. Vishnu XXX, 47.

12. 'As fire consumes dry grass, even so the Veda, asked for, (but) not honoured, (destroys the enquirer). Let him not proclaim the Veda to that man, who does not show him honour according to his ability.'

13. The (lawful) occupations of a Brâhma*n*a are six,

14. Studying the Veda, teaching, sacrificing for himself, sacrificing for others, giving alms, and accepting gifts.

15. (The lawful occupations) of a Kshatriya are three,

16. Studying, sacrificing for himself, and bestowing gifts;

17. And his peculiar duty is to protect the people with his weapons; let him gain his livelihood thereby.

18. (The lawful occupations) of a Vai*s*ya are the same (as those mentioned above, Sûtra 16),

19. Besides, agriculture, trading, tending cattle, and lending money at interest,

20. To serve those (superior castes) has been fixed as the means of livelihood for a *S*ûdra.

21. (Men of) all (castes) may wear their hair arranged according to the customs fixed (for their family), or allow it to hang down excepting the lock on the crown of the head.

---

13. K*ri*sh*n*apa*nd*ita wrongly connects the word brâhma*n*asya with the next Sûtra. For this and the next seven Sûtras, compare Vish*n*u II, 4–14.

14. K*ri*sh*n*apa*nd*ita by mistake leaves out the word 'dânam.'

20. I read 'teshâm pari*k*aryâ,' with the majority of the MSS., instead of K*ri*sh*n*apa*nd*ita's 'teshâ*m* *k*a pari*k*aryâ.'

21. In illustration of this Sûtra K*ri*sh*n*apa*nd*ita quotes a verse of Laugâkshi, which states that Brâhma*n*as belonging to the Vasish*th*a family wore the top-lock on the right side of the head, and the members of the Atri family allowed it to hang down on

22. Those who are unable to live by their own lawful occupation may adopt (that of) the next inferior (caste),

23. But never (that of a) higher (caste).

24. (A Brâhmana and a Kshatriya) who have resorted to a Vaisya's mode of living and maintain themselves by trade (shall not sell) stones, salt, hempen (cloth), silk, linen (cloth), and skins,

25. Nor any kind of dyed cloth,

26. Nor prepared food, flowers, fruit, roots, perfumes, substances (used for) flavouring (food); nor water, the juice extracted from plants; nor Soma, weapons, poison; nor flesh, nor milk, nor preparations from it, iron, tin, lac, and lead,

27. Now they quote also (the following verse): 'By (selling) flesh, lac, and salt a Brâhmana at once becomes an outcast; by selling milk he becomes (equal to) a Sûdra after three days.'

28. Among tame animals those with uncloven hoofs, and those that have an abundance of hair, (must not be sold), nor any wild animals, (nor) birds, nor beasts that have tusks (or fangs).

29. Among the various kinds of grain they mention sesamum (as forbidden).

---

both sides, while the Bhrigus shaved their heads, and the Âṅgirasas wore five locks (*kûdâ*) on the crown of the head. Cf. Max Müller, Hist. Anc. Sansk. Lit., p. 53.

22. Vishnu II, 15.

24. For this and the following four Sûtras, see Gautama VII, 8–21.

26. Rasâh, 'substances used for flavouring,' i. e. 'molasses, sugar-cane, sugar, and the like.'—Krishnapandita. See also note on Gautama VII, 9.

27. Identical with Manu X, 92.

29. Vishnu LIV, 18; Âpastamba I, 7, 20, 13. Krishnapandita wrongly connects this Sûtra with the preceding one.

30. Now they quote also (the following verse): 'If he applies sesamum to any other purpose, but food, anointing, and charitable gifts, he will be born again as a worm and, together with his ancestors, be plunged into his own ordure.'

31. Or, at pleasure, they may sell (sesamum), if they themselves have produced it by tillage.

32. For that purpose he shall plough before breakfast with two bulls whose noses have not been pierced.

33. (If he ploughs) in the hot season, he shall water (his beasts even in the morning).

34. The plough is attended by strong males, provided with a useful share and with a handle (to be held) by the drinker of Soma; that raises (for him) a cow, a sheep, a stout damsel, and a swift horse for the chariot.

35. The plough is attended by strong males, i. e. is attended by strong men and bullocks, provided with a useful share—for its share is useful (because) with the share it raises, i. e. pierces deep—and provided with a handle for the drinker of Soma,—for Soma reaches him,—possessing a handle for him. That raises a cow, a sheep, goats, horses, mules, donkeys and camels, and a stout damsel, i. e. a beautiful, useful maiden in the flower of her youth.

36. For how could the plough raise (anything for him) if he did not sell grain?

---

30. Manu X, 91. 31. Manu X, 90.

34. Vâgasaneyi-sa*m*hitâ XII, 71. The translation follows the explanation given in the next Sûtra as closely as possible, though the latter is without doubt erroneous. The purpose for which Vasish*th*a introduces it, is to show that a Vedic text permits agriculture to a Brâhma*n*a who offers Soma-sacrifices.

37. Substances used for flavouring may be bartered for (other) substances of the same kind, be it for one more valuable or for one worth less.

38. But salt must never (be exchanged) for (other) substances used for flavouring (food).

39. It is permitted to barter sesamum, rice, cooked food, learning, and slaves (each for its own kind and the one for the other).

40. A Brâhma*n*a and a Kshatriya shall not lend (anything at interest acting like) usurers.

41. Now they quote also (the following verses): 'He who acquiring property cheap, gives it for a high price, is called a usurer and blamed among those who recite the Veda.'

42. '(Brahman) weighed in the scales the crime of killing a learned Brâhma*n*a against (the crime of) usury; the slayer of the Brâhma*n*a remained at the top, the usurer sank downwards.'

43. Or, at pleasure, they may lend to a person who entirely neglects his sacred duties, and is exceedingly wicked,

44. Gold (taking) double (its value on repayment, and) grain trebling (the original price).

37-39. Gautama VII, 16-21.

40. Manu X, 117. K*r*ish*n*apa*n*d*i*ta reads with MS. B., vârdhushi*m* na dadyâtâm, and explains it by v*r*iddhi*m* naiva prayogayetâm, 'they shall not take interest.' I read with the other MSS. vârdhushî, and translate that term by 'usurers.' Below, Sûtra 42, vârdhushi is used likewise in this its usual sense.

43. Manu X, 117.

44-47. Vish*n*u VI, 11-17; Colebrooke I, Dig. LXVI, where 'silver and gems' have been added after gold, and rasâ*h*, 'flavouring substances,' been translated by 'fluids.' The translation differs also in other respects, because there the Sûtras stand by themselves, while here the nouns in Sûtras 44 and 47 are governed by the preceding dadyâtâm, 'they may lend.' They, i.e. a Brâhma*n*a

45. (The case of) flavouring substances has been explained by (the rule regarding) grain,

46. As well as (the case of) flowers, roots, and fruit.

47. (They may lend) what is sold by weight, (taking) eight times (the original value on repayment).

48. Now they quote also (the following verses): 'Two in the hundred, three and four and five, as has been declared in the Smriti, he may take as interest by the month according to the order of the castes.'

49. 'But the king's death shall stop the interest on money (lent);'

50. 'And after the coronation of (a new) king the capital grows again.'

---

and a Kshatriya. The rule, of course, refers to other castes also, and to those cases where no periodical interest is taken, but the loan returned in kind.

47. The Ratnâkara quoted by Colebrooke loc. cit. takes 'what is sold by weight' to be 'camphor and the like.' Krishnapandita thinks that 'clarified butter, honey, spirituous liquor, oil, molasses, and salt' are meant. But most of these substances fall under the term rasâh, 'flavouring substances.' The proper explanation of the words seems to be, 'any other substance not included among those mentioned previously, which is sold by weight.'

48. Vishnu VI, 2, and especially Manu VIII, 142. The lowest rate of interest is to be taken from the highest caste, and it becomes greater with decreasing respectability. According to Krishnapandita and the commentators on the parallel passage of Vishnu, Manu, and other Smritis, this rule applies only to loans for which no security is given—a statement which is doubtlessly correct.

49–50. Both the reading and the sense of this verse, which in some MSS. is wanting, are somewhat doubtful. I read with my best MSS.,

rågâ tu mritabhâvena dravyavriddhim vinâsayet ı
punâ râgâbhishekena dravyamûlam ka vardhate ıı

and consider that it gives a rule, ordering all money transactions to be stopped during the period which intervenes between the death of a king and the coronation of his successor. I am, however, unable to point out any parallel passages confirming this

51. 'Hear the interest for a money-lender declared by the words of Vasishtha, five mâshâs for twenty (kârshâpanas may be taken every month); thus the law is not violated.'

Chapter III.

1. (Brâhmanas) who neither study nor teach the Veda nor keep sacred fires become equal to Sûdras;

2. And they quote a verse of Manu on this (subject), 'A twice-born man, who not having studied the Veda applies himself to other (and worldly study), soon falls, even while living, to the condition of a Sûdra, and his descendants after him.'

3. '(A twice-born man) who does not know the

---

view. Krishnapandita's text shows two important various readings, 'bhritibhâvena' and 'râgâbhîshikena,' which I think are merely conjectures, unsupported by the authority of MSS. He explains the verse as follows: 'The king shall destroy, i.e. himself not take, the interest on money by giving [it away] as a salary. But, after thus giving away interest received, he may increase his capital by [an extra tax imposed on] the cultivators, i.e. take from them the highest rate, consisting of one-fourth of the produce.'

51. Gautama XII, 29; Colebrooke I, Dig. XXIV. The rule given in this Sûtra refers, as Krishnapandita correctly states, to loans, for which security is given. The rate is 1¼ per cent for the month, or 15 per annum; see the note to Gautama loc. cit. Manu, VIII, 140, especially mentions that this rate is prescribed by Vasishtha.

III. 1. I read Sûdrasadharmânah, 'equal to Sûdras,' instead of sûdrakarmânah, which occurs in MS. B. only. Krishnapandita explains the latter reading by sûdravatkarma yeshu te sûdravatteshvâkaranîyamityarthah, 'shall be treated like Sûdras.' But the verses quoted in the following Sûtras show that the former reading is the better one.

2. Identical with Manu II, 168.

3. This and the following nine verses are, as the word 'iti,' which the best MSS. give at the end of Sûtra 12, quotations.

Veda (can)not be (called) a Brâhma*n*a, nor he who lives by trade, nor he who (lives as) an actor, nor he who obeys a *S*ûdra's commands, nor (he who like) a thief (takes the property of others), nor he who makes his living by the practice of medicine.'

4. 'The king shall punish that village where Brâhma*n*as, unobservant of their sacred duties and ignorant of the Veda, subsist by begging; for it feeds robbers.'

5. 'Many thousands (of Brâhma*n*as) cannot form a (legal) assembly (for declaring the sacred law), if they have not fulfilled their sacred duties, are unacquainted with the Veda, and subsist only by the name of their caste.'

6. 'That sin which dunces, perplexed by ignorance and unacquainted with the sacred law, declare (to be duty) shall fall, increased a hundredfold, on those who propound it.'

7. 'What four or (even) three (Brâhma*n*as) who have completely studied the Vedas proclaim, that must be distinctly recognised as the sacred law, not (the decision) of a thousand fools.'

8. 'Offerings to the gods and to the manes must always be given to a *S*rotriya alone. For gifts

---

An*ri*k, 'who does not know the Veda,' means, literally, 'unacquainted with the *Ri*g-veda.'

5. This verse, which is identical with Manu XII, 114, and the next two are intended to show that a Brâhma*n*a who neglects the study of the Veda, is unfit to decide points of the sacred law, which are not settled either by the Sm*ri*ti or the *S*ruti, and become a member of a parishad or 'Pa*ñk*.'

6. The verse contains a better version of Manu XII, 115.

7. Regarding the term Vedapâraga, see Gautama V, 20, note. Itareshâm, 'fools,' means literally, 'different from (those who have mastered the Vedas).'

bestowed on a man unacquainted with the Veda, reach neither the ancestors nor the gods.'

9. 'If a fool lives even in one's house and a (Brâhmana) deeply learned in the Veda lives at a great distance, the learned man shall receive the gift. The sin of neglecting (a Brâhmana is not incurred) in (the case of) a fool.'

10. 'The offence of neglecting a Brâhmana cannot be committed against a twice-born man who is ignorant of the Veda. For (in offering sacrifices) one does not pass by a brilliant fire and throw the oblations into ashes.'

11. 'An elephant made of wood, an antelope made of leather, and a Brâhmana ignorant of the Veda, those three have nothing but the name (of their kind).'

12. 'Those kingdoms, where ignorant men eat the food of the learned, will be visited by drought; or (some other) great evil will befall (them).'

13. If anybody finds treasure (the owner of) which is not known, the king shall take it, giving one sixth to the finder.

14. If a Brâhmana who follows the six (lawful) occupations, finds it, the king shall not take it.

9–10. Regarding the crime of 'neglecting a Brâhmana,' see Manu VIII, 392–393, where fines are prescribed for neglecting to invite to dinner worthy neighbours and Srotriyas.

10. A learned Brâhmana resembles a sacrificial fire, see e.g. below, XXX, 2–3; Âpastamba I, 1, 3, 44.

11. Manu II, 157. Krishnapandita and MS. B. give the ungrammatical construction which occurs in Manu and other Dharmasâstras, while the other MSS. read more correctly, 'yaska kâshthamayo h. yaska karmamayo m.' &c.

13–14. This rule agrees exactly with Gautama X, 45; see also Vishnu III, 56–61. The matter is introduced here in order to show the prerogative of a learned Brâhmana. Regarding the six lawful occupations, see above, II, 13–14.

15. They declare that the slayer commits no crime by killing an assassin.

16. Now they quote also (the following verses): 'An incendiary, likewise a poisoner, one who holds a weapon in his hand (ready to kill), a robber, he who takes away land, and he who abducts (another man's) wife, these six are called assassins (âtatâyin).'

17. 'He may slay an assassin who comes with the intention of slaying, even though he knows the whole Veda together with the Upanishads; by that (act) he (does) not (incur the guilt of) the slayer of a Brâhma*n*a.'

18. 'He who slays an assassin learned in the Veda and belonging to a noble family, does not incur by that act the guilt of the murderer of a learned Brâhma*n*a; (in) that (case) fury recoils upon fury.'

19. Persons who sanctify the company are, a Tri*n*â*k*iketa, one who keeps five fires, a Trisupar*n*a, one who (knows the texts required for) the four sacrifices (called A*s*vamedha, Purushamedha, Sarvamedha, and Pit*ri*medha), one who knows the Vâ*g*asaneyi-*s*âkhâ of the White Ya*g*ur-veda, one who knows the six Aṅgas, the son of a female married according to the Brâhma-rite, one who knows the first part of the Sâma-veda Sa*m*hitâ, one who sings the *G*yesh*th*a-sâman, one who knows the Sa*m*hitâ and the Brâhma*n*a, one who studies (the treatises on) the sacred law, one whose ancestors to the ninth degree, both

15. Vish*n*u V, 189–192. The connexion of this subject with the main topic consists therein that it furnishes an instance where learning does not protect a Brâhma*n*a.

17. I read with the majority of the MSS., 'api vedântapâragam,' instead of 'vedântaga*m* ra*n*e,' as K*ri*sh*n*apa*n*dita has.

19. For the explanations of the terms left untranslated, see the

C 2

on the mother's and on the father's side, are distinctly known to have been *S*rotriyas, and learned men and Snâtakas.

20. (Four students of) the four Vedas, one who knows the Mîmâ*m*sâ, one who knows the Aṅgas, a teacher of the sacred law, and three eminent men who are in three (different) orders, (compose) a (legal) assembly consisting at least of ten (members).

21. He who initiates (a pupil) and teaches him the whole Veda is called the teacher (â*k*ârya).

22. But he who (teaches) a portion (of the Veda only is called) the sub-teacher (upâdhyâya);

23. So is he who (teaches) the Aṅgas of the Veda.

24. A Brâhma*n*a and a Vai*s*ya may take up arms in self-defence, and in (order to prevent) a confusion of the castes.

25. But that (trade of arms) is the constant (duty) of a Kshatriya, because he is appointed to protect (the people).

26. Having washed his feet and his hands up to

---

note on Âpastamba II, 8, 17, 22; Gautama XV, 28; and the notes on Vish*n*u LXXXIII, 2–21. Regarding the meaning of *Kh*andoga, 'one who knows the first part of the Sâma-veda Sa*m*hitâ,' see Weber, Hist. Ind. Lit., p. 63, note 59. 'One who knows the Sa*m*hitâ and the Brâhma*n*a, i. e. of the Rig-veda.'—K*ri*sh*n*apa*nd*ita. Regarding the various classes of Snâtakas, see Âpastamba I, 11, 30, 1–3.

20. Manu XII, 111. K*ri*sh*n*apa*nd*ita reads *k*âturvidyas trikalpî *k*a, 'one who knows the four Vedas and one who knows three different Kalpa-sûtras.' My translation follows the reading of the MSS., *k*âturvidya*m* vikalpî *k*a, which is corroborated by the parallel passage of Baudhâyana I, 1, 8, '*k*âturvaidya*m* vikalpî *k*a.' The explanation of the latter word is derived from Govindasvâmin. 'Men who are in three orders, i. e. a student, a householder, and ascetic,' see Gautama XXVIII, 49.

21–23. Vish*n*u XXIX, 1–2. 24. Gautama VII, 25.
25. Vish*n*u II, 6. 26–34. Vish*n*u LXII, 1–9.

the wrist, and sitting with his face turned towards the east or towards the north, he shall thrice sip water out of the Tîrtha sacred to Brahman, (i.e.) the part of the hand above the root of the thumb, without uttering any sound;

27. He shall twice wipe (his mouth with the root of the thumb);

28. He shall touch the cavities (of the head) with water;

29. He shall pour water on his head and on the left hand;

30. He shall not sip water while walking, standing, lying down or bending forward.

31. A Brâhma*n*a (becomes pure) by (sipping) water, free from bubbles and foam, that reaches his heart,

32. But a Kshatriya by (sipping water) that reaches his throat,

33. A Vai*s*ya by (sipping water) that wets his palate,

34. A woman and a *S*ûdra by merely touching water (with the lips).

35. Water (for sipping may) even (be taken) out of a hole in the ground, if it is fit to slake the thirst of cows.

36. (He shall not purify himself with water) which has been defiled with colours, perfumes, or flavouring substances, nor with such as is collected in unclean places.

---

30. K*ri*sh*n*apa*nd*ita is probably right in thinking that the word vâ, 'or,' inserted before 'bending forward,' is intended to forbid other improper acts, gestures or postures, which are reprehended in other Sm*ri*tis.

35. Vish*n*u XXIII, 43; Manu V, 128.

36. 'Collected in unclean places, e.g. in a burial-ground.'—K*ri*sh*n*apa*nd*ita.

37. Drops (of saliva) falling from the mouth, which do not touch a limb of the body, do not make (a man) impure.

38. If, after having sipped water, he sleeps, eats, sneezes, drinks, weeps or bathes, or puts on a dress, he must again sip water,

39. Likewise, if he touches (that part of) the lips on which no hair grows.

40. No defilement is caused by the hair of the moustache (entering the mouth).

41. If (remnants of food) adhere to the teeth, (they are pure) like the teeth, and he is purified by swallowing those which (become detached) in the mouth.

42. He is not defiled by the drops which fall on his feet, while somebody gives to others water for sipping; they are stated to be equally (clean) as the ground.

43. If, while occupied with eatables, he touches any impure substance, then he shall place that thing (which he holds in his hand) on the ground, sip water and afterwards again use it.

44. Let him sprinkle with water all objects (the purity of) which may be doubtful.

45. 'Both wild animals killed by dogs, and fruit thrown by birds (from the tree), what has been spoilt by children, and what has been handled by women,'

37. Gautama I, 41. 38. Gautama I, 37.
39. Âpastamba I, 5, 16, 10. 40. Âpastamba I, 5, 16, 11.
41. Gautama I, 38–40. 42. Manu V, 142.

43. Vishnu XXIII, 55. 'Occupied with eatables,' i.e. 'eating.'—Krishnapandita.

45. Vishnu XXIII, 50. This and the following two Sûtras are a quotation, as appears from the use of the particle iti at the end of Sûtra 47.

46. 'A vendible commodity tendered for sale and what is not dirtied by gnats and flies that have settled on it,'

47. 'Likewise water collected on the ground that quenches the thirst of cows,—enumerating all these things, the Lord of created beings has declared them to be pure.'

48. Anything defiled by unclean (substances) becomes pure when the stains and the smell have been removed by water and earth.

49. (Objects) made of metal must be scoured with ashes, those made of clay should be thoroughly heated by fire, those made of wood should be planed, and (cloth) made of thread should be washed.

50. Stones and gems (should be treated) like objects made of metal,

51. Conch-shells and pearl-shells like gems,

52. (Objects made of) bone like wood,

53. Ropes, chips (of bamboo), and leather become pure (if treated) like clothes,

54. (Objects) made of fruits, (if rubbed) with (a brush of) cow-hair,

55. Linen cloth, (if smeared) with a paste of yellow mustard (and washed afterwards with water).

---

46. Manu V, 129. 47. Vishnu XXIII, 43.

48. Gautama I, 42. For the explanation of the term amedhya, 'unclean substances,' see Manu V, 135, and the passage from Devala translated in Professor Jolly's note on Vishnu XXIII, 38.

49. Gautama I, 29; Vishnu XXIII, 26, 33, 27, 18.

50–51. Gautama I, 30.

52. Gautama I, 31 and note; Vishnu XXIII, 4.

53. Gautama I, 33.

54. Vishnu XXIII, 28. Cups and bottles made of the shell of the cocoa-nut or of the Bilva (Bel) fruit and of bottle-gourds are meant.

55. Vishnu XXIII, 22.

56. But land becomes pure, according to the degree of defilement, by sweeping (the defiled spot), by smearing it with cowdung, by scraping it, by sprinkling (water) or by heaping (pure earth) on (it).

57. Now they quote also (the following verses): 'Land is purified by these four methods, by digging, burning, scraping, being trodden on by cows, and fifthly by being smeared with cowdung.'

58. 'A woman is purified by her monthly discharge, a river by its current, brass by (being scoured with) ashes, and an earthen pot by another burning.'

59. 'But an earthen vessel which has been defiled by spirituous liquor, urine, ordure, phlegm, pus, tears, or blood cannot be purified even by another burning.'

60. 'The body is purified by water, the internal organ by truth, the soul by sacred learning and austerities, and the understanding by knowledge.'

61. Gold is purified by water alone,

62. Likewise silver,

---

56. Vishnu XXIII, 56–57. Krishnapandita takes upakarana, 'heaping (pure earth) on (the defiled spot),' to mean 'lighting a fire on it' or 'digging it up.' The translation given above rests on the parallel passages of Gautama I, 32, and of Baudhâyana I, 5, 52, bhûmes tu sammârganaprokshanopalepanâvastaranopalekhanair-yathâsthânam doshaviseshât prâyatyam, 'land becomes pure, according to the degree of the defilement, by sweeping the (defiled) spot, by sprinkling it, by smearing it with cowdung, by scattering (pure earth) on it, or by scraping it.' Bhûmi, 'land,' includes also the mud-floor of a house or of a verandah.

57. Some MSS. have instead of gharshât, 'by scraping,' varshât, 'by rain;' see also note on Gautama I, 32.

58. Vishnu XXII, 91. 59. Vishnu XXIII, 5.

60. Identical with Manu V, 109, and Vishnu XXII, 92.

61–62. Vishnu XXIII, 7. Krishnapandita points out that these

63. Copper is cleansed by acids.

64. The Tîrtha sacred to the Gods lies at the root of the little finger,

65. That sacred to the *Ri*shis in the middle of the fingers,

66. That sacred to Men at the tips of the fingers,

67. That sacred to Agni (fire) in the middle of the hand,

68. That sacred to the Manes between the forefinger and the thumb.

69. He shall honour (his food at) the evening and morning meals (saying), 'It pleases me,'

70. At meals in honour of the Manes (saying), 'I have dined well,'

71. At (a dinner given on the occasion of) rites procuring prosperity (saying), 'It is perfect.'

CHAPTER IV.

1. The four castes are distinguished by their origin and by particular sacraments.

2. There is also the following passage of the Veda, 'The Brâhma*n*a was his mouth, the Kshatriya formed his arms, the Vai*s*ya his thighs; the *S*ûdra was born from his feet.'

3. It has been declared in (the following passage

---

two rules and that given in the next Sûtra refer to cases in which gold, silver, and copper have not been stained by impure substances.

63. Vish*n*u XXIII, 25.

64–68. Vish*n*u LXII, 1–4; Âpastamba II, 2, 3, 11.

69. Vish*n*u LXVIII, 42. The Sûtra is also intended to prescribe that the number of the daily meals is two only.

70. Manu III, 251.

71. The rites referred to are, according to K*ri*sh*n*apa*nd*ita, marriages, feeding Brâhma*n*as, Nândî*s*râddhas, and the like.

IV. 1. Manu I, 87. 2. Rig-veda X, 90, 12.

of) the Veda that (a Sûdra) shall not receive the sacraments, 'He created the Brâhmana with the Gâyatrî (metre), the Kshatriya with the Trishtubh, the Vaisya with the Gagatî, the Sûdra without any metre.'

4. Truthfulness, suppression of anger, liberality, abstention from injuring living beings, and the procreation of offspring (are duties common to) all (castes).

5. The Mânava (Sûtra states), 'Only when he worships the manes and the gods, or honours guests, he may certainly do injury to animals.'

6. 'On offering a Madhuparka (to a guest), at a sacrifice, and at the rites in honour of the manes, but on these occasions only may an animal be slain; that (rule) Manu proclaimed.'

---

4. Vishnu II, 17.

5. Mânavam, 'the Mânava (Sûtra),' means literally 'a work proclaimed by Manu' (manunâ proktam). It is probable that the work referred to by Vasishtha is the lost Dharma-sûtra of the Mânava Sâkhâ, which is a subdivision of the Maitrâyanîyas, and on which the famous metrical Mânava Dharmasâstra is based. The words of the Sûtra may either be a direct quotation or a summary of the opinion given in the Mânava-sûtra. I think the former supposition the more probable one, and believe that not only Sûtra 5, but also Sûtras 6-8 have been taken bodily from the ancient Dharma-sûtra. For Sûtra 6 agrees literally with a verse of the metrical Manusmriti, and at the end of Sûtra 8 several MSS. have the word iti, the characteristic mark that a quotation is finished, while the language of Sûtra 8 is more antiquated than Vasishtha's usual style. If my view is correct, it follows that the lost Mânava Dharma-sûtra consisted, like nearly all the known works of this class, partly of prose and partly of verse.

6. Identical with Manu V, 41; Vishnu LI, 64; and Sânkhâyana Grihya-sûtra II, 16, 1. I take pitridaivata, against Kullûka's and Krishnapandita's view, as a bahuvrîhi compound, and dissolve it by pitaro daivatam yasmimstat, literally 'such (a rite) where the manes are the deities.' The other explanation, '(rites)

7. 'Meat can never be obtained without injuring living beings, and to injure living beings does not procure heavenly bliss; therefore the (sages declare) the slaughter (of beasts) at a sacrifice not to be slaughter (in the ordinary sense of the word).'

8. 'Now he may also cook a full-grown ox or a full-grown he-goat for a Brâhma*n*a or Kshatriya guest; in this manner they offer hospitality to such (a man).'

9. Libations of water (must be poured out) for all (deceased relatives) who completed the second year and (their death causes) impurity.

10. Some declare that (this rule applies also to children) that died after teething.

11. After having burnt the body (of the deceased, the relatives) enter the water without looking at (the place of cremation),

12. Facing the south, they shall pour out water with both hands on (those days of the period of impurity) which are marked by odd numbers.

---

to the manes or to the gods,' which is also grammatically correct, recommends itself less, because the rites to the gods are already included by the word *yagñe*, 'at a sacrifice.' As to the Madhuparka, see Âpastamba II, 4, 8, 8–9, and below XI, 1.

7. Manu V, 48, and Vish*n*u LI, 71, where, however, the conclusion of the verse has been altered to suit the ahi*m*sâ-doctrines of the compilers of the metrical Sm*ri*tis. The reason why slaughter at a sacrifice is not slaughter in the ordinary sense may be gathered from Vish*n*u LI, 61, 63.

8. *S*atapatha-brâhma*n*a III, 4, 1, 2; Yâ*g*ñavalkya I, 109.

9–10. Vish*n*u XIX, 7; Manu V, 58. Regarding the length of the period of impurity, see below, Sûtras 16, 26–29.

11. Vish*n*u XIX, 6.

12. Vish*n*u XIX, 7; Gautama XIV, 40. 'On those days of the period of impurity which are marked by odd numbers,' i. e. 'on the first, third, fifth, seventh, and ninth, as has been declared by Gautama.'—K*ri*sh*n*apa*nd*ita.

13. The south, forsooth, is the region sacred to the manes.

14. After they have gone home, they shall sit during three days on mats, fasting.

15. If they are unable (to fast so long), they shall subsist on food bought in the market or given unasked.

16. It is ordered that impurity caused by a death shall last ten days in the case of Sapi*nd*a relations.

17. It has been declared in the Veda that Sapi*nd*a relationship extends to the seventh person (in the ascending or descending line).

18. It has been declared in the Veda that for married females it extends to the third person (in the ascending or descending line).

19. Others (than the blood-relations) shall perform (the obsequies) of married females,

20. (The rule regarding impurity) should be exactly the same on the birth of a child for those men who desire complete purity,

21. Or for the mother and the father (of the child alone); some (declare that it applies) to the

---

14. Vish*n*u XIX, 16; Gautama XIV, 37.

15. Vish*n*u XIX, 14. 17. Vish*n*u XXII, 5.

19. Gautama XIV, 36; Pâraskara G*ri*hya-sûtra III, 10, 42. 'Others than the blood-relations,' i. e. 'the husband and his relatives.' The MSS. have another Sûtra following this, which K*ri*sh*n*apa*nd*ita leaves out. Tâ*s*ka teshâm, 'and they (the married females shall perform the obsequies) of those (i. e. their husbands and his Sapi*nd*as).' It seems to me very probable that the passage is genuine, especially as Pâraskara, G*ri*hya-sûtra III, 10, 43, has the same words.

20. Vish*n*u XXII, 1.

21. Gautama XIV, 15–16. The Sûtra ought to have been divided into two.

mother (only), because she is the immediate cause of that (event).

22. Now they quote also (the following verse): 'On the birth (of a child) the male does not become impure if he does not touch (the female); on that (occasion) the menstrual excretion must be known to be impure, and that is not found in males.'

23. If during (a period of impurity) another (death or birth) happens, (the relatives) shall be pure after (the expiration of) the remainder of that (first period);

24. (But) if one night (and day only of the first period of impurity) remain, (they shall be pure) after two (days and nights);

25. (If the second death or birth happens) on the morning (of the day on which the first period of impurity expires, they shall be purified) after three (days and nights).

26. A Brâhmana is freed from impurity (caused by a death or a birth) after ten days,

27. A Kshatriya after fifteen days,

28. A Vaisya after twenty days,

29. A Sûdra after a month.

30. Now they quote also (the following verses): 'But (a twice-born man) who has eaten (the food) of a Sûdra during impurity caused by a death or a

---

23. Vishnu XXII, 35. 24. Vishnu XXII, 36.

25. Vishnu XXII, 37. Krishnapandita explains prabhâte, 'on the morning (of the day on which the first period of impurity expires),' in accordance with Nandapandita's explanation of Vishnu's text by 'during the last watch (of the last night of the period of impurity).' See also the slightly different explanation of the identical words by Haradatta, Gautama XIV, 8.

26. Vishnu XXII, 1. 29. Vishnu XXII, 4.

birth, will suffer dreadful (punishment in) hell and be born again in the womb of an animal.'

31. 'A twice-born man who eats by appointment in the house of a stranger whose ten days of impurity, caused by a death, have not expired, after death will become a worm and feed on the ordure of that (man who fed him).'

32. It has been declared in the Veda, '(Such a sinner) becomes pure by reciting the Samhitâ of the Veda for twelve months or for twelve half-months while fasting.'

33. On the death of a child of less than two years or on a miscarriage, the impurity of the Sapindas lasts three (days and) nights.

34. Gautama (declares that on the former occasion they become) pure at once.

35. If (a person) dies in a foreign country and (his Sapindas) hear (of his death) after ten days (or a longer period), the impurity lasts for one (day and) night.

36. Gautama (declares that) if a person who has kindled the sacred fire dies on a journey, (his Sapindas shall) again celebrate his obsequies, (burning a dummy made of leaves or straw), and remain impure (during ten days) as if (they had actually buried) his corpse.

37. When he has touched a sacrificial post, a pyre, a burial-ground, a menstruating or a lately confined woman, impure men or (Kândâlas and so forth), he shall bathe, submerging both his body and his head.

---

32. Regarding the penance prescribed here, the so-called anasnatpârâyana, see below XX, 46, and Baudhâyana III, 9.

33. Vishnu XXII, 27–30.

34. Gautama XIV, 44, and introduction to Gautama, p. liii.

36. Introduction to Gautama, pp. liii and liv.

37. Vishnu XXII, 69. Krishnapandita and MS. B. read pûya,

Chapter V.

1. A woman is not independent, the males are her masters. It has been declared in the Veda, 'A female who neither goes naked nor is temporarily unclean is paradise.'

2. Now they quote also (the following verse): 'Their fathers protect them in childhood, their husbands protect them in youth, and their sons protect them in age; a woman is never fit for independence.'

3. The penance (to be performed) by a (wife) for being unfaithful to her husband has been declared in the (section on) secret penances.

'pus,' instead of yûpa, 'a sacrificial post.' The reading is, however, wrong, because the parallel passages of most Smritis enjoin that a man who has touched a sacrificial post shall bathe. The cause of the mistake is probably a mere clerical error. The MSS. repeat the last word of this chapter, apa ityapah. The reason is not, as Krishnapandita imagines, that the author wishes to indicate the necessity of bathing when one touches a person who has touched some impure thing or person. It is the universal practice of the ancient authors to repeat the last word of a chapter in order to mark its end, see e.g. Gautama note on I, 61. If it is neglected in the earlier chapters of the Vâsishtha Dharma-sûtra, the badness of the MSS. is the cause.

V. 1. Vishnu XXV, 12. The second clause ought to have been given as a separate Sûtra. 'A female who no longer goes naked,' i.e. one who has reached the age of puberty. Amritam, 'is paradise,' i.e. procures bliss in this life and heaven after death through her children.

2. Vishnu XXV, 13. Identical with Manu IX, 3.

3. 'The penance which has been ordained in case a wife is unfaithful to her husband, i.e. goes to a lover and so forth, must be performed in secret, i.e. in solitary places.'—Krishnapandita. The explanation is clearly erroneous. Rahasyeshu cannot mean 'in secret' or 'in secret places.' It might refer either to a work or works called Rahasyâni or to the rahasyâni prâyaskittâni. As

4. For month by month the menstrual excretion takes away her sins.

5. A woman in her courses is impure during three (days and) nights.

6. (During that period) she shall not apply collyrium to her eyes, nor anoint (her body), nor bathe in water; she shall sleep on the ground; she shall not sleep in the day-time, nor touch the fire, nor make a rope, nor clean her teeth, nor eat meat, nor look at the planets, nor smile, nor busy herself with (household affairs), nor run; she shall drink out of a large vessel, or out of her joined hands, or out of a copper vessel.

7. For it has been declared in the Veda, 'When Indra had slain (Vritra) the three-headed son of Tvashtri, he was seized by Sin, and he considered himself to be tainted with exceedingly great guilt. All beings cried out against him (saying to him),

---

the next Sûtra contains a half-verse taken from the section on secret penances, XXVIII, 4, it is evident that Vasishtha here makes a cross-reference. Similar cross-references occur further on.

4. Yâgñavalkya I, 72, and below, XXVIII, 4.

5. Vishnu XXII, 72.

6. Taitt. Samh. II, 5, 1, 6–7. I read with the majority of the MSS., grahânna nirîksheta instead of grihân na nirîksheta, which latter phrase Krishnapandita renders by 'she shall not look out of the house.' My reading is confirmed by his quotation from the Smritimañgarî, where grahânâm nirîkshanam, 'looking at the planets, i. e. the sun, moon,' &c., is forbidden. 'A large vessel,' i. e. an earthen jar.—Krishnapandita.

7. Taitt. Samh. II, 5, 1, 2–5. The name 'slayer of a learned Brâhmana' is applied to Indra, because Vritra is said to have been deeply versed in the Vedas. Regarding the 'proper season of women,' see Manu III, 46–48. In the clause 'That guilt of Brâhmana-murder appears,' &c., I read âvir bhavati with the majority of the MSS. For the prohibition to accept food from a ragasvalâ, see Vishnu LI, 16–17.

'O thou slayer of a learned Brâhma*n*a! O thou slayer of a learned Brâhma*n*a!' He ran to the women for protection (and said to them), 'Take upon yourselves the third part of this my guilt (caused by) the murder of a learned Brâhma*n*a.' They answered, 'What shall we have (for doing thy wish)?' He replied, 'Choose a boon.' They said, 'Let us obtain offspring (if our husbands approach us) during the proper season, at pleasure let us dwell (with our husbands) until (our children) are born.' He answered, 'So be it.' (Then) they took upon themselves (the third part of his guilt). That guilt of Brâhma*n*a-murder appears every month as the menstrual flow. Therefore let him not eat the food of a woman in her courses; (for) such a one has put on the shape of the guilt of Brâhma*n*a-murder.

8. (Those who recite the Veda) proclaim the following (rule): 'Collyrium and ointment must not be accepted from her; for that is the food of women. Therefore they feel a loathing for her (while she is) in that (condition, saying), "She shall not approach."'

9. 'Those (Brâhma*n*as in) whose (houses) menstruating women sit, those who keep no sacred fire,

---

8. Taitt. Sa*m*h. II, 5, 1; 6. I read the text of this Sûtra as follows: 'Tadâhu*h*—a*ñg*anâbhya*ñg*anam evâsyâ na pratigrâhya*m* taddhi striyâ annam iti—tasmât tasyai *k*a tatra *k*a bîbhatsante meyam upâgâd iti.' The MSS. give the following readings in the second clause: tasmât tasmai *k*a (B. Bh. E. F.), tatra na (F.), medhamupâgâd (Bh. F.), medha upâgâd (E.), seyamupâgâd (B.) K*ri*sh*n*apa*nd*ita follows as usually MS. B. His explanation of the whole Sûtra is erroneous. 'That is the food of women,' i. e. that is as necessary to women as their food, because to beautify themselves is one of their duties.

9. The meaning of the Sûtra is that a Brâhmanical beggar must not accept any alms from Brâhma*n*as whose wives are in their

and those in whose family there is no Srotriya,—all these are equal to Sûdras.'

CHAPTER VI.

1. (To live according to) the rule of conduct is doubtlessly the highest duty of all men. He whose soul is defiled by vile conduct perishes in this world and in the next.

2. Neither austerities, nor (the study of) the Veda, nor (the performance of) the Agnihotra, nor lavish liberality can ever save him whose conduct is vile and who has strayed from this (path of duty).

3. The Vedas do not purify him who is deficient in good conduct, though he may have learnt them all together with the six Aṅgas; the sacred texts depart from such a man at death, even as birds, when full-fledged, leave their nest.

4. As the beauty of a wife causes no joy to a blind man, even so all the four Vedas together with the six Aṅgas and sacrifices give no happiness to him who is deficient in good conduct.

---

courses, who keep no sacred fire, and do not attend to the duty of Veda-study. Regarding sinners of the latter two kinds, see also Âpastamba I, 6, 18, 32–33.

VI. 1. Manu IV, 155. The word âkâra, which has been variously translated by 'conduct,' 'rule of conduct,' and 'good conduct,' includes the observance of all the various rules for every-day life, taught in the Smritis, and the performance of the prescribed ceremonies and rites.

4. I read with MSS. Bh. and E., shadaṅgâstvakhilâh sayagñâh. The reading of MS. B., which Krishnapandita adopts, shadaṅgâh sakhilâh means, 'together with the six Aṅgas, (and) the Khila (spurious) portions of the Veda.'

5. The sacred texts do not save from sin the deceitful man who behaves deceitfully. But that Veda, two syllables of which are studied in the right manner, purifies, just as the clouds (give beneficent rain) in the month of Isha.

6. A man of bad conduct is blamed among men, evils befal him constantly, he is afflicted with disease and short-lived.

7. Through good conduct man gains spiritual merit, through good conduct he gains wealth, through good conduct he obtains beauty, good conduct obviates the effect of evil marks.

8. A man who follows the rule of conduct established among the virtuous, who has faith and is free from envy, lives a hundred years, though he be destitute of all auspicious marks.

---

5. Isha is another name for Âsvina, the month September–October. Though the rainy season, properly so called, is over in September, still heavy rain falls in many parts of India, chiefly under the influence of the beginning north-east monsoon, and is particularly important for the Rabi or winter crops. I think, therefore, that it is not advisable to take, as Krishnapandita does, yathâ ishe 'bdâh both with the first and the second halves of the verse, and to translate, 'As the clouds (in general remain barren) in the month of Isha, even so the texts of the Veda do not save from evil the deceitful man who behaves deceitfully. But that Veda, two syllables of which have been studied in the right manner, sanctifies, just as the clouds in the month of Isha, (which shed a few drops of rain on the day of the Svâti conjunction, produce pearls).' 'In the right manner,' i. e. with the due observance of the rules of studentship.

6. Identical with Manu IV, 157.

7. Manu IV, 156. By the 'inauspicious marks' mentioned in this verse, and the 'auspicious marks' occurring in the next, the various lines on the hands and feet &c. are meant, the explanation of which forms the subject of the Sâmudrika Sâstra.

8. Identical with Manu IV, 158; Vishnu LXXI, 92.

9. But a man who knows the sacred law shall perform in secret all acts connected with eating, the natural evacuations and dalliance with (his wife); business to be accomplished by speech or intellect, likewise austerities, wealth, and age, must be most carefully concealed.

10. And a man shall void both urine and fæces, facing the north, in the day-time, but at night he shall do it turning towards the south; for (if he acts) thus, his life will not be injured.

11. The intellect of that man perishes who voids urine against a fire, the sun, a cow, a Brâhmana, the moon, water, and the morning or evening twilights.

12. Let him not void urine in a river, nor on a path, nor on ashes, nor on cowdung, nor on a ploughed field, nor on one which has been sown, nor on a grass-plot, nor in the shade (of trees) that afford protection (to travellers).

13. Standing in the shade (of houses, clouds, and so forth), when it is quite dark, and when he fears for his life, a Brâhmana may void urine, by day and by night, in any position he pleases.

14. (Afterwards) he shall perform the necessary (purification) with water fetched for the purpose (from a tank or river, and with earth).

15. For a bath water not fetched for the purpose (may also be used).

16. (For the purpose of purification) a Brâhmana

10. Vishnu LX, 2. I read with the majority of the MSS., na rishyati.

11. Identical with Manu IV, 52.

12. Vishnu LX, 3–22.

13. Identical with Manu IV, 51. 14. Vishnu LX, 24.

15. I.e. one may bathe also in a tank or river.

shall take earth that is mixed with gravel, from the bank (of a river).

17. Five kinds of earth must not be used, viz. such as is covered by water, such as lies in a temple, on an ant-hill, on a hillock thrown up by rats, and that which has been left by one who cleaned himself.

18. The organ (must be cleaned by) one (application of) earth, the (right) hand by three, but both (feet) by two, the anus by five, the one (i.e. the left hand) by ten, and both (hands and feet) by seven (applications of earth).

19. Such is the purification ordained for householders; it is double for students, treble for hermits, but quadruple for ascetics.

20. Eight mouthfuls are the meal of an ascetic, sixteen that of a hermit, but thirty-two that of a householder, and an unlimited quantity that of a student.

21. An Agnihotrin, a draught-ox, and a student, those three can do their work only if they eat (well); without eating (much), they cannot do it.

22. (The above rule regarding limited allowances of food holds good) in the case of penances, of self-imposed restraint, of sacrifices, of the recitation of the Veda, and of (the performance of other) sacred duties.

---

18. Vish*n*u LX, 25.

19. Identical with Vish*n*u LX, 26, and Manu V, 137.

20-21. Identical with Âpastamba II, 5, 9, 13, and S. 21, with *S*ânkhâyana G*ri*hya-sûtra II, 16, 5.

22. 'Penances (vrata), i.e. the K*rikkh*ras and the rest; self-imposed restraint (niyama), i.e. eating certain food in accordance with a vow, and so forth, during a month or any other fixed period . . . . sacred duties (dharma), i.e. giving gifts and the like.'—K*ri*sh*n*apa*nd*ita.

23. The qualities by which a (true) Brâhmana may be recognised are, the concentration of the mind, austerities, the subjugation of the senses, liberality, truthfulness, purity, sacred learning, compassion, worldly learning, intelligence, and the belief (in the existence of the deity and of a future life).

24. One may know that bearing grudges, envy, speaking untruths, speaking evil of Brâhmanas, backbiting, and cruelty are the characteristics of a Sûdra.

25. Those Brâhmanas can save (from evil) who are free from passion, and patient of austerities, whose ears have been filled with the texts of the Veda, who have subdued the organs of sensation and action, who have ceased to injure animated beings, and who close their hands when gifts are offered.

26. Some become worthy receptacles of gifts through sacred learning, and some through the practice of austerities. But that Brâhmana whose stomach does not contain the food of a Sûdra, is even the worthiest receptacle of all.

27. If a Brâhmana dies with the food of a Sûdra in his stomach, he will become a village pig (in his next life) or be born in the family of that (Sûdra).

28. For though a (Brâhmana) whose body is nourished by the essence of a Sûdra's food may

24. Krishnapandita connects brâhmanadûshanam, translated above by 'speaking evil of Brâhmanas,' with sûdralakshanam, and renders the two words thus, 'the characteristics of a Sûdra which degrade a Brâhmana.'

25. 'Close their hands,' i.e. are reluctant to accept.

26. Krishnapandita takes kimkit, translated by 'some,' to mean 'somewhat,' 'to a certain degree,' i.e. neither very distinguished nor very despicable.

daily recite the Veda, though he may offer (an Agnihotra) or mutter (prayers, nevertheless) he will not find the path that leads upwards.

29. But if, after eating the food of a *S*ûdra, he has conjugal intercourse, his sons will belong to the giver of the food, and he shall not ascend to heaven.

30. They declare that he is worthy to receive gifts, who (daily) rises to recite the Veda, who is of good family, and perfectly free from passion, who constantly offers sacrifices in the three sacred fires, who fears sin, and knows much, who is beloved among the females (of his family), who is righteous, protects cows, and reduces himself by austerities.

31. Just as milk, sour milk, clarified butter, and honey poured into an unburnt earthen vessel, perish, owing to the weakness of the vessel, and neither the vessel nor those liquids (remain),

32. Even so a man destitute of sacred learning, who accepts cows or gold, clothes, a horse, land, (or) sesamum, becomes ashes, as (if he were dry) wood.

33. He shall not make his joints or his nails crack,

34. Nor shall he make a vessel ring with his nails.

35. Let him not drink water out of his joined hands.

36. Let him not strike the water with his foot or his hand,

37. Nor (pour) water into (other) water.

38. Let him not gather fruit by throwing brick-bats,

39. Nor by throwing another fruit at it.

40. He shall not become a hypocrite or deceitful.

---

32. Manu IV, 188. Read in the text 'eva*m* gâ vâ' instead of 'eva*m* gâvo.'

33. Gautama IX, 51.

35. Gautama IX, 9.

40. Manu IV, 177.

41. Let him not learn a language spoken by barbarians.

42. Now they quote also (the following verses): 'The opinion of the *S*ish*t*as is, that a man shall not be uselessly active, neither with his hands and his feet, nor with his eyes, nor with his tongue and his body.'

43. 'Those Brâhma*n*as, in whose families the study of the Veda and of its supplements is hereditary, and who are able to adduce proofs perceptible by the senses from the revealed texts, must be known to be *S*ish*t*as.'

44. 'He is a (true) Brâhma*n*a regarding whom no one knows if he be good or bad, if he be ignorant or deeply learned, if he be of good or of bad conduct.'

CHAPTER VII.

1. There are four orders,

2. Viz. (that of) the student, (that of) the householder, (that of) the hermit, and (that of) the ascetic.

3. A man who has studied one, two, or three Vedas without violating the rules of studentship, may enter any of these (orders), whichsoever he pleases.

4. A (professed) student shall serve his teacher until death;

5. And in case the teacher dies, he shall serve the sacred fire.

---

42. Manu IV, 177; Gautama IX, 50-51.

43. Manu XII, 109.

VII. 1-2. Gautama III, 2. 3. Gautama III, 1.

4. Vish*n*u XXVIII, 43.

5. Vish*n*u XXVIII, 46. I agree with K*ri*sh*n*apa*nd*ita in thinking that the apparently purposeless particle 'and,' which is used in

6. For it has been declared in the Veda, 'The fire is thy teacher.'

7. (A student, whether professed or temporary), shall bridle his tongue;

8. He shall eat in the fourth, sixth, or eighth hour of the day.

9. He shall go out in order to beg.

10. He shall obey his teacher.

11. He either (may wear all his hair) tied in a knot or (keep merely) a lock on the crown of his head tied in a knot, (shaving the other parts of the head.)

12. If the teacher walks, he shall attend him walking after him; if the teacher is seated, standing; if the teacher lies down, seated.

13. He shall study after having been called (by the teacher, and not request the latter to begin the lesson).

14. Let him announce (to the teacher) all that he has received (when begging), and eat after permission (has been given to him).

---

this Sûtra, indicates Vasish*th*a's approval of the rules given in other Sm*ri*tis, according to which the student, on the death of the teacher, shall serve the teacher's son, a fellow-student, or the teacher's wife, and the service of the sacred fire is the last resource only. See Vish*n*u XXVIII, 44–45; Gautama III, 7–8.

6. These words form part of one of the Mantras which the teacher recites at the initiation of the student; see e.g. *S*âṅkhâyana G*ri*hya-sûtra.

7. Gautama II, 13, 22.

8. According to K*ri*sh*n*apa*nd*ita a kâla, 'hour,' is the eighth part of a day.

9. Vish*n*u XXVIII, 9.

10. Vish*n*u XXVIII, 7.

11. Gautama I, 27; Vish*n*u XXVIII, 41.

12. Vish*n*u XXVIII, 18–22.

13. Vish*n*u XXVIII, 6.

14. Vish*n*u XXVIII, 10; Âpastamba I, 1, 3, 25.

15. Let him avoid to sleep on a cot, to clean his teeth, to wash (his body for pleasure), to apply collyrium (to his eyes), to anoint (his body), and to wear shoes or a parasol.

16. (While reciting his prayers) he shall stand in the day-time and sit down at night.

17. Let him bathe three times a day.

CHAPTER VIII.

1. (A student who desires to become) a householder shall bathe, free from anger and elation, with the permission of his teacher, and take for a wife a young female of his own caste, who does neither belong to the same Gotra nor has the same Pravara, who has not had intercourse (with another man),

2. Who is not related within four degrees on the mother's side, nor within six degrees on the father's side.

3. Let him kindle the nuptial fire.

---

15. Gautama II, 13.

16. Vishnu XXVIII, 2-3. The prayers intended are the so-called Sandhyâs, which are recited at daybreak and in the evening.

17. Gautama II, 8. 'Three times a day,' i.e. morning, noon, and evening. Krishnapandita thinks that he shall perform three ablutions at midday.

VIII. 1. Vishnu XXIV, 9; Gautama IV, 1-2. Regarding the bath at the end of the studentship, see Vishnu XXVIII, 42, and Professor Jolly's note.

2. Vishnu XXIV, 10; Gautama IV, 2.

3. Vishnu LIX, 1, and Professor Jolly's note. The fire intended is the grihya or smârta, the sacred household fire, which according to this Sûtra must be kindled on the occasion of the marriage ceremony, while other Smritis permit of its being lighted on the division of the paternal estate.

4. Let him not turn away a guest who comes in the evening.

5. (A guest) shall not dwell in his house without receiving food.

6. If a Brâhma*n*a who has come for shelter to the house of a (householder) receives no food, on departure he will take with him all the spiritual merit of that (churlish host).

7. But a Brâhma*n*a who stays for one night only is called a guest. For (the etymological import of the word) atithi (a guest) is 'he who stays for a short while only.'

8. A Brâhma*n*a who lives in the same village (with his host) and a visitor on business or pleasure (are) not (called guests. But a guest), whether he arrives at the moment (of dinner) or at an inopportune time, must not stay in the house of a (householder) without receiving food.

9. (A householder) who has faith, is free from covetousness, and (possesses wealth) sufficient for (performing) the Agnyâdheya-sacrifice, must become an Agnihotrin.

10. He (who possesses wealth) sufficient for (the expenses of) a Soma-sacrifice shall not abstain from offering it.

---

4. Vish*n*u LXVII, 28–29. 5. Vish*n*u LXVII, 30.

6. Vish*n*u LXVII, 33.

7. Identical with Vish*n*u LXVII, 34; Manu III, 102.

8. Vish*n*u LXVII, 35; Manu III, 105.

9. Vish*n*u LIX, 2. The Agnihotra which is here intended is, of course, the *S*rauta Agnihotra, to be performed with three fires. The Agnyâdheya is one of the Haviryag*ñ*as with which the *S*rautâgnihotrin has to begin his rites.

10. Vish*n*u LIX, 8.

11. (A householder) shall be industrious in reciting the Veda, offering sacrifices, begetting children, and (performing his other duties).

12. Let him honour visitors (who come) to his house by rising to meet them, by (offering them) seats, by speaking to them kindly and extolling their virtues,

13. And all creatures by (giving them) food according to his ability.

14. A householder alone performs sacrifices, a householder alone performs austerities, and (therefore) the order of householders is the most distinguished among the four.

15. As all rivers, both great and small, find a resting-place in the ocean, even so men of all orders find protection with householders.

16. As all creatures exist through the protection afforded by their mothers, even so all mendicants subsist through the protection afforded by householders.

17. A Brâhma*n*a who always carries water (in his gourd), who always wears the sacred thread, who daily recites the Veda, who avoids the food of outcasts, who approaches (his wife) in the proper season, and offers sacrifices in accordance with the

11. I agree with K*r*ishn*a*pa*nd*ita that the word 'and' used in this enumeration serves the purpose of calling to mind that there are other minor duties. The three named specially are the so-called 'three debts;' see below, XI, 48.

12. Vish*n*u LXVII, 45; Gautama V, 38–41.

13. Vish*n*u LXVII, 26.

14–17. Vish*n*u LIX, 27–30; Manu VI, 89.

15. Identical with Manu VI, 90.

17. 'Who always carries water (in his gourd)' (nityodakî) may also be translated, 'who always keeps water (in his house);' see Âpastamba II, 1, 1, 15. 'Who always wears the sacred thread'

rules (of the Veda, after death) never falls from Brahman's heaven.

Chapter IX.

1. A hermit shall wear (his hair in) braids, and dress (in garments made of) bark and skins;

2. And he shall not enter a village.

3. He shall not step on ploughed (land).

4. He shall gather wild growing roots and fruit (only).

5. He shall remain chaste.

6. His heart shall be full of meekness.

7. He shall honour guests coming to his hermitage with alms (consisting of) roots and fruit.

8. He shall only give, not receive (presents).

9. He shall bathe at morn, noon, and eve.

10. Kindling a fire according to the (rule of the) *S*râma*n*aka (Sûtra), he shall offer the Agnihotra.

11. After (living in this manner during) six months,

---

may also mean 'who always wears his upper in the manner required at a sacrifice,' i.e. passes it over the left and under the right arm.

IX. 1. Vish*n*u XCIV, 8–9; Gautama III, 34. K*ri*sh*n*apa*nd*ita takes *k*îra, 'bark,' to mean '(made of) grass,' e.g. of Mu*ñg*a or Balva*g*a.

2. Gautama III, 33. The particle 'and' probably indicates that the hermit is not to enter any other inhabited place.

3. Gautama III, 32. 4. Vish*n*u XCV, 5.

5. Vish*n*u XCV, 7. 6. Manu VI, 8.

7. Gautama III, 30. 9. Vish*n*u XCV, 10.

10. Gautama III, 27. K*ri*sh*n*apa*nd*ita and MSS. B. F. read *s*râva*n*akena, and the rest âvar*n*akena. I read *s*râma*n*akena, 'according to the rule of the *S*râma*n*aka Sûtra,' in accordance with Gautama's text. Baudhâyana, too, uses the same word.

11. Manu VI, 25.

he shall dwell at the root of a tree, keeping no fire and having no house.

12. He (who in this manner) gives (their due) to gods, manes, and men, will attain endless (bliss in) heaven.

Chapter X.

1. Let an ascetic depart from his house, giving a promise of safety from injury to all animated beings.

2. Now they quote also (the following verses): 'That ascetic who wanders about at peace with all creatures, forsooth, has nothing to fear from any living being.'

3. 'But he who becomes an ascetic and does not promise safety from injury to all beings, destroys the born and the unborn; and (so does an ascetic) who accepts presents.'

4. 'Let him discontinue the performance of all religious ceremonies, but let him never discontinue the recitation of the Veda. By neglecting the Veda he becomes a Sûdra; therefore he shall not neglect it.'

5. '(To pronounce) the one syllable (Om) is the best (mode of reciting the) Veda, to suppress the breath is the highest (form of) austerity; (to subsist on) alms is better than fasting; compassion is preferable to liberality.'

6. (Let the ascetic) shave (his head); let him have no property and no home.

X. 1. Manu VI, 39; Yâgñavalkya III, 61.

2. Manu VI, 40.

3. 'The born and the unborn,' i.e. his ancestors who lose heaven, and his descendants who lose their caste.

4. Manu VI, 39. 5. Manu II, 83.

6. Gautama III, 11, 22. The term parigraha, 'home,' includes the wife, the family, attendants, and a house.

7. Let him beg food at seven houses which he has not selected (beforehand),

8. (At the time) when the smoke (of the kitchen-fire) has ceased and the pestle lies motionless.

9. Let him wear a single garment,

10. Or cover his body with a skin or with grass that has been nibbled at by a cow.

11. Let him sleep on the bare ground.

12. Let him frequently change his residence,

13. (Dwelling) at the extremity of the village, in a temple, or in an empty house, or at the root of a tree.

14. Let him (constantly) seek in his heart the knowledge (of the universal soul).

15. (An ascetic) who lives constantly in the forest,

16. Shall not wander about within sight of the village-cattle.

17. 'Freedom from future births is certain for him who constantly dwells in the forest, who has subdued his organs of sensation and action, who has renounced all sensual gratification, whose mind is fixed in meditation on the Supreme Spirit, and who is (wholly) indifferent (to pleasure and pain).'

18. (Let him) not (wear) any visible mark (of his order), nor (follow) any visible rule of conduct.

19. Let him, though not mad, appear like one out of his mind.

20. Now they quote also (the following verses): 'There is no salvation for him who is addicted to

---

7. Vishnu XCVI, 3.

8. Vishnu XCVI, 6; Manu VI, 56.

9. Vishnu XCVI, 13. It is very probable that the single garment mentioned in the Sûtra is, as Krishnapandita thinks, a small strip of cloth to cover the ascetic's nakedness.

12–13. Vishnu XCVI, 10–12. 14. Manu VI, 43, 65.

20. I read 'ramyâvasathapriyasya,' with the majority of the MSS.

the pursuit of the science of words, nor for him who rejoices in captivating men, nor for him who is fond of (good) eating and (fine) clothing, nor for him who loves a pleasant dwelling.'

21. 'Neither by (explaining) prodigies and omens, nor by skill in astrology and palmistry, nor by casuistry and expositions (of the Sâstras), let him ever seek to obtain alms.'

22. 'Let him not be dejected when he obtains nothing, nor glad when he receives something. Let him only seek as much as will sustain life, without caring for household property.'

23. 'But he, forsooth, knows (the road to) salvation who cares neither for a hut, nor for water, nor for clothes, nor for the three Pushkaras' (holy tanks), nor for a house, nor for a seat, nor for food.'

24. In the morning and in the evening he may eat as much (food) as he obtains in the house of one Brâhmana, excepting honey and meat,

25. And he shall not (eat so much that he is quite) satiated.

26. At his option (an ascetic) may (also) dwell in a village.

27. Let him not be crooked (in his ways); (let him) not (observe the rules of) impurity on account

---

21. Identical with Manu VI, 50.

22. Vishnu XCVI, 4. Identical with Manu VI, 57.

23. There are three Tîrthas called Pushkara; see Professor Jolly's note on Vishnu LXXXV, 1.

24. Krishnapandita thinks that this rule is a concession to those ascetics who are unable to subsist on one meal a day, as Manu VI, 55 prescribes.

25. Manu VI, 59. 26. Manu VI, 94-95.

27. The text is here probably corrupt. But I follow Krishnapandita. Several MSS. read asatho, 'he shall not be a rogue,' for asavo, 'he shall not observe the rules of impurity.'

of deaths (or births); let him not have a house; let him be of concentrated mind.

28. Let him not enjoy any object of sensual gratification.

29. Let him be (utterly) indifferent, avoiding to do injury or to show kindness to any living being.

30. To avoid backbiting, jealousy, pride, self-consciousness, unbelief, dishonesty, self-praise, blaming others, deceit, covetousness, delusion, anger, and envy is considered to be the duty of (men of) all orders.

31. A Brâhma*n*a who wears the sacred thread, who holds in his hand a gourd filled with water, who is pure and avoids the food of *S*ûdras will not fail (to gain) the world of Brahman.

Chapter XI.

1. Six persons are (particularly) worthy to receive the honey-mixture (madhuparka),

2. (Viz.) an officiating priest, the bridegroom of one's daughter, a king, a paternal uncle, a Snâtaka, a maternal uncle, as well as (others enumerated elsewhere).

3. (A householder) shall offer, both at the morning and the evening (meals, a portion) of the prepared (food) to the Vi*s*ve Devas in the (sacred) domestic fire.

30. Vish*n*u II, 16–17.

31. K*r*ish*n*apa*nd*ita believes that this Sûtra again refers to ascetics. But that is hardly possible, as ascetics are not allowed to wear a sacrificial thread (see above, Sûtra 18). I think that it is meant to emphatically assert that a Brâhma*n*a who is free from the shortcomings enumerated in the preceding Sûtra, and who follows the rule of conduct, will obtain salvation, whether he passes through the order of Sa*m*nyâsins or not.

XI. 1–2. Gautama V, 27–30. The persons enumerated elsewhere are the teacher, the father-in-law, and so forth. Regarding the Snâtaka, see Âpastamba I, 11, 30, 1–4.

3. Vish*n*u LXVII, 1–3.

4. Let him give a Bali-offering to the (guardian) deities of the house,

5. (Thereafter) let him give a portion, one Pala in weight, to a *S*rotriya or to a student, (and afterwards an offering) to the manes.

6. Next let him feed his guests in due order, the worthiest first,

7. (Thereafter) the maidens, the infants, the aged, the half-grown members of his family, and pradâtâs,

8. Then the other members of his family.

9. (Outside the house) he shall throw (some food) on the ground for the dogs, *K*â*nd*âlas, outcasts, and crows.

10. He may give to a *S*ûdra either the fragments (of the meal) or (a portion of) fresh (food).

11. The master of the house and his wife may eat what remains.

---

4. Vish*n*u LXVII, 4-22.

5. Vish*n*u LIX, 14; LXVII, 23, 27. K*ri*sh*n*apa*nd*ita does not take 'agrabhâga' as a technical term, but explains it by 'a first portion, sufficient for a dinner, or as much as one is able to spare.'

6. Vish*n*u LXVII, 28, 36-38.

7. Vish*n*u LXVII, 39. The majority of the MSS. read bâlav*ri*ddhataru*n*apradâtâs [tato]. K*ri*sh*n*apa*nd*ita corrects the last word to pradâtâ, while the editor of the Calcutta edition writes prabhrit*îm*s [tato]. Both conjectures are inadmissible. As the same phrase occurs once more, below, XIX, 23 (where K*ri*sh*n*apa*nd*ita writes pradâtâra*h*), I think that it is not permissible to change the text. Pradâtâ*h* must be the correct reading, and a technical name for a class of female relatives. Etymologically it may mean 'those who have been perfectly cleansed.' But I am unable to trace its precise technical import, and have left it untranslated.

8. Vish*n*u LXVII, 41. 9. Vish*n*u LXVII, 26.

10. Gautama V, 25, and note. 'A *S*ûdra, i.e. one who is his servant.'—K*ri*sh*n*apa*nd*ita. It is, however, possible, that a visitor of the *S*ûdra caste is meant; see Âpastamba II, 2, 4, 19-20.

11. Vish*n*u LXVII, 41.

12. A fresh meal for which all (the same materials as for the first) are used (may be prepared), if a guest comes after the Vaisvadeva has been offered. For such a (guest) he shall cause to be prepared food (of a) particularly (good quality).

13. For it has been declared in the Veda, 'A Brâhma*n*a guest enters the house resembling the Vais*v*ânara fire. Through him they obtain rain, and food through rain. Therefore people know that the (hospitable reception of a guest) is a ceremony averting evil.'

14. Having fed the (guest), he shall honour him.

15. He shall accompany him to the boundary (of the village) or until he receives permission (to return).

16. Let him present (funeral offerings) to the manes during the dark half of the month (on any day) after the fourth.

17. After issuing an invitation on the day preceding (the *S*râddha, he shall feed on that occasion) three ascetics or three virtuous householders, who are *S*rotriyas, who are not very aged, who do not follow forbidden occupations, and neither (have been his) pupils, nor are (living as) pupils in his house.

18. He may also feed pupils who are endowed with good qualities.

19. Let him avoid men neglecting their duties,

---

12. Âpastamba II, 3, 6, 16; Gautama V, 32, 33. A guest, i.e. one to whom the definition given above, VIII, 6, 7, applies. I read according to my MSS. puna*h*pâko instead of puna*h*pâke.

14–15. Gautama V, 38.

16. Vish*n*u LXXVI, 1–2; Gautama XV, 3.

17. Vish*n*u LXXIII, 1; LXXXII, 2–4; LXXXIII, 5, 19; Gautama XV, 10; Âpastamba II, 7, 17, 4.

18. Âpastamba II, 7, 17, 6.

19. Gautama XV, 16, 18. The explanation of the word nagna,

those afflicted with white leprosy, eunuchs, blind men, those who have black teeth, those who suffer from black leprosy, (and) those who have deformed nails.

20. Now they quote also (the following verses): 'Now, if a (Brâhmana) versed in the Vedas is afflicted with bodily (defects) which exclude him from the company, Yama declares him to be irreproachable. Such (a man) sanctifies the company.'

21. 'At a funeral sacrifice the fragments (of the meal) must not be swept away until the end of the day. For streams of nectar flow (from them, and the manes of) those who have received no libations of water drink (them).'

22. 'But let him not sweep up the fragments (of the meal) before the sun has set. Thence issue rich streams of milk for those who obtain a share with difficulty.'

23. 'Manu declares that both the remainder (in the vessels) and the fragments (of the meal) certainly are the portion of those members of the family who died before receiving the sacraments.'

24. 'Let him give the fragments that have fallen on the ground and the portion scattered (on the blades of Kusa grass), which consists of the wipings

---

'neglecting their duties,' is doubtful. I have followed Krishnapandita, who quotes the Mârkandeya Purâna in support of his view. The word occurs in the same connexion, Vishnu LXXXII, 27, where it is rendered by 'naked.' Possibly it may refer to ascetics who go entirely naked.

20. The Sûtra gives an exception to the preceding rule.

21. I read 'skyotante hi' instead of 'skyotante vai.'

22. 'Those who receive a share with difficulty,' i. e. the manes of uninitiated children, mentioned in the next verses.

23-24. Vishnu LXXXII, 22; Manu III, 245-246. These rules, however, do not fully agree with the teaching of our Manu-smriti,

and water, as their food, to the manes of those who died without offspring and of those who died young.'

25. 'The malevolent Asuras seek an opportunity (to snatch away) that food intended for the manes, which is not supported with both hands;'

26. 'Therefore let him not offer it (to the Brâhmanas) without holding (a spoon) in his hand; or let him stand, holding the dish (with both hands, until) leavings of both kinds (have been produced).'

27. 'He shall feed two (Brâhmanas) at the offering to the gods, and three at the offering to the manes, or a single man on either occasion; even a very wealthy man shall not be anxious (to entertain) a large company.'

28. 'A large company destroys these five (advantages), the respectful treatment (of the invited guests, the propriety of) time and place, purity and (the selection of) virtuous Brâhmana (guests); therefore he shall not (invite a large number).'

29. 'Or he may entertain (at a Srâddha) even a single Brâhmana who has studied the whole Veda, who is distinguished by learning and virtue, and is free from all evil marks (on his body).'

---

as the latter assigns the fragments on the ground to honest and upright servants. Sûtra 24 I read with the majority of the MSS. 'lepanodakam' for 'lepamodakam,' and 'annam preteshu' for 'anupreteshu.'

25. Manu III, 225.

26. Manu III, 224. The meaning of the last clause seems to be that the sacrificer shall stand before the Brâhmanas until they have done eating.

27. Identical with Manu III, 125; see also Vishnu LXXIII, 3. The offering to the gods is the Vaisvadeva offering which precedes the Srâddha.

28. Identical with Manu III, 126. 29. Manu III, 129.

30. '(But) how can the oblation to the gods be made if he feeds a single Brâhmana at a funeral sacrifice? Let him take (a portion) of each (kind of) food that has been prepared (and put it) into a vessel;'

31. 'Let him place it in the sanctuary of a god and afterwards continue (the performance of) the funeral sacrifice. Let him offer that food in the fire or give it (as alms) to a student.'

32. 'As long as the food continues warm, as long as they eat in silence, as long as the qualities of the food are not declared (by them), so long the manes feast on it.'

33. 'The qualities of the food must not be declared as long as the (Brâhmanas who represent the) manes are not satiated. Afterwards when they are satisfied, they may say, "Beautiful is the sacrificial food."'

34. 'But an ascetic who, invited to dine at a sacrifice of the manes or of the gods, rejects meat, shall go to hell for as many years as the slaughtered beast has hairs.'

35. 'Three (things are held to) sanctify a funeral sacrifice, a daughter's son, the midday, and sesamum grains; and they recommend three (other things) for it, purity, freedom from anger and from precipitation.'

36. 'The eighth division of the day, during which the sun's (progress in the heavens) becomes slow, one must know to be midday; what is (then) given to the manes lasts (them) for a very long time.'

37. 'The ancestors of that man who has inter-

32. Identical with Vishnu LXXXII, 20, and Manu III, 237.

34. Manu V, 35. 35. Identical with Manu III, 235.

37. Vishnu LXIX, 2-4.

course with a woman after offering or having dined at a *S*râddha, feed during a month from that (day) on his semen.'

38. 'A child that is born from (intercourse immediately) after offering a *S*râddha or partaking of a funeral repast, is unable to acquire sacred learning and becomes short-lived.'

39. 'The father and the grandfather, likewise the great-grandfather, beset a descendant who is born to them, just as birds (fly to) a fig tree;'

40. '(Saying), "He will offer to us funeral repasts with honey and meat, with vegetables, with milk and with messes made of milk, both in the rainy season and under the constellation Maghâ*h*."'

41. 'The ancestors always rejoice at a descendant who lengthens the line, who is zealous in performing funeral sacrifices, and who is rich in (images of the) gods and (virtuous) Brâhma*n*a (guests).'

42. 'The manes consider him to be their (true) descendant who offers (to them) food at Gayâ, and (by the virtue of that gift) they grant him (blessings), just as husbandmen (produce grain) on well-ploughed (fields).'

43. He shall offer (a *S*râddha) both on the full moon days of the months *S*râva*n*a and Âgrahâya*n*a and on the Anvash*t*akî.

39-40. Vish*n*u LXXVIII, 51-53.

41. 'Who lengthens the line,' i. e. who himself begets sons. Read instead of nuyanta*m* pit*ri*karma*n*i (v. l. muyanta*m* and *tri*panta*h*), 'udyata*m*.'

42. Vish*n*u LXXXV, 4, 66-67.

43. *S*râva*n*a, i.e. July-August; Âgrahâya*n*a, i.e. Mârga*s*îrsha or November-December. Anvash*t*akî means the day following the Ash*t*akâ, or eighth day, i. e. the ninth day of the dark halves of Mârga*s*îrsha, Pausha, Mâgha, and Phâlguna. The form of the word is usually anvash*t*akâ.

44. There is no restriction as to time, if (particularly suitable) materials and (particularly holy) Brâhma*n*as are at hand, or (if the sacrificer is) near (a particularly sacred) place.

45. A Brâhma*n*a must necessarily kindle the three sacred fires.

46. He shall offer (in them) the full and new moon sacrifices, the (half-yearly) Âgraya*n*a Ish*t*i, the *K*âturmâsya-sacrifice, the (half-yearly) sacrifices at which animals are slain, and the (annual) Soma-sacrifices.

47. For all this is (particularly) enjoined (in the Veda), and called by way of laudation 'a debt.'

48. For it is declared in the Veda, 'A Brâhma*n*a is born, loaded with three debts,' (and further, 'He owes) sacrifices to the gods, a son to the manes, the study of the Veda to the *Ri*shis; therefore he is free from debt who has offered sacrifices, who has begotten a son, and who has lived as a student (with a teacher).'

49. Let him (ordinarily) initiate a Brâhma*n*a in the eighth (year) after conception,

50. A Kshatriya in the eleventh year after conception,

51. A Vai*s*ya in the twelfth year after conception.

52. The staff of a Brâhma*n*a (student may) optionally (be made) of Palâ*s*a wood,

---

44. Gautama XV, 5. 45. Vish*n*u LIX, 2.

46. Vish*n*u LIX, 4-9.

47. Manu IV, 257. I read *rin*asa*m*stuta*m* with MS. E.

48. Taitt. Sa*m*h. VI, 3, 10, 5; *S*atapatha-brâhma*n*a I, 7, 2, 11.

49-51. Vish*n*u XXVII, 15-17.

52-54. Vish*n*u XXVII, 29. Regarding other kinds of sticks, see Gautama I, 22-24.

53. (That) of a Kshatriya optionally of the wood of the Banyan tree,

54. (That) of a Vaisya optionally of Udumbara wood.

55. (The staff) of a Brâhmana shall (be of such a length as to) reach the hair,

56. (That) of a Kshatriya the forehead,

57. (That) of a Vaisya the (tip of the) nose.

58. The girdle of a Brâhmana shall be made of Muñga grass,

59. A bowstring (shall be that) of a Kshatriya,

60. (That) of a Vaisya shall be made of hempen threads.

61. The upper garment of a Brâhmana (shall be) the skin of a black antelope,

62. (That) of a Kshatriya the skin of a spotted deer,

63. (That) of a Vaisya a cow-skin or the hide of a he-goat.

64. The (lower) garment of a Brâhmana (shall be) white (and) unblemished,

65. (That) of a Kshatriya dyed with madder,

66. (That) of a Vaisya dyed with turmeric, or made of (raw) silk;

67. Or (a dress made of) undyed (cotton) cloth may be worn by (students of) all (castes).

68. A Brâhmana shall ask for alms placing (the word) 'Lady' first,

---

55–57. Vishnu XXVII, 22. 58–60. Vishnu XXVII, 18.

61–63. Vishnu XXVII, 20.

64–67. Vishnu XXVII, 19; Gautama I, 17–21. 'Unblemished,' i. e. new, without holes and seams.

68–70. Vishnu XXVII, 25. I. e. 'Lady, give alms;' 'Give, O lady, alms;' and 'Give alms, lady.'

69. A Kshatriya placing (the word) 'Lady' in the middle,

70. A Vaisya placing (the word) 'Lady' at the end (of the formula).

71. The time (for the initiation) of a Brâhmana has not passed until the completion of the sixteenth year,

72. (For that) of a Kshatriya until the completion of the twenty-second,

73. (For that) of a Vaisya until the completion of the twenty-fourth.

74. After that they become 'men whose Sâvitrî has been neglected.'

75. Let him not initiate such men, nor teach them, nor sacrifice for them; let them not form matrimonial alliances (with such outcasts).

76. A man whose Sâvitrî has not been performed, may undergo the Uddâlaka-penance.

77. Let him subsist during two months on barley-gruel, during one month on milk, during half a month on curds of two-milk whey, during eight days on clarified butter, during six days on alms given without asking, (and) during three days on water, and let him fast for one day and one night.

78. (Or) he may go to bathe (with the priests) at the end of an Asvamedha (horse-sacrifice).

79. Or he may offer a Vrâtya-stoma.

71–73. Vishnu XXVII, 26.

74. Vishnu XXVII, 27. Sâvitrî, literally 'the *Rik* sacred to Savitri' (Rig-veda III, 62, 10), means here 'the initiation,' see Gautama I, 12 note.

75. Âpastamba I, 1, 1, 28. The plural vivâhayeyuh, 'let them (not) form matrimonial alliances,' indicates that orthodox Brâhmanas must neither give their daughters to Patitasâvitrîkas nor take the daughters of such persons.

78. Gautama XIX, 9.

79. Gautama XIX, 8.

CHAPTER XII.

1. Now, therefore, the duties of a Snâtaka (will be explained).

2. Let him not beg from anybody except from a king and a pupil.

3. But let him ask, if pressed by hunger, for some (small gift) only, a cultivated or uncultivated field, a cow, a goat or a sheep, (or) at the last extremity, for gold, grain or food.

4. But the injunction (given by those who know the law) is, 'A Snâtaka shall not be faint with hunger.'

5. Let him not dwell together with a person whose clothes are foul;

6. (Let him not cohabit) with a woman during her courses,

7. Nor with an unfit one.

8. Let him not be a stay-at-home.

XII. 1. 'Now' marks the beginning of a new topic. 'Therefore,' i. e. because the duties of a Snâtaka have to be taught after those of a student.

2. Manu IV, 33; Gautama IX, 63.

3. Manu X, 113–114. 4. Manu IV, 34; Vish*n*u III, 79.

5. K*ri*sh*n*apa*nd*ita, whom I have followed in the translation of this Sûtra, thinks that it indicates the obligation of wearing clean clothes, see e. g. Vish*n*u LXXI, 9. It seems to me, however, probable that its real sense is, 'Let him not cohabit with a woman during her courses,' and that the next Sûtra has to be read nâragasvalayâ, 'Nor with one of immature age.'

7. 'An unfit one,' i. e. 'one of low caste' (hînâ).—K*ri*sh*n*apa*nd*ita. Probably a sick wife is meant, Gautama IX, 28.

8. Gautama IX, 53. K*ri*sh*n*apa*nd*ita gives besides the above interpretation of the Sûtra from Haradatta's Gautamîyâ Mitâksharâ, another one, according to which it means, 'Let him not forsake his own family and enter another one (by adoption and so forth).' A third

9. Let him not step over a stretched rope to which a calf (or cow) is tied.

10. Let him not look at the sun when he rises or sets.

11. Let him not void excrements or urine in water,

12. Nor spit into it.

13. Let him ease himself, after wrapping up his head and covering the ground with grass that is not fit to be used at a sacrifice, and turning towards the north in the day-time, turning towards the south at night, sitting with his face towards the north in the twilight.

14. Now they quote also (the following verses): 'But Snâtakas shall always wear a lower garment and an upper one, two sacrificial threads, (shall carry) a staff and a vessel filled with water.'

15. 'It is declared, that (a vessel becomes) pure (if cleaned) with water, or with the hand, or with a stick, or with fire. Therefore he shall clean (his) vessel with water and with his (right) hand.'

16. 'For Manu, the lord of created beings, calls (this mode of cleaning) encircling it with fire.'

17. 'He who is perfectly acquainted with (the rules of) purification shall sip water (out of this vessel), after he has relieved the necessities of nature.'

18. Let him eat his food facing the east.

---

explanation is given by Nârâyana on Sâṅkhâyana Grihya-sûtra IV, 12, 11, who takes it to mean, 'Let him not go from one house to the other.'

9. Gautama IX, 52; Vishnu LXIII, 42.

10. Vishnu LXXI, 17–18. 11–12. Vishnu LXXI, 35.

13. Gautama IX, 37–38, 41–43; Vishnu LX, 2–3.

14. Vishnu LXXI, 13–15. 18. Vishnu LXVIII, 40.

19. Silently let him swallow the entire mouthful, (introducing it into the mouth) with the four fingers and with the thumb;

20. And let him not make a noise (while eating).

21. Let him approach his wife in the proper season, except on the Parva days.

22. Let him not commit a crime against nature (with her).

23. Now they quote also (the following verse): 'The ancestors of a man who commits an unnatural crime with a wedded wife, feed during that month on his semen. All unnatural intercourse is against the sacred law.'

24. It is also declared in the Kâ*th*aka, '(When) the women (asked) Indra, "May even those among us, who are soon to be mothers, (be allowed to) cohabit with their husbands," he granted that wish.'

25. Let him not ascend a tree.

26. Let him not descend into a well.

27. Let him not blow the fire with his mouth.

28. Let him not pass between a fire and a Brâhma*n*a,

29. Nor between two fires;

30. Nor between two Brâhma*n*as; or (he may do it) after having asked for permission.

31. Let him not dine together with his wife. For it is declared in the Vâ*g*asaneyaka, 'His children will be destitute of manly vigour.'

---

19. K*ri*sh*n*apa*nd*ita thinks that this rule refers to the first five mouthfuls only.

21. Vish*n*u LXIX, 1. The Parva days are the eighth, fourteenth, and fifteenth of each half-month.

25–27. Gautama IX, 32. 28. Âpastamba II, 5, 12, 6.

30. Âpastamba II, 5, 12, 7–8.

31. *S*atapatha-brâhma*n*a X, 5, 2, 9; Vish*n*u LXVIII, 46.

32. Let him not point out (a rainbow calling it) by (its proper) name, 'Indra's bow.'

33. Let him call it 'the jewelled bow' (*mani*-dhanu*h*).

34. Let him avoid seats, clogs, sticks for cleaning the teeth, (and other implements) made of Palâ*s*a wood.

35. Let him not eat (food placed) in his lap.

36. Let him not eat (food placed) on a chair.

37. Let him carry a staff of bamboo,

38. And (wear) two golden earrings.

39. Let him not wear any visible wreath excepting a golden one;

40. And let him disdain assemblies and crowds.

41. Now they quote also (the following verse): 'To deny the authority of the Vedas, to carp at the teaching of the *Ri*shis, to waver with respect to any (matter of duty), that is to destroy one's soul.'

42. Let him not go to a sacrifice except if he is chosen (to be an officiating priest. But) if he goes, he must, on returning home, turn his right hand (towards the place).

43. Let him not set out on a journey when the sun stands over the trees.

32-33. Gautama IX, 22. 34. Gautama IX, 44.
35. Vish*n*u LXVIII, 21. 36. Gautama IX, 32.
37. Vish*n*u LXXI, 13. 38. Vish*n*u LXXI, 16.
39. Gautama IX, 32.

40. I read sabhâsamavâyâ*m*s*k*âva*g*ayeta. The corrupt readings of Bh. samavâyâ*s**k*a *g*avîyan and of F. samavâyâ*m*s*k*a vakshîyanna point to this version, the sense of which agrees with the parallel passages of other Sm*ri*tis, see e. g. Âpastamba I, 11, 32, 19.

41. Vish*n*u LXXI, 83. 42. Gautama IX, 54-55, 66.

43. Vish*n*u LXIII, 9. According to K*ri*sh*n*apa*nd*ita the time intended is midday.

44. Let him not ascend an unsafe boat, or (any unsafe conveyance).

45. Let him not cross a river, swimming.

46. When he has risen in the last watch (of the night) and has recited (the Veda) he shall not lie down again.

47. In the Muhûrta sacred to Pra*g*âpati a Brâhma*n*a shall fulfil some sacred duties.

Chapter XIII.

1. Now, therefore, the Upâkarman (or the rite preparatory to the study) of the Veda (must be performed) on the full moon day of the month *S*râva*n*a or Praush*th*apada.

2. Having kindled the sacred fire, he offers (therein) unground (rice) grains,

3. To the gods, to the *Ri*shis, and to the *Kh*andas.

4. Let them begin to study the Vedas, after having made Brâhma*n*as (invited for the purpose) wish 'welfare' (svasti), and after having fed them with sour milk,

5. (And continue the Veda-study) during four

44. Vish*n*u LXIII, 47.

45. Vish*n*u LXIII, 46. K*ri*sh*n*apa*nd*ita omits this Sûtra which is found in the majority of the MSS.

46. Âpastamba I, 11, 32, 15; Vish*n*u XXX, 27.

47. Manu IV, 92; Vish*n*u LX, 1. The Muhûrta sacred to Pra*g*âpati is the same as the Brâhma-muhûrta, and falls in the last watch of the night.

XIII. 1. Vish*n*u XXX, 1. *S*râva*n*a, July–August. Praush*th*apada, i. e. Bhâdrapada, August–September. K*ri*sh*n*apa*nd*ita improperly combines this Sûtra with the next.

5. Gautama XVI, 2.

months and a half or during five months and a half.

6. After (the expiration of) that (period), he may study (the Vedas) during the bright half of each month,

7. But the supplementary treatises (Aṅgas) of the Veda at pleasure (both during the bright and the dark halves of each month).

8. Interruptions of the (Veda-study shall take place),

9. If it thunders during the twilight,

10. During (both) the twilights (of each day),

11. In towns where a corpse (lies) or *K*â*nd*âlas (stay).

12. At pleasure (he may study seated) in (a place) which has been smeared with cowdung and around which a line has been drawn.

13. (Let him not study) near a burial-ground,

14. (Nor) lying down,

15. Nor when he has eaten or received a gift at a funeral sacrifice;

16. And with reference to this (subject) they quote a verse of Manu, 'Be it fruit, or water, or

---

6–7. Manu IV, 98.

9. Âpastamba I, 3, 9, 20.

10. Gautama XVI, 12.

11. Gautama XVI, 19; Vish*n*u XXX, 10. The above translation follows K*ri*sh*n*apa*nd*ita's gloss. But the Sûtra may also be taken differently: 'In (villages) where a corpse lies or a *K*â*nd*âla stays (and) in towns.' For the prohibition to study in towns is mentioned by Gautama XVI, 45; Manu IV, 116; and Âpastamba I, 3, 9, 4.

12. Âpastamba I, 3, 9, 5. The rule refers to places, such as high-roads, where studying is ordinarily forbidden.

13. Vish*n*u XXX, 15; Âpastamba I, 3, 9, 6.

14. Gautama XVI, 17.

15. Gautama XVI, 34.

16. Manu IV, 117 somewhat resembles the verse quoted. But

sesamum, or food, or whatever be the (gift) at a *S*râddha, let him not, having just accepted it, recite the Veda; for it is declared in the Sm*ri*ti, that the hand of a Brâhma*n*a is his mouth.'

17. (Let him not recite the Veda) while he runs, (nor) while a foul smell and the like (are perceptible, nor) on barren ground,

18. (Nor) when he has ascended a tree,

19. (Nor) in a boat or in a camp,

20. Nor after meals while his hands are moist,

21. (Nor) while the sound of a Vâ*n*a (is heard),

22. (Nor) on the fourteenth day (of each half-month, nor) on the new moon day, (nor) on the eighth day (of each half-month, nor) on an Ash*t*akâ,

23. (Nor) while he stretches his feet out, (nor) while he makes a lap, (nor) while he leans against (something), nor (in any other unbecoming posture),

24. (Nor) close to his Gurus,

25. (Nor) during that night in which he has had conjugal intercourse,

26. (Nor) dressed in that garment which he had on during conjugal intercourse, except if it has been washed,

---

its altered form shows clearly that the Mânava Dharma*s*âstra known to Vasish*th*a differed from the work which at present goes by that name. Compare also *S*âṅkhâyana G*ri*hya-sûtra IV, 7, 55.

17. Yâ*gñ*avalkya I, 150; Gautama XVI, 19; Manu IV, 120.

18. Âpastamba I, 3, 11, 16.

19. Vish*n*u XXX, 18; Manu IV, 121.

20. Âpastamba I, 3, 10, 25.

21. Gautama XVI, 7, and note.

22. Vish*n*u XXX, 4; Gautama XVI, 37–38. The Ash*t*akâs are the eighth days of the dark halves of the winter months, Mârga*s*îrsha, Pausha, Mâgha, and Phâlgu*n*a.

23. Vish*n*u XXX, 17; Manu IV, 112. 26. Manu IV, 116.

27. (Nor) at the extremity of a village,

28. (Nor) after (an attack of) vomiting,

29. (Nor) while voiding urine or fæces.

30. (Let him not recite) the Rig-veda, the Yagur-veda, and (the Atharva-veda) while the sound of the Sâman melodies (is audible), nor (the Sâman while the other Vedas are being recited).

31. (Let him not study) before (his food is) digested,

32. (Nor) when a thunderbolt falls,

33. (Nor) when an earthquake happens,

34. Nor when the sun and the moon are eclipsed.

35. When a preternaturally loud sound is heard in the sky, when a mountain falls, (and) when showers of stones, blood or sand (fall from the sky, the Veda must not be read) during the twenty-four hours (immediately succeeding the event).

36. If meteors and lightning appear together, (the interruption shall last) three (days and) nights.

37. A meteor (alone and) a flash of lightning (alone cause an interruption lasting) as long as the sun shines (on that or the next day).

38. (If rain or other celestial phenomena come) out of season, (the Veda must not be read) during the twenty-four hours (immediately succeeding the event).

---

27. Gautama XVI, 18. 28. Vishnu XXX, 19.

29. Gautama XVI, 11. Krishnapandita improperly divides the Sûtra into two.

30. Vishnu XXX, 26. 31. Vishnu XXX, 21.

32–34. Vishnu XXX, 5; Gautama XVI, 22.

35. Gautama XVI, 22; Manu IV, 105, 115. Krishnapandita mentions digdâha, 'when the sky appears preternaturally red,' as a various reading for 'dignâda.'

38. Âpastamba I, 3, 11, 29.

39. If the teacher has died, (he shall not study the Veda) during three (days and) nights.

40. If the teacher's son, a pupil, or a wife (have died, he shall not study) during a day and a night.

41. Let him honour an officiating priest, a father-in-law, paternal and maternal uncles, (though they may be) younger than himself, by rising and saluting them,

42. Likewise the wives of those persons whose feet must be embraced, and the teacher's (wives),

43. And his parents.

44. Let him say to one acquainted with (the meaning of) a salute, 'I N. N. ho! (salute thee);'

45. But him who does not know it (he shall address with the same formula, omitting his name).

46. When a salute is returned, the last vowel (of the noun standing) in the vocative is produced to the length of three moras, and if it is a diphthong (e or o) changeable according to the Sandhi rules, it becomes ây or âv, e.g. bho, bhâv.

47. A father who has committed a crime causing loss of caste must be cast off. But a mother does not become an outcast for her son.

48. Now they quote also (the following verses):

---

39. Âpastamba I, 3, 10, 2–4. 40. Vishnu XXXII, 4.

42. The persons intended are, the teacher and so forth. See Âpastamba I, 4, 14, 7, note.

44. Gautama VI, 5.

45. Âpastamba I, 4, 14, 23. K*r*ish*n*apa*nd*ita combines this Sûtra with the preceding.

46. Âpastamba I, 2, 5, 18. In returning a salute, the name of the person addressed is pronounced, and if it ends in a, the vowel is made pluta, while e and o are changed to âya and âva, e.g. Hare to Harâya.

47. Gautama XX, 1; XXI, 15; Âpastamba I, 10, 28, 9.

48. Manu II, 145.

'The teacher (âkârya) is ten times more venerable than a sub-teacher (upâdhyâya), the father a hundred times more than the teacher, and the mother a thousand times more than the father.'

49. 'A wife, sons, and pupils who are defiled by sinful deeds, must first be reproved, and (if they do not amend, then) be cast off. He who forsakes them in any other way, becomes (himself) an outcast.'

50. An officiating priest and a teacher who neglect to teach the recitation of the Veda, or to sacrifice, shall be cast off. If he does not forsake them, he becomes an outcast.

51. They declare that the male offspring of outcasts are (also) outcasts, but not the females.

52. For a female enters (the family of) a stranger.

53. He may marry such a (female) without a dowry.

54. 'If the teacher's teacher is near, he must be treated like the teacher (himself). The Veda declares that one must behave towards the teacher's son just as towards the teacher.'

55. A Brâhmana shall not accept (as gifts) weapons, poison, and spirituous liquor.

56. Learning, wealth, age, relationship, and occupation must be honoured.

57. (But) each earlier named (quality) is more venerable than (the succeeding ones).

58. If he meets aged men, infants, sick men, load-carriers, women, and persons riding in chariots, he

49. Âpastamba I, 2, 8, 29–30. 50. Gautama XXI, 12.
51. Âpastamba I, 10, 29, 14.
53. Manu II, 238; Yâgñavalkya III, 261.
54. Vishnu XXVIII, 29, 31. 56. Vishnu XXXII, 16.
58–59. Vishnu LXIII, 51.

must make way (for them, i.e.) for each later (named before those enumerated earlier).

59. If a king and a Snâtaka meet, the king must make (way) for the Snâtaka.

60. All (must make way) for a bride who is being conveyed (to her husband's house).

61. Grass, room (for resting), fire, water, a welcome, and kind words never fail in the houses of good men.

CHAPTER XIV.

1. Now, therefore, we will declare what may be eaten and what may not be eaten.

2. Food given by a physician, a hunter, a woman of bad character, a mace-bearer, a thief, an Abhi*s*asta, a eunuch, (or) an outcast must not be eaten,

3. (Nor that given) by a miser, one who has performed the initiatory ceremony of a *S*rauta-sacrifice, a prisoner, a sick person, a seller of the Soma-plant, a carpenter, a washerman, a dealer in spirituous liquor, a spy, a usurer, (or) a cobbler,

4. Nor (that given) by a *S*ûdra,

5. Nor (that given) by one who lives by his weapons,

6. Nor (that given) by the (kept) paramour of a

61. Âpastamba II, 2, 4, 14; Gautama V, 35–36.

XIV. 2. Vish*n*u LI, 7, 10–11. Da*nd*ika, 'a mace-bearer,' may mean 'a police officer' or 'a messenger.' I read with MSS. Bh. and F. sha*ndh*a, 'a eunuch,' instead of *sath*a, 'a rogue,' the reading of the other MSS. and of K*ri*sh*n*apa*nd*ita.

3. Vish*n*u LI, 8–9, 12, 19; Gautama XVII, 17. I write sû*k*aka, 'a spy,' instead of sû*k*ika, 'a tailor,' according to the other Sm*ri*tis, e.g. Vish*n*u LI, 12; Âpastamba I, 6, 18, 30

4. Âpastamba I, 6, 18, 13. 5. Âpastamba I, 6, 18, 19.

6. Vish*n*u LI, 16; Gautama XVII, 18. I read with the majority

married woman, or by a husband who allows a paramour (to his wife),

7. Nor (that given) by an incendiary,

8. Nor (that given) by (a ruler) who does not slay those worthy of capital punishment,

9. Nor (food) offered publicly with these words, 'Who is willing to eat?'

10. Nor food given by a multitude of givers, or by harlots, and so forth.

11. Now they quote also (the following verse): 'The gods do not eat (the offerings) of a man who keeps dogs, nor of him whose (only) wife is of the *S*ûdra caste, nor of him who lives in subjection to his wife, nor of (a husband) who (permits) a paramour (of his wife to reside) in his house.'

12. He may accept (the following presents even) from such (people, viz.) firewood, water, fodder, Ku*s*a grass, parched grain, (food) given without asking, a vehicle, (shelter in) the house, small fish, millet, a garland, perfumes, honey, and meat.

13. Now they quote also (the following verse): 'For the sake of a Guru, when he desires to save his wife (and family from starvation), when he wishes to honour the gods or guests, he may accept (presents) from anybody; but let him not satisfy his (own hunger) with such (gifts).'

---

of the MSS. ya*sk*opapati*m* [patti*m* F.] manyate, instead of B.'s and K*r*ish*n*apa*nd*ita's ya*sk*opari manyate.

9. Âpastamba I, 6, 18, 17.

10. Vish*n*u LI, 7. 'And so forth (iti), i.e. by cruel men and the like.'—K*r*ish*n*apa*nd*ita.

11. Vish*n*u LI, 15.

12. Gautama XVII, 3; Vish*n*u LVII, 10.

13. Vish*n*u LVII, 13; Manu IV, 251.

14. Food given by a hunter who uses the bow must not be rejected.

15. For it is declared in the Veda, 'At a sacrificial session (sattra), which lasted one thousand years, Agastya went out to hunt. He had sacrificial cakes prepared with the meat of beasts and fowls good (to eat).'

16. With reference to this (subject) they quote also some verses proclaimed by Pra*g*âpati, 'Pra*g*âpati (the Lord of created beings) has declared that food freely offered and brought (by the giver himself) may be eaten, though (the giver) be a sinful man, provided the gift has not been asked for beforehand.'

17. 'Food offered by a man who has faith must certainly be eaten, even though (the giver) be a thief, but not that given by (a Brâhma*n*a) who sacrifices for many and who initiates many.'

18. 'The manes do not eat during fifteen years (the food) of that man who disdains a (freely offered gift), nor does the fire carry his offerings (to the gods).'

19. 'But alms, though offered without asking, must not be accepted from a physician, from a hunter, from a surgeon or a (very) wicked man, from a eunuch, and from a faithless wife.'

20. Fragments of food left by other persons than the teacher must not be eaten,

21. Nor remnants of one's own (meal) and food touched by leavings,

15. Manu V, 22–23. I connect vi*gñ*âyate with this Sûtra, instead of with the preceding one, as K*ri*sh*n*apa*nd*ita does.

16. Vish*n*u LVII, 11; Manu IV, 248; Âpastamba I, 6, 19, 14.

18. Vish*n*u LVII, 12; Manu IV, 249; Âpastamba I, 6, 19, 14.

19. Âpastamba I, 6, 19, 15. 20. Vish*n*u XXVIII, 11.

22. Nor (food) defiled by contact with a garment, hair, or insects.

23. But at pleasure he may use (such food) after taking out the hair and the insects, sprinkling it with water, dropping ashes on it, and (after it has been declared) fit for use by the word (of a Brâhma*n*a).

24. With reference to this (subject) they quote also some verses proclaimed by Pra*g*âpati, 'The gods created for Brâhma*n*as three means of purifying (defiled substances), viz. ignorance (of defilement), sprinkling (them) with water, and commending (them) by word of mouth.'

25. 'Let him not throw away that food which, at a procession with images of the gods, at weddings, and at sacrifices, is touched by crows or dogs.'

26. 'After the (defiled) portion has been removed, the remainder shall be purified, liquids by straining them, but solid food by sprinkling it with water.'

27. 'What has been touched by the mouth of a cat is even pure.'

28. (Cooked food which has become) stale (by being kept), what is naturally bad, what has been placed once only in the dish, what has been cooked more than once, raw (food), and (food) insufficiently cooked (must not be eaten).

29. But at pleasure he may use (such food) after pouring over it sour milk or clarified butter.

---

22. Âpastamba I, 5, 16, 28; Gautama XVII, 9.

23. Vish*n*u XXIII, 38; Yâ*gñ*avalkya I, 189.

24. Yâ*gñ*avalkya I, 191.

26. Vish*n*u XXIII, 30. K*ri*sh*n*apa*nd*ita thinks that plâvanena, 'by straining them (through a cloth),' may also mean 'by heating them on the fire.'

28. Gautama XVII, 13, and note, 15–16.

29. Manu V, 24.

30. With reference to this (subject) they quote also some verses proclaimed by Pra*g*âpati, 'A Brâhma*n*a shall not eat clarified butter or oil which drips from the nails (of the giver). Yama has declared such (food to be) impure; (to eat it is as sinful) as to partake of cow's flesh.'

31. 'But fatty substances, salt, and condiments proffered with the hand do not benefit the giver, and he who partakes of them will eat sin.'

32. 'Let him give, therefore, such substances placed on a leaf or on grass, but never with his hands or in an iron vessel.'

33. For eating garlic, onions, mushrooms, turnips, *S*leshmântaka, exudations from trees, the red sap flowing from incisions (in trees or plants), food pecked at by crows or worried by dogs, or the leavings of a *S*ûdra, an Atik*rikkh*ra (penance must be performed).

34. (Let him not drink) the milk of a cow that is in heat, nor of one whose calf has died,

35. Nor that which cows, buffalo-cows, and goats give during the first ten days (after giving birth to young ones),

36. Nor water collected at the bottom of a boat.

37. Let him avoid wheat-cakes, (fried) grain, porridge, barley-meal, pulse-cakes, oil, rice boiled in milk, and vegetables that have turned sour (by standing),

---

33. Vish*n*u LI, 34, 36; Gautama XVII, 32–33. Regarding the Atik*rikkh*ra penance, see below, XXIV, 1.

34. Vish*n*u LI, 40. For other explanations of the term sandhinî, 'a cow that is in heat,' see Âpastamba I, 5, 17, 23; Vish*n*u LI, 40.

35. Vish*n*u LI, 39. The Sûtra implies that the milk of other animals must not be drunk under any circumstances.

37–38. Vish*n*u LI, 35, 42.

38. Likewise other kinds of (sour) food prepared with milk and barley-flour.

39. Among five-toed animals, the porcupine, the hedgehog, the hare, the tortoise, and the iguana may be eaten,

40. Among (domestic) animals those having teeth in one jaw only, excepting camels.

41. And among fishes, the long-nosed crocodile, the Gavaya, the porpoise, the alligator, and the crab (must not be eaten),

42. Nor those which are misshaped or have heads like snakes,

43. Nor the bos Gaurus, the Gayal, and the *S*arabha,

44. Nor those that have not been (specially mentioned (as fit for food),

45. Nor milch-cows, draught-oxen, and animals whose milk teeth have not dropped out.

46. It is declared in the Vâ*g*asaneyaka, that (the flesh of) milch-cows and oxen is fit for offerings.

47. But regarding the rhinoceros and the wild boar they make conflicting statements.

48. And among birds, those who seek their food by scratching with their feet, the web-footed ones, the Kalaviṅka, the water-hen, the flamingo, the

---

39. Gautama XVII, 27. Haradatta on Âpastamba and Gautama explain *s*vâvidh, 'the porcupine,' to be a kind of boar, and *s*alyaka, 'the hedgehog,' to be 'the porcupine.'

40. Vish*n*u LI, 30; Manu V, 18.

41–42. Gautama XVII, 36; Âpastamba I, 5, 17, 38–39.

43. Âpastamba I, 5, 17, 29. 44. Manu V, 11, 17.

45. Gautama XVII, 30–31. 46. Âpastamba I, 5, 17, 31.

48. Gautama XVII, 34–35; Vish*n*u LI, 28–31. I read mândhâla, 'the flying fox,' while K*ri*sh*n*apa*nd*ita gives mâghâra, a

Brahma*n*î duck, the Bhâsa, the crow, the blue pigeon, the osprey, the *K*âtaka, the dove, the crane, the black partridge, the grey heron, the vulture, the falcon, the white egret, the ibis, the cormorant, the peewit, the flying-fox, those flying about at night, the woodpecker, the sparrow, the Railâtaka, the green pigeon, the wagtail, the village-cock, the parrot, the starling, the cuckoo, those feeding on flesh, and those living about villages (must not be eaten).

CHAPTER XV.

1. Man formed of uterine blood and virile seed proceeds from his mother and his father (as an effect) from its cause.

2. (Therefore) the father and the mother have power to give, to sell, and to abandon their (son).

3. But let him not give or receive (in adoption) an only son;

4. For he (must remain) to continue the line of the ancestors.

5. Let a woman neither give nor receive a son except with her husband's permission.

6. He who desires to adopt a son, shall assemble

---

reading which he cannot explain. The MSS. read as follows: B. E. mâghâra, Bh. F. mâdhâ*m*, I. O. 913 (*t*i*t*ibh)ândha (nakta*m*). Haradatta on Âpastamba I, 5, 17, 33 explains plava, 'the water-hen,' to be a kind of heron, called also *s*aka*t*abila.

XV. 1–9. Vyavahâramayûkha IV, 5, 16; Colebrooke V, Digest CCLXXIII; Dattakamîmâ*m*sâ IV, 14; V, 31–40.

3. Colebrooke, Mitâksharâ I, 11, 11; Dattakamîmâ*m*sâ IV, 2–3.

4. Dattakamîmâ*m*sâ IV, 4. I. e. to offer funeral sacrifices to his ancestors and to have sons who do it after him.

5. Dattakamîmâ*m*sâ I, 15; IV, 9.

6. Colebrooke, Mitâksharâ I, 11, 13, and note; Dattakamî-

his kinsmen, announce his intention to the king, make burnt-offerings in the middle of the house, reciting the Vyâhritis, and take (as a son) a not remote kinsman, just the nearest among his relatives.

7. But if a doubt arises (with respect to an adopted son who is) a remote kinsman, (the adopter) shall set him apart like a Sûdra.

8. For it is declared in the Veda, 'Through one he saves many.'

9. If, after an adoption has been made, a legitimate son be born, (the adopted son) shall obtain a fourth part,

10. Provided he be not engaged in (rites) procuring prosperity.

---

mâmsâ II, 51; Dattakakandrikâ II, 11. 'To the king,' i.e. to the person who holds the village, either to the king of the country or to the feudal chief (Thâkor) who holds it under the sovereign. 'Reciting the Vyâhritis,' i.e. saying with the first oblation *Om* bhûh svâhâ, with the second *Om* bhuvah svâhâ, with the third *Om* svah svâhâ, and with the fourth *Om* bh., bh., sv. svâhâ; see Vyavahâramayûkha IV, 5, 42. 'A not remote kinsman, just the nearest among his relatives,' i.e. a boy as nearly related as possible, in the first instance a Sapinda, on failure of such a one, a Samânodaka or a Sagotra.

7. Dattakamîmâmsâ II, 18; Dattakakandrikâ II, 11. 'If a doubt arises,' i.e. if the adopter afterwards feels uncertain regarding the caste or other qualifications of his adopted son. 'Set him apart like a Sûdra,' i.e. shall neither have him initiated nor employ him for any sacred rites.

8. Dattakakandrikâ II, 11.

9. Colebrooke, Mitâksharâ I, 11, 24. Dattakamîmâmsâ X, 1; Dattakakandrikâ II, 11; V, 17. For the explanation of the term 'a fourth part,' see Colebrooke, Mitâksharâ I, 77.

10. 'Rites procuring prosperity,' i.e. Srâddhas, expiatory rites, &c. See also above, III, 71, and Gautama XI, 17. According to Krishnapandita the estate is in this case to be divided equally between the legitimate son and the adopted son. An entirely

11. He who divulges the Veda (to persons not authorised to study it), he who sacrifices for *S*ûdras, (and all those) who have fallen from the rank of the highest caste (shall be excommunicated by the ceremony of) emptying the water-vessel.

12. A slave or the son of a wife of a lower caste, or a relative not belonging to the same caste, who is destitute of good qualities, shall fetch a broken pot from a heap of vessels unfit for use, place Ku*s*a grass, the tops of which have been cut off, or Lohita grass (on the ground), and empty the pot for the (outcast, overturning it) with his left foot;

13. And the relatives of the (outcast), allowing their hair to hang down, shall touch him who empties (the pot).

14. Turning (when they leave) their left hands towards (that spot), they may go home at pleasure.

15. Let them not afterwards admit the (excommunicated person) to sacred rites.

16. Those who admit him to sacred rites become his equals.

17. But outcasts who have performed (the prescribed) penance (may be) readmitted.

18. Now they quote also (the following verse):

---

different explanation, 'Provided (the estate) may not have been expended in acts of merit,' is given Dattaka*k*andrikâ V, 17–18. It is doubtlessly erroneous, for 'the estate' is nowhere mentioned in the preceding Sûtras.

11. Gautama XX, 1.

12. Gautama XX, 4. 'For the (outcast),' i. e. pronouncing his name, and saying, 'I deprive N. N. of water.'

13. Gautama XX, 5. K*r*ish*n*apa*n*d*i*ta takes the Sûtra differently, but his explanation is refuted by the parallel passage of Gautama and Haradatta's commentary thereon.

14. Gautama XX, 7.

15. Gautama XX, 8–9.

'Let him walk before those who readmit him, like one gamboling and laughing. Let him walk behind those who excommunicate him, like one weeping and sorrowing.'

19. Those who strike their teacher, their mother, or their father may be readmitted in the following manner, either after being pardoned by the (persons offended) or after expiating their sin.

20. Having filled a golden or an earthen vessel (with water taken) from a sacred lake or river, they pour (the water) over him, (reciting the three verses) 'Ye waters are' &c.

21. All the (other ceremonies to be performed on the) readmission of one who has bathed (in this manner) have been explained by (those ordained on) the birth of a son.

Chapter XVI.

1. Now (follow the rules regarding) legal proceedings.

2. Let the king (or) his minister transact the business on the bench.

3. When two (parties) have a dispute, let him not be partial to one of them.

---

20. Gautama XX, 10–14. I read 'puṇyahradât,' instead of 'pûrṇâhradât,' as the MSS. and Kṛishṇapaṇḍita have. The passage of the Veda referred to occurs Rig-veda X, 9, 1.

21. I. e. the person readmitted shall receive all the various sacraments just like a new-born child.

XVI. 2. Vishṇu III, 72–73. Kṛishṇapaṇḍita gives a second explanation of the Sûtra, which also appears admissible, 'Let the king transact the business on the bench, taking counsel (with learned Brâhmaṇas as assessors);' see Vishṇu III, 72.

3. Translated as above the Sûtra is nearly equivalent to Gautama

4. Let him reason properly regarding an offence; finally the offence (will become evident thereby).

5. He who properly reasons regarding an offence, in accordance with the sum of the science of the first two castes, is equitable towards all created beings.

6. And let him protect what has been gained;

7. (Likewise) the property of infants (of the) royal (race).

XI, 5. But the phrase 'when two parties have a dispute' may also indicate, as K*r*ishn*a*pa*nd*ita suggests, that the king or judge shall not promote litigation, see Gautama XIII, 27. As K*r*ish*n*a-pa*nd*ita states, the Sûtra may, however, mean also, 'When one case is being argued, let him not begin another (without finishing the first);' see Manu VIII, 43. Owing to the particular nature of the Sûtra style and the inclination of the Brâhmanical mind to double-entendres, I do not think it improbable that the author may have intended, both in this and in the preceding Sûtras, that his words should be interpreted in two ways.

4. Gautama XI, 23-24. I divide the words of the text, as follows, 'yathâsanam (i. e. yathâ-âsanam) aparâdhohî; antena aparâdha*h*,' and interpolate syât at the end of the first clause.

5. K*r*ish*n*apa*nd*ita wrongly divides this Sûtra into two, and wrongly adopts the reading of MSS. B. and E., consequently he obtains a sense only by the most astonishing tricks of interpretation. I read with MSS. Bh. and F., yathâsanam aparâdhohyâdya-var*n*ayor vidyântata*h*, to which the reading of I. O. 913 âdya-var*n*ayor vidhânata*h* points also. The meaning of the expression, 'according to the sum of the science of the first two castes,' I take to be according to the rules of sacred learning and of the mîmâ*m*sâ, which is peculiar to the Brâhma*n*as and of logic (ânvîkshikî) and polity (da*nd*anîti), which are peculiar to or at least recommended to the particular attention of the Kshatriyas.

6. I read with MSS. Bh. and F., sa*m*panna*m* *k*a rakshayet. I consider this Sûtra to contain an admonition addressed to the king for himself; see Manu VII, 99. K*r*ish*n*apa*nd*ita and B. read sapattra*m* *k*a rakshayet, 'Let him protect that which is attested by writings,' i. e. the donations of former kings, attested by writings; see Vish*n*u III, 83.

7. K*r*ish*n*apa*nd*ita thinks that the rule refers to the property of

8. (Likewise the property) of persons unfit to transact legal business (minors, widows, and so forth).

9. But if (a minor) comes of age, his property must be made over to him.

10. 'It is declared in the Smriti that there are three kinds of proof which give a title to (property, viz.) documents, witnesses, and possession; (thereby) an owner may recover property which formerly belonged to him (but was lost).'

11. From fields through which (there is a right of) road (a space sufficient for the road) must be set apart, likewise a space for turning (a cart).

12. Near new-built houses (and) other things (of the same description there shall be) a passage three feet broad.

13. In a dispute about a house or a field, reliance (may be placed on the depositions of) neighbours.

14. If the statements of the neighbours disagree, documents (may be taken as) proof.

---

the infant children of a hostile king who has been conquered and slain. It is, however, not improbable that it has a wider sense, and exhorts the king to look after the property of the children of his predecessor and of deceased feudal barons.

8–9. Gautama X, 48; Vishnu III, 65.

10. Yâgñavalkya II, 22.

11. Krishnapandita quotes in illustration of this Sûtra the following passage of Sankha and Likhita: 'In a field through which (there is a right of) road, (space) for the road must be set apart, and on the king's high-road a space sufficient for turning a chariot.'

12. Arthântareshu, 'near other things (of the same description),' means, according to Krishnapandita, 'near pleasure-gardens and the like.' No doubt, buildings of all kinds, fenced or walled gardens, and so forth are meant. I read tripâdamâtram.

13. Manu VIII, 258, 262; Yâgñavalkya II, 150, 152, 154.

15. If conflicting documents are produced, reliance (may be placed) on (the statements of) aged (inhabitants) of the village or town, and on (those of) guilds and corporations (of artisans or traders).

16. Now they quote also (the following verse): 'Property inherited from a father, a thing bought, a pledge, property given to a wife after marriage by her husband's family, a gift, property obtained for performing a sacrifice, the property of reunited coparceners, and wages as the eighth.'

17. Whatever belonging to these (eight kinds of property) has been enjoyed (by another person) for ten years continuously (is lost to the owner).

18. They quote also (a verse) on the other side: 'A pledge, a boundary, and the property of minors, an (open) deposit, a sealed deposit, women, the property of a king, (and) the wealth of a *S*rotriya are not lost by being enjoyed (by others).'

19. Property entirely given up (by its owner) goes to the king.

20. If it be otherwise, the king with his ministers and the citizens shall administer it.

---

15. Manu VIII, 259.

16. In translating anvâdheya by 'property given to a wife by her husband or his family after marriage,' I have followed K*ri*sh*n*apa*nd*ita's explanation. It may, however, mean also 'a deposit to be delivered to a third person' (anvâhita or anvâdhi). Pratigraha, 'a gift,' is elsewhere explained as 'property promised, but not actually given.'

17. Yâ*gñ*avalkya II, 24; see also Vish*n*u V, 187; Manu VIII, 148.

18. Identical with Manu VIII, 149; Yâ*gñ*avalkya II, 25.

19. Manu VIII, 30.

20. 'If it be otherwise,' i.e. if the owner gave his property up temporarily only, e.g. went on a journey or a pilgrimage, leaving it without anybody to take care of.

21. A king will be superior even to Brahman if he lives surrounded by servants (who are keen-eyed) like vultures.

22. But a king will not be exalted if he lives surrounded by servants (who are greedy) like vultures.

23. Let him live surrounded by servants (who are keen-eyed) like vultures, let him not be a vulture surrounded by vultures.

24. For through his servants blemishes become manifest (in his kingdom),

25. (Such as) theft, robbery, oppression, and (so forth).

26. Therefore let him question his servants beforehand.

27. Now (follow the rules regarding) witnesses:

28. *S*rotriyas, men of unblemished form, of good character, men who are holy and love truth (are fit to be) witnesses,

29. Or (men of) any (caste may give evidence) regarding (men of) any (other caste).

30. Let him make women witnesses regarding women; for twice-born men twice-born men of the same caste (shall be witnesses), and good *S*ûdras for *S*ûdras, and men of low birth for low-caste men.

31. Now they quote also (the following verse): 'A son need not pay money due by a surety, anything idly promised, money due for losses at play or for spirituous liquor, nor what remains unpaid of a fine or a toll.'

32. 'Depose, O witness, according to the truth; expecting thy answer, thy ancestors hang in suspense;

---

28. Vish*n*u VIII, 8; Yâg*ñ*avalkya II, 68; Manu VIII, 62–63.

29. Yâg*ñ*avalkya II, 69. 30. Manu VIII, 68.

31. Vish*n*u VI, 41; Manu VIII, 159; Yâg*ñ*avalkya II, 47.

(in accordance with its truth or falsehood) they will rise (to heaven) or fall (into hell).'

33. 'Naked and shorn, tormented with hunger and thirst, and deprived of sight shall the man who gives false evidence go with a potsherd to beg food at the door of his enemy.'

34. 'He kills five by false testimony regarding a maiden; he kills ten by false testimony regarding kine; he kills a hundred by false evidence regarding a horse, and a thousand by false evidence regarding a man.'

35. (Men) may speak an untruth at the time of marriage, during dalliance, when their lives are in danger or the loss of their whole property is imminent, and for the sake of a Brâhma*n*a; they declare that an untruth spoken in these five cases does not make (the speaker) an outcast.

36. Those who give partial evidence in a judicial proceeding for the sake of a relative or for money, deprive the ancestors of their spiritual family and those of their natural family of their place in heaven.

---

33. Identical with Manu VIII, 93.

34. Identical with Manu VIII, 98. Regarding the explanation of the words 'he kills,' see Manu VIII, 97, and Haradatta on Gautama XIII, 14.

35. Gautama XXIII, 29. Between this and the preceding Sûtras the MSS. as well as K*ri*sh*n*apa*nd*ita insert another one, which is so corrupt that I am unable to translate it. K*ri*sh*n*apa*nd*ita's explanation is opposed to all rules of interpretation, and not worth giving.

36. This verse, too, is corrupt, though the general sense is not doubtful. I read svaganasyârthe yadi vârthaheto*h* pakshâ*s*raye*n*aiva vadanti kâryam—te *s*abdava*ms*asya kulasya pûrvân svargasthitâ*m*stânapi pâtayanti. 'The ancestors of their spiritual family,' i. e. the teacher, the teacher's teacher, and so forth.

G 2

CHAPTER XVII.

1. The father throws his debts on the (son) and obtains immortality if he sees the face of a living son.

2. It is declared in the Veda, 'Endless are the worlds of those who have sons; there is no place for the man who is destitute of male offspring.'

3. There is a curse (in the Veda), 'May our enemies be destitute of offspring.'

4. There is also (the following) passage of the Veda, 'May I obtain, O Agni, immortality by offspring.'

5. 'Through a son he conquers the worlds, through a grandson he obtains immortality, but through his son's grandson he gains the world of the sun.'

6. There is a dispute (among the wise; some say), 'The son belongs to the husband of the wife;' (and some say), 'The son belongs to the begetter.'

7. With respect to this (matter) they quote also on both sides verses like the following:

8. (Some say), 'If (one man's) bull were to beget a hundred calves on another man's cows, they would belong to the owner of the cows; in vain would the bull have spent his strength.'

XVII. 1. Identical with Vishnu XV, 45; Manu IX, 107; Colebrooke V, Dig. CCCIV.

2. The latter part of the quotation occurs Aitareya-brâhmana VII, 3, 9.

3. Rig-veda I, 21, 5.

4. Rig-veda V, 4, 10; Taittirîya-samhitâ I, 4, 46, 1.

5. Identical with Manu IX, 137, and Vishnu XV, 46.

6. The same point is argued Manu IX, 31–56.

8. Identical with Manu IX, 50.

9. (Others say), 'Carefully watch the procreation of your offspring, lest strangers sow seed on your soil; in the next world the son belongs to the begetter; (by carelessness) a husband makes (the possession of) offspring in vain.'

10. If amongst many brothers who are begotten by one father, one have a son, they all have offspring through that son; thus says the Veda.

11. If among many wives of one husband, one have a son, they all have offspring through that son; thus says the Veda.

12. Twelve (kinds of) sons only are noticed by the ancients.

13. The first (among these is the son) begotten by the husband himself on his legally married wife.

14. The second is the son of a wife (who is begotten) on failure of the (first) on a (wife or widow duly) authorised (thereto, by a kinsman).

15. The third is an appointed daughter.

---

9. Âpastamba II, 6, 13, 7.

10. Vish*n*u XV, 42. 11. Vish*n*u XV, 41.

12. Colebrooke V, Dig. CXCIII; Vish*n*u XV, 1. Elsewhere the expression purâ*n*adrish*t*â*h*, 'noticed by the ancients,' has been taken to mean 'seen in the Purâ*n*a' ('the holy writ,' Colebrooke).

13. Colebrooke V, Dig. CXCIII; Vish*n*u XV, 2.

14. Colebrooke V, Dig. CCXXX; Vish*n*u XV, 3.

15. Colebrooke V, Dig. CCIII; Mitâksharâ I, 11, 3; Vyavahâra Mayûkha IV, 4, 43. The curious fact that Vasish*th*a here calls the appointed daughter a son may perhaps be explained by a custom which, though rarely practised, still occurs in Ka*s*mîr, and by which a brotherless maiden is given a male name. A historical instance of this kind is mentioned in the Râ*g*atarangi*n*î, where it is stated that Kalyâ*n*adevî, princess of Gau*d*a and wife of king *G*ayâpî*d*a, was called by her father Kalyâ*n*amalla. When I collated this passage with the help of a Ka*s*mîrian, I was told that a certain Brâhma*n*a, still living in *S*rinagar, had changed the

16. It is declared in the Veda, 'A maiden who has no brothers comes back to the male ancestors (of her own family); returning she becomes their son.'

17. With reference to this (matter there is) a verse (to be spoken by the father when appointing his daughter), 'I shall give thee a brotherless damsel, decked with ornaments; the son whom she may bear, shall be my son.'

18. The fourth is the son of a remarried woman.

19. She is called remarried (punarbhû) who leaving the husband of her youth, and having lived with others, re-enters his family;

20. And she is called remarried who leaving an impotent, outcast or mad husband, or after the death of her husband takes another lord.

21. The fifth is the son of an unmarried damsel.

22. They declare that the son whom an unmarried damsel produces through lust in her father's house, is the son of his maternal grandfather.

---

name of his only child, a daughter called Amrî, to the corresponding masculine form, Amargû, in order to secure to himself through her the same spiritual benefits as if he had a son. It seems to me not improbable that Vasishtha's Sûtra alludes to the same legal fiction, and that he recommends in the first instance that the father is to make his daughter a son by changing her name, and next to secure for himself her son, by the verse quoted Sûtra 17.

16. Colebrooke V, Dig. CCIII, where the preceding Sûtra has been placed after this. Compare Rig-veda I, 124, 5.

17. Colebrooke V, Dig. CCXVI; Mitâksharâ I, 11, 3; Dâyabhâga X, 4; Vyavahâra Mayûkha IV, 4, 43; Vishnu XV, 5.

18. Vishnu XV, 7.

19. Nârada XII, 48 (Jolly), where, however, kaumâram patim has been wrongly translated by 'an infant husband.'

20. Manu IX, 175.

21. Colebrooke V, Dig. CCLIX; Vishnu XV, 10.

22. Colebrooke V, Dig. CCLIX; Vishnu XV, 11.

23. Now they quote also (the following verse): 'If an unmarried daughter bear a son begotten by a man of equal caste, the maternal grandfather has a son through him; he shall offer the funeral cake, and take the wealth (of his grandfather).'

24. (A male child) secretly born in the house is the sixth.

25. They declare that these (six) are heirs and kinsmen, preservers from a great danger.

26. Now among those (sons) who are not heirs, but kinsmen, the first is he who is received with a pregnant bride.

27. (The son of a damsel) who is married pregnant (is called) a son received with the bride (saho*dh*a).

28. The second is the adopted son,

29. (He) whom his father and his mother give (in adoption).

30. (The son) bought is the third.

31. That is explained by (the story of) *S*una*h*-*s*epa.

32. 'Haris*k*andra, forsooth, was a king. He bought the son of A*g*îgarta Sauyavasi.

33. The fourth is (the son) self-given.

---

24. Vish*n*u XV, 13.

25. 'From a great danger,' i.e. 'from the danger of losing heaven through failure of the funeral oblations.'

26. Vish*n*u XV, 15.

28. Vish*n*u XV, 18.

29. Vish*n*u XV, 19.

30. Vish*n*u XV, 20.

32. The MSS. and editions read the last word of the Sûtra as follows: B. vikrîyya; Ben. ed. vikrîya; Bh. E. F. vikrâdya; Calc. ed. and I. O. 913 vikrâyya svaya*m* krîtavân. I believe that, as the letters *k*a and va are constantly mistaken by the copyists the one for the other, the original reading was *k*ikrâya. Regarding the story told in this Sûtra and continued below, Sûtra 35, see Max Müller, History of Ancient Sanskrit Literature, pp. 408–416 and 573–588.

33. Vish*n*u XV, 22.

34. That is (likewise) explained by (the story of) *S*una*h*sepa.

35. '*S*una*h*sepa, forsooth, when tied to the sacrificial stake, praised the gods; there the gods loosened his bonds. To him spoke (each of) the officiating priests, "He shall be my son." He did not agree to their (request. Then) they made him make (this) agreement, "He shall be the son of him whom he chooses." Visvâmitra was the Hot*ri* priest at that (sacrifice). He became his son.'

36. The son cast off is the fifth.

37. (He is called so) who, cast off by his father and his mother, is received (as a son).

38. They declare that the son of a woman of the *S*ûdra caste is the sixth. These (six) are kinsmen, not heirs.

39. Now they quote also (the following rule): 'These (last-mentioned) six (sons) shall take the heritage of him who has no heir belonging to the first-mentioned six (classes).

40. Now (follow the rules regarding) the partition of the (paternal) estate among brothers:

41. And (let it be delayed) until those (widows) who have no offspring, (but are supposed to be pregnant), bear sons.

42. Let the eldest take a double share,

43. And a tithe of the kine and horses.

36–37. Colebrooke V, Dig. CCXC; Vish*n*u XV, 24–25.

38. Colebrooke V, Dig. CCXCII; Dattaka*k*andrikâ V, 14; Vish*n*u XVII, 27; Manu IX, 178–179; Gautama XXVIII, 39.

40. Colebrooke V, Dig. L; Vyavahâra Mayûkha IV, 4, 37.

41. Colebrooke V, Dig. CXVII; Vyavahâra Mayûkha IV, 4, 37.

42–45. Colebrooke V, Dig. L; Dâyabhâga II, 41; Gautama XXVIII, 9 and 5–7.

44. The goats, the sheep, and the house belong to the youngest,

45. Black iron, the utensils, and the furniture to the middlemost.

46. Let the daughters divide the nuptial present of their mother.

47. If a Brâhma*n*a has issue by wives belonging to the Brâhma*n*a, Kshatriya, and Vai*s*ya classes respectively,

48. The son of the Brâhma*n*a wife shall receive three shares,

49. The son of the Kshatriya wife two shares,

50. The other (sons) shall inherit equal shares.

51. And if one of the (brothers) has gained something by his own (effort), he shall receive a double share.

52. But those who have entered a different order receive no share,

53. Nor (those who are) eunuchs, madmen, or outcasts.

54. Eunuchs and madmen (have a claim to) maintenance.

55. The widow of a deceased person shall sleep

---

46. Colebrooke V, Dig. CCCCXCII; Dâyabhâga IV, 2, 15; Vish*n*u XVII, 21.

47–50. Colebrooke V, Dig. CLIV; Vish*n*u XVIII, 1–5.

51. Colebrooke V, Dig. LXXV, CXXXVIII, CCCLVI; Dâyabhâga II, 41; Vyavahâra Mayûkha IV, 7, 8. 'By his own effort,' i.e. by learning or disputations with learned men, by bravery in battle, &c.

52. Colebrooke V, Dig. CCCXXXVIII; Mitâksharâ II, 8, 7; 10, 3; Vyavahâra Mayûkha IV, 11, 5. The persons intended are a perpetual student, a hermit, and ascetic.

53. Vyavahâra Mayûkha IV, 11, 10.

54. Vyavahâra Mayûkha IV, 11, 10; Vish*n*u XV, 33.

55. 'Practising religious vows,' i.e. 'eating only once a day, and so forth.'—K*ri*sh*n*apa*nd*ita.

on the ground during six months, practising religious vows and abstaining from pungent condiments and salt.

56. After the completion of six months she shall bathe, and offer a funeral oblation to her husband. (Then) her father or her brother shall assemble the Gurus who taught or sacrificed (for the deceased) and his relatives, and shall appoint her (to raise issue to her deceased husband).

57. Let him not appoint a (widow who is) mad, ill-conducted, or diseased,

58. Nor one who is very aged.

59. Sixteen years (after maturity is the period for appointing a widow);

60. Nor (shall an appointment be made) if the (male entitled to approach the widow) is sickly.

61. Let him approach (the widow) in the muhûrta sacred to Pragâpati, (behaving) like a husband, without (amorously) dallying with her, and without abusing or ill-treating her.

62. Let her obtain (the expenses for) food, raiment, baths, and unguents from (the estate of) her former (husband).

63. They declare that a son begotten on (a widow who has) not been (duly) appointed, belongs to the begetter.

---

56. Gautama XVIII, 4-7. The Gurus intended are the teacher, sub-teachers (upâdhyâya), and officiating priests.

57. Avasâm, 'ill-conducted,' may also mean 'out of her mind through grief or any other passion.' The former explanation has been adopted by Krishnapandita, whom I have followed above.

61. Manu IX, 60. Regarding the muhûrta sacred to Pragâpati, see above, XII, 47.

63. Gautama XVIII, 9-12.

64. If she was (appointed, the child belongs) to both the males connected with the appointment.

65. No appointment (shall be made) through a desire to obtain the estate.

66. Some say, 'Or, one may appoint (a widow out of covetousness), after imposing a penance.'

67. A maiden who has attained puberty shall wait for three years.

68. After three years (have passed), she may take a husband of equal caste.

69. Now they quote also (the following verses): 'But if through a father's negligence a maiden is here given away after the suitable age has passed, she who was waiting (for a husband) destroys him who gives her away, just as the fee which is paid too late to the teacher (destroys the pupil).'

70. 'Out of fear of the appearance of the menses let the father marry his daughter while she still runs about naked. For if she stays (in the house) after the age of puberty, sin falls on the father.'

---

64. Gautama XVIII, 13. 'To both the males connected with the appointment,' i.e. to the deceased husband for whose sake the appointment is made, and to the natural father of the child, to whom the widow is made over.

65. Colebrooke, Mitâksharâ II, 1, 11. K*ri*sh*n*apa*nd*ita thinks that the Sûtra forbids an appointment which is made with the intention to secure the estate or a share of the estate of the natural father, from whom the kshetra*g*a son inherits also (Yâ*gñ*avalkya II, 127). But it seems equally probable that it is intended to prevent a widow from agreeing to an appointment in order to obtain control over her husband's estate.

66. K*ri*sh*n*apa*nd*ita thinks that the rule refers to all cases of appointment.

67–68. Vish*n*u XXIV, 40, and note.

70. Gautama XVIII, 23.

71. 'As often as the courses of a maiden, who is filled with desire, and demanded in marriage by men of equal caste, recur, so often her father and her mother are guilty of (the crime of) slaying an embryo; that is a rule of the sacred law.'

72. 'If the betrothed of a maiden die after she has been promised to him verbally, and by (a libation of) water, but before she was married with (the recitation of) sacred texts, she belongs to her father alone.'

73. 'If a damsel has been abducted by force, and not been wedded with sacred texts, she may lawfully be given to another man; she is even like a maiden.'

74. 'If a damsel at the death of her husband had been merely wedded by (the recitation of) sacred texts, and if the marriage had not been consummated, she may be married again.'

75. The wife of an emigrant shall wait for five years.

76. After five years (have passed), she may go (to seek) her husband.

77. If for reasons connected with spiritual or with money matters she be unwilling to leave her home, she must act in the same manner as if (her husband were) dead.

78. In this manner a wife of the Brâhma*n*a caste who has issue (shall wait) five years, and one who has no issue, four years; a wife of the Kshatriya caste who has issue, five years, and one who has no issue, three years; a wife of the Vai*s*ya caste who

71. Colebrooke IV, Dig. XVI; Dâyabhâga XI, 2, 6; Yâ*gñ*avalkya I, 64.

72. Colebrooke IV, Dig. CLXXIV.

75–76. Colebrooke IV, Dig. CLVI, where the Sûtras have been altered intentionally; Gautama XVIII, 15–12.

has issue, four years, and one who has no issue, two years; a wife of the *S*ûdra caste who has issue, three years, and one who has no issue, one year.

79. After that among those who are united (with her husband) in interest, or by birth, or by the funeral cake, or by libations of water, or by descent from the same family, each earlier named person is more venerable than the following ones.

80. But while a member of her family is living, she shall certainly not go to a stranger.

81. Let the Sapi*nd*as or the subsidiary sons divide the heritage of him who has no heir of the first-mentioned six kinds.

82. On failure of them the spiritual teacher and a pupil shall take the inheritance.

83. On failure of those two the king inherits.

84. But let the king not take (the estate) of a Brâhma*n*a.

85. For the property of a Brâhma*n*a is a terrible poison.

86. 'Poison they do not call the (worst) poison; the property of a Brâhma*n*a is said to be the (most destructive) poison. Poison destroys only one person, but the property of a Brâhma*n*a (him who takes it) together with sons and grandsons.'

---

79. The persons intended are, (1) brothers united in interest with her husband and other coparceners, (2) separated brothers of the husband, (3) separated blood-relations of the husband within six degrees, (4) separated blood-relations of the husband within fourteen degrees, and (5) persons bearing the same family name or, in the case of Brâhma*n*as, descended from the same *Ri*shi.

81. Gautama XXVIII, 21; Vish*n*u XVII, 10. The subsidiary sons are those mentioned above, 26–38, who under ordinary circumstances do not inherit; see also above, Sûtra 39, and Gautama XXVIII, 34.

82. Âpastamba II, 6, 14, 3. 83–84. Vish*n*u XVII, 13.

87. He should give it to men who are well versed in the three Vedas.

Chapter XVIII.

1. They declare that the offspring of a *S*ûdra and of a female of the Brâhma*n*a caste becomes a *K*â*nd*âla,

2. (That of a *S*ûdra and) of a female of the Kshatriya caste, a Vai*n*a,

3. (That of a *S*ûdra and) of a female of the Vai*s*ya caste, an Antyâvasâyin.

4. They declare that the (son) begotten by a Vai*s*ya on a female of the Brâhma*n*a caste becomes a Râmaka,

5. (The son begotten by the same) on a female of the Kshatriya caste, a Pulkasa.

6. They declare that the (son) begotten by a Kshatriya on a female of the Brâhma*n*a caste becomes a Sûta.

7. Now they quote also (the following verse): 'One may know by their deeds those who have been begotten secretly, and to whom the stigma of springing from unions in the inverse order of the castes attaches, because they are destitute of virtue and good conduct.'

---

87. Vish*n*u XVII, 14.

XVIII. 1. Vish*n*u XVI, 6.

4. K*ri*sh*n*apa*nd*ita reads Romaka, 'a Roman,' for Râmaka, and the B. MS. supports him. The other MSS., including I. O. 913, give the reading adopted above. I prefer it, as there is no reason to assume that the Vâsish*th*a Dharma*s*âstra belongs to the late period when the Hindus had become aware of the existence of the Roman empire. On the other hand, it may be urged that Romaka is a correction which would easily suggest itself to a Pandit, who was unable to find a parallel passage in which the word Râmaka occurs.

6. Vish*n*u XVI, 6.   7. Manu X, 40.

8. (Children) begotten by Brâhma*n*as, Kshatriyas, and Vai*s*yas on females of the next lower, second lower, and third lower castes become (respectively) Ambash*th*as, Ugras, and Nishâdas.

9. (The son of a Brâhma*n*a and) of a *S*ûdra woman (is) a Pâra*s*ava.

10. They declare that the condition of a Pâra*s*ava is that of one who, though living, is (as impure) as a corpse.

11. Some call that *S*ûdra race a burial-ground.

12. Therefore (the Veda) must not be recited in the presence of a *S*ûdra.

13. Now they quote also the (following) verses, which Yama proclaimed:

'The wicked *S*ûdra-race is manifestly a burial-ground. Therefore (the Veda) must never be recited in the presence of a *S*ûdra.'

14. 'Let him not give advice to a *S*ûdra, nor what remains from his table, nor (remnants of) offerings (to the gods); nor let him explain the holy law to such a man, nor order him (to perform) a penance.'

15. 'He who declares the law to such a man, and he who instructs him in (the mode of) expiating (sin), sinks together with that very man into the dreadful hell, (called) Asa*m*v*ri*ta.'

16. 'If ever a worm is produced in an open wound (on his body), he shall purify himself by the Prâ*g*â-patya penance, and give gold, a cow, (and) a garment as presents (to Brâhma*n*as).'

---

8. Gautama IV, 16.

10. I omit the words *s*ava iti m*ri*tâkhyâ, 'a corpse is another name for one who has died,' as an interpolation.

11. Âpastamba I, 3, 9, 9. 12. Vish*n*u XXX, 14.

14–15. Identical with Manu IV, 80–81.

16. A Prâ*g*âpatya penance, i. e. a K*rikkh*ra, see below, XXI, 20.

17. Let him not approach a wife of the *S*ûdra caste after he has built the fire-altar for a *S*rauta-sacrifice.

18. For a *S*ûdra-wife who belongs to the black race, (is espoused) for pleasure, not in order to fulfil the law.

CHAPTER XIX.

1. The particular duty of a king is to protect (all) beings; by fulfilling it (he obtains) success (in this world and in the next).

2. Those learned (in the sacred law) declare that to be free from fear and pity is, indeed, a life-long sacrificial session (sattra, to be performed by the king).

3. Therefore let him appoint a domestic priest to (perform the rites) obligatory on the order of householders.

4. It is declared in the Veda, 'A realm where a Brâhma*n*a is appointed domestic priest, prospers;'

5. For thus both (the special duties of a king and those of a householder) will be fulfilled,

6. And (the king alone is) unable (to do both).

7. Let the king, paying attention to all the laws of countries, (subdivisions of) castes (*g*âti) and families, make the four castes (var*n*a) fulfil their (respective) particular duties.

The verse belongs rather to the section on penances, and seems to have been entered here merely because it stood in Yama's text with the other two, and the author, to use a homely Indian comparison, 'did not disdain to catch a fish, though he went to fetch water.'

XIX. 1. Vish*n*u III, 2. 2. Manu VIII, 306.
3. Vish*n*u III, 70. 4. Gautama XI, 14.
7. Vish*n*u III, 3; Gautama XI, 20.

8. Let him punish those who stray from (the path of duty).

9. But punishment must be awarded in cases of assault and abuse after (due consideration of) the particular place and time (where and when the offence was committed), of the duties, age, learning (of the parties), and the seat (of the injury),

10. In accordance with (the precepts of) the (sacred) records and with precedents.

11. Let him not injure trees that bear fruit or flowers.

12. (But) he may injure them in order to extend cultivation and (for sacrifices).

13. The measures and weights of objects necessary for households must be guarded (against falsification).

14. Let him not take property for his own use from (the inhabitants of) his realm.

15. The measures and price (of such property) only shall be liable to deductions (in the shape of taxes).

---

8. Vish*n*u III, 37.

9. Gautama XII, 51. K*ri*sh*n*apa*nd*ita has two Sûtras instead of one, and reads the second hi*m*sâkro*s*ayo*h* kalpa*h*. The majority of the MSS. have, however, kalpâ(*h*), which I consider to be a mistake for kalpya*h*, 'must be awarded.'

11. Vish*n*u V, 55–56. The meaning of the Sûtra is that the king is to punish those who commit such acts.

12. The explicit permission to cut down trees for sacrificial purposes is given Vish*n*u LI, 63.

13. Manu VIII, 403.

14–15. The translation of these two Sûtras is not certain, because the words nîhâra and naihârika are not found elsewhere in the sense which has been attributed to them here. Still I think it very probable that K*ri*sh*n*apa*nd*ita's explanation nirhâra and nirhâre sâdhu is right, and that the king is exhorted not to take the property of his subjects by force, but to levy taxes according to the value or the measure of the articles sold.

16. . . . .

17. On the march against the enemy the army which consists of companies of ten, shall be able to perform a double (duty).

18. In every (camp) there shall be places where water is distributed.

19. Let him make one hundred men at the least engage in battle.

20. The wives (of slain soldiers) shall be provided for.

21. . . . .

22. A ferry shall be taken away (from a river) in which there is no water.

23. A *S*rotriya is free from taxes, (and so are) a servant of the king, one who has no protector,

16. The Sûtra has been left out, as the text is corrupt, and I am unable to suggest any emendation. K*ri*sh*n*apa*nd*ita's explanation is not worth giving.

17. 'The army which consists of companies of ten,' i. e. the lowest subdivision of which consists of ten parts, viz. one elephant, one chariot, two horsemen, and three foot soldiers. Such a body is called a patti. The larger divisions, like the senâmukha, 'battalion,' &c., are formed by three, nine, or twenty-seven pattis. Though I am unable to adduce any positive proof for it, vâha must, according to the connexion in which it stands, be a synonym of patti. 'The double duty' of the army is, according to K*ri*sh*n*apa*nd*ita, marching and fighting.

21. The Sûtra is utterly corrupt, and cannot be restored with the help of the MSS. at my disposal. It probably referred to the amount of duties to be levied on goods sold in the market.

22. The meaning of the Sûtra seems to be, that on those rivers, where the water either runs off or is very low during the dry season, the ferrymen must not be allowed to exact a toll from people crossing without their help. Such a rule would not be superfluous, as most Indian rivers are perfectly fordable between December and June, but impassable without boats in the other five months.

23. Âpastamba II, 10, 26, 10, 12–17; Manu VIII, 394. K*ri*sh*n*a-

one who has left (the order of householders), an infant, a very aged man, a young man (who studies), and pradâtâs;

24. (Moreover widows) who return to their former (family), unmarried maidens, and the wives of servants,

25. He who swims with his arms (across a river in order to escape payment of a toll at a ferry) shall pay one hundred times (the amount due).

26. No taxes (shall be paid) on the usufruct of rivers, dry grass, forests, (places of) combustion, and mountains;

27. Or those who draw their subsistence from them may pay (something),

28. But he shall take a monthly tax from artisans.

29. And when a king has died, let him give what is required for the occasion.

---

pa*nd*ita correctly points out that, though according to I, 43, all Brâhma*n*as are to be free from taxes, the *S*rotriya or Vaidik is mentioned once more in order to show that a king, however distressed, must not take anything from him (Manu VII, 133). K*ri*shn*a*pa*nd*ita reads instead of pradâtâs, pradâtâra*h*, 'very liberal men.' Manu loc. cit. exempts 'those who confer great benefits on priests of eminent learning' from paying taxes. His emendation would, therefore, be acceptable if the word pradâtâ*h* did not occur in the same connexion above, XI, 7.

24. Âpastamba II, 10, 26, 11.

25. I read with the majority of the MSS. bâhubhyâmuttarañ*kh*atagunam dadyât.

26. K*ri*sh*n*apa*nd*ita explains dâha, '(places of) combustion,' by agni, 'fire.' I am not certain what he means thereby. To me it seems most probable that Vasish*th*a intends 'a place of cremation' (dâhasthala), though it is just possible to refer the expression to the jungle fires, which the aboriginal tribes light in the forests, in order to sow their Nâglî in the ground manured by the ashes.

28. Gautama X, 31.

29. K*ri*sh*n*apa*nd*ita refers this and the following five Sûtras to

30. It is hereby explained that (his) mother (must receive) maintenance.

31. Let the king maintain the paternal and maternal uncles of the chief-queen,

32. As well as her other relatives.

33. The wives of the (deceased) king shall receive food and raiment,

34. Or if they are unwilling, they may depart.

35. Let the king maintain eunuchs and madmen,

36. Since their property goes to him.

37. Now they quote also a verse proclaimed by Manu, which refers to duties and taxes, 'No duty (is paid) on a sum less than a Karshâpana, there is no tax on a livelihood gained by art, nor on an infant, nor on a messenger, nor on what has been received as alms, nor on the remnants of property left after a robbery, nor on a Srotriya, nor on an ascetic, nor on a sacrifice.'

---

the case where a king has conquered a foreign country; compare also Vishnu III, 47-48. I think that Sûtras 30-31 conclusively show that these rules are intended to regulate the conduct of a king on the death of his predecessor and his own accession to the throne.

34. Krishnapandita thinks that the queens unwilling to accept a bare subsistence may go wherever they like. I think the word used in the text points rather to their becoming ascetics.

35. This rule refers apparently to eunuchs and insane persons left with money, but without near relatives, with whom they are united in interest. Vishnu III, 65.

37. I translate the one word sulka by 'duties and taxes.' The term has a great many different meanings in the law books, and is in this verse apparently used in two senses. Krishnapandita is of a different opinion, and thinks that the persons named are free from paying a sulka in case they trade. The chief objection is that trading ascetics and Srotriyas are not known to the ancient writers, though they are common enough in modern India.

38. A thief becomes free from guilt by entering (the royal presence) after (his deed and asking to be punished).

39. But according to some (lawyers) he (who is caught) with weapons in his hands, with stolen goods in his possession, or covered with wounds is proved (to be a criminal).

40. In case (a criminal) worthy of punishment is allowed to go free, the king shall fast during one (day and one) night;

41. (And) his domestic priest during three (days and) nights.

42. If an innocent man is punished, the domestic priest (shall perform) a K*rikkh*ra penance;

43. (And) the king (shall fast) during three (days and) nights.

44. Now they quote also (the following verses): 'The slayer of a learned Brâhma*n*a casts his guilt on him who eats his food; an adulterous wife on her (negligent) husband; a student and a sacrificer on an (ignorant) teacher (and officiating priest); and a thief on the king (who pardons him).'

45. 'But men who have committed offences and have received from kings the punishment (due to them), go pure to heaven, and (become) as holy as the virtuous.'

46. 'The guilt falls on the king who pardons an

---

38. This Sûtra apparently alludes to a penitent thief who confesses his crime and asks for punishment; see below, XX, 41.

39. Manu IX, 270; Nârada V, 29–33 (Jolly). As given in the MSS. and by K*r*ishn*a*pa*nd*ita, the Sûtra is doubtlessly corrupt. I read vra*n*asampanno vyapadish*t*a*h*.

44. Identical with Manu VIII, 317.

45. Identical with Manu VIII, 318.

offender. If he causes him to be slain, he destroys sin in accordance with the sacred law.'

47. 'It is ordained that kings become at once pure (by bathing) when they have done acts causing death. They are likewise (pure while engaged in business) not causing death. Time is the reason for that.'

48. And with reference to this (matter) they quote a verse proclaimed by Yama, 'No taint of impurity, forsooth, falls on kings, on those engaged in practising vows, or on those engaged in the performance of sacrificial session (sattra); for (the first) are seated on the throne of Indra, (and the others) are always equal to Brahman.'

Chapter XX.

1. A penance (shall be performed) for an offence committed unintentionally.

2. Some (declare that it shall be performed) also for (a fault) committed intentionally.

3. 'The spiritual teacher corrects the learned; the king corrects the evil-minded; but Yama, the son of Vivasvat, forsooth, punishes those who offend secretly.'

4. And among those (sinful persons), let him who slept at sunrise stand during the (following) day and recite the verse sacred to Savitri.

---

47. Vishnu XXII, 48; Manu V, 94.

48. Identical with Manu V, 93. 'Those engaged in practising vows' are, according to Kullûka and Krishnapandita, students learning the Veda.

XX. 1–2. Manu XI, 45; Yâgñavalkya III, 226.

4. 'Among those,' i.e. the sinful men (enasvinah) enumerated above, I, 18; Vishnu LIV, 11.

5. Let him who slept at sunset remain in a sitting posture during the (next) night, likewise (reciting the Gâyatrî).

6. But let a man with deformed nails or black teeth perform a K*rikkh*ra penance of twelve days' duration.

7. He whose younger brother married first shall perform a K*rikkh*ra penance during twelve days, marry and take to himself even that (woman whom his brother wedded).

8. Now he who has taken a wife before his elder brother shall perform a K*rikkh*ra penance and an Atik*rikkh*ra penance, give (his wife) to that (elder brother), marry again, and take (back) the same (woman whom he wedded first).

9. The husband of a younger sister married before her elder sister shall perform a K*rikkh*ra penance during twelve days, marry and take to him that (elder sister).

10. The husband of an elder sister married after the younger one shall perform a K*rikkh*ra penance and an Atik*rikkh*ra penance, give (his wife) to that (husband of the younger sister and marry again).

5–10. Manu XI, 201.

6. Regarding the K*rikkh*ra penance, see below, XXI, 20.

7–8. Vish*n*u LIV, 16. According to K*r*ish*n*apa*nd*ita both brothers shall perform penances. The elder brother shall marry after his penance is finished. The younger one shall offer his wife to the elder, in order to atone for the slur put upon the elder. The latter shall accept her for form's sake and return her to the younger brother, who must once more wed her. Regarding the Atik*rikkh*ra penance, see below, XXIV, 2.

10. Vish*n*u LIV, 16. K*r*ish*n*apa*nd*ita thinks that he should marry another wife, but adds that others say that, after offering his wife to the husband of the younger sister and receiving his permission, he should wed her once more.

11. We shall declare below (the penance prescribed for) him who extinguishes the sacred fire.

12. He who has forgot the Veda (by neglecting to recite it daily), shall perform a *Kri*kkh*ra penance of twelve days' duration, and again learn it from his teacher.

13. He who violates a Guru's bed shall cut off his organ, together with the testicles, take them into his joined hands and walk towards the south; wherever he meets with an obstacle (to further progress), there he shall stand until he dies.

14. Or, having shaved all his hair and smeared his body with clarified butter, he shall embrace the heated (iron) image (of a woman). It is declared in the Veda that he is purified after death.

15. The same (expiation is prescribed if the offence was committed) with the wife of the teacher, of a son, and of a pupil.

16. If he has had intercourse with a female (who is considered) venerable in the family, with a female friend, with the female friend of a Guru, with an Apapâtra female, or with an outcast, he shall perform a K*ri*kkh*ra penance during three months.

17. The same (penance must be performed) for eating food given by a *K*â*nd*âla or by an outcast. Afterwards the initiation (must be performed) once more; but the tonsure and the rest may be omitted.

11. See below, XXI, 27. 12. Vish*n*u LIV, 13.
13. Gautama XXIII, 10. 14. Gautama XXIII, 9, 11.
15–16. Gautama XXIII, 12.
16. K*ri*sh*n*apa*nd*ita explains sakhîm, 'a female friend,' by 'a woman who has affection (for the offender), i. e. a sister and so forth.' Apapâtras are low-caste people, whose vessels must not be used; see Âpastamba I, 1, 3, 25, note.

18. And with reference to this (matter) they quote a verse proclaimed by Manu, 'The tonsure, (the tying on of) the sacred girdle, (the wearing of) a staff, and the begging of alms, these acts may be omitted on a second initiation.'

19. If (a Brâhma*n*a) intentionally (drinks) other spirituous liquor than that distilled from rice, or if he unintentionally (drinks) spirituous liquor extracted from rice (surâ), he (must perform) a K*rikkh*ra and an Atik*rikkh*ra, and, after eating clarified butter, be initiated again.

20. The same (expiation is prescribed) for swallowing ordure, urine, and semen.

21. If a Brâhma*n*a drinks water which has stood in a vessel used for (keeping) spirituous liquor, he becomes pure by drinking, during three days, water (mixed with a decoction) of lotus, Udumbara, Bilva, and Palâ*s*a (leaves).

22. But a Brâhma*n*a who repeatedly (and intentionally partakes) of liquor extracted from rice, shall drink (liquor of) the same (kind) boiling hot. 'He becomes pure after death.'

23. We will declare (who must be considered) the slayer of a learned Brâhma*n*a (bhrû*n*ahan). He is called Bhrû*n*ahan who kills a Brâhma*n*a or destroys an embryo (the sex of) which is unknown.

24. 'For embryos (the sex of) which is unknown

---

18. Identical with Manu XI, 152, and Vish*n*u LI, 5.

19–20. Manu XI, 151; Vish*n*u LI, 2. Regarding the other of liquors, see Manu XI, 95–96.

21. Manu XI, 148.

22. Gautama XXIII, 1.

23. Gautama XXII, 13. It must be understood a real Brâhma*n*a who knows the Veda is meant.

24. 'Therefore they offer burnt-oblations for the production of males,' i. e. they perform the Pu*m*savana, one of the sacraments;

become males; therefore they offer burnt-oblations for the production of males.'

25. Let the slayer of a learned Brâhmana kindle a fire and offer (therein the following eight oblations, consisting of portions of his own body),

26. The first (saying), 'I offer my hair to Death, I feed Death with my hair;' the second (saying), 'I offer my skin to Death, I feed Death with my skin;' the third (saying), 'I offer my blood to Death, I feed Death with my blood;' the fourth (saying), 'I offer my flesh to Death, I feed Death with my flesh;' the fifth (saying), 'I offer my sinews to Death, I feed Death with my sinews;' the sixth (saying), 'I offer my fat to Death, I feed Death with my fat;' the seventh (saying), 'I offer my bones to Death, I feed Death with my bones;' the eighth (saying), 'I offer my marrow to Death, I feed Death with my marrow.'

27. (Or) let him (fight) for the sake of the king, or for the sake of Brâhmanas, and let him die in battle with his face turned (to the foe).

28. It is declared in the Veda, '(A murderer) who remains thrice unvanquished or is thrice defeated (in battle) becomes pure.'

29. 'A sin which is openly proclaimed becomes smaller.'

---

see e.g. Âsvalâyana I, 13. The Sûtra is marked as a quotation, and probably belongs to some Vedic work.

25. Âpastamba I, 9, 25, 12. 27. Gautama XXII, 8.

28. Âpastamba I, 9, 24, 21.

29. Taken by itself the Sûtra would seem to refer to the maxim that a free confession reduces the guilt of the offender (Manu XI, 228). But on account of the next Sûtra it is necessary to assume, with Krishnapandita, that half the guilt of a crime, of which another man justly accuses an offender, falls on the accuser, while the

30. To this (effect) they quote also (the following verse): 'By saying to an outcast, "O thou outcast!" or to a thief, "O thou thief!" a man incurs a guilt as great as (that of the offender). (If he) falsely (accuses anybody of such offences), his guilt will be twice as great.'

31. In like manner having slain a Kshatriya, he shall perform (a penance) during eight years,

32. For (killing) a Vaisya during six (years),

33. For (killing) a Sûdra, during three (years),

34. For killing a female of the Brâhmana caste who is an Âtreyî, and a Kshatriya or a Vaisya, engaged in a sacrifice (the same penance must be performed as for killing a learned Brâhmana).

35. We will explain (the term) Âtreyî. They declare that she who has bathed after temporary uncleanness is an Âtreyî.

36. 'For if (the husband) approaches her at that (time), he will have offspring.'

---

offender's guilt becomes less by the publication of his misdeed. It is, however, not improbable that the text is here defective, and one or several Sûtras have been left out.

30. Gautama XXI, 17–18.

31. Vishnu L, 12. The text is here evidently defective. The Sûtra or Sûtras left out must have contained the description of another penance for the murder of a Brâhmana, which is mentioned in nearly all the Smritis (see Vishnu L, 1–6, 15, and the parallel passages). Its chief conditions are, that the murderer is to live separate for twelve years, and to subsist on alms given by people who are acquainted with his crime. Without such an additional rule this and the following Sûtras are utterly unintelligible.

32. Vishnu L, 13.

33. Vishnu L, 14.

34. Vishnu L, 7, 9.

36. The author means to say that the word âtreyî is derived from atra, 'at that time,' and the verb i, 'to approach.' The etymology is worthy of the Nirukta.

37. (For killing a female of the Brâhmana caste) who is not an Âtreyî, (the penance prescribed) for the murder of a Kshatriya (must be performed),

38. (For killing) a female of the Kshatriya caste, (the penance prescribed) for the murder of a Vaisya,

39. (For killing) a female of the Vaisya caste, (the penance prescribed) for the murder of a Sûdra.

40. (For killing) a female of the Sûdra caste (let him perform) during one year (the penance prescribed for the murder of a Brâhmana).

41. If a man has stolen gold belonging to a Brâhmana, he shall run, with flying hair, to the king, (exclaiming) 'Ho, I am a thief; sir, punish me!' The king shall give him a weapon made of Udumbara wood; with that he shall kill himself. It is declared in the Veda that he becomes pure after death.

42. Or (such a thief) may shave off all his hair, anoint his body with clarified butter, and cause himself to be burnt from the feet upwards, in a fire of dry cowdung. It is declared in the Veda that he becomes pure after death.

43. Now they quote also (the following verses): 'Hear, (how) the bodies of those who having committed various crimes died a long time ago, and were (afterwards) born again, are (marked);'

37–40. Gautama XXII, 17.

41. Vishnu LII, 1–2. Krishnapandita remarks that Sûlapâni explains audumbaram, 'made of Udumbara wood,' by 'made of copper,' and that the weapon intended is a club. The last remark is probably true, as the parallel passages of the other Smritis state that the thief is to take a club to the king, with which he is to be struck.

42. Âpastamba I, 9, 25, 6.

44. 'A thief will have deformed nails, the murderer of a Brâhma*n*a will be afflicted with white leprosy, but he who has drunk spirituous liquor will have black teeth, and the violator of his Guru's bed will suffer from skin diseases.'

45. Property received from outcasts, after forming alliances with them either by (teaching) the Veda (and by sacrificing) or by marriage, must be relinquished. Let him not associate with such (men).

46. It is declared in the Veda that (he who has associated with outcasts) becomes pure by reciting the Sa*m*hitâ (of his Veda), proceeding in a northerly direction and fasting.

47. They quote also (a verse) to this (effect), 'A sinner is liberated from guilt by tormenting his body, by austerities, and by reciting the Veda; he becomes also free by bestowing gifts. That has been declared in the Veda.'

Chapter XXI.

1. If a *S*ûdra approaches a female of the Brâhma*n*a caste, (the king) shall cause the *S*ûdra to be tied up in Vîra*n*a grass and shall throw him into a fire. He shall cause the head of the Brâhma*n*î to be shaved, and her body to be anointed with butter; placing her naked on a black donkey, he shall cause her to be conducted along the highroad. It is declared that she becomes pure (thereby).

44. Manu XI, 49; Vish*n*u XLV, 4, 5, 6.

45. Vish*n*u LIV, 28. 46. Manu XI, 194.

XXI. 1–5. Gautama XXIII, 15. K*r*ish*n*apa*nd*ita reads, instead of prâsyet, 'he shall throw,' prâ*s*yet, and explains it by dâhayet, 'he shall cause to be burnt.' It must be understood that these

2. If a Vaisya approaches a female of the Brâhmana caste, (the king) shall cause the Vaisya to be tied up in Lohita grass and shall throw him into a fire. He shall cause the head of the Brâhmanî to be shaved, and her body to be anointed with butter; placing her naked on a yellowish donkey, he shall cause her to be conducted along the highroad. It is declared in the Veda that she becomes pure (thereby).

3. If a Kshatriya approaches a female of the Brâhmana caste, (the king) shall cause the Kshatriya to be tied up in leaves of Sara grass and shall throw him into a fire. He shall cause the head of the Brâhmanî to be shaved, and her body to be anointed with butter; placing her naked on a white donkey, he shall cause her to be conducted along the highroad. It is declared in the Veda that she becomes pure (thereby).

4. A Vaisya who offends) with a female of the Kshatriya class (shall be treated) in the same manner,

5. And a Sûdra (who offends) with females of the Kshatriya or Vaisya castes.

6. If (a wife) has been mentally unfaithful to her husband, she shall live on barley or rice boiled in milk during three days, and sleep on the bare ground. After the three days (have expired), the (husband) shall offer eight hundred burnt-oblations, (reciting) the Sâvitrî (and the Mantra called) Siras, while she is immersed in water. It is declared in the Veda that she becomes pure (thereby).

---

extreme punishments are to be inflicted in particularly bad cases only.

6. 'Afterwards in order to purify her who is immersed in water, i. e. has plunged into water, he shall offer eight hundred, i. e. (such)

7. If (a wife) has held an (improper) conversation (with another man), she must perform the same penance during a month. After (the expiration of) the month, (the husband) shall offer four times eight hundred burnt-oblations, (reciting) the Sâvitrî (and the Mantra called) *S*iras, while she is immersed in water. It is declared in the Veda that she becomes pure (thereby).

8. But if (a wife) has actually committed adultery, she shall wear during a year a garment smeared with clarified butter, and sleep on a mat of Ku*s*a grass, or in a pit filled with cowdung. After (the expiration of) the year, (the husband) shall offer eight hundred burnt-oblations, (reciting) the Sâvitrî (and the Mantra called) *S*iras, while she is immersed in water. It is declared in the Veda that she becomes pure (thereby).

9. But if she commits adultery with a Guru, she is forbidden (to assist her husband) in (the fulfilment of) his sacred duties.

10. But (these) four (wives) must be abandoned, (viz.) one who yields herself to (her husband's) pupil or to (his) Guru, and especially one who attempts

---

a number of burnt-oblations with the *S*iras, i. e. (the words) "Om, ye waters, who are splendour, juice, and ambrosia," &c., which are joined to the Gâyatrî.'—K*r*ish*n*apa*nd*ita. The *S*iras, or 'head,' is again mentioned below, XXV, 13; see also Vish*n*u LV, 9. This and the following two rules refer to offences committed with males of equal caste.

9. Yâg*ñ*avalkya I, 70. Colebrooke IV, Dig. LXXVI, where a different reading, vyavâyatîrthagamanadharmebhya*h*, has been adopted, and the Sûtra has been combined with the next. The first clause may also be translated, 'If she actually commits adultery, (and especially) if she converses with a Guru.'

10. Colebrooke loc. cit.; Manu IX, 80; Yâg*ñ*avalkya I, 72.

the life of her lord, or who commits adultery with a man of a degraded caste.

11. That woman of the Brâhmana caste who drinks spirituous liquor, the gods will not admit (after death) to the same abode with her husband; losing all spiritual merit she wanders about in this world and is born again as a leech or a pearl-oyster.

12. The wives of Brâhmanas, Kshatriyas, and Vaisyas who commit adultery with a Sûdra may be purified by a penance in case no child is born (from their adulterous intercourse), not otherwise.

13. (Those who have committed adultery) with a man of lower caste shall perform a Krikkhra penance, succeeded by one, two, or three Kândrâyanas.

14. Faithful wives who are constantly pure and truthful (reside after death) in the same abodes with their husbands; those who are unfaithful are born as jackals.

15. Half the body of the husband falls if his wife

---

11. Colebrooke IV, Dig. CXIII, where sûkarî, 'a sow,' is read instead of suktikâ, 'a pearl-oyster.'

13. Manu XI, 178. Krishnapandita states correctly that kândrâyanottaram, 'succeeded by one, two, or three Kândrâyanas,' may also mean 'following one, two, or three Kândrâyanas,' and that the number of Kândrâyanas to be performed depends on the caste of the person with whom the adultery was committed. Thus a Brâhmanî must perform one Krikkhra and one Kândrâyana for adultery with a Kshatriya, one Krikkhra and two Kândrâyanas for adultery with a Vaisya, and one Krikkhra and three Kândrâyanas for adultery with a Sûdra. His view that the rule refers to wives who commit the sin without intent or against their will, is open to doubt. It is probably an alternative, to be adopted in lighter cases, for the public punishment prescribed above, XXI, 1–3. Regarding the Kândrâyana, see below, XXIV, 44.

14. Colebrooke IV, Dig. CVIII; Manu V, 164–165.

15. Manu IX, 80; Yâgñavalkya I, 73.

drinks spirituous liquor. No purification is prescribed for the half which has fallen.

16. If a Brâhma*n*a unintentionally commits adultery with the wife of a Brâhma*n*a, (he shall perform) a K*rikkh*ra penance in case (the husband) fulfils the religious duties (of his caste), and an Atik*rikkh*ra penance in case (the husband) does not fulfil his religious duties.

17. The same (penances are prescribed) for Kshatriyas and Vai*s*yas (for adultery with women of their respective castes).

18. If he kills a cow, let him perform, during six months, a K*rikkh*ra or a Taptak*rikkh*ra, dressed in the raw hide of that (cow).

19. The rule for these two (penances is as follows):

20. 'During three days he eats in the day-time (only), and during the (next) three days at night (only), he subsists during (another) period of three days on food offered without asking, and (finally) he fasts during three days.' That is a K*rikkh*ra penance.

21. 'Let him drink hot water during three days; let him drink hot milk during the (next) three days; after drinking during (another) period of three days hot clarified butter, he shall subsist on air during the (last) three days.' That is a Taptak*rikkh*ra penance.

22. And he shall give (to a Brâhma*n*a) a bull and a cow.

23. Now they quote also (the following verse): 'Through killing a spotted deer, a he-goat, and

16. Vish*n*u LIII, 2.

18. Vish*n*u L, 16–24; Gautama XXII, 18.

20. Vish*n*u XLVI, 10. 21. Vish*n*u XLVI, 11.

23. The above translation follows the commentary of K*ri*sh*n*a-

a bird three maladies (befal men), viz. jealousy, hunger, and old age; (therefore) let him (who is guilty of such an offence) perform (a penance) during ninety-eight (days).'

24. Having slain a dog, a cat, an ichneumon, a snake, a frog, or a rat, let him perform a K*rikkh*ra penance of twelve days' duration, and give something (to a Brâhma*n*a).

25. But having slain a quantity of boneless animals, equal to the weight of a cow, let him perform a K*rikkh*ra penance of twelve days' duration, and give something (to a Brâhma*n*a).

26. But (the same penance must be performed) for each single (slain animal) that possesses bones.

27. He who extinguishes the (sacred) fires shall perform a K*rikkh*ra penance of twelve days, and cause them to be kindled again (by priests engaged for the occasion).

28. He who falsely accuses a Guru shall bathe, dressed in his clothes, and ask his Guru's pardon. It is declared in the Veda that he becomes pure by the Guru's forgiving him.

29. An atheist shall perform a K*rikkh*ra penance of twelve days' duration, and give up his infidelity.

---

pa*nd*ita, who further states that the penance to be performed shall consist of a diet of barley gruel. I feel by no means certain that his interpretation, especially that of the last clause, is correct. Possibly ash*t*ânavatim âharet may mean 'he shall offer ninety-eight oblations.'

24. Vish*n*u L, 30, 31.

25. Gautama XXII, 21. 'Something' means eight handfuls of grain.

26. Gautama XXII, 22.

27. Vish*n*u LIV, 13; Gautama XXII, 34.

28. Vish*n*u LIV, 14; Yâg*ñ*avalkya III, 283.

29-30. Vish*n*u LIV, 15.

30. But he who receives subsistence from infidels (shall perform) an Atik*rikkh*ra penance (and not repeat his offence).

31. (The rule applicable to) a seller of Soma has been explained hereby.

32. A hermit, on violating the rules of his order, shall perform a K*rikkh*ra penance of twelve days' duration, and continue (the observances obligatory on him) in a great forest.

33. Ascetics, (offending in the same manner) as hermits, shall perform for a protracted period (the vow of regulating the quantity of their food according to) the growth of the moon, and shall again be initiated, in accordance with (the rules of) the Institutes applicable to them.

Chapter XXII.

1. Now, indeed, man (in) this (world) speaks an untruth, or sacrifices for men unworthy to offer a sacrifice, or accepts what ought not to be accepted, or eats forbidden food, or practises what ought not to be practised.

31. Vish*n*u LIV, 17.

33. The penance prescribed appears to be similar to the *K*ândrâya*n*a. The offender must eat one mouthful on the first lunar day, two on the second, and so forth. But it is not clear for how long a period the rule is to be observed. The Sûtra is interesting as it furnishes corroborative evidence for Pâ*n*ini's statement (IV, 3, 110) that Bhikshu-sûtras which contained the rules applicable to Bhikshus formerly existed.

XXII. 1. As this chapter is almost identical with and probably copied from Baudhâyana III, 10, and Gautama XIX, the division of the Sûtras has not been made in accordance with K*r*ish*n*a-pa*nd*ita's commentary, but agrees with that of the chapter in Gautama's Dharma*s*âstra. The notes to the translation of the

2. They are in doubt if he shall perform a penance for such (a deed), or if he shall not do it.

3. (Some) declare that he shall not do it,

4. Because the deed does not perish.

5. (The correct view is, that) he shall perform (a penance), because it is enjoined in the revealed texts,

6. 'He who offers a horse-sacrifice conquers all sin, he destroys the guilt of the murder of a Brâhma*n*a.'

7. (Moreover), 'Let an Abhi*s*asta offer a Gosava or an Agnish*t*ut-sacrifice.'

8. Reciting the Veda, austerity, a sacrifice, fasting, giving gifts are the means for expiating such a (blamable act).

9. (The purificatory texts are) the Upanishads, the Vedântas, the Sa*m*hitâ-text of all the Vedas, the (Anuvâkas called) Madhu, the (hymn of) Aghamar-

---

latter work must be consulted for the explanation of the more difficult passages.

5-7. The text appears here to be corrupt. After Sûtra 5, Baudhâyana III, 10, 6 (Gautama XIX, 7), Puna*h* stomena *y*a*g*eta puna*h* savanamâyântîti vi*gñ*âyate, 'It is declared in the Veda, "Let him offer a Puna*h*stoma-sacrifice, (those who offer it) again come to partake of (the libations of) Soma,"' has been left out. This omission caused the insertion of the words tasmâ*kkh*rutinidar*s*anât [dar*s*anât, Bh. F.], ('because it is enjoined in the revealed texts,') at the end of Sûtra 5. The proof that the sixth Sûtra of Baudhâyana has been accidentally omitted is furnished by the fact that several MSS. of Vasish*th*a read iti *k*a after yo '*s*vamedhena *y*a*g*ate (Vas. XXII, 6). This *k*a has no meaning, except if another Vedic passage preceded Sûtra 6. In order to escape this difficulty, K*ri*sh*n*apa*nd*ita writes yo '*s*vamedhena ya*g*ata iti, and begins the next Sûtra with iti *k*a, which he explains by 'moreover.'

9. K*ri*sh*n*apa*nd*ita gives before 'Vedântas' another word vedâdaya*h*, which he explains by 'the Vedas, Sm*ri*tis, and Purâ*n*as.'

sha*n*a, the Atharva*s*iras, the (Anuvâkas called) Rudras, the Purusha-hymn, the two Sâmans called Râ*g*a*n*a and Rauhi*n*eya, the Kûshmâ*nd*as, the Pâvamânîs, and the Sâvitrî.

10. Now they quote also (the following verse): 'He who performs once in each season the offerings to Vai*s*vânara and Vratapati and the Pavitresh*t*i sanctifies ten ancestors.'

11. To live on milk alone, as if one were fasting, to eat fruit only, (to live on) barley gruel prepared of a handful of grain, to eat gold, to drink Soma (are modes of subsistence which) purify.

12. All mountains, all rivers, holy lakes, places of pilgrimage, the dwellings of *Ri*shis, cowpens, and temples of the gods (are) places (which destroy sin).

13. A year, a month, twenty-four days, twelve days, six days, three days, a day and a night are the periods (for penances).

14. These (acts) may be optionally performed when no (particular penance) has been prescribed,

15. (Viz.) for great sins difficult (penances), and for trivial faults easy ones.

16. The K*rikkh*ra and the Atik*rikkh*ra (as well as) the *K*ândrâya*n*a are penances for all (offences).

CHAPTER XXIII.

1. If a student has approached a woman, he shall slay in the forest, in a place where four roads meet,

10. K*ri*sh*n*apa*nd*ita takes the last word da*s*apûrusham to mean ten ancestors and ten descendants.

11. 'As if one were fasting,' i. e. in small quantities.—K*ri*sh*n*apa*nd*ita.

XXIII. 1. Gautama XXIII, 17.

(kindling) a common fire, an ass for the Rakshas (the goblins),

2. Or he may offer an oblation of rice (*k*aru) to Nir*ri*ti (the goddess of hell).

3. Let him throw into the fire (four oblations consisting) of that (sacrificial food, saying), 'To Lust svâhâ; to him who follows his lust svâhâ; to Nir*ri*ti svâhâ; to the divine Rakshas svâhâ.'

4. If, before returning home (from his teacher, a student) voluntarily defiles himself, sleeps in the day-time, or practises any other vow (than that of studentship), the same (penance must be performed).

5. If he has committed a bestial crime, he shall give a white bull (to a Brâhma*n*a).

6. The guilt incurred by a bestial crime with a cow, has been explained by the (rule regarding) the killing of a female of the *S*ûdra caste.

7. A student breaks his vow by performing funeral rites,

8. Excepting those of his mother and his father.

9. If a (student) is sick, he may eat, at his pleasure, all that is left by his teacher as medicine.

10. If (a student) who is employed by his teacher (to perform some duty), meets with his death, (the teacher) shall perform three K*rikkh*ra penances.

---

4. Manu XI, 121.

5. Vish*n*u LIII, 7; Gautama XXII, 36.

6. Vish*n*u LIII, 3; Gautama XXIII, 12.

7. Manu V, 88. 8. Manu V, 91.

9. The object of the Sûtra is to permit during sickness a relaxation of the rules regarding forbidden food. Hence a sick student may eat honey, meat, &c.

10. Yâ*g*ñavalkya III, 283. 'Meets with his death,' e.g. is killed by a wild animal or a snake, while collecting fuel in the forest.

11. If a student eats meat which has been given to him as leavings (by his teacher), he shall perform a K*rikkh*ra penance of twelve days' duration, and afterwards finish his vow.

12. The same (penance must be performed) if he eats food given at a *S*râddha or by a person who is impure on account of a recent death or birth.

13. It is declared in the Veda, that honey given without asking does not defile (a student) of the Vâ*g*asaneyi-*s*âkhâ.

14. For him who committing suicide becomes an Abhi*s*asta, his blood-relations (sapi*nd*a) shall not perform the funeral rites.

15. He is called a suicide who destroys himself by means of wood, water, clods of earth, stones, weapons, poison, or a rope.

16. Now they quote also (the following verse): 'The twice-born man who out of affection performs the last rites for a suicide, shall perform a *K*ândrâ-ya*n*a penance together with a Taptak*rikkh*ra.'

17. We shall describe the *K*ândrâya*n*a below.

18. A fast of three days (must be performed) for resolving to die by one's own hand.

---

11. Manu XI, 159; Yâ*gñ*avalkya III, 282; see also Âpastamba's discussion on the subject, I, 1, 4, 5.

12. Manu XI, 158.

13. This Sûtra may also mean, 'It is declared that, according to the Vâ*g*asaneyaka, honey given (to a student) without his asking for it does not defile him.' But a parallel passage of Devala, which K*r*ish*n*apa*nd*ita quotes, makes, I think, the version given above appear preferable. In either case the passage is explained by the fact that, according to the *S*atapatha-brâhma*n*a, *S*vetaketu, one of the great teachers of the White Ya*g*ur-veda, strongly pleaded for the use of honey; see Weber, Indische Studien X, 123 seq.

14. Vish*n*u XXII, 56; Gautama XIV, 12.

16. Vish*n*u XXII, 58–59. 17. See below, Sûtra 45.

19. 'He who attempts suicide, but remains alive, shall perform a Krikkhra penance during twelve days. (Afterwards) he shall fast for three (days and) nights, being dressed constantly in a garment smeared (with clarified butter), and suppressing his breath, he shall thrice recite the Aghamarshana;'

20. Or, following the same rule, he may also frequently recite the Gâyatrî;

21. Or, having kindled a fire, he may offer clarified butter with the Kûshmândas.

22. 'And the guilt (of) all (offences) excepting mortal sins is removed thereby.'

23. Now he may also sip water in the morning, thinking of (the Mantra), 'May fire and wrath and the lords of wrath protect me,' &c., and meditating on his sin; (then) he may mutter the Vyâhritis that end with satya (truth), prefixing (the syllable) Om (to each), or he may recite the Aghamarshana.

24. If he touches a human bone to which fat still adheres, he becomes impure during three (days and) nights;

25. But (on touching a bone) to which no fat adheres, a day and a night,

26. Likewise if he has followed a corpse (to the burial-ground).

27. If he passes between men reciting the Veda, he shall fast during a day and a night.

28. (Those who recite the Veda) shall sprinkle each other with water and stay away (from their houses) during three (days and) nights.

---

22. Regarding the efficacy of the Kûshmânda texts, see above, XXII, 9.

23. The text occurs Taitt. Âr. X, 24, 1.

24–25. Manu V, 87; Vishnu XXII, 75.

26. Manu V, 101.

28. Gautama I, 58.

29. (The same penance must be performed) for a day and night, if a dog, a cat, or an ichneumon pass quickly (between those who recite the Veda).

30. If he has swallowed the flesh of a dog, a cock, a village pig, a grey heron, a vulture, a Bhâsa, a pigeon, a man, a crow or an owl, (he must) fast during seven days, (and thus) empty his entrails; (afterwards he must) eat clarified butter, and be initiated again.

31. 'But a Brâhma*n*a who has been bitten by a dog, becomes pure, if he goes to a river that flows into the ocean, (bathes there), suppresses his breath one hundred times, and eats clarified butter.'

32. 'Time, fire, purity of mind, water, looking at the sun, and ignorance (of defilement) are the six means by which created beings are purified.'

33. It is declared in the Veda that, on touching a dog, a *K*â*nd*âla, or an outcast, he becomes at once pure, if he bathes, dressed in his clothes.

34. If (while reciting the Veda) they hear noises

---

29. Gautama I, 59.

30. Vish*n*u LI, 3-4; Gautama XXIII, 4-5; Manu XI, 157. The Sûtra is badly corrupted in K*ri*sh*n*apa*nd*ita's edition. I read kaṅka instead of vaṅka, leave out vâyasa after bhâsa, and change kâkolûkânâ*m* sâdane to kâkolûkamâ*m*sâdane. The latter change is absolutely necessary; firstly, because the penances for killing dogs and men have been given above; secondly, because the word mânusha requires a noun which it qualifies at the end of the compound; thirdly, because the penance which is prescribed, fasting until the entrails are empty, is absurd for murder, but appropriate for eating forbidden food; and fourthly, because the parallel passages of other Sm*ri*tis actually do prescribe it for eating the flesh of excessively impure animals and for cannibalism. The change of amâ to ânâ is a very common mistake in Devanâgarî MSS.

31. Vish*n*u LIV, 12. 32. Vish*n*u XXII, 88.

33. Âpastamba I, 5, 15, 16.

made by outcasts or *Kândâlas*, they shall sit silent and fasting during three days;

35. Or if they repeat that (text of the Gâyatrî) at least one thousand times, they become pure; thus it is stated in the Veda.

36. By this rule (the penance to be performed by) those who teach or sacrifice for vile men has been explained. It is declared in the Veda that they become pure by also relinquishing the fees (which they received).

37. By this same (rule the penance prescribed for) an Abhisasta, (one accused of a heinous crime,) has been explained.

38. (If he has been accused of) killing a learned Brâhma*n*a, let him subsist during twelve days on water (only), and fast during (another) twelve days.

39. If he has falsely accused a Brâhma*n*a of a crime which causes loss of caste, or of a minor offence which does not cause loss of caste, he shall subsist during a month on water (only), and constantly repeat the (*Rik*as called) *S*uddhavatîs;

40. Or he may go to bathe (with the priests) at (the conclusion of) a horse-sacrifice.

41. By this (rule the penance for) intercourse with a female of the *Kândâ*la caste has been declared.

42. Now (follows the description of) another K*rikkh*ra penance, applicable to all (men), where (the rule given above) has been altered.

43. On one day (let him eat) in the morning (only), on the (following) day at night (only), on the (next) day food given without asking, and on the (fourth) day (let him) fast; the succeeding (three) periods of

36. Vish*n*u LIV, 25, 28. 38. Yâg*ñ*avalkya III, 287.
39. Yâg*ñ*avalkya III, 286. 41. Vish*n*u LIII, 5, 6.

four days (must be passed) in the same manner. Wishing to show favour to the Brâhma*n*as, Manu, the chief among the pillars of the law, has thus described the *S*isuk*rikkh*ra (the hard penance of children) for infants, aged, and sick men.

44. Now follows the rule for (the performance of) the *K*ândrâya*n*a (lunar penance).

45. On the first day of the dark half (of the month) let him eat fourteen (mouthfuls), let him diminish the (number of) mouthfuls (each day by one), and continue in this manner until the end of the fortnight. In like manner let him eat one mouthful on the first day of the bright half, and (daily) increasing (the number of) mouthfuls, continue until the end of the fortnight.

46. Meanwhile let him sing Sâmans, or mutter the Vyâh*ri*tis.

47. A month during which he thus performs a *K*ândrâya*n*a, the *Ri*shis have called by way of laudation, 'a means of purification' (pavitra). It is prescribed as an expiation of all (offences) for which no (special penance) has been mentioned.

Chapter XXIV.

1. Now (follows the description of) an Atik*rik-kh*ra penance.

2. Let him eat as much as he can take at one (mouthful, and follow the rules given) above for a K*rikkh*ra, (viz.) to eat during three days in the morning, (during another three days) in the evening, (during further three days) food given without

44–47. Vish*n*u XLVII. It must be understood that during the bright half of the month the number of mouthfuls must be increased every day by one.

XXIV. 1–2. Gautama XXVI, 18–19. 'Above,' i. e. XXI, 20.

asking, and to fast during the last three days. That is an Atikrikkhra.

3. A Krikkhra penance (during the performance of which one) subsists on water (only is called) a Krikkhrâtikrikkhra.

4. The peculiar observances (prescribed during the performance) of Krikkhra penances (are as follows):

5. 'Having cut his nails, (the performer) shall cause his beard and all his hair to be shaved off, excepting the eyebrows, the eyelashes, and the lock at the top of the head; (wear) one garment only; he shall eat blameless food; what one obtains by going to beg once (is called) blameless food; he shall bathe in the morning, at noon, and in the evening; he shall carry a stick (and) a waterpot; he shall avoid to speak to women and Sûdras; carefully keeping himself in an upright or sitting posture, he shall stand during the day, and remain seated during the night.' Thus speaks the divine Vasishtha.

6. Let him not instruct in these Institutes of the sacred law anybody but his son or a pupil who stays (in his house at least) for a year.

7. The fee (for teaching it) is one thousand (panas), (or) ten cows and a bull, or the worship of the teacher.

Chapter XXV.

1. I will completely explain the purification of those whose guilt has not been made public, both from great crimes and for minor offences.

---

3. Gautama XXVI, 20; see also Vishnu XLVI, 13–14.

4–5. Gautama XXVI, 6, 8; Vishnu XLVII, 24–25.

6. The MSS. read in the beginning of this Sûtra, satayânudeti or satayâtudeta, while Krishnapandita, probably as a guess, writes satapâ nudati. I do not think that his correction is satisfactory, and propose in its stead, sa tadyadetad (dharmasâstram).

2. A penance prescribed in (the section on) secret (penances) is for an Agnihotrin, an aged and a learned man, who have subdued their senses; but other men (must perform the expiations) described above.

3. Those constantly engaged in suppressing their breath, reciting purificatory texts, giving gifts, making burnt-oblations, and muttering (sacred texts) will, undoubtedly, be freed from (the guilt of) crimes causing loss of caste.

4. Seated with Kusa grass in his hands, let him repeatedly suppress his breath, and again and again recite purificatory texts, the Vyâhritis, the syllable Om, and the daily portion of the Veda.

5. Always intent on the practice of Yoga, let him again and again suppress his breath. Up to the ends of his hair and up to the ends of his nails let him perform highest austerity.

6. Through the obstruction (of the expiration) air is generated, through air fire is produced, then through heat water is formed; hence he is internally purified by (these) three.

7. Neither through severe austerities, nor through the daily recitation of the Veda, nor through offering sacrifices can the twice-born reach that condition which they attain by the practice of Yoga.

8. Through the practice of Yoga (true) knowledge is obtained, Yoga is the sum of the sacred law, the practice of Yoga is the highest and eternal austerity; therefore let him always be absorbed in the practice of Yoga.

XXV. 4. Read prânâyâmân in the text.

5. The MSS. read at the end of this verse, tapas tapyatam uttamam, while Krishnapandita gives tapas tapyât tu uttamam. The correct reading is probably tapas tapyatu uttamam.

9. For him who is constantly engaged in (reciting the syllable) Om, the seven Vyâhritis, and the three-footed Gâyatrî no danger exists anywhere.

10. The Vedas likewise begin with the syllable Om, and they end with the syllable Om, the syllable Om is the sum of all speech; therefore let him repeat it constantly.

11. The most excellent (portion of the) Veda, which consists of one syllable, is declared to be the best purificatory text.

12. If the guilt of all sins did fall on one man, to repeat the Gâyatrî ten thousand times (would be) an efficient means of purification.

13. If, suppressing his breath, he thrice recites the Gâyatrî together with the Vyâhritis together with the syllable Om and with the (text called) Siras, that is called one suppression of breath.

CHAPTER XXVI.

1. If, untired, he performs three suppressions of his breath according to the rule, the sins which he committed during a day and a night are instantly destroyed.

2. Seated during the evening prayer, he removes by (three) suppressions of his breath all guilt which

9. I read with the MSS. bhayam for bhave.

10. Manu II, 74.

13. Identical with Vishnu LV, 9. Regarding the text called Siras, see above, XXI, 6.

XXVI. 1. The verb dhârayet, 'performs,' seems to be used in order to indicate that, according to the Yogasâstra, three Prânâyâmas make one Dhâranâ; see Yâgñavalkya III, 201.

2-3. Regarding the position at the Sandhyâ prayers, see also above.

he incurred during the day by deeds, thoughts, or speeches.

3. But standing during the morning prayer, he removes by (three) suppressions of his breath all guilt which he incurred during the night by deeds, thoughts, or speeches.

4. But sixteen suppressions of breath, accompanied by (the recitation of) the Vyâh*ri*tis and the syllable Om, repeated daily, purify after a month even the slayer of a learned Brâhma*n*a.

5. Even a drinker of spirituous liquor becomes pure, if he mutters the (hymn seen) by Kutsa, 'Apa na*h* *s*o*s*u*k*ad agham,' and (the hymn seen) by Vasish*th*a (which begins with the word) 'Prati,' the Mâhitra (hymn), and the *S*uddhavatîs.

6. Even he who has stolen gold becomes instantly free from guilt, if he once mutters (the hymn beginning with the words) 'Asya vâmasya' and the *S*ivasa*m*kalpa.

7. The violator of a Guru's bed is freed (from sin) if he repeatedly recites the (hymn beginning) 'Havish pântam a*g*aram' and that (beginning) 'Na tam a*m*ha*h*' and mutters the hymn addressed to Purusha.

8. Or plunging into water he may thrice mutter the Aghamarsha*n*a. Manu has declared that the (effect is the) same as if he had gone to bathe at a horse-sacrifice.

---

4. Identical with Manu XI, 249; see also Vish*n*u LV, 2.

5. Identical with Manu XI, 250. The Vedic texts mentioned are Rig-veda I, 97, 1; VII, 80; X, 185; VIII, 84, 7–9.

6. Manu LI, 251. The Vedic texts alluded to are Rig-veda I, 164; and an Upanishad.

7. Identical with Manu XI, 252. The Vedic texts mentioned are Rig-veda X, 88; X, 126; X, 90.

8. Manu XI, 260–261; Vish*n*u LV, 7.

9. An offering consisting of muttered prayers is ten times more efficacious than a sacrifice at which animals are killed; a (prayer) which is inaudible (to others) surpasses it a hundred times, and the mental (recitation of sacred texts) one thousand times.

10. The four Pâkayag*ñ*as and those sacrifices which are enjoined by the rules of the Veda are all together not equal in value to the sixteenth part of a sacrifice consisting of muttered prayers.

11. But, undoubtedly, a Brâhma*n*a reaches the highest goal by muttering prayers only; whether he perform other (rites) or neglect them, he is called a Brâhma*n*a who befriends all creatures (maitra).

12. The sins of those who are intent on muttering prayers, of those who offer burnt-oblations, of those who are given to meditation, of those who reside in sacred places, and of those who have bathed after performing the vows called *S*iras, do not remain.

13. As a fire, fanned by wind, burns brighter, and (as its flame grows) through offerings (of butter), even so a Brâhma*n*a who is daily engaged in

9. Manu II, 85; Vish*n*u LV, 19. The term ârambhayag*ñ*a, translated by 'an offering at which animals are slain,' is taken by K*r*ishn*a*pa*nd*ita to mean pâ*th*ayag*ñ*a, 'an offering consisting of Vedic mantras recited aloud.' The word may be taken in several ways, but the various reading vidhiyag*ñ*a in Manu's verse induces me to adopt the translation given above.

10. Identical with Manu II, 86, and Vish*n*u LV, 20. Regarding the four Pâkayag*ñ*as, see Professor Jolly's note on Vish*n*u. In my opinion the four classes of rites huta, ahuta, prahuta, and prâ*s*ita are meant.

11. Identical with Manu II, 87.

12. 'After performing the vows (called) *S*iras,' i.e. those which are known in the Upanishads, which are called agnidhâra*n*a and so forth, and whose head (*s*iras) consists in the worship of the teacher.—K*r*ish*n*apa*nd*ita. Mu*nd*aka Upanishad III, 2, 10.

muttering sacred texts shines with a brilliant lustre.

14. The destruction of those who fulfil the duty of daily study, who constantly restrain themselves, who mutter prayers and offer sacrifices has never been known (to happen).

15. Let him who is desirous of purification repeat, though he be charged with all sins, the divine (Gâyatrî), at the most one thousand times, or one hundred times as a medium (penance), or at least ten times (for trivial faults).

16. A Kshatriya shall pass through misfortunes which have befallen him by the strength of his arms, a Vai*s*ya and *S*ûdra by their wealth, the highest among twice-born men by muttered prayers and burnt-oblations.

17. As horses (are useless) without a chariot, as chariots (are useless) without horses, even so austerity (is useless) to him who is destitute of sacred learning, and sacred learning to him who practises no austerities.

18. As food mixed with honey, or honey mixed with food, even so are austerities and learning, joined together, a powerful medicine.

19. No guilt taints a Brâhma*n*a who possesses learning, practises austerities, and daily mutters sacred texts, though he may constantly commit sinful acts.

CHAPTER XXVII.

1. If a hundred improper acts, and even more, have been committed, and the (knowledge of the)

---

14. Manu IV, 146.
XXVII. 1-2. Manu XI, 247.

Veda is retained, the fire of the Veda destroys all (the guilt) of that man just as a (common) fire consumes fuel.

2. As a fire that burns strongly consumes even green trees, even so the fire of the Veda destroys one's guilt caused by (evil) deeds.

3. A Brâhma*n*a who remembers the Rig-veda is not tainted by any guilt, though he has destroyed these (three) worlds and has eaten the food of all, (even of the most sinful) men.

4. If (a Brâhma*n*a) relies on the power of the Veda, he cannot find pleasure in sinful acts. Guilt (incurred) through ignorance and negligence is destroyed, not (that of) other (intentional offences).

5. If a hermit subsisting on roots and fruit practises austerities in a forest, and (a householder) recites a single *Rik*, the merit of the acts of the one and of the other is equal.

6. Let him strengthen the Veda by (studying) the Itihâsas and Purâ*n*as. For the Veda fears a man of little learning, (thinking) 'He will destroy me.'

7. The daily recitation of the Veda and the performance, according to one's ability, of the series of Mahâya*gñ*as quickly destroy guilt, even that of mortal sins.

8. Let him daily perform, without tiring, his particular rites which the Veda enjoins. For if he does that according to his ability, he will reach the most blessed state.

9. Through sacrificing for wicked people, through teaching them, through intermarrying with them, and through receiving gifts from them, (learned)

3. Identical with Manu XI, 262.

8. 'The most blessed state,' i.e. final liberation, or moksha.

Brâhmanas do not contract guilt, for (a learned Brâhmana) resembles a fire and the sun.

10. I will now declare the purification prescribed for (eating) food, regarding which doubts have arisen, whether it may be called fit to be eaten or not. Listen to my words!

11. Let a Brâhmana drink during three days the astringent decoction of the Brahmasuvarkalâ plant, unmixed with salt or pungent condiments, and (a decoction of) the Sankhapushpî plant, together with milk.

12. Let him drink water, after boiling in it Palâsa and Bilva leaves, Kusa grass, and (leaves of) lotuses and Udumbara trees; after three days and no more he becomes pure.

13. (Subsisting) during one day on each (of the following substances), cow's urine, cowdung, milk, sour milk, butter, and water in which Kusa grass has been boiled, and fasting on the seventh day purify even (him who fears that he has partaken of the food of) a Svapâka.

14. He who lives during five days on cow's urine, cowdung, milk, sour milk, and clarified butter, is purified by means of (that) Pañkagavya, (the five products of the cow.)

15. He who, in accordance with the rule, uses barley (for his food), becomes pure even by ocular proof. (For) if he is pure, those (barley grains) will be white, if he is impure they will be discoloured.

16. (If he makes) three morning meals of food

12. Vishnu XLVI, 23. I read abhogyabhogyasamgñake.

13. Vishnu XLVI, 19.

15. The rule is described by Vishnu XLVIII.

16. The meaning of the Sûtra is that each mode of subsistence is to be continued during three days.

fit for a sacrifice and three evening meals in like manner, and if food given without asking (is his subsistence) in the same manner, (he will thus perform) three fasts.

17. Now if he is in haste to make (himself pure), (let him) subsist on air during a day, and pass the night standing in water; (that penance) is equal to a Prâgâpatya (Krikkhra).

18. But if at sunrise he mutters the Gâyatrî eight thousand times, he will be freed from all mortal sins, provided he be not the slayer of a Brâhmana.

19. He, forsooth, who has stolen (the gold of a Brâhmana), has drunk spirituous liquor, has slain a learned Brâhmana, or has violated his Guru's bed, will become free from all (these) mortal sins if he studies the Institutes of the sacred law.

20. For unlawful acts, for unlawful sacrifices, and for great sins (let him perform) a Krikkhra and a *K*ândrâyana, which destroy all guilt.

21. Let him add daily one mouthful (to his food) during the bright (half of the month), let him diminish it (daily by one mouthful) during the dark (half), and let him fast on the new-moon day; that is the rule for the *K*ândrâyana (or lunar penance).

CHAPTER XXVIII.

1. A woman is not defiled by a lover, nor a Brâhmana by Vedic rites, nor water by urine and ordure, nor fire by consuming (impure substances).

---

18. Ashtasahasram, 'eight thousand times,' may also mean 'one thousand and eight times.'

21. See above, XXIII, 44-47.

XXVIII. 1. 'Is not defiled by a lover,' i. e. does not become irrevocably an outcast, but may be restored to her position after

2–3. A wife, (though) tainted by sin, whether she be quarrelsome, or have left the house, or have suffered criminal force, or have fallen into the hands of thieves, must not be abandoned; to forsake her is not prescribed (by the sacred law). Let him wait for the time of her courses; by her temporary uncleanness she becomes pure.

4. Women (possess) an unequalled means of purification; they never become (entirely) foul. For month by month their temporary uncleanness removes their sins.

5. Women belong first to three gods, Soma (the moon), the Gandharva, and Fire, and come afterwards into the possession of men; according to the law they cannot be contaminated.

6. Soma gave them cleanliness, the Gandharva their melodious voice, and Fire purity of all (limbs); therefore women are free from stains.

7. Those versed in the sacred law state that there are three acts (only) which make women outcasts, (viz.) the murder of the husband, slaying a learned Brâhma*n*a, and the destruction of the fruit of their womb.

8. A calf is pure when the milk flows, a bird when it causes fruit to fall, women during dalliance, and a dog when he catches a deer.

9. Pure is the mouth of a goat and of a horse, pure is the back of a cow, pure are the feet of a Brâhma*n*a, but women are pure in all (limbs).

---

performing a penance, provided her lover was a man of equal caste.—K*r*ish*n*apa*nd*ita.

2–3. For the last clause compare Yâ*g*ñavalkya I, 72.

4. See above, V, 3–4.

5. Pâraskara G*r*ihya-sûtra I, 4, 16.

6. Yâ*g*ñavalkya I, 71.

7. Yâ*g*ñavalkya I, 72.

8. Vish*n*u XXIII, 49.

9. Vish*n*u XXIII, 40.

10. I will now declare the purificatory texts (which are found) in each Veda; by muttering them or reciting them at a burnt-oblation (men) are doubtlessly cleansed (from sin).

11. (They are) the Aghamarshana, the Devakrita, the Suddhavatîs, the Taratsamas, the Kûshmândas, the Pâvamânîs, and the Durgâsâvitrî;

12. The Atîshangas, the Padastobhas, and the Sâmans (called) Vyâhriti, the Bhârunda Sâmans, the Gâyatra (Sâman), and the Raivata;

13. The Purushavrata and the Bhâsa, and likewise the Devavrata (Sâmans), the Ablinga, the Bârhaspatya, the hymn addressed to Vâk, likewise the *Rik*as (called) Madhu;

14. The Satarudriya, the Atharvasiras, the Trisuparna, the Mahâvrata, the Gosûkta, and the Asvasûkta, and the two Sâmans (called) Suddhâsuddhîya.

15. The three (Sâmans called) Âgyadohas, the Rathantara, the Agnervrata, the Vâmadevya, and the Brihat, being muttered, purify (all) living beings. (He who sings them) may obtain the recollection of former existences, if he desires it.

16. Gold is the firstborn of Fire, through Vishnu exists the earth, and the cows are children of the

---

10–15. Vishnu LVI, and preface, p. xviii. The explanation of the various terms used will be found in the notes to Professor Jolly's translation of Vishnu.

12. MSS. and Krishnapandita, Abhishangâh. Krishnapandita and MS. B. bhâradandâni; E. bhâdâni; Bh. and F. omit vv. 12 and 13 a.

13. Krishnapandita and B. artvigam; Bh. E. F. as above. The Bhâsa begins, according to Krishnapandita, agne vratapate.

14. Krishnapandita and B. indrasuddhe; Bh. E. F. suddhamsuddhena.

Sun; he who bestows as gifts gold, a cow, and land will obtain rewards without end for them.

17. A cow, a horse, gold, (and) land, bestowed on an unlearned Brâhma*n*a who neglects his sacred duties, prevent the giver (from attaining heaven).

18–19. (If he presents), on the full moon of the month of Vai*s*âkha, (to) seven or five Brâhma*n*as, black or white sesamum grains (mixed) with honey, (saying), 'May the king of justice (Yama) rejoice!' or (expressing) some other (wish) which he may have in his mind, the guilt which he has incurred during his (whole) life will instantly vanish.

20. But hear (now) the reward of the merit acquired by that man who gives the skin of a black antelope, to which the hoofs are (still) attached and the navel of which is adorned with gold, covering it with sesamum grains.

21. 'Without doubt he has bestowed (through that gift) the four-faced earth, together with its caves filled with gold, and together with its mountains, groves, and forests.'

22. 'He who, placing on the skin of a black antelope, sesamum, gold, honey, and butter, gives it to a Brâhma*n*a, overcomes all sin.'

---

17. Manu IV, 190, 193–194. K*r*ish*n*apa*nd*ita and MSS. B. and E. read uparudanti dâtâra*m*, MSS. Bh. and F. uparundanti. I change the latter reading to uparundhanti.

18–19. Vish*n*u XC, 10.

20–22. Vish*n*u LXXXVII, 8–10, and Professor Jolly's preface, p. xviii.

21. 'The four-faced earth,' i. e. the earth which is surrounded by the four oceans.

CHAPTER XXIX.

1. Through liberality (man) obtains all his desires,

2. (Even) longevity, (and he is born again as) a student of the Veda, possessed of beauty.

3. He who abstains from injuring (sentient beings) obtains heaven.

4. By entering a fire the world of Brahman (is gained).

5. By (a vow of) silence (he obtains) happiness.

6. By staying (constantly) in water he becomes a lord of elephants.

7. He who expends his hoard (in gifts) becomes free from disease.

8. A giver of water (becomes) rich by (the fulfilment of) all his desires.

9. A giver of food (will have) beautiful eyes and a good memory.

10. He who gives a promise to protect (somebody) from all dangers (becomes) wise.

11. (To bestow gifts) for the use of cows (is equal to) bathing at all sacred places.

12. By giving a couch and a seat (the giver becomes) master of a harem.

13. By giving an umbrella (the giver) obtains a house.

XXIX. 4. This Sûtra, which recommends self-cremation, is of some importance, as it confirms the teaching of the Purâṇas and explains the accounts of the Greeks regarding the self-immolation of Brâhmaṇas who visited Europe.

9. Vishṇu XCII, 21.

12. Vishṇu XCII, 27; Manu IV, 232. 'Master of a harem,' i. e. the possessor of many beautiful wives and concubines.

14. He who gives a house obtains a town.

15. He who gives a pair of shoes obtains a vehicle.

16. Now they quote also (the following verses): 'Whatever sin a man distressed for livelihood commits, (from that) he is purified by giving land, (be it) even "a bull's hide."'

17. 'He who gives to a Brâhma*n*a a vessel filled with water for sipping, will obtain after death complete freedom from thirst and be born again as a drinker of Soma.'

18. 'If a gift of one thousand oxen fit to draw a carriage (has been bestowed) according to the rule on a perfectly worthy man, that is equal to giving a maiden.'

19. 'They declare that cows, land, and learning are the three most excellent gifts. For to give learning is (to bestow) the greatest of all gifts, and it surpasses those (other gifts).'

20. 'A learned man who, free from envy, follows this rule of conduct which procures endless rewards, and which through final liberation frees him from transmigration;'

21. 'Or who, full of faith, pure, and subduing his

---

14. Vish*n*u XCII, 31. 15. Vish*n*u XCII, 28.

16. Vish*n*u XCII, 4. K*r*ish*n*apa*n*d*i*ta quotes a passage of the Matsya-purâ*n*a according to which 'a bull's hide' is a measure equal to 140 square hastas; see, however, notes to Vish*n*u loc. cit. and V, 183.

17. Manu IV, 229.

18. Read in the text vidhivaddânam kanyâdânena tatsamam.

19. K*r*ish*n*apa*n*d*i*ta wrongly makes two Sûtras out of this verse.

20. K*r*ish*n*apa*n*d*i*ta and MS. B. read, against the metre and sense, yoginâ*m* sampûritam vidvân, another reading yoginâ*m* sa*m*matam vidvân. F. reads *y*onasa*m*yurima*m* vidvân. I read yo 'nasûyurima*m* vidvân.

senses, remembers or even hears it, will, freed from all sin, be exalted in the highest heaven.'

CHAPTER XXX.

1. Practise righteousness, not unrighteousness; speak truth, not untruth; look far, not near; look towards the Highest, not towards that which is not the Highest.

2. A Brâhma*n*a is a fire.

3. For the Veda (says), 'Agni, forsooth, is a Brâhma*n*a.'

4. And how is that?

5. And it is also declared in the Kâ*th*aka, 'On that (occasion) the body of the Brâhma*n*a who represents the sacrificial seat is the altar, the vow to perform the rite is the sacrifice, the soul is the animal to be slain, the intellect the rope (with which the animal is bound), the mouth of (the Brâhma*n*a) who represents the seat is the Âhavanîya fire, in his navel (is the Dakshi*n*â fire), the fire in his abdomen is the Gârhapatya fire, the Prâ*n*a is the Adhvaryu priest, the Apâna the Hot*ri* priest, the Vyâna the Brahman, the Samâna the Udgât*ri* priest, the organs of sensation the sacrificial vessels. He who knowing this offers a sacrifice to the organs through the organs.' . . .

6. Now they quote also (the following verses): 'An offering placed in the mouth-fire of a Brâh-

XXX. 2. See above, III, 10.

3. *S*atapatha-brâhma*n*a I, 4, 22.

5. K*ri*sh*n*apa*nd*ita divides the passage into thirteen Sûtras, and connects tatra, 'on that occasion,' with the preceding Sûtra. 'On that (occasion),' i. e. if a Brâhma*n*a is fed.

mana which is rich in Veda-fuel, protects and saves the giver and (the eater) himself from sin.'

7. 'But the offering made through the mouth of a Brâhmana, which is neither spilt nor causes pain (to sentient creatures), nor assails him (who makes it), is far more excellent than an Agnihotra.'

8. After performing a mental sacrifice at which meditation (takes the place of the sacred) fire, truthfulness (the place of) the sacred fuel, patience (the place of) the oblation, modesty (the place of) the sacrificial spoon, abstention from injuring living beings (the place of the) sacrificial cake, contentment (the place of) the sacrificial post, (and a promise of) safety given to all beings which is hard to keep (the place of) the reward given to the priests, a wise man goes to his (eternal) home.

9. The hair of an aging man shows signs of age, (and) the teeth of an aging man show signs of age, (but) the desire to live and the desire for wealth do not decay even in an aging man.

---

7. Manu VII, 84; Yâgñavalkya I, 315. Krishnapandita's reading, nainam adhyâkate ka yah, which occurs also in B., is nonsense. I read with Bh. nainamadhyâpatekka yat, and take adhyâpatet, 'assails (the giver),' in the sense of 'troubles him by causing the performance of penances, on account of mistakes committed.' Manu's version, na vinasyati karhikit, 'and never perishes,' is of course an easier one, but it seems to me doubtful whether it is older than Vasishtha's.

8. The passage, which is probably a quotation from an Upanishad, is very corrupt in the MSS. and Krishnapandita's text. I correct it as follows:

Dhyânâgnih satyopakayanam kshântyâhutih
sruvamhrih purodâsamahimsâ samtosho
yûpah krikkhram bhûtebhyo 'bhayadâkshinyam iti
kritvâ kratum mânasam yâti kshayam budhah.

But I am not confident that all the difficulties have been removed.

10. Happiness (is the portion) of that man who relinquishes (all) desire, which fools give up with difficulty, which does not diminish with age, and which is a life-long disease.

11. Adoration to Vasish*th*a *S*atayâtu, the son of Mitra and Varu*n*a and Urva*s*î!

BAUDHÂYANA.

BAUDHÂYANA.

Prasna I, Adhyâya 1, Kandikâ 1.

1. The sacred law is taught in each Veda.

2. We will explain (it) in accordance with that.

3. (The sacred law), taught in the Tradition (Smriti, stands) second.

4. The practice of the *S*ish*t*as (stands) third.

5. *S*ish*t*as, forsooth, (are those) who are free from envy, free from pride, contented with a store of grain sufficient for ten days, free from covetousness, and free from hypocrisy, arrogance, greed, perplexity, and anger.

6. '(Those are called) *S*ish*t*as who, in accordance with the sacred law, have studied the Veda together

---

1. 1. Vasish*th*a I, 4. Each Veda, i.e. each *s*âkhâ or redaction of the Veda.—Govinda.

3. Vasish*th*a I, 4. Govinda takes smriti, 'the tradition,' in the sense of works (grantha) explaining the recollections of the *R*ishis, and is no doubt right in doing so.

4. Vasish*th*a I, 5. The explanation of âgama by 'practice' rests on the authority of Govinda and the parallel passages where *s*îla and â*k*âra, 'conduct,' are used.

5. Âpastamba I, 7, 20, 8; Gautama XXVIII, 48. Kumbhîdhânya, translated according to Govinda by 'contented with a store of grain sufficient for ten days,' means, according to others, 'contented with a store of grain sufficient for six days or for a year.'

6. Vasish*th*a VI, 43. Govinda omits the word 'iti,' given by the

with its appendages, know how to draw inferences from that, (and) are able to adduce proofs perceptible by the senses from the revealed texts.'

7. On failure of them, an assembly consisting at least of ten members (shall decide disputed points of law).

8. Now they quote also (the following verses): 'Four men, who each know one of the four Vedas, a Mîmâmsaka, one who knows the Aṅgas, one who recites (the works on) the sacred law, and three Brâhmanas belonging to (three different) orders, (constitute) an assembly consisting, at least, of ten members.'

9. 'There may be five, or there may be three, or there may be one blameless man, who decides (questions regarding) the sacred law. But a thousand fools (can)not (do it).'

10. 'As an elephant made of wood, as an antelope made of leather, such is an unlearned Brâhmana: those three having nothing but the name (of their kind).'

MSS. after the verse, whereby it is marked as a quotation. 'The appendages,' i.e. the Itihâsas and Purânas.—Govinda.

8. Vasishtha III, 20. Govinda, quoting Gautama XXVIII, 49, says that Vânaprasthas cannot serve as members of Parishads, because they live in the forest. He also notices a different reading, not found in my MSS., 'Âsramasthâs trayo mukhyâh.' He asserts that thereby professed students are intended, because professed students are declared to be particularly holy in the Dharmaskandhabrâhmana.

9. Vasishtha III, 7. Itare, translated by 'fools,' means literally, 'those different from the persons enumerated in the preceding verse.' Govinda remarks that according to Sûtra 12 one learned Brâhmana must be taken only in cases of the most pressing necessity.

10. Vasishtha III, 11.

11. 'That sin which dunces, perplexed by ignorance and unacquainted with the sacred law, declare (to be duty), falls, increased a hundredfold, on those who propound it.'

12. 'Narrow and difficult to find is the path of the sacred law, towards which many gates lead. Hence, if there is a doubt, it must not be propounded by one man (only), however learned he may be.'

13. 'What Brâhma*n*as, riding in the chariot of the law (and) wielding the sword of the Veda, propound even in jest, that is declared to be the highest law.'

14. 'As wind and sun will make water, collected on a stone, disappear, even so the sin that (cleaves) to an offender completely vanishes like water.'

15. 'He who knows the sacred law shall fix the penances with discernment, taking into consideration the constitution, the strength, the knowledge, and the age (of the offender), as well as the time and the deed.'

---

11. Vasish*th*a III, 6.

12. The 'gates' of the sacred law are the Vedas, the Sm*ri*tis, and the practice of the *S*ish*t*as. They are many, because the redactions of the Vedas and Sm*ri*tis are numerous and the practices vary in different countries.

14. I. e. provided the offender performs the penance imposed by learned and virtuous Brâhma*n*as. Pra*n*â*s*ayet, 'will make disappear,' is ungrammatical, as the subject stands in the dual. Grammatical accuracy has probably been sacrificed to the exigencies of the metre.

15. Vasish*th*a XIX, 9. *S*arîram, literally 'the body,' means here the constitution, which may be bilious, 'windy,' and so forth. Âyu*h*, literally 'life' or 'long life,' has been translated by 'knowledge,' in accordance with Govinda's explanation, *g*ñânam. As the word vaya*h*, 'age,' also occurs in this verse, it is clear that âyu*h* cannot have its usual meaning.

16. 'Many thousands (of Brâhma*n*as) cannot form a (legal) assembly (for declaring the sacred law), if they have not fulfilled their sacred duties, are unacquainted with the Veda, and subsist only by the name of their caste.'

Pra*s*na I, Adhyâya 1, Ka*nd*ikâ 2.

1. There is a dispute regarding five (practices) both in the south and in the north.

2. We will explain those (peculiar) to the south.

3. They are, to eat in the company of an uninitiated person, to eat in the company of one's wife, to eat stale food, to marry the daughter of a maternal uncle or of a paternal aunt.

4. Now (the customs peculiar) to the north are, to deal in wool, to drink rum, to sell animals that have teeth in the upper and in the lower jaws, to follow the trade of arms, to go to sea.

---

16. Vasish*th*a III, 5. The two copies of the commentary omit this Sûtra, though it is quoted in the explanation of Sûtra 9. The best MSS. repeat the last words of the Sûtra in order to show that the Ka*nd*ikâ ends here. The same practice is observed, though not quite regularly, in the sequel.

2. 1. The boundary between the north and south of India is, as Govinda also points out, the river Narmadâ.

3. Some of the customs mentioned here still prevail in parts of southern India. Thus the marriages between cousins occur among the De*s*astha and Karhâ*d*â Brâhma*n*as of the Dekhan.

4. The first two customs mentioned still prevail in the north, especially in Ka*s*mîr, where Brâhma*n*as commonly deal in wool and woollen cloth. Spirituous liquor is not now drunk openly, but its use is sanctioned in the Ka*s*mîrian Nîlamata-purâ*n*a. Many Brâhmanical families in the north, especially in the North-western Provinces, subsist by enlisting as soldiers in the British and native armies.

5. He who follows (these practices) in any other country than where they prevail, commits sin.

6. For each (of these customs) the (rule of the) country should be (considered) the authority.

7. Gautama declares that that is false.

8. And one should not take heed of either (set of practices) because they are opposed to the tradition of the *S*ish*t*as.

9. The country of the Âryas (Âryâvarta) lies to the east of the region where (the river Sarasvatî) disappears, to the west of the Black-forest (Kâlakavana), to the north of the Pâripâtra (mountains), to the south of the Himâlaya. The rule of conduct which (prevails) there, is authoritative.

10. Some (declare) the country between the (rivers) Yamunâ and Ganges (to be the Âryâvarta).

11. Now the Bhâllavins quote also the (following) verse:

12. 'In the west the boundary-river, in the east the region where the sun rises,—as far as the black antelopes wander (between these two limits), so far spiritual pre-eminence (is found).'

5–6. A similar argument is given by the Ka*s*mîrians for the lawfulness of the consumption of meat, which they justify by a de*s*agu*n*a or 'virtue of their country.'

7. Gautama XI, 20.

9. Vasish*th*a I, 8, 10. Many MSS., and among them the Telugu copy of the commentary, read Pâriyâtra instead of Pâripâtra, which latter I consider to be the correct form of the word.

10. Vasish*th*a I, 12.

11. Vasish*th*a I, 14. Govinda remarks that the Bhâllavins are a school studying the Sâma-veda. See also Max Müller, Hist. Anc. Sansk. Lit., pp. 193, 364.

12. Vasish*th*a I, 15. There is a great uncertainty in the MSS. about the word following sindhu*h*. I have adopted the reading of

13. The inhabitants of Avantî, of Aṅga, of Magadha, of Surâshṭra, of the Dekhan, of Upâvṛit, of Sindh, and the Sauvîrâs are of mixed origin.

14. He who has visited the (countries of the) Âraṭṭas, Kâraskaras, Puṇḍras, Sauvîras, Vaṅgas, Kaliṅgas, (or) Prânûnas shall offer a Punastoma or a Sarvapṛishṭhâ (ishṭi).

15. Now they quote also (the following verses): 'He commits sin through his feet, who travels to the (country of the) Kaliṅgas. The sages declare the Vaiṣvânarî ishṭi to be a purification for him.'

M., sindhur vidharaṇî, 'the boundary-river,' which occurs also in the parallel passage of Vasishṭha. The Dekhan and Gugarât MSS. read vikaraṇî or vikaraṇâ, and the two copies of the commentary visaraṇî. The sense of these various readings appears to be 'the river that vanishes or looses itself,' i. e. the Sarasvatî.

13. This and the following two Sûtras are intended to show that the customs prevailing in the countries named have no authority and must not be followed. Avanti corresponds to western Mâlvâ, Aṅga to western Bengal, Magadha to Bihâr, and Surâshṭra to southern Kâṭhiâvâḍ. The Sauvîras, who are always associated with the Sindhians, probably dwelt in the south-west of the Pañgâb, near Multân. The Upâvṛits probably are the same as the Upâvṛittas mentioned Mahâbhârata VI, 49. But I am unable to determine their seats.

14. The Âraṭṭas dwelt in the Pañgâb (Lassen, Ind. Alth. I, p. 973, sec. ed.), and are greatly blamed, Mahâbhârata VIII, 44, 36 seq. The Kâraskaras are named in the same chapter of the Mahâbhârata as a degraded tribe, but seem to belong to the south of India. The Kaliṅgas are the inhabitants of the eastern coast of India, between Orissa and the mouth of the Kṛishṇâ river. The Puṇḍras, who are mentioned as a degraded tribe in the Aitareya-brâhmaṇa VII, 18, and occur frequently in the Mahâbhârata, and the Vaṅgas belong to Bengal (see Lassen, Ind. Alth. I, 669, sec. ed.; Cunningham, Anc. Geog. p. 480). Regarding the Punastoma, see Gautama XIX, 7 note; and regarding the Sarvapṛishṭhâ ishṭi, Taittirîya-saṃhitâ II, 3, 7, 1-2.

15. Âpastamba I, 11, 32, 18.

16. 'Even if many offences have been committed, they recommend for the removal of the sin the Pavitreshti. For that (sacrifice) is a most excellent means of purification.'

17. Now they quote also (the following verse): 'He who performs (by turns) in each season the Vaisvânarî (ishti), the Vrâtapatî (ishti), and the Pavitreshti is freed from (all) sins.'

Prasna I, Adhyâya 2, Kandikâ 3.

1. The (term of the) studentship for (learning the) Veda, as kept by the ancients, (is) forty-eight years,

2. (Or) twenty-four (years), or twelve for each Veda,

3. Or at the least one year for each Kânda,

4. Or until (the Veda has been) learned; for life is uncertain.

5. A passage of the revealed texts declares, 'Let him kindle the sacred fires while his hair is (still) black.'

---

17. Vasishtha XXII, 10. The meaning is that in each of the three seasons of the year, Grîshma, Varsha, Hemanta, one of the three sacrifices is to be offered.

3. 1. Âpastamba I, 1, 2, 12. Govindasvâmin gives four explanations of the adjective paurânam, 'kept by the ancients,' viz. 1. old, i.e. kept by the men of the Krita or Golden age; 2. revealed to and kept by the ancients, such as Manu; 3. found in the ancient, i.e. eternal Veda; 4. found in the known Itihâsas and Purânas.

2. Âpastamba I, 1, 2, 14-16.

3. Each Kânda, i.e. each of the seven books of the Taittirîya-samhitâ.

4. Manu III, 1.

5. The object of the Sûtra is to prove that the period of studentship must not be protracted too long, lest the duty of offering the Srauta Agnihotra be neglected.

6. They do not put any (religious) restrictions on the acts of a (child) before the investiture with the girdle (is performed). For he is on a level with a *S*ûdra before (his second) birth through the Veda.

7. The number of years (must be calculated) from the conception. Let him initiate a Brâhma*n*a in the eighth (year) after that,

8. A Kshatriya three (years) later (than a Brâh-ma*n*a),

9. A Vai*s*ya one year later than a (Kshatriya).

10. Spring, summer, and autumn are the seasons (for the initiation) according to the order of the castes.

11. (Let him perform the initiation reciting), according to the order (of the castes), a Gâyatrî, a Trish*t*ubh, (or) a *G*agatî (verse).

12. Up to the sixteenth, the twenty-second, and the twenty-fourth (years) respectively (the time for the initiation) has not passed.

13. The girdles (shall consist of a rope) made of Mu*ñg*a grass, a bow-string, (or a rope) made of hemp.

14. The skins (shall be) those of a black antelope, of a spotted deer, (or) of a he-goat.

15. The staff shall reach the crown of the head, the forehead, (or) the tip of the nose, (and be made) of a tree fit for a sacrifice. The details have been stated above.

---

6. Vasish*th*a II, 6; Gautama II, 1.

7–9. Vasish*th*a XI, 49–51.

10. Âpastamba I, 1, 1, 18. 12. Vasish*th*a XI, 71–73.

13. Vasish*th*a XI, 58–60. With this and the next two Sûtras the words 'according to the order of the castes' must be understood.

14. Vasish*th*a XI, 61–63.

15. Vasish*th*a XI, 55–57. The details referred to are to be

16. Let him beg, (employing a formula) consisting of seven syllables, with the word bhavat in the beginning, with the word bhikshâ in the middle, and with the (verb expressing) the request at the end; and let him not pronounce loudly (the syllables) kshâ and hi.

17. A Brâhma*n*a (student) shall ask for alms, placing (the word) 'Lady' first, a Kshatriya placing

---

found in the Baudhâyana G*ri*hya-sûtra II, 7, where the various kinds of trees from which the staff may be taken are specified. The Sûtra shows that the G*ri*hya-sûtra preceded the Dharma-sûtra in the collection.

16. The text of this Sûtra is corrupt. I read, 'bhavatpurvâ*m* bhikshâmadhyâ*m* yâ*k*ñântâ*m* *k*aret saptâksharâ*m* bhikshâ*m* kshâ*m* *k*a hi*m* *k*a na vardhayet.' The various readings of the MSS. are, bhikshâ*m* madhyâ*m* ya*kkh*â*m*tâ*m* *k*aret saptâksharâ*m* bhim *k*a na vardhayet, C. T.;—yâ*k*ñâ*m*tâ*m* *k*aret saptâksharam*m*i kshâ*m* *k*a bhim *k*a narvyayet, D.;—yâ*k*ñâ*m*tâ*m* *k*aret saptâksharâ*m*sti*m* rkshâ ba hi*m* na vardhayet, K.;—yâ*k*ñâ*m*tâ*m* tikshâ*m* *k*aret saptâksharân kshâ*m* *k*a hi*m* *k*a na vardhayan, M.;—yâ*k*anâ*s*kâ*m*tâ*m* *k*aret saptâksharân bhikshâ*m* *k*a hi*m* *k*a na vardhayet, C. I. The most serious corruption lies in the syllables following saptâksharâ*m*, and I am not certain that my emendation bhikshâ*m* is correct. The commentary on the first half of the Sûtra runs as follows: bhikshâmantra*m* vyaktam evo*kk*aret bhava*kkh*abdapûrvâm bhikshâ*s*abdamadhyâ*m* yâ*k*ñâpratipa[pâ]daka*s*abdâ*m*tâ*m* *s*abdâksharâ*m* [saptâksharâ*m*] *k*a eva*m* hi bhavati bhikshâ*m* dehi sa*m*panno bhavati, 'let him pronounce distinctly the formula employed in begging, beginning with the word bhavat, having the word bhikshâ in the middle, and ending with the word conveying the sense of giving, and containing seven syllables. For thus (the formula), "Lady, give alms," becomes complete.' It is curious that Govinda says nothing about the form saptâksharâm and the feminine terminations of the other adjectives, which do not agree with mantram, a masculine.

17. Vasish*th*a XI, 68–70; Gautama II, 35. Govinda thinks that a student should, if possible, beg from people of his own caste. Three castes only are intended by the term 'from all castes.' But see Âpastamba I, 1, 3, 25; Gautama VII, 1 seqq.

it in the middle, (and) a Vaisya placing it at the end (of the formula), from (men of) all castes.

18. The (persons fit to be asked) are Brâhmanas and so forth, who follow (their lawful) occupations.

19. Let him daily fetch fuel out of the forest and offer (it in the sacred fire).

20. (A student shall be) truthful, modest, and devoid of pride.

21. He shall rise before (his teacher in the morning) and go to rest after (him in the evening).

22. He shall never disobey the words of his teacher except (when he is ordered to commit) a crime causing loss of caste.

23. Let him converse with women so much (only) as his purpose requires.

24. Let him avoid dancing, singing, playing musical instruments, the use of perfumes, garlands, shoes, (or) a parasol, applying collyrium (to his eyes), and anointing (his body).

25. Let him take hold (of his teacher's) right (foot) with the right (hand), and of the left (foot) with the left hand.

26. If he desires long life and (bliss in) heaven,

---

19. Vishnu XXVIII, 4.

20. Gautama II, 8; Âpastamba I, 1, 3, 20.

21. Vishnu XXVIII, 13.

22. Âpastamba I, 1, 2, 19; Vasishtha VII, 10.

23. Âpastamba I, 1, 3, 16.

24. Vishnu XXVIII, 11; Vasishtha VII, 15.

25. Vishnu XXVIII, 15. The details regarding the times when this kind of salutation is to be performed are found Âpastamba I, 2, 5, 21 seqq.

26. The two copies of the commentary connect the clause, 'if he is desirous of long life and (bliss in) heaven,' with the preceding Sûtra. But see Âpastamba I, 2, 5, 15, where the identical words

(he may act) at his pleasure (in the same manner) towards other holy (men), after having received permission from his teacher.

27. (Let him say), 'I N. N., ho! (salute thee),' touching his ears, in order to compose the internal organ.

28. (Let him embrace his teacher's leg) below the knee down to the feet.

29. (A student shall not embrace his teacher) when he (himself) is seated, or lying down, or impure, nor when (his teacher) is seated, lying down, or impure.

30. If he can (find water to sip), he shall not remain impure even during a muhûrta.

31. If he carries a load of fuel or holds a pot, flowers, or food in his hands, he shall not salute; nor (shall he do it) on similar occasions.

32. Let him not salute (the teacher) standing too close,

33. Nor, if he has reached the age of puberty, the young wives of brothers and the young wives of the teacher.

---

occur. The commentary omits the remainder of the Sûtra, which all my MSS. give here, and inserts it below, after Sûtra 29.

27. Âpastamba I, 2, 5, 12; Vasish*th*a XIII, 44. Regarding the phrase, 'in order to compose his internal organ,' see Manu II, 120.

28. Âpastamba I, 2, 5, 22. The meaning seems to be that the pupil is first to stroke his teacher's legs from the knee downwards, and then to take hold of it at the ankle.

29. Âpastamba I, 4, 14, 14–20. 30. Âpastamba I, 5, 15, 8.

31. Âpastamba I, 4, 14, 22. 'On similar occasions,' i.e. when he himself is engaged in the worship of the manes, of the gods, or of the fire, or when his teacher is occupied in that way.

33. The salutation which is meant, is probably the embrace of the feet; see also Gautama II, 32. Govinda thinks that the words samavâye 'tyantya*s*a*h*, 'standing too close,' must be understood.

34. To sit together with (these persons) in a boat, on a rock, on a plank, on an elephant, on the roof of a house, on a mat, or in wheeled vehicles is permissible.

35. (The pupil) must assist his teacher in making his toilet, shampoo him, attend him while bathing, eat his leavings, and so forth.

36. (But he) should avoid the remnants of food left by his (teacher's) son, though he may know the Veda together with the Aṅgas,

37. And to assist at the toilet of, to shampoo, to attend in the bath, and to eat the remnants of food left by a young wife of his (teacher).

38. Let him run after (his teacher) when he runs, walk after him when he walks, attend him standing when he stands.

39. Let him not sport in the water while bathing.

40. Let him swim (motionless) like a stick.

41. To study under a non-Brâhmanical teacher (is permitted) in times of distress.

---

34. Govinda adds that to sit with young wives of his teachers on other occasions is sinful.

35. I read utsâdana, 'to shampoo,' while the MSS. have either a lacuna or read u*kkh*âdana, and the commentary â*kkh*âdana, which is explained by *kh*attradhâra*n*a, 'to hold a parasol,' or malâpakarsha*n*a, 'to clean.' The *kkh*a is, however, merely owing to a very common faulty pronunciation of tsa. Govinda remarks correctly that the word 'iti,' which follows the enumeration of the services to be performed by the pupil, has the force of 'and so forth.'

36–37. The meaning of the two Sûtras is that the pupil shall serve the son of his teacher, especially if he is learned, and aged wives of his teacher, but not eat their leavings. The explanation of anû*k*âna, 'who knows the Aṅgas,' is given by Baudhâyana, G*ri*hya-sûtra I, 11, 4.

38. Âpastamba I, 2, 6, 7–9; Vasish*th*a VII, 12.

39–40. Âpastamba I, 1, 2, 30; Vish*n*u XXVIII, 5.

41. Âpastamba II, 2, 4, 25. Govinda combines this Sûtra with the next two and makes one of the three.

42. (The pupil shall) obey and walk after him as long as the instruction (lasts).

43. (According to some this is improper, because) just that (mutual relation) sanctifies both of them.

44. And (the behaviour) towards brothers, sons, and (other) pupils (of the teacher shall be regulated) in the same manner.

45. But officiating priests, a father-in-law, paternal and maternal uncles who are younger than (oneself must be honoured by) rising and (by being) addressed.

46. Kâtya (declares that) the salutation shall be returned.

47. For (the propriety of that rule) is apparent (from the story) about *S*isu Âṅgirasa.

Prasna I, Adhyâya 2, Ka*nd*ikâ 4.

1. If merit and wealth are not (obtained by teaching), nor (at least) the due obedience, one should die with one's learning; one should not sow it on barren soil.

---

42. Âpastamba II, 2, 4, 26; Gautama VII, 2–3.

43. The words between brackets belong to Govinda.

44. I. e. if they are younger than oneself.

45. Instead of pratyutthâyâbhibhâsha*n*am, '(shall be honoured by) rising and being addressed,' which is the reading of the two copies of the commentary and of M., the MSS. from the Dekhan and Gu*g*arât read, pratyutthâyâbhivâdanam. The latter reading might be translated by 'shall be saluted by rising;' see Gautama VI, 9. Govinda says, in explanation of this rule: 'This restrictive rule also (refers) to teachers only, officiating priests, and the rest; to address (means) to use words such as "welcome."'

46. 'Kâtya, i.e. a descendant of the *R*ishi Kata. He was of opinion that officiating priests and the rest must return the salute. As the return of a salute is prescribed for them, it is understood that the other (party) must salute.'—Govinda.

47. The story of *S*isu Âṅgirasa is told, Manu II, 151–153.

4. 1. Manu II, 112.

2. As fire consumes dry grass, even so the Veda, asked for, (but) not honoured, (destroys the enquirer). Therefore let him not proclaim the Veda to those who do not show him honour according to their ability.

3. They proclaim to him a command to the following effect;

4. 'Brahman, forsooth, made the created beings over to Death. The student alone it did not make over to him.' He (Death) spake, 'Let me have a share in him.' (Brahman answered), 'That night in which he may neglect to offer a piece of sacred fuel (shall belong to thee).'

5. 'Therefore a student who passes a night without offering a piece of sacred fuel, cuts it off from the length of his life. Therefore let the student offer a piece of sacred fuel, lest he spend a night, shortening his life.'

6. 'A long sacrificial session begins he who commences his studentship. That (night) in which, after being initiated, he (first) offers a piece of sacred fuel corresponds to the Prâya*n*îya (Âtirâtra of a sacrificial session); that night in which (he offers it last), intending to take the final bath, corresponds to the Udayanîya (Âtirâtra). Those nights which (lie) between (these two terms correspond) just to the nights of his sacrificial session.'

---

2. Vasish*th*a II, 12.

3. 'They, i.e. the Vâ*g*asaneyins; to him, i.e. to the student.'—Govinda.

4. The quotation, which begins here and ends with the end of the section, is taken from *S*atapatha-brâhma*n*a XI, 2, 6. In the text the word Brahman is a neuter.

6. MSS. M. and K., as well as the commentary, read dîrghasat-

7. 'A Brâhma*n*a who becomes a student of the Veda, enters existent beings in a fourfold manner, (viz.) with one quarter (he enters) Fire, with one quarter Death, with one quarter the Teacher, the fourth quarter remains in the Soul. When he offers to Fire a piece of sacred fuel, he thereby buys back even that quarter which (resides) in Fire, hallowing it, he places it in himself; that enters into him. Now when making himself poor and, becoming shameless, he asks for alms (and) lives as a student of the Veda, he thereby buys back the quarter which (resides) in Death; hallowing it, he places it in himself; that enters into him. Now when he obeys the orders of his Teacher, he thereby buys back that quarter which (resides) in the Teacher; hallowing it, he places it in himself; that enters into him. [Now when he recites the Veda, he thereby buys back the quarter which resides in the Soul. Hallowing it, he places it in himself; that enters into him.] Let him not go to beg, after he has bathed (on finishing his studentship). . . . If he does not find another woman whom he can ask for alms, let him beg even from his own teacher's wife or from his own mother. The seventh (night) shall not pass without his asking for alms. [(He commits) sin if he does not go out to ask for alms and does not place fuel on the fire. If he neglects that during seven (days and) nights, he must perform the

tram ha vâ esha upaiti, while the MSS. from the Dekhan and Gugarât, like the printed edition of the *S*at. Br., omit the particle 'ha.' Prâya*n*îya means, literally, 'initial,' and udayanîya, 'final.' Each sattra or sacrificial session begins and ends with an Âtirâtra sacrifice.

7. This portion of the quotation shows, besides some minor deviations from the published text of the Mâdhyandinas, several

penance prescribed for one who has broken the vow of studentship.] All the Vedas come to him who knows that and acts thus.'

8. 'As a blazing fire shines, even so shines he who, knowing this, thus fulfils the duties of studentship, after he has bathed (on leaving his teacher).' Thus speaks the Brâhma*n*a.

Prasna I, Adhyâya 3, Ka*nd*ikâ 5.

1. Now (follow the duties) of a Snâtaka.

---

interpolations and corruptions. The minor discrepancies are, 'brâhma*n*o vai brahma*k*aryam upayan' (upaya*kkh*an, C. I. and T.); padâtmanyeva *k*aturtha*h* pâda*h*; yadagnaye samidham âdadhâti; atha yad âtmâna*m* daridrîk*ri*tyâhrîr bhûtvâ bhikshate brahma*k*arya*m* *k*arati; atha yad â*k*âryava*k*a*h* karoti ya evâsyâ*k*ârye. In the second passage the Dekhan MSS. read, however, like the printed text. The interpolations are, 'Now when he recites the Veda,' &c., and the verse, 'He commits sin if he neglects,' &c. The former passage entirely destroys the sense of the whole and the connexion of the parts. Both have, however, been retained, as they occur in all the MSS. and the two copies of the commentary, and have been enclosed in brackets. The corrupt passage is so bad that it makes no sense at all. The best MSS. read as follows: 'api hi vai snâtvâ bhikshâ*m* *k*aratyavi*g*ñânanâ*s*anâyayâ pitrî*n*â-manyabhya*h* kriyâbhya*h*' sa yadanyâm, &c., D.; 'api ha vai snâtvâ bhish*t*â*m* *k*arasapi *g*ñâni nâ*s*anâya yâ [vâ sec. m.] pit*r*î*n*âm anyâbhya*h* kriyâbhya*h*,' K.; api ha vai snâtvâ bhikshâ*ñ* *k*arati—pa*g*ñâtî—nâ*m* *s*anâyâpi pit*r*i*n*âm anyâbhya*h* kriyâsas, M.; api ha vai snâtvâ bhikshâ*m* *k*aratyavi*g*ñâtînâma*s*anayâpi pit*r*i*n*âm anyâbhya kriyâbhya*h*, C. I. As it is by no means certain that Baudhâyana's reading agreed with that of the printed text, I have left the passage out.

5. 1. Regarding the term Snâtaka, see Âpastamba I, 11, 30, 1–4. Govinda thinks that the following rules are intended to apply in the first instance to a student who has performed the Samâvartana on completion of his studentship and lives unmarried at home. For though the Sm*ri*ti declares it necessary for a student to enter, on completing his term, at once into one of the remaining three

2. He shall wear a lower garment and upper garment.

3. Let him carry a staff made of bamboo,

4. And a pot filled with water.

5. Let him wear two sacrificial threads.

6. (He shall possess) a turban, an upper garment (consisting of) a skin, shoes, and a parasol. (He shall keep) a sacred fire and (offer) the new and full moon (Sthâlîpâkas).

7. He shall cause the hair of his head, of his beard, and of his body, and his nails to be cut on the Parva days.

8. His livelihood (he shall obtain in the following manner):

9. Let him beg uncooked (food) from Brâhma*n*as, Kshatriyas, Vai*s*yas, or carpenters,

10. Or (cooked) food (even from many).

11. Let him remain silent (when he goes to beg).

12. Let him perform with that all Pâkaya*gñ*as, offered to the gods and manes, and the rites, securing welfare.

---

orders, it may happen, as the commentator observes, that the Snâtaka's marriage cannot take place immediately. The correctness of this view is proved by Âpastamba I, 2, 8, and by the fact that below, II, 3, 5, the rules for a married Snâtaka are given separately.

2–5. Vasish*th*a XII, 14. 6. Âpastamba I, 2, 8, 2.

7. Regarding the Parva days, see Vasish*th*a XII, 21 note.

8. Vasish*th*a XII, 2–4. 'Though the Snâtaka is the subject of the discussion, the word "his" is used (in this Sûtra) in order to introduce the remaining duties of a householder also.'—Govinda.

9. The carpenter (rathakâra) is a *S*ûdra, but connected with the Vedic sacrifices.

10. '"Food" (bhaiksham), i.e. a quantity of begged food. The meaning is that in times of distress he may beg from many.'—Govinda.

12. With that, i.e. with the food obtained by begging. Regarding

13. Baudhâyana declares that by (following) this rule the most excellent sages reach the highest abode of Pragâpati Parameshthin.

Prasna I, Adhyâya 4, Kandikâ 6.

1. Now (those who know the law) prescribe the carrying of a waterpot.

2. It is declared (in the Vedas) that fire (resides) in the right ear of a goat, in the right hand of a Brâhmana, likewise in water (and) in a bundle of Kusa grass. Therefore after personal purification let him wipe (his water-vessel) on all sides with his (right) hand, (reciting the mantra), 'Blaze up, O fire;' for that (is called) encircling it with fire and is preferable to heating (the pot on the fire).

3. With reference to this matter they prescribe also (the following rules): 'If he thinks in his heart that (the pot) has been slightly defiled, let him light Kusa or (other) grass and heat (the pot) on all sides, keeping his right hand turned towards it.'

4. 'If (pots) have been touched by crows, dogs, or

---

the Pâkayagñas, see Gautama VIII, 18. Govinda gives as an instance of the rites securing welfare (bhûtikarmâni) the âyushya-karu, a rice-offering intended to procure long life.

13. Govinda explains Baudhâyana by Kânvâyana, and adds that either the author speaks of himself in the third person or a pupil must have compiled the book.

6. 1. As Govinda observes, the rules regarding the waterpot (kamandalu) are introduced here in connexion with I, 3, 5, 4.

2. Vasishtha XII, 15–16. The mantra is found, Taittirîya-Âranyaka X, 1, 4.

3. The word upadisanti, 'they prescribe,' stands at the end of Sûtra 4, as it refers to both rules.

4. Vasishtha III, 59. The paryagnikarana is the rite prescribed in Sûtra 2.

other (unclean animals, they shall be heated, until they are of) the colour of fire, after the (paryagnikara*n*a has been performed).'

5. (Pots) which have been defiled by urine, ordure, blood, semen, and the like must be thrown away.

6. If his waterpot has been broken, let him offer one hundred (oblations) reciting the Vyâh*ri*tis, or mutter (the Vyâh*ri*tis as often).

7. (Reciting the text), 'Earth went to earth, the mother joined the mother; may we have sons and cattle; may he who hates us be destroyed,' he shall collect the fragments, throw them into water, repeat the Gâyatrî at least ten times and take again another (pot).

8. Taking refuge with Varu*n*a, (he shall recite the mantra), 'That (belongs) to thee, Varu*n*a; again to me, Om,' (and) meditate on the indestructible.

---

5. Vasish*th*a III, 59.

6. Regarding the Vyâh*ri*tis, see Gautama I, 51.

7. Govinda says that Vâmadeva is the *Ri*shi of the mantra. The fragments of the pot are to be thrown into a river or tank, in order to preserve them from defilement. See also Journ. Bo. Br. Roy. As. Soc., No. XXXIV A, p. 55 note.

8. 'Taking refuge with Varu*n*a, i. e. saying, "I flee for safety to Varu*n*a." (The words), "That for thee, Varu*n*a, again to me, Om," (are) the mantras (to be recited) on taking (a new vessel). Its meaning is this: "Those fragments which I have thrown into the water shall belong to thee, Varu*n*a." (Saying), "Come, thou (who art) a lord of water-vessels, again to me, Om," he shall meditate on another visible pot as indestructible, i. e. at the end of the Vedic (word) "Om," let him meditate, (i. e.) recollect, that not everything will be turned topsy-turvy, (but that some things are) also indestructible, i. e. that that is not destroyed, does not perish.'—Govinda. The explanation of the last clause of our Sûtra seems to be that, on pronouncing the syllable (akshara) Om, the reciter is

9. 'If he has received (the new vessel) from a *S*ûdra, let him recite (the Gâyatrî) one hundred (times). (If he has received it) from a Vai*s*ya, fifty (repetitions of the Gâyatrî) are prescribed, but (on receiving it) from a Kshatriya twenty-five, (and on taking it) from a Brâhma*n*a ten.'

10. Those who recite the Veda are doubtful whether he shall fetch water after the sun has set or shall not fetch it.

11. The most excellent (opinion is) that he may fetch it.

12. Let him restrain his breath, while he fetches water.

13. Fire, forsooth, takes up water.

14. It is declared (in the Veda), 'When he has washed his hands and feet with water from his water-vessel, he is impure for others, as long as the moisture (remains). He purifies himself only. Let him not perform other religious rites (with water from his pot).'

---

to recollect the etymological import of the word akshara, 'indestructible,' and thus to guard the new vessel against the mishap which befell the old one.

9. According to Govinda, either the pra*n*ava, the syllable Om, or the Gâyatrî are the mantras to be recited, and the recitation is a penance to be performed when the vessel is received. The MSS. of the text mark the verse as a quotation by adding the word 'iti,' which the commentary omits.

13. According to Govinda, a Brâhma*n*a who goes to fetch water at night, which he may want for personal purification, is ordered to restrain his breath, because thereby the air in the body becomes strong, and fire or heat (agni) is produced. Now as at night the sun is stated to enter the fire and to become subject to it, a Brâhma*n*a, who by restraining his breath has produced fire, has secured the presence of the sun, when he goes to fetch water.

14. Govinda expressly states that the word vig*ñ*âyate, 'it is declared,'

15. Baudhâyana (says), 'Or if on the occasion of each personal purification (he washes himself with other water) up to the wrist, (he will become) pure.'

16. Now they quote also (the following verses):

Prasna I, Adhyâya 4, Kandikâ 7.

1. 'Formerly (the use of) a waterpot has been prescribed by Brahman and the chief sages for the purification of twice-born men. Therefore he shall always carry one.'

'He who desires his own welfare, shall use it without hesitation, for purifying (his person), for drinking, and for performing his twilight devotions.'

2. Let him do it with a believing heart; a wise man must not corrupt his mind. The self-existent

---

literally, 'it is distinctly known,' always indicates that the passage quoted is taken from the Veda. The rites for which water from the waterpot is not to be used, are libations to the manes, the gods, and the fire. See also below, I, 4, 7, 5.

15. The words enclosed between parentheses are Govinda's.

7. 1. The division of this chapter into two sections occurs in the M. manuscript only. The Dekhan MSS., which give the division into Kandikâs, do not note it, and have at the end of the Prasna the figure 20, while M. has 21 and in words ekavimsatih after the enumeration of the Pratîkas.

2. 'A wise man must not corrupt his mind,' i. e. must not doubt or adopt erroneous views regarding the teaching of the Sâstras with respect to the waterpot. It seems to me that this passage indicates the existence of an opposition to the constant carrying of the waterpot in Baudhâyana's times. This is so much more probable, as the custom is now obsolete, and is mentioned in some Purânas and versified Smritis as one of the practices forbidden in the Kali age; see e.g. the general note appended to Sir W. Jones' translation of Manu.

(Brahman) came into existence with a water-vessel. Therefore let him perform (his rites) with a water-vessel.

3. Let him hold it in his right hand when he voids urine and excrements, in the left when he sips water. That is (a) settled (rule) for all good men.

4. For as the sacrificial cup (*k*amasa) is declared to be pure on account of its contact with the Soma-juice, even so the water-vessel is constantly pure through its contact with water.

5. Therefore let him avoid (to use) it for the worship of the manes, the gods, and the fire.

6. Therefore let him not go on a journey without a waterpot, nor to the boundary of the village, nor from one house to the other.

7. Some (declare that he must not go without it) a step further than the length of an arrow.

8. Baudhâyana (says that he shall not go without it) if he wishes to fulfil his duties constantly.

9. (The divine) Word declares that (this is confirmed) by a *Ri*k-shaped (passage).

Prasna I, Adhyâya 5, Ka*nd*ikâ 8.

1. Now (follows the description of) the means of purification.

5. According to Govinda the word 'therefore' refers back to Sûtra I, 4, 6, 14.

9. '*Ri*gvidham, "a *Ri*k-shaped (passage)," means *Ri*gvidhânam, "a prescription consisting of a *Ri*k." The Brâhma*n*a is indicated by (the word) vâk, ("the goddess of) speech." The meaning is, "The Brâhma*n*a says that there is also a *Ri*k-verse to this effect. That is as follows, tasyaishâ bhavati yat te *s*ilpam ityâdi' (Taittirîya-Âra*n*yaka I, 7, 1).—Govinda.

2. The body is purified by water, the understanding by knowledge, the soul by abstention from injuring living beings, the internal organ by truth.

3. Purifying the internal organ (is called) internal purification.

4. We will explain (the rules of) external purification.

5. The sacrificial thread (shall be made) of Kusa grass, or cotton, (and consist) of thrice three strings.

6. (It shall hang down) to the navel.

7. (In putting it on) he shall raise the right arm, lower the left, and lower the head.

8. The contrary (is done at sacrifices) to the manes.

9. (If the thread is) suspended round the neck, (it is called) nivîta.

10. (If it is) suspended below (the navel, it is called) adhopavîta.

11. Let him perform (the rite of personal) purification, facing the east or the north, (and) seated in a pure place; (let him) place his right arm between his knees and wash both hands up to the wrist and both feet (up to the ankles).

12. Let him not use for sipping the remainder of the water with which he has washed his feet.

13. But if he uses (that) for sipping, let him do it, after pouring (a portion of it) on the ground.

---

8. 2. Vasishtha III, 60. 7–9. Manu II, 63.

11. Vasishtha III, 26. Govinda points out that the word saukam, '(rite of) purification,' has here the meaning of âkamanam, 'sipping water.' He thinks that the ka, 'and,' which stands after pâdau, 'both feet,' indicates that other portions of the body which have been defiled must be washed also.

14. He shall sip out of the Tîrtha sacred to Brahman.

15. The part (of the hand) at the root of the thumb (is called) the Tîrtha sacred to Brahman.

16. The part above the thumb (is called the Tîrtha) sacred to the manes, the part at the tips of the fingers that sacred to the gods, the part at the root of the fingers that sacred to the *Ri*shis.

17. (Let him not use for sipping water that has trickled) from the fingers, nor (water) that is covered with bubbles or foam, nor (water that is) hot, or alkaline, or salt, or muddy, or discoloured, or has a bad smell or taste.

18. (Let him not sip water) laughing, nor talking, nor standing, nor looking about, nor bending his head or his body forward, nor while the lock on his crown is untied, nor while his throat is wrapped up, nor while his head is covered, nor when he is in a hurry, nor without wearing the sacrificial thread, nor stretching his feet out, nor while his loins are girt (with a cloth), nor without holding his right arm between his knees, nor making a sound.

19. Let him thrice drink water that reaches his heart.

20. Let him wipe (his lips) thrice.

21. Some (declare that he shall do it) twice.

---

14. Vasish*th*a III, 26.

16. Vish*n*u LXII, 3-4. All the MSS. except M. place the Tîrtha sacred to the gods at the root of the fingers, and that sacred to the *Ri*shis at the tips of the fingers, and Govinda has the same erroneous reading.

17. Vasish*th*a III, 36. 18. Vasish*th*a III, 30.

19-20. Vasish*th*a III, 26; Âpastamba I, 5, 16, 3.

21. Vasish*th*a III, 27; Âpastamba I, 5, 16, 4.

22. A woman and a *S*ûdra (shall perform) both (acts) once (only).

23. Now they quote also (the following verse): 'A Brâhma*n*a is purified by water that reaches his heart, a Kshatriya by (water) reaching his throat, a Vai*s*ya by (water barely) taken into the mouth, a woman and a *S*ûdra by touching (it) with the extremity (of the lips).

24. 'If (drops) adhere to his teeth, (they must be considered pure) like the teeth, because they are fixed (in the mouth) like the teeth. Let him not sip water on their account in case they fall. If they flow out, he will be pure.'

25. Now they quote also (the following verse): 'If anything adheres to the teeth, (it is pure) like the teeth; and if he swallows (it or) whatever else may be in the mouth (or) may remain after sipping water, (he will become) pure.'

26. (After sipping) he shall touch the cavities (of the head) with water, the feet, the navel, the head, (and) lastly the left hand.

27. If he becomes impure while holding (a vessel) made of metal, he shall put it down, sip water and sprinkle it, when he is going to take it up.

28. Now if he becomes impure (while he is occupied) with food, he shall put it down, sip water and sprinkle it, when he is going to take it up.

29. Now if he becomes impure (while occupied)

---

23. Vasish*th*a III, 31–34.

24. The MSS. read in the last pâda of this verse, teshâ*m* sa*m*srâye [ya or va]-*kk*u*k*i*s*iti. I think sa*m*srâva*n*â*kkh*u*k*ir iti is the correct reading.

25. Vasish*th*a III, 41.

26. Vasish*th*a III, 28–29.

28. Vasish*th*a III, 43–44.

with water, he shall put it down, sip water and sprinkle it, when he is going to take it up.

30. That is contrary (to the rule) in (the case of an earthen) vessel.

31. In (the case of a vessel) made of wood there is an option.

32. Defiled (objects) made of metal must be scoured with cowdung, earth, and ashes, or with one of these (three).

33. Copper, silver, and gold (must be cleaned) with acids.

34. Earthen vessels must be heated.

35. (Objects) made of wood must be planed.

36. (Objects) made of bamboo (must be cleaned) with cowdung,

37. (Objects) made of fruits with a rope of cow-hair,

38. Skins of black deer with (ground) Bel nut and rice,

39. Blankets (of the hair of the mountain goat) with Areka nuts,

40. (Cloth) made of (sheep's) wool by the (rays of the) sun,

41. Linen (cloth) with a paste of yellow mustard,

---

30. '(The word) amatram, literally "a vessel," denotes here an earthen vessel. The meaning is that such a one, if it is very much defiled, shall only be put down and not be taken back. Any other (earthen vessel) shall be heated.'—Govinda.

32. Vasish*th*a III, 49.

33. Manu V, 114; Vasish*th*a III, 63.

34–35. Vasish*th*a III, 49. 36. Vasish*th*a III, 53.

37. Vasish*th*a III, 54. Govinda thinks that the word *raggu*, 'a rope,' is used here in the sense of 'a conglomeration,' and merely indicates that a quantity of cowhair must be used.

39. Manu V, 120. 41. Vasish*th*a III, 55.

42. Cotton cloth with earth,

43. Skins (other than deer-skins shall be treated) like cotton cloth,

44. Stones and gems like (objects) made of metal,

45. Bones like wood,

46. Conch-shells, horn, pearl-shells, and ivory like linen cloth.

47. Or (they may be cleaned) with milk.

48. (Objects) which have been defiled by urine, ordure, blood, semen, or a dead body, (but) are agreeable to the eye and the nose, shall be rubbed seven times with one of the substances mentioned above.

49. (Objects) not made of metal which are in the same condition must be thrown away.

50. The cups and vessels (used) at a sacrifice (must be cleaned) according to the injunction (of the Veda).

51. The Veda (declares), 'They do not become impure through Soma.'

52. 'Time, fire, purity of mind, water and the like (fluids), smearing with cowdung and ignorance (of defilement) are declared to be the sixfold (means of) purification for created beings.'

53. Now they quote also (the following verse):

---

42. Vasish*th*a III, 49.
43. Vasish*th*a III, 53.
44. Vasish*th*a III, 50.
45. Vasish*th*a III, 52.
46. Vasish*th*a III, 51.
49. Vasish*th*a III, 59.

50. Govinda explains this Sûtra differently. He says: 'The fault of defilement by remnants does not affect sacrificial cups and vessels. This must be understood. If they are defiled by urine and the like, they must be thrown away.' My explanation is based on the parallel passage of Âpastamba I, 5, 17, 13. See also below, I, 6, 13, 11 seq.

52. Vish*n*u XXII, 88.

'A clever man, who knows (the rules of) purification and is desirous of righteousness, shall perform (the rites of) purification, after having fully considered the time, and the place (of the defilement); likewise himself, (as well as) the object (to be cleaned) and the substance (to be employed), the purpose of the object, the cause (of the defilement), and the condition (of the thing or person defiled).'

Prasna I, Adhyâya 5, Kandikâ 9.

1. The Veda declares that the hand of an artisan is always pure, so is every vendible commodity exposed for sale and food obtained by begging, which a student holds in his hand.

2. A calf is pure on the flowing (of the milk), a bird on the fall of the fruit, women at the time of dalliance, and a dog when he catches a deer.

3. All mines and places of manufacture are pure excepting distilleries of spirituous liquor; continuously flowing streams of water and dust raised by the wind cannot be contaminated.

4. The flowers and fruit of flowering and fruit-bearing trees which grow in unclean places are likewise not impure.

9. 1. Vishnu XXIII, 48.

2. Vishnu XXIII, 49.

3. Vishnu XXIII, 48. The term âkara, translated by 'mines and places of manufacture,' is explained in the commentary by 'places of production, i.e. of sugar and honey.' It is no doubt intended to apply to any place where articles of consumption or use are produced. Govinda adds that as 'continuous streams of water' are always pure, one must take care that the water for sipping flows out of the vessel in an unbroken stream.

5. On touching a tree standing on a sacred spot, a funeral pile, a sacrificial post, a *K*a*n**d*âla or a person who sells the Veda, a Brâhma*n*a shall bathe dressed in his clothes.

6. One's own couch, seat, clothes, wife, child, and waterpot are pure for oneself; but for strangers they are impure.

7. A seat, a couch, a vehicle, ships (and boats), the road and grass are purified by the wind, if they have been touched by *K*a*n**d*âlas or outcasts.

8. Grain on the threshing-floor, water in wells and reservoirs, and milk in the cowpen are fit for use even (if they come) from a person whose food must not be eaten.

9. The gods created for Brâhma*n*as three means of purification, (viz.) ignorance of defilement, sprinkling with water, and commending by word of mouth.

10. Water collected on the ground with which

5. Vasish*th*a IV, 37. *K*aityav*ri*ksha, 'a tree standing on sacred ground,' means literally, 'a memorial-tree.'

7. Govinda points out that couches and seats and the like, on which *K*a*n**d*âlas and outcasts have lain or sat down, must be purified.

8. 'That must be referred to grain on a threshing-floor, and so forth, which has been produced by men whose food must not be eaten, and again is considered to be common to all. In this case, too, what has been received from outcasts and *K*a*n**d*âlas, that is defiled. Milk which has been received just at milking-time may be drunk out of a vessel that stands in the cowpen.'—Govinda. As regards the grain produced by low-caste people, the rule probably refers to cases where the land of an Agrahâra or other village is cultivated by men of the lowest castes. The author means to say that in such cases a Brâhma*n*a may take his share from the threshing-floor, where the whole produce of the village-land is stored, without hesitation.

9. Vasish*th*a XIV, 24; Manu V, 127.

10. Vasish*th*a III, 35-36.

cows slake their thirst is a means of purification, provided it is not strongly mixed with unclean (substances), nor has a (bad) smell, nor is discoloured, nor has a (bad) taste.

11. But land becomes pure, according to the degree of the defilement, by sweeping the (defiled) spot, by sprinkling it with water, by smearing it with cowdung, by scattering (pure earth) on it, or by scraping it.

12. Now they quote also (the following verse):

PRASNA I, ADHYÂYA 5, KANDIKÂ 10.

1. 'A drop of water which is allowed to fall (on the ground) purifies a bull's hide of land, whether (the land) has been (previously) swept or not, provided no impure substance is visible on it.'

2. Food which is cooked out of sight must be illuminated (with fire) and be sprinkled with water,

3. Likewise eatables bought in the market.

4. For the Veda (declares), 'For the gods who are (easily) disgusted and desirous of purity do not

---

11. Vasishtha III, 56.

10. 1. Regarding the term 'a bull's hide' of land, see Vishnu V, 181-183, XCII, 4.

2. Âpastamba II, 2, 3, 9. 'Out of sight,' i.e. not before the eyes of him who eats it.'—Govinda. It would, however, seem that this rule refers to food prepared by Sûdras, without the supervisions of Âryans. For Âpastamba's Sûtra, which contains the same word, paroksham, 'out of sight,' certainly has reference to that case only, and there is no reason why food prepared by Brahman cooks should be purified before it is eaten.

3. Âpastamba I, 5, 17, 19. The eatables here intended are, according to Govinda, Lâdus and other sweet-meats which are frequently bought ready made.

enjoy the offerings made by a man destitute of faith.'

5. After reflecting (for a long time on the respective value of) the (food) of a pure man destitute of faith and of an impure person who has faith, the gods declared both to be equal. But the Lord of created beings said to them, 'That is not equal, it is unequal. The food of a man destitute of faith is worthless, that which is purified by faith is preferable.'

6. Now they quote also (the following verses): 'Want of faith is the greatest sin; for faith is the highest austerity. Therefore the gods do not eat offerings given without faith.'

7. 'A foolish man does not reach heaven, though he may offer (sacrifices) or give (gifts).'

8. 'He is called a foolish man whose conduct is blemished by doubts, and who, clinging to his own fancies, transgresses (the rules of) the *S*âstras, because he opposes the fulfilment of the sacred law.'

9. But pot-herbs, flowers, fruit, roots, and annual plants (must be) sprinkled (with water).

10. Having placed dry grass, wood of trees unfit for sacrifices or a clod of earth (on the ground), let him void faeces or urine, turning his face during the day towards the north and at night towards the south and wrapping up his head.

---

8. Dharmatantra, translated 'the fulfilment of the sacred law,' is explained in the commentary by dharmasya tantram anush*th*ânam, by 'the performance of the sacred duties.' It may also mean 'the doctrine of or the treatises on the sacred law.' The *S*âstras are the Vedas and the whole body of the sacred literature.

9. Vish*n*u XXIII, 15. 10. Vasish*th*a VI, 10.

11. (After voiding) urine he shall clean (the organ once) with earth and water,

12. The hand three times.

13. In like manner (he shall clean himself with earth and water after voiding) faeces.

14. The number (of the applications of both is) thrice three for both feet and the hand.

15. After an effusion of semen (he shall purify himself) in the same manner as after voiding urine.

16. He shall wash himself, after he has untied or put on the cloth round his loins,

17. Or he may touch moist grass, cowdung, or earth.

18. While he is engaged in (the performance of) religious rites, he shall avoid to touch (the part of his body) below the navel.

19. The Veda (declares), 'A man's (body) is pure above the navel, it is impure below the navel.'

20. *S*ûdras living in the service of Âryans shall trim (their hair and nails) every month; their mode

---

11–12. Vasish*th*a VI, 14, 18. According to Govinda one application of water suffices for the left hand and two for both together.

13–14. Vasish*th*a VI, 18. Govinda reads in Sûtra 14, against the authority of all the MSS., pâyo*h*, 'for the anus,' instead of pâdayo*h*, 'for both feet.'

15. Âpastamba I, 5, 15, 23.

16. Âpastamba I, 5, 16, 14. 17. Âpastamba I, 5, 16, 15.

18. Vish*n*u XXIII, 51.

19. Taittirîya Sa*m*hitâ VI, 1, 3, 4.

20. Âpastamba II, 1, 2, 4–5. The above translation follows Govinda's explanation. But âryâdhish*th*itâ*h*, 'living in the service of Âryans,' may also mean 'superintended by Âryans,' and the rule be taken to refer to the special case of *S*ûdra cooks, as in the parallel passage of Âpastamba.

of sipping water (shall be) the same as that of Âryans.

21. A Vaisya may live by usury.

22. But (a sum of) twenty-five (kârshâpanas shall bear an interest) of five mâshas (per mensem).

23. Now they quote also (the following verses): 'He who, acquiring property cheap, employs (it so that it yields) a higher price, is called a usurer, and blamed in all (treatises on) the sacred law.' '(Brahman) weighed in the scales the crime of killing a learned Brâhmana against (the crime of) usury; the slayer of the Brâhmana remained at the top, the usurer sank downwards.'

24. 'Let him treat Brâhmanas who tend cattle, those who live by trade, (and) those who are artisans, actors (and bards), servants or usurers, like Sûdras.'

25. But men of the first two castes may, at their pleasure, lend (money at interest) to one who neglects his sacred duties, to a miser, to an atheist, or to a very wicked man.

26. Through the neglect of sacrifices, of (lawful) marriages, of the study of the Veda, and of (learned) Brâhmanas, (noble) families (even) are degraded.

27. The offence of neglecting a Brâhmana cannot be committed against a fool who is unacquainted

21. Vasishtha II, 19. 22. Vasishtha II, 51.

23. Vasishtha II, 41-42. 24. Vasishtha III, 3.

25. Vasishtha II, 43. M. reads na dadyâtâm, 'shall not lend.' According to Govinda, 'a very wicked man' is equivalent to 'a Sûdra.'

26. Manu III, 63. Govinda says that this Sûtra is introduced in connexion with the expression, 'one who neglects his sacred duties,' which occurs in Sûtra 25.

27. Vasishtha III, 9 note, 10. This Sûtra is added in explanation of the term 'the offence of neglecting a Brâhmana.'

with the Veda. For (in offering sacrifices) one does not pass by a brilliant fire and throw the oblations into ashes.

28. Families which are deficient in (the knowledge of) the Veda, are degraded by (keeping) cows, horses and vehicles, by agriculture and by serving the king.

29. But even poor families which are rich in (the knowledge of) the Veda obtain rank among the (noble) families and gain great fame.

30. The (study of) the Veda impedes (the pursuit of) agriculture, (the pursuit of) agriculture impedes (the study of) the Veda. He who is able (to do it), may attend to both; but he who is unable (to attend to both), shall give up agriculture.

31. A fat, bellowing, raging humped bull, who does not restrain himself, who hurts living creatures and speaks according to his pleasure, forsooth, does not reach the (abode of) the gods; (but) those who are small like atoms, (being) emaciated (by austerities and fasts), go thither.

32. If, erring, in his youth he commits at any time good or evil acts of any kind, (they will all remain without result). (For) if in his later age he lives righteously, he will obtain (the reward of) that (virtuous conduct) alone, not (the punishments of his former) crimes.

33. Let him always be sorrowing in his heart, when he thinks of his sins, (let him) practise austerities and be careful; thus he will be freed from sin.

34. 'Where drops of water touch the feet of a

28-29. Manu III, 64, 66. 34. Vasish*th*a III, 42.

man who offers water for sipping to others, no defilement is caused by them. They are equally (pure) as (water) collected on the ground.'

Prasna I, Adhyâya 5, Kandikâ 11.

1. Referring to deaths and births, they declare that the impurity of Sapi*nd*as lasts ten days; excepting officiating priests, men who have performed the initiatory ceremony of a Soma-sacrifice, and students of the Veda.

2. But amongst Sapi*nd*as Sapi*nd*a-relationship (extends) to the seventh person.

3. (If children die) before the completion of the seventh month or before teething, (the relatives) shall bathe.

4. In (the case of a child) that dies before the completion of its third year or before teething, offerings of funeral cakes and water are not prescribed, and one should not burn its (body);

5. Nor when unmarried maidens die.

6. Some do it in the case of married daughters.

7. That (is done) in order to gain the good-will

---

11. 1. Vasish*th*a IV, 16. Officiating priests, Soma-sacrificers, and students do not become impure by deaths or births occurring among their relatives; see Vasish*th*a XIX, 48; Gautama XIV, 1.

2. Vasish*th*a IV, 17. For the specification of the extent of the Sapi*nd*a-relationship, see below, Sûtra 9.

3. Vish*n*u XXII, 27.

4. Vish*n*u XXII, 28; Gautama XIV, 34, 43.

6. Gautama XIV, 36. 'That refers to the Sapi*nd*as on the father's side.'—Govinda.

7. Manu IX, 18.

of the people. Women are considered to have no business with the sacred texts.

8. 'The relatives of unmarried women become pure after three days. But the uterine brothers become pure by (following) the rule mentioned before.'

9. Moreover, the great-grandfather, the grandfather, the father, oneself, the uterine brothers, the son by a wife of equal caste, the grandson, (and) the great-grandson—these they call Sapi*nd*as, but not the (great-grandson's) son;—and amongst these a son and a son's son (together with their father are) sharers of an undivided oblation.

10. The sharers of divided oblations they call Sakulyas.

---

8. This verse, which occurs in all my MSS. of the text, is left out in the two copies of Govinda's commentary.

9. Colebrooke, Dâyabhâga XI, 1, 37; V. Digest CCCXCVII. The text on which Colebrooke's two versions are based differs from that of my MSS. and of Govinda by reading avibhaktadâyâdân instead of teshâ*m k*a putrapautram [v. l. °pautrakam] avibhaktadâyam. The meaning of the latter clause, which is placed parenthetically before sapi*nd*ân â*k*akshate, '(these) they call Sapi*nd*as,' seems to be that a father with his son and grandson share the cakes offered at one funeral sacrifice by the fourth descendant. Its object is to show that the group called Sapi*nd*as consists of two such subdivisions, between whom the middlemost forms the connecting link. For the middlemost, the svayam, 'oneself,' of the text, first offers the cakes to his three ancestors and later receives the cakes, together with his first two descendants, from his great-grandson. Govinda gives no help. He merely remarks that the Sûtra contains a paribhâshâ or technical rule of interpretation, and that the words api *k*a, 'moreover,' indicate that it is an expansion of Sûtra 2.

10. Colebrooke, loc. cit. According to *G*îmûtavâhana the Sakulyas are the three ascendants beyond the great-grandfather and the three descendants beyond the great-grandson. Others, among

11. If no other (relations) are living, the property (of a deceased male) descends to them (the Sapi*nd*as).

12. On failure of Sapi*nd*as, the Sakulyas (inherit).

13. On failure of them, the teacher who (holds the place of a spiritual) father, a pupil, or an officiating priest shall take it,

14. On failure of them, the king. Let him give that property to persons well-versed in the three Vedas.

15. But the king should never take for himself the property of a Brâhma*n*a.

16. Now they quote also (the following verse): 'The property of a Brâhma*n*a destroys (him who

---

whom Govinda takes his place, explain the word sakulya to mean 'members of one family' in general. Govinda says, sambandhavi*s*esha*g*ñâne sati sapi*nd*â u*k*yante I sambandhamâtra*g*ñâne sakuly*âh* II Ata*s* *k*a sapi*nd*â api sakulyâ*h* II 'If a particular relationship is known, they are called Sapi*nd*as; and if (the fact) only is known that relationship exists, Sakulyas. Hence the Sapi*nd*as are also Sakulyas.'

11. Colebrooke, loc. cit. Both the Dâyabhâga and the Digest read satsvanga*g*eshu, 'when there is male issue,' and the Vîramitrodaya, fol. 218, p. 2, l. 7, agrees with them. The MSS. read all satsv anyeshu, which may, however, be taken with Govinda for asatsv anyeshu, because the preceding word ends in *e*. Govinda explains anyeshu, 'others,' by aurasâdishu, 'legitimate sons of the body, and so forth.'

12. Colebrooke, Dâyabhâga, loc. cit. The digest omits this Sûtra.

13. Colebrooke, loc. cit. *G*îmûtavâhana wrongly reads pitâ *k*â*k*âryah, 'the father and the teacher.' Govinda gives the explanation adopted above. Regarding the spiritual fatherhood of the teacher, see e. g. Vasish*th*a II, 4.

14. Colebrooke, loc. cit. Govinda reads satsvam, 'the property of a holy man,' instead of tatsvam, 'that property.'

15. Colebrooke V, Dig. CCCCXLIV; Vasish*th*a XVII, 86.

N 2

takes it), together with sons and grandsons; poison kills one man only. (Therefore) they do not declare poison to be (the worst) poison. The property of a Brâhma*n*a is called (the worst) poison.'

17. If a birth and a death occur together, one and the same period of ten (days and) nights (shall serve for both).

18. Now if (other deaths or births) happen before the completion of the ten (days and) nights (of impurity), the first period of ten (days and) nights (shall suffice, provided the new cause of impurity occurs) before the end of the ninth day.

19. On a birth, indeed, the parents (alone) become impure during ten days.

20. Some (declare that) the mother (alone becomes impure), because (people) avoid (lying-in women alone).

21. Others (say that) the father (alone becomes impure) because the semen is the chief cause (of the generation).

22. For sons who were born without mothers, are mentioned in the revealed texts.

23. But (the correct opinion is that) both the parents (become impure) because they are equally connected (with the event).

---

18. Vasish*th*a IV, 23–25. Govinda points out that in case the second birth or death happens after the completion of the ninth day, the rule given (Gautama XIV, 7) applies.

19. Vasish*th*a IV, 20–21.

20. Vasish*th*a IV, 21–22. Tatpariharanât, literally, 'because she is avoided, i.e. because people avoid newly-confined women (not their husbands).'—Govinda.

21. E.g. Agastya and Vasish*th*a. See Rig-veda VII, 33, 11, and Sâya*n*a's commentary thereon.

24. But when a death (has happened, the relatives of the deceased), allowing the youngest to begin, shall pass their sacrificial threads over the right shoulder and under the left arm, descend into the water at a bathing-place, submerge (their bodies), emerge (out of the water), ascend the bank, sip water, pour out libations for the (deceased, repeating the last four acts) severally three times thereafter, ascend the bank, sip water, touch a coal, water or the like at the door of their house, and sit during ten days on mats, eating food that does not contain pungent condiments or salt.

25. (Let him perform) a funeral sacrifice on the eleventh or the twelfth (day).

26. In (performing) the remaining rites (one should) conform to (the customs of) the people.

27. In case of a (death) let him also keep (a period of impurity) for (persons who are) not (his) Sapi*nd*as, according to the degree of nearness, three (days and) nights, a day and a night, one day and so forth,

---

24. Vasish*th*a IV, 9–15. When the libations of water are poured out, the name of the deceased must be pronounced. Govinda correctly states that iti, 'or the like,' which stands after 'a coal, water,' is intended to include 'cowdung, and yellow mustard seed,' which are mentioned by Yâg*ñ*avalkya III, 13. Regarding the clause sak*ri*ttri*h*, '(repeating these last four acts) severally three times,' see Âpastamba II, 6, 15, 10.

25. Vish*n*u XXI, 2 seq., and especially 19.

26. Govinda, in explanation of this Sûtra, refers to the last words of Âpastamba II, 6, 15, 10, where it is said that relatives 'shall perform those rites for the dead which the women declare to be necessary,' and to Âpastamba II, 11, 29, 15.

27. Gautama XIV, 20. Govinda is of opinion that the duration of the impurity shall depend on the good qualities, learning, &c. of the deceased.

28. For a teacher, a sub-teacher (upâdhyâya), and their sons, three (days and) nights,

29. Likewise for officiating priests,

30. Let him keep on account of a pupil, for one who has the same spiritual guide, for a fellow-student (sabrahma*k*ârin) three (days and) nights, one day and a night, one day and so forth (as periods of impurity).

31. On a miscarriage females (remain impure) as many (days and) nights as months (elapsed after conception).

32. If he unintentionally touches the corpse of a stranger, he becomes at once pure after bathing dressed in his clothes.

33. (If he does it) intentionally, (he will remain impure) during three (days and) nights.

34. And (the same rules apply if he touches a woman) during her courses.

35. A son who is born from (intercourse with a temporarily unclean woman) becomes an Abhi*s*asta. Thereby the penances (to be performed) by him have been explained.

---

28. Vish*n*u XXII, 42, 44. Govinda asserts that the impurity on account of an Upâdhyâya lasts one night, together with the preceding and following days, and on account of a teacher's or Upâdhyâya's sons one day only. It looks as if he had read the words pakshi*n*yekâham in his text.

29. Govinda asserts that *k*a, 'likewise,' indicates that the rule applies also on the death of persons for whom one sacrifices.

30. Vish*n*u XXII, 44. Govinda explains satîrthya to mean 'one who has the same guru or spiritual guide,' while according to others it means 'one who studies under the same sub-teacher' (upâdhyâya). See also the Kâ*s*ikâ on Pâ*n*ini IV, 4, 117, and note.

31. Vish*n*u XXII, 25. 32-33. Gautama XIV, 27.

34. Vish*n*u XXII, 69.

36. On touching one who sells the Veda, a sacrificial post, an outcast, a funeral pile, a dog, or a *Kand*âla he shall bathe.

37. Now if a worm is produced in an open wound that is filled with pus and sanies, how shall, in that case, a penance be performed?

38. He who is bitten by a worm will become pure on bathing (daily) during three days and drinking (a mixture of) cow's urine, cowdung, milk, sour milk, butter, and water boiled with Ku*s*a grass.

39. He who has been touched by a dog shall bathe dressed in his clothes;

40. Or he becomes pure by washing that spot (where he has been touched), by touching it with fire, by (afterwards) again washing it and his feet, and by sipping water.

41. Now they quote also (the following verses): 'But a Brâhma*n*a who has been bitten by a dog, is purified if he goes to a river that flows into the ocean, (bathes there and) suppresses his breath one hundred times and (afterwards) eats clarified butter. He will (also) become pure at once on bathing (in water brought) in golden or silver (vessels), or in a cow's horn, or in new (earthen pots).'

---

36. This verse, which is another version of I, 5, 9, 5, is left out in the Dekhan and Gugarât MSS.; I consider its genuineness very doubtful.

37. Vasish*th*a XVIII, 16.

39–40. Âpastamba I, 5, 15, 16–17. Govinda, too, states that the second mode of purification is to be adopted, if the dog touches any part of the body below the navel.

41. Vasish*th*a XXIII, 31.

Prasna I, Adhyâya 5, Kandikâ 12.

1. Tame animals must not be eaten,

2. Nor carnivorous and (tame) birds,

3. Nor (tame) cocks and pigs;

4. Goats and sheep (are) excepted (from the above prohibition).

5. Five five-toed animals may be eaten, (viz.) the porcupine, the iguana, the hare, the hedgehog, the tortoise and the rhinoceros, excepting the rhinoceros,

6. Likewise five animals with cloven hoofs, (viz.) the white-footed antelope (Nîl-gâi), the (common ravine) deer, the spotted deer, the buffalo, the (wild) boar and the black antelope, excepting the black antelope,

7. (Likewise) five (kinds of) birds that feed scratching with their feet, (viz.) the partridge, the blue rock-pigeon, the francoline partridge, the (crane called) Vârdhrâ*n*asa, the peacock and the Vâra*n*a, excepting the Vâra*n*a,

---

12. 1. Vasish*th*a XIV, 40.

2. Vasish*th*a XIV, 48. Govinda says that the particle *k*a, 'and,' is used in order to indicate that the word 'tame' must be understood.

3. Âpastamba I, 5, 17, 29, 32.

5. Vasish*th*a XIV, 39. Another explanation of the word *s*vâvi*t*, 'the porcupine' (see also Gautama XVII, 27), is given in the commentary, which says that it is a wild animal resembling a dog, and belonging to the boar species. Govinda points out that there is a dispute among the learned regarding the rhinoceros (Vasish*th*a XV, 47), and that the peculiar wording of the Sûtra is intended to indicate that.

6. The permissibility of the last-named animal is again doubtful.

7. Gautama XVII, 35. The case of the last-mentioned bird, the Vâra*n*a, is again doubtful. From the first rock-edict of A*s*oka

8. (And the following) fishes, (viz.) the Silurus Pelorius (Sahasradamsh*t*rin), the *K*ili*k*ima, the Varmi, the B*ri*ha*kkh*iras, the Masakari(?), the Cyprinus Rohita, and the Râ*g*i.

9. The milk of a (female animal) whose offspring is not ten days old, and of one that gives milk while big with a young one, must not be drunk,

10. Nor that of a (cow) that has no calf or that (suckles) a strange calf.

11. (The milk) of sheep, camels, and one-hoofed animals must not be drunk.

12. If (he has) drunk (milk) which ought not to be drunk, excepting cow's milk, (he must perform) a K*rikkh*ra (penance).

13. But if (he has drunk) cow's milk (that is unfit for use, he shall) fast during three (days and) nights.

14. Stale (food must not be eaten or drunk) excepting pot-herbs, broths, meat, clarified butter, cooked grain, molasses, sour milk, and barley-meal,

15. Nor (substances) which have turned sour, nor molasses which have come into that state.

16. After performing the ceremony preparatory

---

it appears that peacocks, now considered inviolable, were actually eaten in the third century A. D.

8. Vasish*th*a XIV, 41–42. The names are much corrupted in the MSS., and for Masakari, which I do not find in the dictionaries, Samasakari or Samasakari is also read. The B*ri*ha*kkh*iras is probably the Indian salmon, the Mâhsir.

9–10. Vasish*th*a XIV, 34–35; Gautama XVII, 22. The meaning of sandhinî, 'a female animal that gives milk while big with young,' is uncertain. See also Vish*n*u LI, 40; Âpastamba I, 5, 17, 23.

11. Gautama XVII, 24. 12. Vish*n*u LI, 38–41.

14. Gautama XVII, 16. 15. Vasish*th*a XIV, 37–38.

16. Vasish*th*a XIII, 1–5. Govinda states that this Sûtra has been introduced here, because the purity of one's food ensures

to the beginning of the Veda-study (upâkarman) on the (full moon of the month) of *S*râva*n*a or of Âshâ*dh*a, they shall close the term on the full moon of Taisha or Mâgha.

PRA*S*NA I, ADHYÂYA 6, KA*N*D*I*KÂ 13.

1. The gods enjoy a pure sacrifice (only);

2. For the gods are desirous of purity and (themselves) pure.

3. The following (*Rik*) declares that, 'To you, O Maruts, the pure ones, pure viands; to you, the pure ones, I offer a pure sacrifice. They who love the pious rites, who are of pure origin, (themselves) pure and purifiers (of others), came duly to the truthful (worshipper).'

4. (He will be) pure (if there is) no blemish on his clothes, therefore let him perform all (acts) that are connected with sacrificing, (dressed) in unblemished clothes.

5. The sacrificer and his wife as well as the officiating priests shall put on dresses which have been washed, and dried by the wind, and which are not in a bad condition.

---

purity of one's soul, and purity of soul gives strength of memory, and thereby makes one fit to study the Veda.

13. 1–2. See also above, I, 5, 10, 4. This Adhyâya and the next ought to have been given in the *S*rauta Sûtra.

3. Rig-veda VII, 56, 12; Taittirîya-brâhma*n*a II, 8, 5, 5. The meaning of the last portion of the verse is somewhat doubtful. Sâya*n*a gives two different explanations and Govinda a third.

4. Govinda points out that the dresses of the sacrificer and of his priests must be white, because farther on (Sûtras 9–10) other colours are specially prescribed.

5. Govinda thinks that the word *k*a, 'as well as,' is intended to include the lookers-on.

6. (It shall be) thus from the (beginning of the) Prakrama,

7. And thus at the long Soma-sacrifices and the Sattras;

8. And (on other occasions other dresses must be used) in accordance with the injunction (of the Veda),

9. Thus at (all) Ish*t*is, animal sacrifices, and Soma-sacrifices which may be used as spells (against enemies), the priests shall perform (the sacred rites), wearing red turbans and red dresses; (when reciting the hymn seen by) V*ri*shâkapi (he shall) wear a dress and a mantle of many colours and so forth.

10. At the Agnyâdhâna (sacrifice) the clothes (shall be made) of flax; on failure of such, (dresses) made of cotton or of wool are used.

11. Clothes defiled by urine, ordure, blood, semen and the like (shall be) cleaned with earth, water and the like.

12. (Dresses) made of T*ri*pa-bark and v*ri*kala (shall be treated) like cotton-cloth,

---

6. Regarding the ceremony called Prakrama, literally 'stepping forward from the Gârhapatya fire,' see Sâya*n*a on Taitt. Br. I, 1, 4, 1. It opens the Agnyâdhâna rite.

9. Govinda states that the words iti *k*a, 'and so forth,' are intended to include other incantations. The V*ri*shâkapi hymn is found Rig-veda X, 86.

11. Govinda states that the word iti, 'and the like,' is intended to include cowdung, cow's urine, and other substances used for purification.

12. Govinda states that there is a tree called T*ri*pa, the bark of which is used for dresses. V*ri*kala, which has been left untranslated, is explained by *s*akama, a word which is not found in our dictionaries.

13. Deer-skins like (dresses) made of bark.

14. (Let him) not (use) a mantle which has been wrapped (round the loins, or) on which he has been lying (in his bed), without washing it.

15. Let him not employ for the gods anything used by men without beating it on a stone.

16. If solid earth is defiled, (it must be) smeared with cowdung.

17. Loose (earth must be cleansed by) ploughing,

18. Moist (earth) by bringing pure (earth) and covering (it with that).

19. Land is purified in four (ways), by being trod on by cows, by digging, by lighting a fire on it, by rain falling on it,

20. Fifthly by smearing it with cowdung; and sixthly through (the lapse of) time.

21. Grass placed on unconsecrated ground (must be) washed.

22. (Grass) defiled out of one's sight, (shall be) sprinkled (with water).

23. Small pieces of sacred fuel (shall be purified) in the same manner.

24. Large pieces of wood (must be) washed and dried.

---

13. Govinda says that, as the treatment of valkala, 'bark-dresses,' has not been prescribed, the meaning of the Sûtra can only be, that bark-dresses and black-buck skins are to be treated alike, i.e. that they are to be cleaned with Bel-nut and rice; see above.

15. Govinda explains apalpûlitam by 'without beating it with the hand on a stone.' He mentions as an instance the skin which is used in preparing the Soma.

16. According to Govindâ, solid earth is such on which the fire-altars are built.

21. E.g. grass intended for the barhis, if it has been placed on a spot which has not been sprinkled with water.

22. 'Defiled out of one's sight,' i.e. brought by Sûdras.

25. But a great quantity (of wood shall be) sprinkled (with water).

26. Wooden vessels which have been touched by impure men (shall be) scraped;

27. (And) those which are defiled by stains of remnants (shall be) planed.

28. (Wooden vessels) defiled by urine, ordure, blood, semen, and the like (very impure substances shall be) thrown away.

29. These (rules must be followed) except in case a (special) injunction (is given);

30. Thus, for instance, (purification by) washing with Kusa grass and water (is prescribed) on all the following (occasions, viz.) at the Agnihotra, the Gharmo*kkh*ish*t*a, the Dadhigharma, the Ku*nd*apâyinâm Ayana, the Utsargi*n*âm Ayana, the Dâkshâya*n*a sacrifice, the Ardhodaya, the *K*atus*k*akra, and the Brahmaudanas,

31. (Again) at all Soma-sacrifices (the cups must be) cleaned with water only on (the heap of earth called) the Mâr*g*âlîya;

32. If these same (cups are defiled) by urine, ordure,

27. Govinda says that this rule is optional.

28. Govinda adds that fuel, Kusa grass, and the like, which have been defiled in this manner, must also be thrown away.

30. Regarding the Dadhigharma, a homa, see Vaitâna Sûtra 21, 18; regarding the Ku*nd*apâyinâm Ayana, Âsvalâyana *S*rauta Sûtra XII, 4; and regarding the Dâkshâya*n*a sacrifice, a variety of the new and full-moon offering, Âsvalâyana II, 14. The Ardhodaya is possibly the vrata of that name mentioned in the Purâ*n*as. According to Govinda, the *K*atus*k*akra, which is otherwise known as a Tântric rite, is a sacrifice, ish*t*akâkosh*t*a (?) madhyavasanto ya*g*ante tathetaradaya*h* (?). Regarding the Brahmaudana, see Âsvalâyana *S*rauta Sûtra I, 4.

32. Govinda says that the injunction to throw away defiled

blood, semen, and the like (they must be) thrown away.

PRASNA I, ADHYÂYA 6, KANDIKÂ 14.

1. Earthen vessels that have been touched by impure persons (must be) exposed to (the flame of) a fire of Kusa grass.

2. Those which have been defiled by stains of remnants (of food must be) exposed to another burning.

3. Those which have been defiled by urine, ordure, blood, semen, and the like (must be) thrown away.

4. (Vessels) made of metal (must be) washed, after having been scrubbed as (directed) above.

5. The materials (to be used) for scrubbing (are) cowdung, earth, ashes, and so forth.

6. Those which have been defiled by urine, ordure, blood, semen, and the like (must be) recast,

7. Or (they must) be kept during seven (days and) nights completely immersed in cow's urine,

8. Or in a great river for as long (a period).

9. (Vessels) made of stone or of fruits, (i. e.) gourds, Bel-fruit, and Vinâlas, (shall be) brushed with (a brush of) cow's hair.

---

vessels has been repeated, in order to prevent a misconception. For as Soma is said to be a great means of purification, it might be supposed that it was powerful enough to prevent the defilement of vessels into which it is poured at a sacrifice. But compare the next Sûtras.

14, 8. A great river, i. e. one which directly flows into the ocean.—Govinda.

9. A Vinâla, i. e. (a vessel) made of bamboo or Vidagdhanala; it is called a 'long vessel' (dirghabhâganam), and is used for carrying the Pranîta water and the like purposes.—Govinda. The vessel

10. (Sacrificial implements made of) plaited Na*l*a-reeds, bamboo, or *S*ara-reeds (shall be) washed with cowdung, water, and the like.

11. If unhusked rice has been defiled, (it must be) washed (and afterwards be) dried.

12. But a great quantity (of unhusked rice must be) sprinkled.

13. Husked rice (which has been defiled must be) thrown away.

14. The same (rule applies) to cooked sacrificial viands.

15. But if a great quantity has been defiled by (the touch of) dogs, crows, and the like (unclean beings), one must throw away that portion (as) food for men, and sprinkle (the rest with water), reciting the Anuvâka, 'Pavamâna*h* suvarganа*h*.'

16. Hydromel and preparations of milk (are) purified by pouring them from one vessel into another.

---

intended is no doubt the flask made of a bamboo which is cut below the joint, and is commonly used as a bottle for oil. Govinda adds that this mode of purification is to be adopted in case the vessels have been touched by impure persons.

10. Na*l*a-reeds, i.e. Amphidonax Karka; *S*ara, i.e. Saccharum Sara. Govinda says that the rule applies to cases where such implements have been defiled by remnants of food (u*kkh*isht*a*-lepa).

11. 'Defiled, i.e. touched by a *Kand*âla.' (The rule) refers to a quantity less than a Dro*n*a (66 or 132 lbs.).—Govinda.

13. 'If it has been defiled by urine and the like and the quantity is small;' this must be understood, because he will declare (below, Sûtra 15) that if there is a great quantity (the defiled) portion only shall be thrown away.—Govinda.

14. This, too, refers to small quantities only.

15. The Anuvâka referred to is Taittirîya-brâhma*n*a I, 4, 8.

16. 'Hydromel, i.e. sour milk, honey, clarified butter, water, and

17. In like manner let him pour oil and clarified butter which have been touched by an impure (person) into water, and (afterwards) use them.

18. If (any) impure (substance) is thrown (into the sacrificial fire) let him place (the two Aranis one) on (the other), produce fire by friction, (and offer) a Pavamâneshti.

19. If (the rules regarding) purity, the proper place, the mantras, the series of actions, the object, the materials, (their) consecration, and the proper time are conflicting, each earlier-named (point) is more important (than the following ones).

Prasna I, Adhyâya 7, Kandikâ 15.

1. The sacred fires (shall be) approached from the north,

2. (And be) left in the same manner.

3. The contrary (proceeding should be adopted at sacrifices offered) to the manes.

---

grain; a preparation of milk, i.e. curd of two-milk whey (âmikshâ), if these are blemished by the fault of men, and that (blemish must have been caused by) the touch of an impure (person, ukkhishta) only.'—Govinda.

17. 'And that must be done in such a manner that the oil and the clarified butter are not lost.'—Govinda.

18. 'Any impure substance, i.e. urine, ordure, and the like.'—Govinda.

19. Âvrit, 'the series of actions,' i.e. the growth (prâmsubhâva) of the ceremonial (prayoga).—Govinda.

15. 1. Mânava Srauta Sûtra I, 1, 1, and Kumârila thereon in Professor Goldstücker's lithographed copy and Kâtyâyana Srauta Sûtra I, 8, 24. See also Professor Haug's map of 'the sacrificial compound,' Aitareya-brâhmana, vol. i.

3. I.e. the entrance and exit are to be made to the south of the fires.

4. Let him wash that which has been touched with (his) foot.

5. Let him touch water, in case he touches his body or the hem (of his garment).

6. Likewise (let him touch water) after cutting, splitting, digging or removing (anything, or offering oblations) to the manes, to the Râkshasas, to Nir*ri*ti, to Rudra, (and after performing sacrifices) intended as spells (against enemies).

7. Let him not turn round himself a sacrificial implement (the use of) which is accompanied by the recitation of mantras.

8. (For) the sacrificial implements (are) more nearly (connected with the sacrifice),

9. The priests, more remotely.

10. The sacrificer and his wife are even nearer than the priests.

11. After the sacrificial implements (follows) the clarified butter, after the clarified butter the sacrificial viands, after the sacrificial viands the animal to be slain, after the animal the Soma, after the Soma the sacred fires.

---

5. Govinda explains si*k*, 'the hem of the garment,' by the garment wrapped round the loins (parihita*m* vâsa*h*).

7. The meaning is that the priest must hold the sacrificial implements, such as the sru*k* and sruva ladles, between himself and the fires, and not place himself between them and the fires (âtmano bahir na kûryât agner antara*h* svaya*m* na bhaved iti yâvat).

8. 'He gives the reason for that (rule), "For the sacrificial implements (are) nearer" than the priests, that must be understood.'—Govinda.

10. 'For they obtain the reward of the sacrifice. The instances (referring) to those two are the Vaisar*g*anas and the Dâkshi*n*as.'—Govinda.

11. Kâtyâyana *S*rauta Sûtra I, 8, 31. 'If the space on the

12. If there is work for them, the priests shall not turn away from the sacred fires.

13. If he faces the east, let him turn towards his right shoulder,

14. If he faces the west, towards the left.

15. The entrance to the sacrificial (enclosure lies) between the *K*âtvâla and the Utkara,

16. (When one comes) from the *K*âtvâla, (it lies between) the Âhavanîya fire and the Utkara.

17. The officiating (priests), the sacrificer, and his wife shall enter by that (road),

18. As long as the sacrificial rite is not completed.

19. When it has been finished (they shall) pass to and fro on the side where there is no Utkara (i.e. on the western side of the enclosure).

Uttaravedi and the rest is confined, the Soma is made ready immediately after the fire, after that the meat and so forth, after that the grain for the sacrificial cakes, then the clarified butter, and after that the spoons called sruva, sru*k*, and so forth.'—Govinda.

12. 'It is indicated hereby that, if there is work (to be done) there, they shall not turn away from the sacred fires except in cases of absolute necessity.'—Govinda.

13. 'This rule (refers to the case) when he walks with the sacred fires. It must be understood that he shall not turn his back on the fires.'—Govinda.

14. 'This rule (is to be interpreted) in the same manner (as the preceding one). Or it is prescribed by these two Sûtras that the men engaged (in the sacrifice) shall go out, turning their right hand towards (the fires).'—Govinda.

15. Kâtyâyana *S*rauta Sûtra V, 1, 11.

16. I read with the MSS. of the text '*k*âtvâlâd âhavanîyotkarau.' The two copies of the commentary give *k*âtvâla*h* âhavanîyotkarau. Govinda says that the words antare*n*a tîrtham must be understood. For the position of the *K*âtvâla and the Utkara, see Professor Haug's map, where the road of the priests is also marked, though somewhat differently.

20. Let him not put on the fire logs or Samidhs which have not been sprinkled (with water),

21. The Brahman (priest) and the sacrificer shall enter in front of the Âhavanîya fire.

22. Some (declare that they shall enter) behind the Âhavanîya fire.

23. The seat of the Brahman (priest is situated) to the south of the Âhavanîya fire, (that) of the sacrificer to the west of him.

24. (The seat) of the Hotri (priest is situated) to the north of the northern Sroni (of the Vedi),

25. (That) of the Âgnîdhra priest near the Utkara,

26. (That) of the (sacrificer's) wife behind the Gârhapatya fire.

27. He scatters Darbha grass on these (seats) as often as (they are used).

28. A vessel filled with water, for the purpose of sipping, shall be appropriated to (the use of) each (person).

29. He who has been initiated (to the performance of a sacrifice shall) keep the (following) vows:

30. Let him not proclaim the guilt of other men; let him not become angry; let him not weep; let him not look at urine and ordure.

31. If he has looked at any unclean (substance), he mutters (the verse), 'Unrestrained is the internal

23. For the seats of the priests and the other persons named in this and the following rules, see Professor Haug's plan, and Dr. Hillebrandt's Altindische Neu und Vollmondopfer, p. 190.

24. 'The northern Sroni of the Vedi, i. e. the north-western corner of the Vedi.'—Govinda.

31. Taittirîya Samhitâ III, 1, 1, 2, where the rule also is given. M. alone adds another Sûtra, the text of which is corrupt. But it ended with the mantra undatîr balam dhatta, &c. Taitt. S. ibid. 3.

O 2

organ, wretched (my) eye-sight; the sun is the chief of the (heavenly) lights; O Dîkshâ, do not forsake me!'

Prasna I, Adhyâya 8, Kandikâ 16.

1. There are four castes (varna, viz.) Brâhmanas, Kshatriyas, Vaisyas, and Sûdras.

2. (Males) belonging to them (may take) wives according to the order of the castes, (viz.) a Brâhmana four,

3. A Kshatriya three,

4. A Vaisya two,

5. A Sûdra one.

6. Sons begotten on (wives) of equal or of the next lower castes (are called) Savarnas (of equal caste).

7. (Those born) of (wives) of the second or third lower castes (become) Ambashthas, Ugras, and Nishâdas.

8. Of females wedded in the inverse order of the castes (are born) Âyogavas, Mâgadhas, Vainas, Kshattris, Pulkasas, Kukkutakas, Vaidehakas, and Kandâlas.

9. An Ambashtha (begets) on a female of the first (caste) a Svapâka,

10. An Ugra on a female of the second (caste) a Vaina,

11. A Nishâda on a female of the third (caste) a Pulkasa.

---

16. 1. Vasishtha II, 1. 2-5. Vasishtha I, 24-25.

6. Gautama IV, 16. 7. Vasishtha XVIII, 8.

8-12. Vasishtha XVIII, 1-6; Gautama IV, 17-21. In the I. O. copy of the commentary there is a break, which extends from Sûtra 8 to the beginning of Adhyâya 10.

12. In the contrary case a Kukku*t*aka (is produced).

13. . . . .

14. . . . .

15. . . . .

16. Now they quote also (the following verse): 'But those sons whom an uninitiated man begets, the wise call Vrâtyas, who are excluded from the Sâvitrî; (that is a rule which refers) in an equal manner to the three (highest) castes.'

Pras*n*a I, Adhyâya 9, Ka*nd*ikâ 17.

1. The Rathakâra (carpenter), the Ambash*th*a, the Sûta (charioteer), the Ugra, the Mâgadha, the Âyogava, the Vai*n*a, the Kshatt*ri*, the Pulkasa, the Kukku*t*a, the Vaidehaka, the *K*a*nd*âla, and so forth,

2. Among these, sons of equal caste (spring) from women of equal caste.

3. A Brâhma*n*a (begets) on a female of the Kshatriya caste a Brâhma*n*a, on a female of the Vais*y*a caste an Ambash*th*a, on a female of the *S*ûdra caste a Nishâda,

4. (According to) some a Pâras*a*va.

13–15. The text of the three Sûtras is exceedingly corrupt, and the Telugu copy of the commentary affords no help. It is, however, clear that the passage left out contained something which corresponded to Gautama IV, 22–23, and treated of the possibility of raising persons of a lower caste to a higher one by intermarriages continued for five or seven generations. The reading of K., which perhaps is the best, will show this: 'nishâdena nishâdyâd â pañ*k*amâ*gg*âtâ bhavanti tam upanayet shash*th*a*m* yâ*g*ayet saptamo 'vik*ri*tâ*g*îsama*m*gito saptamauñ*g*îsama ity ekeshâ*m* sa*m*gñâ krame*n*a nipatanti.'

16. Manu X, 20.

17. 1–2. Manu X, 26–27. 3–6. See above, I, 8, 16, 6–7.

5. A Kshatriya (begets) on a female of the Vaisya caste a Kshatriya, on a female of the *S*ûdra caste an Ugra.

6. A Vai*s*ya (begets) on a female of the *S*ûdra caste a Rathakâra.

7. A *S*ûdra begets on a female of the Vai*s*ya caste a Mâgadha, on a female of the Kshatriya caste a Kshatt*ri*, but on a female of the Brâhma*n*a caste a *K*a*nd*âla.

8. A Vai*s*ya begets on a female of the Kshatriya caste an Âyogava, on a female of the Brâhma*n*a caste a Sûta.

9. If among these an Ambash*th*a (male) and an Ugra (female) unite, (their son) will be born in the direct order of the castes (Anuloma).

10. If a Kshatt*ri* (male) and a Vaidehaka (female) unite, (their son will be) born against the order of the castes (Pratiloma).

11. An Ugra (begets) on a female of the Kshatt*ri* caste a *S*vapâka,

12. A Vaidehaka on a female of the Ambash*th*a caste a Vai*n*a,

13. A Nishâda on a female of the *S*ûdra caste a Pulkasa,

14. A *S*ûdra on a female of the Nishâda caste a Kukku*t*aka.

15. The wise declare those sprung from an intermixture of the castes to be Vrâtyas.

7–8. See above, I, 8, 16, 8.

9–10. I.e. the offspring of individuals of different Anuloma castes again become Anulomas, and the offspring of individuals of different Pratiloma castes, Pratilomas.

11–12. Manu X, 19.

13–14. See above, I, 8, 16, 11–12. 15. Gautama IV, 25.

PRA*S*NA I, ADHYÂYA 10, KA*ND*IKÂ 18.

1. Let the king protect (his) subjects, receiving as his pay a sixth part (of their incomes or spiritual merit).

2. Brahman, forsooth, placed its majesty in the Brâhma*n*as, together with (the duties and privileges of) studying, teaching, sacrificing for themselves, sacrificing for others, liberality, and accepting (gifts), for the protection of the Vedas;

3. In the Kshatriyas (it placed) strength, together with (the duties and privileges of) studying, sacrificing, liberality, (using) weapons, and protecting the treasure (and the life of) created beings, for the growth of (good) government;

4. In the Vai*s*yas (it placed the power of work), together with (the duties of) studying, sacrificing, liberality, cultivating (the soil), trading, and tending cattle, for the growth of (productive) labour.

5. On the *S*ûdras (it imposed the duty of) serving the three higher (castes).

6. For (the Veda states), 'they were created from the feet (of Brahman).'

---

18. 1. Vasish*th*a I, 42-44. Learned Brâhma*n*as do not pay taxes, but the king obtains a sixth part of the spiritual merit which they acquire. Hence Baudhâyana uses the general term, 'a sixth share.'

2. Vasish*th*a II, 13-14. 3. Vasish*th*a II, 15-17.

4. Vasish*th*a II, 18-19. The words 'the power of work' are inserted by Govinda.

5. Vasish*th*a II, 20.

6. Rig-veda X, 90, 12; Taittirîya Âra*n*yaka III, 12, 6.

7. Let (the king) choose a domestic priest (who shall be) foremost in all (transactions).

8. Let him act according to his instructions.

9. Let him not turn back in battle.

10. Let him not strike with barbed or poisoned (weapons).

11. Let him not fight with those who are in fear, intoxicated, insane or out of their minds, (nor with those) who have lost their armour, (nor with) women, infants, aged men, and Brâhma*n*as,

12. Excepting assassins (âtatâyin).

13. Now they quote also (the following verse): 'He who slays an assassin, able to teach (the Veda) and born in a (noble) family, does not (incur) by that (act the guilt of) the murderer of a learned Brâhma*n*a; (in) that (case) fury recoils upon fury.'

14. The duty on goods imported by sea is, after deducting a choice article, ten Pa*n*as in the hundred.

15. Let him also lay just (duties) on other (marketable goods) according to their intrinsic value without oppressing (the traders).

---

7. Vasish*th*a XIX, 3–6. Govinda explains sarvatodhuram, 'foremost in all,' by sarva*gñ*am, 'omniscient.'

8. Vasish*th*a I, 40–41. The rule, of course, refers primarily to advice in spiritual matters.

9. Gautama X, 16. 10. Manu VII, 90.

11. Gautama X, 18. The meaning is that such persons shall not be slain in battle.

12–13. Vasish*th*a III, 18.

14. I take this to mean that the king may take one article which particularly pleases him out of each consignment, and impose on the rest an ad valorem duty of ten per cent. Regarding the tribute in kind to be paid to Indian kings by foreign merchants, see Periplus maris Erythraei, par. 49.

15. Vish*n*u III, 29–30. Govinda interprets anupahatya, 'without

16. Let the king guard the property of men belonging to a non-Brâhmanical caste, the owner of which has disappeared, during a year, and afterwards take it (for himself).

17. A Brâhma*n*a, forsooth, shall not suffer corporal punishment for any offence.

18. In case (a Brâhma*n*a) has slain a Brâhma*n*a, has violated his Guru's bed, has stolen the gold (of a Brâhma*n*a), or has drunk (the spirituous liquor called) Surâ, (the king) shall cause to be impressed with a heated iron the mark of a headless trunk, a female part, a jackal, (or) the sign of a tavern on the forehead (of the offender) and banish him from his realm.

19. If a Kshatriya or (a man of any) other (lower caste) has murdered a Brâhma*n*a, death and the confiscation of all his property (shall be his punishment).

20. If those same (persons) slay men of equal or lower castes, (the king) shall fix suitable punishments in accordance with their ability.

PRA*S*NA I, ADHYÂYA 10, KA*ND*IKÂ 19.

1. For slaying a Kshatriya (the offender) shall

oppressing the traders,' by 'without deducting (anuddh*ri*tya) a choice article.'

16. Vasish*th*a XVI, 19–20. As stated above, I, 5, 11, 15, the king must not take the property of a Brâhma*n*a.

17. Vish*n*u V, 2. 'Corporal punishment,' i.e. capital punishment, mutilation, &c., except branding.

18. Vish*n*u V, 3–7. 19. Âpastamba II, 10, 27, 16.

20. Vasish*th*a XIX, 9. 'Those same persons,' i.e. Kshatriyas, Vai*s*yas, or *S*ûdras.

19. 1. Âpastamba I, 9, 24, 1. Govinda explains vairaniryâta-

give to the king one thousand cows and besides a bull in expiation of his sin,

2. For (slaying) a Vais*y*a one hundred cows, for (slaying) a *S*ûdra ten; and a bull (must be) added (in each case).

3. (The punishment for) the murder of a woman —excepting a (Brâhma*n*î) who had bathed after temporary uncleanness—and for the destruction of a cow have been explained by the (rule regarding the) murder of a *S*ûdra.

4. If he has slain a milch-cow or a draught-ox, he shall perform a *K*ândrâya*n*a (lunar penance) after (paying the prescribed fine).

5. The (punishment for the) murder of a (Brâhma*n*î) who had bathed after temporary uncleanness has been explained by (the rule regarding) the murder of a Kshatriya.

6. For killing a flamingo, a Bhâsa, a peacock, a Brâhma*n*î duck, a Pra*k*alâka, a crow, an owl, a frog, a musk-rat, a dog, (the large ichneumon called) Babhru, a common ichneumon, and so forth, (the offender shall pay) the same (fine) as (for the murder of) a *S*ûdra.

7. In order to gain the good opinion of men, a witness shall give evidence in accordance with what he has seen or heard.

---

nârtham in two ways: 1. in expiation of his sin; 2. in order to remove the enmity of the relatives of the murdered man. He adds all these punishments are really penances (prâyas*k*ittas) to be imposed by the king. Âpastamba has these Sûtras in the section on penances.

2. Âpastamba I, 9, 24, 2–4.

3. Âpastamba I, 9, 24, 5; I, 9, 26, 1.

5. Vasish*th*a XX, 34, 37. 6. Âpastamba I, 9, 25, 13.

7. Vish*n*u VIII, 13–14.

8. Of injustice (in decisions) one quarter falls on the party in the cause, one quarter on his witnesses, one quarter on all the judges, and one quarter on the king.

But where he who deserves condemnation is condemned, the king is guiltless and the judges free from blame; the guilt falls on the offender (alone).

9. (Therefore) a wise man should ask an appointed witness in the following manner:

10. 'The merit which thou hast acquired in the interval between the night in which thou wast born and that in which thou wilt die, all that will go to the king, if thou speakest an untruth.'

11. 'A witness who speaks falsely, slays three fathers and three grandfathers and seven (descendants), both the born and the unborn.'

12. 'By false testimony concerning gold he kills three ancestors; by false testimony regarding (small) cattle he kills five; by false testimony concerning kine he kills ten.'

'He kills a hundred by false evidence regarding horses, (and) a thousand by false evidence concerning a man. A witness who speaks falsely, destroys the whole (world) by false evidence concerning land.'

---

8. Manu VIII, 18–19.

9. I read, with the Telugu copy of the commentary, sâkshi*n*am ṭvevam uddish*t*am. All the MSS. of the text and C. I. read sâkshi*n*am daivam uddish*t*am. Govinda's explanation, adhunâ nirdish*t*ân sâkshi*n*a evam p*rikkh*ed iti padânvaya*h*, 'the construction of the words is, "let him now ask the appointed witnesses in the following manner,"' agrees with the reading adopted.

10. Vasish*th*a XVI, 32–33.

11. 'Three fathers and three grandfathers,' i. e. seven ancestors.

12. Vasish*th*a XVI, 34. Regarding the explanation of the

13. (Men of) the four castes (varna) who have sons may be witnesses excepting Srotriyas, the king, ascetics, and those who are destitute of human (intellect).

14. If (the witness rightly) recollects (the facts of) the case (he will receive) commendation from the most eminent men.

15. In the contrary case (he will) fall into hell.

16. Let him (who has given false evidence), drink hot milk during twelve (days and) nights or offer burnt oblations (reciting) the Kûshmânda (texts).

---

words 'he kills,' see Manu VIII, 97, and Haradatta on Gautama XIII, 14.

13. Vasishtha XVI, 28–30. The text has râganya, 'members of the royal family.' But the parallel passages of other Dharma-sûtras, e.g. Vishnu VIII, 2, make it probable that the king is meant.

14. Âpastamba II, 11, 29, 10. Govinda takes the Sûtra differently. His commentary runs as follows: sâkshidvaye sati râgñâ tatpurushais ka kim kartavyam ity ata âha ॥ smritau pradhânatah pratipattih ॥ prâdhânyatas taponirdishtavidyâdibhih । tadvakanât pratipattir niskayah kârya ityadhyâhârah kâryah ॥ 'What shall the king and his officers do, if there are two witnesses? In order to answer this question he says: "On recollection, according to pre-eminence, reliance." According to pre-eminence, i. e. on account of austerities, (being) appointed (as a witness), learning and the like; in accordance with the evidence of such person's conviction, i. e. the decision must be made. The latter word has to be understood.' Govinda then goes on to quote Manu VIII, 73.

15. Âpastamba II, 11, 29, 9. Govinda and M. read kartripatyam for kartapatyam, the reading of the Dekhan and Gugarât MSS. The explanation of the former term is said to be doshah, 'sin.' Regarding the ancient word kartapatya, which Govinda and the writer of M. have not understood, see Haradatta on Âpastamba I, 2, 5, 3.

16. In accordance with his explanation of Sûtra 14, Govinda thinks that this penance is to be performed by the king and the judges in case they fail to weigh the evidence properly. But

Prasna I, Adhyâya 11, Kandikâ 20.

1. (There are) eight marriage-rites.

2. If (the father) gives (his daughter) to a student (who has not broken his vow of chastity and) who asks for her, after fully enquiring into his learning and character, that (is) the rite of Brahman (brâhma).

3. If (the father gives his daughter away) after clothing her and decking her with ornaments, (saying) 'That (is thy wife), fulfil the law (with her),' that (is) the rite of Pragâpati (prâgâpatya).

4. If (the bridegroom) after offering the first burnt oblation of parched grain (receives the maiden) for a bull and a cow, that is the rite of the *Ri*shis (ârsha).

5. If (a maiden is given) to an officiating priest within the sacrificial enclosure, while the presents are being taken away, that (is) the rite of the gods (daiva).

---

according to Manu VIII, 106, Vish*n*u VIII, 16, the oblations with the Kûshmâ*nd*as (Taitt. Âr. X, 3-5) are to be offered for uttering in evidence a venial falsehood. That is, no doubt, here, too, the real meaning.

20. 1. Vish*n*u XXIV, 17.

2. Vasish*th*a I, 30. The word brahma*k*ârin has, no doubt, as Govinda too contends, been used in the double sense of 'a student of the Veda' and 'chaste.'

3. Vish*n*u XXIV, 22.

4. Vasish*th*a I, 32. 'After the first of the burnt oblations of parched grain, which are prescribed for weddings, has been offered, the bridegroom shall give to him who has power over the maiden a bull and a cow, and receive them back together with the (bride).'—Govinda.

5. Vasish*th*a I, 31. According to this rule the damsel is given

6. The union of a lover with a loving damsel (is called) the rite of the Gandharvas (gândharva).

7. (If the bridegroom receives the maiden) after gladdening (the parents) by money, (that is) the rite of the Asuras (âsura).

8. (If the maiden is wedded) after being forcibly abducted, (that is) the rite of the Râkshasas (râkshasa).

9. If one has intercourse with (a maiden) who is sleeping, intoxicated, or out of her senses (with fear or passion and weds her afterwards, that is) the rite of the Pisâkas (paisâka).

10. Among these (eight rites) the four first (named) are (lawful) for a Brâhmana. Among these also each earlier named is preferable.

11. Among the (four) later (named rites) each succeeding one is more sinful (than the preceding ones).

12. Among these the sixth and the seventh agree with the law of the Kshatriyas. For power is their attribute.

---

as part of the sacrificial fee (dakshinâ) to one of the priests after a sacrifice has been completed. Govinda adds that the recipient has to accept the gift with the six mantras, 'pragâpati striyâm yasah,' Taitt. Brâhmana II, 4, 6, 5. In his commentary on the passage Sâyana makes the same statement. Govinda adds that in this case as well as in those mentioned in the following Sûtras the regular marriage ceremony must be performed later.

6. Vasishtha I, 33. 7. Vasishtha I, 35.

8. Vasishtha I, 34. 9. Vishnu XXIV, 26.

10. Vishnu XXIV, 27.

12. Vishnu XXIV, 28; Vasishtha I, 29, 34. The meaning of the last clause is that as, according to I, 10, 18, 3, Brahman placed power in the Kshatriyas, they may adopt marriage rites by which a disregard of conventionalities or strength is displayed.

13. The fifth and the eighth (are lawful) for Vaisyas and Sûdras.

14. For Vaisyas and Sûdras are not particular about their wives,

15. Because they are allowed (to subsist by such low occupations as) husbandry and service.

16. Some recommend the Gândharva rite for all (castes), because it is based on (mutual) affection.

Prasna I, Adhyâya 11, Kandikâ 21.

1. The Veda declares, 'The quality of the offspring depends on the quality of the marriage rite.'

2. Now they quote also (the following verses): 'It is declared that a female who has been purchased for money is not a wife. She cannot (assist) at sacrifices offered to the gods or the manes. Kâsyapa has stated that she is a slave.'

---

13. 'I.e. the fifth for Vaisyas and the eighth for Sûdras.'—Govinda.

14. 'Those whose spouse, i.e. wife, is not restrained, i.e. not fixed by rule, are called not particular about their wives. The meaning is that there is oneness (dâreshvaikyam) with respect to wives, that fixed rules regarding them there are none (niyamas teshâm na bhavati).'—Govinda.

15. '"Husbandry" includes also trade and the like. Because those two (castes) are permitted to pursue low occupations, therefore their marriage rites are of the same description. That is what the author intends to say.'—Govinda.

21. 1. Âpastamba II, 5, 12, 4.

2. Vasishtha I, 36–38. Govinda inserts after the words 'Now they quote also,' two Sûtras in prose: 1. 'Ten virtuous sons and daughters (spring) from a Daiva marriage, ten from a Prâgâpatya marriage. It is declared in the Veda that the son of a wife wedded according to the Brâhma rite (sanctifies) ten ancestors, ten descendants, and oneself.' 2. 'The power of learning the Veda also

3. 'Those wicked men who, seduced by greed, give away a daughter for a fee, who (thus) sell themselves and commit a great crime, fall (after death) into a dreadful place of punishment and destroy their family down to the seventh (generation). Moreover they will repeatedly die and be born again. All (this) is declared (to happen), if a fee (is taken).'

4. On the day of the full moon, on the eighth day (of each half month), on the day of the new moon, on the appearance of a meteor, on the occasion of an earthquake, on visiting a burial-ground, and on the death of the king of the country, of a *S*rotriya or of one who has the same Guru (satîrthya), the study of the Veda must be discontinued for a day and a night.

5. (The study of the Veda must be interrupted) while (a strong) wind (blows), a foul smell (is perceptible), or hoar-frost (lies on the ground), when dancing (is going on), and while the sounds of singing, musical instruments, weeping, or of the Sâman (melodies are audible).

6. When thunder, lightning, and rain come together, (the interruption shall last) three days except in the rainy season.

---

belongs to such sons.' None of my MSS. of the text has these words, and they are suspicious, because the phrase 'Now they quote also' usually precedes verses only. The Dekhan and Gu*g*arât MSS., except K., omit these and the next Sûtra too.

4. Vasish*th*a XIII, 22, 32–35; Vish*n*u XXX, 23. Govinda explains agnyutpâta, 'on the appearance of meteor,' by 'if a fire breaks out in the village.'

5. Vasish*th*a XIII, 17, 30; Vish*n*u XXX, 7, 13; Âpastamba I, 3, 11, 31; I, 3, 10, 17.

6. Gautama XVI, 41.

7. In the rainy season, too, (the reading must be interrupted) until the same hour of the (next) day or night, (if thunder and lightning come together), not on account of rain.

8. If (he has) received anything or dined on the occasion of a sacrifice in honour of the manes, (he shall not read) during the remainder of the day,

9. (Nor) after meals until (the food) has been digested.

10. For the hand of a Brâhma*n*a is his mouth.

11. Now they quote also (the following verse): 'According to the revealed texts there is no difference whether one has eaten or received (a present at a *S*râddha).'

12. (A student shall discontinue the study of the Veda) during three days in case his father has died.

13. 'Of two kinds, forsooth, is the virile energy of a famous Brâhma*n*a who is learned in the Vedas, (that which resides) above the navel and the other (that resides) below the navel. Through that which

---

7. Govinda takes ahorâtrayo*s k*a tatkâlam to mean until the end of the day or night.

8. Vasish*th*a XIII, 15. Govinda adds that the recitation must be stopped as soon as the invitation to a *S*râddha is received.

9. Vasish*th*a XIII, 31.

10. Vasish*th*a XIII, 16. The word 'for' used in this Sûtra gives the reason for the rule in Sûtra 8.

12. 'This (rule) refers to a student who has not returned home. But on one who has returned home it is obligatory to interrupt the Veda-study until he becomes pure. Here he calls the sub-teacher (upâdhyâya) "father," because he gives the Veda. For (an interruption of) twelve days' duration is prescribed on (the death of) a real father (by the Sûtra); "on the death of the mother, the father, and the teacher twelve days."'—Govinda.

13. Vasish*th*a II, 5. This Sûtra is intended to show how the

(resides) above the navel, his offspring is produced when he initiates Brâhma*n*as, when he teaches them, when he causes them to offer sacrifices, when he makes them holy. All these are his children. But through that which resides below the navel the children of his body are produced. Therefore they never say to a *S*rotriya who is versed in the Vedas, 'Thou art destitute of offspring.'

14. 'Therefore a Brâhma*n*a has two names, two mouths, two kinds of virile energy, and two births.'

15. (Let him discontinue the recitation of the Veda) as long as he is within hearing or sight of *S*ûdras and Apapâtras.

16. When at night the howl of a solitary jackal is heard, he shall not study until he has slept.

17. Let him not study in the evening and morning twilights nor on the Parva-days.

18. He shall not eat meat nor approach his wife (on those days).

19. It is declared in the Veda, 'For on the Parva-days the Râkshasas and the Pi*s*â*k*as roam about (in order to injure men).'

20. And on (the appearance of) other omens and portents (he shall not repeat the Veda), except mentally, during a day and a night.

Upâdhyâya can be called a father. Govinda states that the precise meaning of anû*k*âna, 'versed or learned in the Veda,' is 'one who knows the Veda, its meaning, and the Aṅgas.' See also Baudhâyana G*ri*hya-sûtra I, 10, 5.

15. Vasish*th*a XVIII, 12. Regarding the term Apapâtras, see Âpastamba I, 1, 3, 25 note.

16. Âpastamba I, 3, 10, 17.

17. Vasish*th*a XIII, 22. The explanation of the term Parva-day is given below, Sûtra 22.

18. Vish*n*u LXIX, 1.

21. The mental recitation of the Veda must also be interrupted on births and deaths (occurring in the family).

22. Now they quote also (the following verse): 'The eighth day destroys the teacher, the fourteenth destroys the pupil, the fifteenth destroys learning; therefore let him avoid (studying the Veda) on the Parva-days.'

Prasna II, Adhyâya 1, Kandikâ 1.

1. Now, therefore, the penances (will be described).

2. The murderer of a learned Brâhmana (shall practise the following vow) during twelve years:

3. Carrying a skull (instead of a dish) and the foot of a bedstead (instead of a staff), dressed in the hide of an ass, staying in the forest, making a dead man's skull his flag, he shall cause a hut to be built in a burial-ground and reside there; going to seven houses in order to beg food, while proclaiming his deed, he shall support life with what (he gets there), and shall fast if he obtains nothing;

4. Or he may offer a horse-sacrifice, a Gosava, or an Agnishtut;

22. Vishnu XXX, 29–30. In accordance with the practice usual in Vedic works the best MSS. of the text repeat the beginning of each Kandikâ at the end of the Prasna, giving the last first.

1. 2–3. Gautama XXII, 4–6; Vishnu L, 1–3, 15. The expression 'staying in the forest' means that the sinner shall not stop in the village or the fields during the day-time, but live in some uncultivated tract in the neighbourhood.

4. Gautama XIX, 9–10. The Gosava sacrifice is an Ekâha; see Kâtyâyana Srauta Sûtra XXII, 11, 3.

5. Or he may bathe (with the priests) on the completion of a horse-sacrifice (offered by somebody else).

6. Now they quote also (the following verses): 'He who unintentionally slays a Brâhma*n*a becomes sinful according to the sacred law. The sages declare that he may be purified (if he did it) unintentionally. But no expiation is found for a wilful murderer.'

7. 'He who has raised his hand (against a Brâhma*n*a), shall perform a K*rikkh*ra penance, an Atik*rikkh*ra penance if he strikes, a K*rikkh*ra and a *K*ândrâya*n*a if blood flows. Therefore let him neither raise his hand nor cause blood to flow.'

8. (For killing) a Kshatriya (he shall keep the normal vow of continence) during nine years,

9. (For killing) a Vai*s*ya during three (years),

10. (For killing) a *S*ûdra during one year,

11. Likewise for killing a woman.

12. (The penance for killing) a woman who has bathed after temporary uncleanness (is) the same (as that) for (the murder of) a Brâhma*n*a.

---

5. Gautama XXII, 9. 6. Manu XI, 90.

7. Yâ*gñ*avalkya III, 293. Regarding the penances named, see Vasish*th*a XXI, 20, XXIV, 1-2, XXIII, 45, and below, II, 1, 2, 38, IV, 5, 6.

8-10. Vasish*th*a XX, 31-33. The words 'shall keep the normal vow of continence' have been inserted in accordance with Govinda's explanation, which apparently is based on Gautama XXII, 14. But it is also possible that Baudhâyana, like Vish*n*u (L, 15) and others, may have intended murderers of Kshatriyas, Vai*s*yas, &c., too, to perform the penance prescribed above, Sûtra 4, only for shorter periods.

11. Gautama XXII, 17. Govinda is of opinion that the word *k*a, 'likewise,' is intended to include 'worthless' Kshatriyas and Vai*s*yas.

12. Vasish*th*a XX, 34-35.

13. He who has defiled the bed of a Guru shall place himself on a heated iron bed,

14. Or embrace a red hot image (of a woman),

15. Or cutting off his organ together with the testicles and holding them in his joined hands, he shall walk towards the south-west until he falls down (dead).

16. A thief shall go to the king with flying hair, carrying on his shoulder a club of Sindhraka wood (and say), 'Strike me with that.' (Then the king) shall strike him.

17. Now they quote also (the following verses): 'A thief shall go to the king carrying a club on his shoulder (and say to him), 'Punish me with that, O king, remembering the duty of Kshatriyas.'

'Whether he be punished or be pardoned, the thief is freed from his guilt. But if the king does not punish him, that guilt of the thief falls on him.'

18. If he has drunk (the spirituous liquor called) Surâ, he shall scald himself to death with hot (liquor of the) same (kind).

19. For unintentionally drinking (Surâ), he shall perform K*rikkh*ra penances during three months and be initiated again,

20. And (on this second initiation) the cutting (of

13–15. Gautama XXIII, 8–10; Vasish*th*a XX, 13, 14.

16. Vasish*th*a XX, 41. 'A thief,' i.e. one who has stolen gold from a Brâhma*n*a.

17. Âpastamba I, 9, 25, 4–5.

18. Vasish*th*a XX, 22. Surâ, i.e. the spirituous liquor extracted from rice, to drink which is considered a particularly heinous crime. Vasish*th*a XX, 19, and loc. cit.

19. Vasish*th*a XX, 19.

20. Vish*n*u LI, 5. The vows and restrictive rules, i.e. the Sâvitrya vow, begging, &c.

the hair and nails), the vows, and (the observance of the) restrictive rules may be omitted.

21. Now they quote also (the following verses): 'A Brâhma*n*a, Kshatriya, or Vai*s*ya who has unintentionally drunk (the spirituous liquor called) Vâru*n*î or has swallowed urine or faeces must be initiated a second time.'

22. 'But he who drinks water which has stood in a vessel, used for keeping Surâ, shall live six days on milk in which (leaves of) the *S*ankhapushpî plant have been boiled.'

23. If (a pupil) who is employed by his teacher (on some errand) meets with his death, (the teacher) shall perform three K*rikkh*ra penances.

24. The same (penance) is prescribed for not finishing (the education of the pupil).

25. If a student assists at the burial of anybody except (at that of his) mother, of his father, or of his teacher, he must begin his vow afresh.

26. If a (student) is sick, he may, at his pleasure, eat all the fragments of his teacher's meal as medicine.

27. He may physic himself with any (medicine) which he may desire.

21. Vish*n*u LI, 2–4. 22. Vish*n*u LI, 23.

23. Vasish*th*a XXIII, 10.

24. 'Finishing (the education of the pupil, sa*m*sk*ri*tam), i.e. teaching him the rules of purification, of conduct, and so forth; failing (to do) that (is called) not finishing (the education of the pupil). For that (omission) the same (penance), i.e. three K*rikkh*ras (are to be) performed.'—Govinda.

25. Vasish*th*a XXIII, 7–8. 'Assists at a burial (*s*avakarma), i.e. lays out a corpse, and so forth (ala*m*kara*n*âdi), or carries it out, and so forth.'—Govinda.

26. Vasish*th*a XXIII, 9, and note.

27. 'The meaning is that he may cure himself even with such

28. When he is unable to move, he may worship the sun, after he has risen, reciting this (*Ri*k verse): 'A swan, dwelling in purity.'

29. When he has spent his manly strength in the day-time, let him thrice drink water that reaches his heart, reciting the verses which contain the word retas.

30. A student who approaches a woman (is called) an Avakîr*n*in,

31. Let him offer an ass (in the place of) a sacrificial animal.

32. The sacrificial meat-cake (puro*d*â*s*a shall be offered) to Nir*ri*ti, or to the Râkshasas, or to Yama.

33. It is declared in the Veda, 'The piece to be eaten by the sacrificer (prâ*s*itra, shall be taken) from the organ (of the animal); and the (other) portions shall be offered in water.'

34. 'Or he may also heap (fuel) on the fire in the night of the new moon, perform the preparatory rites required for the Darvîhoma, and offer two

(substances) which are forbidden even to his teacher, e. g. garlic, and so forth.' For a Sm*ri*ti declares, 'He shall protect himself by every means.'—Govinda.

28. 'Unable to move,' i. e. sick. This is a penance to be performed by a sick student when he is unable to fulfil the rules enjoining the morning and evening prayers, and the like; and it applies to other men also because there is no objection. Regarding the Mantra, see Taittirîya Sa*m*hitâ I, 8, 15, 2.

29. The rule refers to intercourse with a wife in the day-time; see Vish*n*u LIII, 4. The Retasyâs occur Taittirîya Âra*n*yaka I, 30.

30. Vasish*th*a XXIII, 1.

33. Weber, Ind. Stud. X, 102; Kâtyâyana *S*rauta Sûtra I, 1, 15.

34. Taitt. Âra*n*yaka II, 18. The Âra*n*yaka has, more appropriately, pra*n*îya, 'having taken out,' before upasamâdhâya, 'may heap (fuel) upon.' The Dekhan and Gugarât MSS. insert the words 'am*ri*ta*m*

oblations of clarified butter (reciting these two sacred texts): "O Lust, I have broken my vow; my vow have I broken, O Lust; to Lust Svâhâ;" "O Lust, I have done evil; evil have I done, O Lust; to Lust Svâhâ."'

35. 'After he has made the offering, he shall address the fire, closely joining his hands, turning sideways (with the following texts): "May the Maruts grant me, may Indra, may B*ri*haspati, may this fire grant me long life and strength, may it make me long-lived!"'

36. Now the relatives shall empty (the water-pot) of a (grievous offender) at a (solemn) meeting (and he shall confess), 'I N. N. am (the perpetrator of) such and such (a deed).' After (the outcast) has performed (his penance) the Brâhma*n*as shall ask him who has touched water, milk, clarified butter, honey, and salt, 'Hast thou performed (thy penance)?' The other (person) shall answer, 'Om' (yes)! They shall admit him who has performed (a penance) to all sacrificial rites, making no difference (between him and others).

37. If he unintentionally marries a female who belongs to his own family (gotra), he shall support her, (treating her) like his mother.

---

vâ â*g*yam am*ri*tam evâtman dhatte,' which occur also in the Âra*n*yaka, after the Mantra. According to Govinda pari*k*esh*t*â, 'preparatory rites,' refers to the consecration of the clarified butter, and so forth. The special rules regarding the Darvîhomas are given Kâtyâyana *S*rauta Sûtra VI, 10, 17 seq.

36. Vasish*th*a XV, 12–21. Govinda thinks that nirvi*s*esha*m* savanîya*m* kuryu*h*, 'they shall admit him to all sacrificial rites, making no difference,' may also be interpreted by 'they shall perform for him the sacraments just as for a new-born child.'

37. Colebrooke V, Dig. CCCXL.

38. If (such a woman) has borne a child, he shall perform K*rikkh*ra penances during three months and offer (two burnt oblations reciting) the two (Mantras), 'That which is the blemish of my soul' (and) 'Fire restored my sight.'

39. 'An elder brother whose younger brother marries first, the younger brother who marries first, the damsel wedded (by the latter), he who gives her away, and fifthly he who sacrifices for them (at the wedding), all sink to a region of torment.'

40. 'The unmarried elder brother and the married younger brother, the giver (of the maiden) and the performer of the sacrifices become pure by undergoing a K*rikkh*ra penance of twelve days, the female (who has been wedded to the younger brother) by (fasting during) three days.'

PRA*S*NA II, ADHYÂYA 1, KA*ND*IKÂ 2.

1. Now (follow the offences) causing loss of caste (patanîya),

2. (Viz.) making voyages by sea,

38. The Mantras are found, Taittirîya Sa*m*hitâ III, 2, 5, 4.

39. Vasish*th*a XX, 7–8. The MSS. read parivitti*h* parivettâ ya*s* *k*ainâm [na*m*] parivindati. But it is absolutely necessary to adopt either the various reading given Manu III, 172, yayâ *k*a parividyate, or to read yâ *k*aina*m* parivindati.

40. The MSS. all read at the end of the verse, tristrirâtre*n*a or dvistrirâtre*n*a. The correct reading appears, however, to be strî t*r*irâtre*n*a; for Govinda says, yayâ saha parivettâ bhûtas [bhûttasya C. I., bhûtassâstri C. T.] tasyâs trirâtre*n*opavâsena *s*uddhi*h*, 'the purification of that female with whom he has become a parivett*ri* takes place through three days, i. e. through fasting (three days).'

2. 1. Âpastamba I, 7, 21, 7–11.

2. Govinda explains samudrasa*m*yânam, 'making voyages by sea,' by 'voyaging by means of ships to another continent (dvîpa).'

3. Stealing the property of a Brâhma*n*a or a deposit,

4. Giving false evidence regarding land,

5. Trading with merchandise of any description (whether forbidden or not),

6. Serving *S*ûdras,

7. Begetting a son on a female of the *S*ûdra caste,

8. And becoming thereby her son.

9. (For those who have) committed one of these (offences the following penance is prescribed):

10. 'They shall eat every fourth meal-time a little food, bathe at the time of the three libations (morning, noon, and evening), passing (the day) standing and (the night) sitting. After the lapse of three years they throw off their guilt.'

11. 'A Brâhma*n*a removes the sin which he committed by serving the black race during one day and one night, if he bathes during three years at every fourth meal-time.'

---

7. The MSS. from Gu*g*arât and the Dekhan read instead of this and the next Sûtras, yas*k*a *s*ûdrâyâm abhipra*g*âyate tadapatya*m* *k*a bhavati, 'and he who begets (offspring) on a *S*ûdra female, and thereby becomes her son.'

8. Govinda explains the Sûtra as a prohibition against allowing oneself to be adopted by a *S*ûdra (*s*ûdraputrabhâva*h* । tavâham putro 'smîty upa*g*îvanam).

9. The Dekhan and Gu*g*arât MSS. again have a different reading, teshâ*m* tu nisvesha*h*, 'but the atonement of these offences (is as follows).'

10. Âpastamba I, 9, 25, 10. All the MSS. read in the last pâda 'tribhir varshais tad apahanti pâpam.' The correct reading is that given by Âpastamba loc. cit., 'tribhir varshair apa pâpa*m* nudante.'

11. Âpastamba I, 9, 27, 11. Govinda explains the Sûtra as referring to cohabitation with a female of the 'black race.' By the latter term he understands a *K*â*n*d*â*lî, adding that others believe

12. Now (follow) the minor offences, entailing loss of caste (upapâtaka),

13. (Viz.) intercourse with females who must not be approached (agamyâ, e. g.) cohabitation with the female friend of a female Guru, with the female friend of a male Guru, with an Apapâtra woman, and a female outcast, following the profession of medicine, sacrificing for many, living by (performances on) the stage, following the profession of a teacher of dancing, singing and acting, tending cows and buffalos, and similar (low occupations, as well as) fornication.

14. The expiation (prescribed) for these (offences is) to live as an outcast during two years.

---

a *S*ûdra female to be intended. It is, however, more probable that Baudhâyana took the verse to forbid twice-born men to serve *S*ûdras.

12. Âpastamba I, 7, 21, 9.

13. Gautama XXI, 11. In explanation of the term agamyâ, 'a female who must not be approached,' Govinda quotes Nârada XII, 73–74, and he takes the four classes of females, who are specially mentioned, not as examples illustrating the term agamyâ, but as not included in and additional to the latter. Physicians and the other professional men enumerated are usually not mentioned among the upapâtakins, but occur in the lists of those whose gifts must not be accepted, and of those who defile the company at a funeral dinner, e. g. Vasish*th*a III, 3; XIV, 2, 3, 11. The expression 'sacrificing for many' (grâmayâ*g*anam) appears to be a description of the so-called Ya*g*amâna V*ri*tti, by which the modern Bha*tt*a*g*îs, or priests who officiate for hire, subsist. In explanation of the term nâ*t*yâ*k*âryatâ, 'following the profession of teaching dancing, music, and acting,' Govinda says that 'instruction in the works of Bharata, Vi*s*âkhila, and others' is intended. Baudhâyana no doubt intends to forbid the instruction of professional dancers and actors in actual works on their art, such as the nâ*t*ya-sûtras mentioned by Pâ*n*ini.

14. 'To live as an outcast, i.e. to subsist by begging.'—Govinda.

15. Now (follow the offences) which make men impure (asu*k*ikara),

16. (Viz.) gambling, performing incantations, subsisting by gleaning corn though one does not perform an Agnihotra, subsisting by alms after one has finished one's studentship, living, after that has been finished, longer than four months in the house of one's teacher, and teaching such a (person who has finished his studentship), gaining one's livelihood by astrology and so forth.

17. But the expiation of these (offences is to perform penances) during twelve months, during twelve fortnights, during twelve times ten days, during twelve se'nnights, during twelve times three days, during twelve days, during six days, during three days, during a day and a night, during one day, in proportion to the offence committed.

18. Now outcasts shall live together and (together) fulfil their duties, sacrificing for each other, teaching each other, and marrying amongst each other. If they have begot sons, they shall say to them, 'Depart from among us; thus you will again reach the Âryas.'

19. For the organs do not become impure together with the man.

20. (The truth of) that may be learned from this (parallel case); a man deficient in limbs begets a son who has the full number of limbs.

21. Hârîta declares that this is wrong.

22. For wives may be (considered) similar to the

---

15. Âpastamba I, 7, 21, 12-19; I, 10, 29, 15.

16. Govinda is probably right in asserting that the word *k*a, 'and (so forth),' is intended to include other not-named offences.

17. Âpastamba I, 10, 29, 17-18.

18-23. Âpastamba I, 10, 29, 8-14.

vessel which contains the curds (for the sacrifice). If one makes impure milk curdle in a milk-vessel and stirs it, the *S*ish*t*as do not use the (curds thus produced) for sacred rites.

23. In like manner no intercourse can be held with that (offspring) which is produced from impure seed.

24. If they desire it, (they may perform) a penance,

25. (Viz. in the case of males) the third part (of the penance prescribed) for crimes causing loss of caste (patanîya); for females the third part (of that).

26. Now they quote also (the following verse): 'If he applies sesamum to any other purpose, but food, anointing, and charitable gifts, he will be born again as a worm and, together with his ancestors, be plunged into the ordure of dogs.'

27. He who sells sesamum, forsooth, sells his ancestors; he who sells rice, forsooth, sells his life; he who gives away his daughter, making a bargain, forsooth, sells portions of his spiritual merit.

28. Grass and wood, in its natural state, may be sold.

29. Now they quote also (the following verse): 'Animals that have teeth in one jaw only, as well as minerals excepting salt, and undyed thread, these, O Brâhma*n*a, are the goods which thou art permitted to sell.'

30. (If he has committed) any offence excepting a

---

25. I. e. males shall live, according to the rules given above in Sûtras 10–11, during one year, and females during four months.

26. Vasish*th*a II, 30. 28. Âpastamba I, 7, 21, 2.

29. The permission to sell 'stones' or minerals contradicts Vasish*th*a II, 24.

30. Regarding the definition of the term 'anû*k*âna,' see above, I, 11, 21, 13.

mortal sin (pâtaka) he may either give to a learned Brâhma*n*a (anû*k*âna) a hairy cow of brown or reddish colour, after sprinkling her with clarified butter and scattering black sesamum seeds over her;

31. Or (he may offer burnt oblations), reciting the Kûshmâ*nd*as, during twelve days.

32. '(Thus) he will be freed from the guilt (of any crime that is) less (heinous) than the murder of a learned Brâhma*n*a.'

33. If one is accused of a mortal sin (pâtaka), a K*rikkh*ra (penance must be performed by the accused).

34. The accuser (shall perform) that (K*rikkh*ra penance during) a year.

35. 'He who during a year associates with an outcast, becomes (likewise) an outcast; not by sacrificing for him, by teaching him or by (forming) a matrimonial (alliance with him), but by using the same carriage or seat.'

36. The penance for eating impure substances is to fast until the entrails are empty. That is attained in seven (days and) nights.

---

31. Regarding the efficacy of the Kûshmâ*nd*a texts, see e.g. Gautama XIX, 12; XXII, 36.

33. Vasish*th*a XXIII, 37–38. 34. Vasish*th*a XXIII, 39.

35. Vasish*th*a I, 22.

36. Âpastamba I, 9, 27, 3–4; Vasish*th*a XXIII, 30. I follow here the Gu*g*arât and Dekhan MSS., which read amedhyaprâ*s*ane prâya*s*/*k*ittir naishpurîshya*m* tat saptarâtre*n*âvâpyate. M. and the two MSS. of the commentary give amedhyaprâ*s*ane prâya*s*/*k*ittam and leave the remainder out. The commentary states that the penance intended is the Taptak*rikkh*ra, described in the next Sûtra. The parallel passages of Âpastamba and others leave no doubt that the northern MSS. in this case have preserved the older form of the text.

37. (Subsisting on) water, milk, clarified butter, (and) fasting,—each for three days,—(and taking the three fluids) hot, that is a Taptak*rikkh*ra penance.

38. (Eating) during three days in the morning only, during the (next) three days in the evening only, (subsisting) during (another) three days (on) food given unasked, and fasting during three days, (that is) a K*rikkh*ra penance.

39. (If the period of twelve days is divided into) three (periods of) four days, that is the K*rikkh*ra penance of women, children, and aged men.

40. If (observing the rule given) above one eats (at each meal) so much only as one can take at one (mouthful), that is an Atik*rikkh*ra penance.

41. (If one) subsists on water only, that is a K*rikkh*râtik*rikkh*ra, the third (in the order of the K*rikkh*ra penances).

42. During a K*rikkh*ra penance (the following rules must be followed, viz.) to bathe at morn, noon, and evening,

43. To sleep on the ground,

44. To wear one garment only, to shave the hair of the head, of the beard, and of the body, and to clip the nails.

45. The same (rules apply) to women except (that referring to) shaving the head.

---

37. Vasish*th*a XXI, 21.

38. Vasish*th*a XXI, 20. M. and the two MSS. of the commentary omit the word '*krikkh*ra*h*' at the end of the Sûtra.

39. Vasish*th*a XXIII, 43. 40. Vasish*th*a XXIV, 2.

41. Vasish*th*a XXIV, 3. Govinda gives another explanation of the word *tri*tîya*h*, 'the third,' according to which it is to refer to the third tryaha*h*, or 'period of three days.'

42–44. Vasish*th*a XXIV, 4–5.

PRA*S*NA II, ADHYÂYA 2, KA*N*D*I*KÂ 3.

1. A Brâhma*n*a who always carries water (in his pot), who always wears the sacred thread, who daily recites the Veda, who avoids the food of *S*ûdras, who approaches (his wife) in the proper season, and offers sacrifices in accordance with the rules (of the Veda, after death) never falls from Brahman's heaven.

2. The Veda (says), 'Manu divided his estate among his sons.'

3. (A father may, therefore, divide his property) equally among all, without (making any) difference;

4. Or the eldest may receive the most excellent chattel.

5. (For) the Veda says, 'Therefore, they distinguish the eldest by (an additional share of the) property.

6. Or the eldest may receive (in excess) one part out of ten;

7. (And) the other (sons) shall receive equal shares.

8. While the father lives, the division of the estate takes place (only) with the permission of the father.

---

3. 1. Vasish*th*a VIII, 17.

2. Taittirîya Sa*m*hitâ III, 1, 9, 4.

3. Colebrooke V, Dig. XL. Govinda points out that this rule refers to sons equal by caste, origin, and virtue.

4. Colebrooke, loc. cit.; Vish*n*u XVIII, 37.

5. Taittirîya Sa*m*hitâ II, 5, 2, 7. See also the discussion on this text, Âpastamba II, 6, 14, 10–13.

6. Colebrooke, loc. cit.; Vasish*th*a XVII, 43.

7. Colebrooke, loc. cit.; Gautama XXVIII, 8.

8. Colebrooke V, Dig. XXII; Dâyabhâga II, 8. In C.'s Digest

9. The (additional) share of the eldest is, (according to the order) of the four castes, a cow, a horse, a goat, and a sheep.

10. If there are sons born of wives of different castes (varna), they should make ten portions of the ancestral property and take four (shares), three, two, (and) one, according to the order (of the castes).

11. But if a legitimate son of the body (aurasa) is born, the (other) sons of equal caste shall obtain one third share (of the estate).

12. If there is a son of equal caste and a son of

---

the first clause is omitted and connected with the following Sûtra. Govinda agrees with *G*îmûtavâhana.

9. Colebrooke V, Dig. XLIX. The rule is an explanation of the term vara*m* rûpam, 'the most excellent chattel,' in Sûtra 4. The meaning probably is, as the Digest states, that among Brâhma*n*as it is usual to give to the eldest a bull, among Kshatriyas a horse, and so forth.

10. Vasish*th*a XVII, 48–50; Vish*n*u XVIII, 2–40; where the several cases that can arise have been fully worked out.

11. I translate according to the reading of K., M., and the two MSS. of the commentary, aurase tûtpanne savar*n*âs [°*n*as, M., K.] t*ri*tîyâ*ms*aharâ*h* [°yâ*ms*a*m* haret, K.] The other MSS. omit the last two words of the Sûtra. The sense of the Sûtra seems to be, that subsidiary sons of equal caste obtain a third of the estate when a legitimate son of the body is born to their father; see also Kâtyâyana V, Dig. CCXVIII. Govinda gives the following explanation: aurasa*h* savar*n*aputrâ*s k*a vakshyante । aurasa*h* savar*n*âyâ*m* sa*m*sk*ri*tâyâ*m* svayam utpâ*d*ita*h* [Sûtra 14] । tasminnutpanne savar*n*âs t*ri*tîyâ*ms*aharâ bhaveyu*h* । sarva*m* dhana*g*âta*m* tredhâ vibha*g*ya teshâm eka*m* sho*d*a*s*a sa*m*pâdya trîn dvâvekam iti kalpayet ॥ 'The legitimate son and the sons of equal caste will be described (below). He is called a legitimate son who is begotten by the husband himself on a wedded wife of equal caste. When such a one is born, the (other) sons of equal caste shall obtain one third share. Dividing the whole property into three parts, and making one of them sixteen (?), he shall give three, two, one.'—Govinda.

12. Colebrooke V, Dig. CLVII; Dâyabhâga IX, 15.

a wife of the next lower caste, the son born of the wife of the next lower caste may take the share of the eldest, provided he be endowed with good qualities.

13. (A son) who possesses good qualities becomes the protector of the rest.

14. One must know a son begotten by (the husband) himself on a wedded wife of equal caste (to be) a legitimate son of the body (aurasa).

Now they quote also (the following verse): 'From the several limbs (of my body) art thou produced, from my heart art thou born; thou art "self" called a son; mayest thou live a hundred autumns.'

15. The (male child) born of a daughter, after an agreement has been made, (one must know to be) the son of an appointed daughter (putrikâputra); any other (male offspring of a daughter they call) a daughter's son (dauhitra).

16. Now they quote also (the following verse): 'The son of an appointed daughter should offer the first funeral cake to his mother, the second to her father, and the third to his father's father.'

17. He who is begotten, by another man, on the wife of a deceased man, of a eunuch, or of one (incurably) diseased, after permission (has been given), is called the son begotten on a wife (kshetra*g*a).

---

13. Colebrooke, loc. cit.

14. Colebrooke V, Dig. CXCVI; Vasish*th*a XVII, 13. The verse is found in the Mahâbhârata and elsewhere.

15. Colebrooke V, Dig. CCXIII; Vasish*th*a XVII, 15–17.

17. Colebrooke V, Dig. CCXXXVII; Dâyabhâga II, 60; Vasish*th*a XVII, 14.

18. Such a (son begotten on a wife) has two fathers and belongs to two families; he has a right to perform the funeral oblations, and to inherit the property of (his) two (fathers).

19. Now they quote also (the following verse): 'The son of two fathers shall give the funeral cakes (to his two fathers, and pronounce) two names with each oblation, and three cakes shall serve for six persons; he who acts thus will not err.'

20. He (is called) an adopted son (datta) who, being given by his father and his mother, or by either of the two, is received in the place of a child.

21. He (is called) a son made (k*ri*trima) whom (a man) himself makes (his son), with the (adoptee's) consent (only), and who belongs to the same caste (as the adopter).

22. He is called a son born secretly (gû*dh*aga) who is secretly born in the house and whose (origin is) afterwards (only) recognised.

23. He is called a son cast off (apaviddha) who, being cast off by his father and his mother, or by either (of them), is received in the place of a child.

24. If anybody approaches an unmarried girl without the permission (of her father or guardian), the son born by such (a woman is called) the son of an unmarried damsel (kânîna).

---

18. Colebrooke Dig., loc. cit. 20. Vasish*th*a XVII, 28.

21. Colebrooke V, Dig. CCLXXXIV; Gautama XXVIII, 32.

22. Vasish*th*a XVII, 24. 23. Vish*n*u XV, 24–25.

24. Colebrooke V, Dig. CCLXI; Vasish*th*a XVII, 21–23. It must be understood that the father must belong to the same caste as the girl.

Q 2

25. If one marries either knowingly or unknowingly a pregnant bride, the child which is born of her is called (a son) taken with the bride (sahod*h*a).

26. He (is called a son) bought (krîta) who, being purchased from his father and his mother, or from either of them, is received in the place of a child.

27. He (is called the son) of a twice-married woman (paunarbhava) who is born of a re-married female, (i. e.) of one who, having left an impotent man, has taken a second husband.

28. He (is called) a self-given (son, svaya*m*-datta) who, abandoned by his father and his mother, gives himself (to a stranger).

29. He who is begotten by (a man of) the first twice-born (caste) on a female of the *S*ûdra caste (is called) a Nishâda.

30. (He who was begotten by the same parents) through lust (is called) a Pâra*s*ava. Thus (the various kinds of) sons (have been enumerated).

31. Now they quote also (the following verses): 'They declare the legitimate son, the son of an appointed daughter, the son begotten on a wife, the adopted son and the son made, the son born secretly and the son cast off, (to be entitled) to share the inheritance.'

32. 'They declare the son of an unmarried damsel and the son received with the bride, the son bought,

25. Vasish*th*a XVII, 27.

26. Colebrooke V, Dig. CCLXXXI; Vasish*th*a XVII, 30–32.

27. Vasish*th*a XVII, 18–20. 28. Vasish*th*a XVII, 33–35.

30. Colebrooke V, Dig. CCXCIII. Govinda points out that the Pâra*s*ava is, according to Baudhâyana, the offspring of a *S*ûdrâ concubine, not of a *S*ûdrâ wife. But see also above, I, 9, 17, 4.

31. Colebrooke V, Dig. CLXXX; Vasish*th*a XVII, 25.

32. Colebrooke V, Dig. CLXXIX; Vasish*th*a XVII, 26.

likewise the son of a twice-married female, the son self-given and the Nishâda, to be members of the family.'

33. Aupagandhani (declares that) the first among them alone (is entitled to inherit, and a member of his father's family).

34. 'Now, O Ganaka, I jealously watch my wives, (though I did) not (do it) formerly; for they have declared in Yama's court that the son belongs to the begetter. The giver of the seed carries off the son, after death, in Yama's hall. Therefore they carefully protect their wives, fearing the seed of strangers.'

35. 'Carefully watch (the procreation of your) offspring, lest strange seed fall on your soil. After death the son belongs to the begetter; through carelessness a husband makes (the procreation of) a son useless.'

36. Let them carefully protect the shares of

33-34. Aupagandhani is one of the ancient teachers of the White Yagur-veda, mentioned in the lists incorporated in the Satapatha-brâhmana XIV, 5, 5, 21; 7, 3, 26. The legends of the White Yagur-veda frequently mention king Ganaka of Videha, and assert that that philosopher king had frequent and intimate intercourse with Yâgñavalkya and other teachers of the Veda which Âditya revealed. It seems to me, therefore, highly probable that Govinda is right in taking the vocative ganaka in Sûtra 34 as a proper name, and in asserting that the verse belongs to a conversation between Aupagandhani and Ganaka. This explanation, which possibly may be based on an ancient tradition of Baudhâyana's school, is certainly preferable to Haradatta's statement on Âpastamba II, 6, 13, 7, that these verses express the sentiments of a husband who had neglected to watch his wives, and later learned that he would not derive any spiritual benefit from their offspring. In the text of Sûtra 34 I read with the Dekhan MSS. and Âpastamba, loc. cit., îrshyâmi, instead of ishyâmi, which M. and the commentary give.

36. Colebrooke V, Dig. CCCCLII; Vasishtha XVI, 8, 9. 'The

those who are minors, as well as the increments (thereon).

37. Granting food, clothes, (and shelter), they shall support those who are incapable of transacting legal business,

38. (Viz.) the blind, idiots, those immersed in vice, the incurably diseased, and so forth,

39. Those who neglect their duties and occupations;

40. But not the outcast nor his offspring.

41. Intercourse with outcasts shall not take place.

42. But he shall support an outcast mother, without speaking to her.

43. The daughters shall obtain the ornaments of their mother, (as many as are) presented according to the custom (of the caste), or anything else (that may be given according to custom).

---

increments, i.e. the proper interest. Thus the money of minors shall bear interest.'—Govinda.

37. Colebrooke V, Dig. CCCXXVIII; Dâyabhâga V, 12; Vyavahâramayûkha IV, 11, 10; Vasish*th*a XVII, 52-54.

38. Colebrooke and Mayûkha, loc. cit. 'The expression "and so forth" includes hunchbacks and other (disabled) persons.'—Govinda. Vyasanin, 'immersed in vice,' may also mean 'afflicted by calamities,' and is perhaps intended to be taken both ways.

39. Colebrooke and Mayûkha, loc. cit. Akarmi*n*as, 'those who neglect their duties and occupations,' i.e. those who though able (to fulfil their duties are) indolent.—Govinda.

40. Colebrooke and Mayûkha, loc. cit.; Burnell, Dâyabhâga 49.

42. Gautama XXI, 15, and note.

43. Colebrooke V, Dig. CXXX; Vasish*th*a XVII, 46. 'Sâmpradâyikam (literally "customary") qualifies (the word) ornaments; sâmpradâyikam (means) what is obtained according to custom; what is given to their mother by the maternal grandfather and grandmother, that (is called) sâmpradâyikam. "Or anything else," (viz.) presented according to custom, (e.g.) a bedstead and the

44. Women do not possess independence.

45. Now they quote also (the following verse): 'Their father protects (them) in childhood, their husband protects (them) in youth, and their sons protect (them) in old age; a woman is never fit for independence.'

46. The Veda declares, 'Therefore women are considered to be destitute of strength and of a portion.'

---

like, a couch, and an outer garment, and the like. So much and nothing else shall the daughters receive.'—Govinda.

44. Vasish*th*a V, 1. All the MSS. of the text read na strîsvâtantryam vidyate, while the text given by the two copies of the commentary has na strî svâtantryam vindate. Govinda asserts that the Sûtra is intended to forbid the independent action of women with respect to things inherited. The correct view probably is that with this Sûtra the topic of the duties and rights of women begins, and that the rule contains a general maxim.

45. Vasish*th*a V, 2.

46. Colebrooke V, Dig. CXXXI. The text is in great confusion. The Dekhan and Gugarât MSS., except K., read, na dâyam nirindriyâ hyadâyâs *k*a striyo matâ iti sruti*h*; K. has, tasmât[n]-nirindriyâ hy. st. m. i. *s*ru. ॥ tasmât striyo nirindriyâ adâyâdîr api pâpât; while M. and the I.O. copy of the commentary have, tasmânnirindriyâ adâyâs *k*a striyo matâ iti *s*ruti*h* [sûti*h*, M.] The Telugu copy is mutilated, and reads nâdayantiriti *s*ruti*h*. Though the reading of the Dekhan MSS. is supported by Mitramisra Vîramitrodaya, fol. 209, p. 1, l. 3, it is certainly not the original one, for there is no verb by which the accusative 'dâyam' is governed. Mitrami*s*ra's attempt to make it depend on 'arhati' in the verse quoted in Sûtra 45 is futile, because, according to the usage of the Sûtrakâras, a Sûtra may be completed by a verb taken from another original aphorism of the author, but cannot be connected with a portion of a quotation taken from some other work. This same principle, of course, applies not only to Sûtras, but to the writings of all other authors, whether Indian or European. The reading of K., M., and of the I. O. copy of the commentary is not open to the objection just mentioned, and therefore preferable. But it seems to me highly probable that, nevertheless, it is not

47. Those (women) who strive (to do what is) agreeable to their husbands will gain heaven.

48. But for a violation (of their duty towards the husband) a K*rikkh*ra penance (must be performed).

49. (For violating it) with a *S*ûdra (a woman) shall perform a lunar penance (*k*ândrâya*n*a);

50. (For violating it) against the order of the castes with a Vai*s*ya and so forth, she shall perform a K*rikkh*ra or an (Atik*rikkh*ra) penance.

51. For male (offenders, i.e.) Brâhma*n*as and so forth, a year's chastity (is prescribed).

---

quite genuine; for the word 'tasmât,' with which it begins, is not required, because its sense is already expressed by the following 'hi,' and because the Sûtra apparently contains half an Anush*t*ubh *S*loka, which the insertion of tasmât destroys. It is also easy to see how it came to be inserted. Every Yagurvedî who read the passage would be reminded of the analogous passage of the Taittirîya Sa*m*hitâ VI, 5, 8, 2, 'tasmât striyo nirindriyâ adâyâdîr api pâpât pu*m*sa*h* upastitaram,' which in K. has actually been inserted after our Sûtra. In the Vedic Mantra 'tasmât' is required, and is certainly the genuine reading. Hence it seems to have been transferred into Baudhâyana's text, possibly by the mistake of some scribe who, according to the habit of his kind, took a marginal reference to the beginning of the Vedic passage for a correction of the text. In my opinion it must be thrown out. The sense of the half verse remains exactly the same. It corresponds to Manu IX, 18. According to Govindasvâmin and others its object is to show that women are incapable of inheriting, and the word dâya, 'portion,' must be taken in the sense of 'a share of the inheritance.' For a full discussion of this point, I refer to the Introductory Note on Book I, Chapter II, Sect. 14 of West and Bühler's Digest of H. L. C., third edition.

47. Vish*n*u XXV, 15, 17; Vasish*th*a XXI, 14.

48–50. Vasish*th*a XXI, 6–13.

51. Govinda points out that this rule refers to adultery with women of equal caste, and thinks that the word 'chastity' indicates that K*rikkh*ra penances are to be performed; Vasish*th*a XXI, 16, 17; Vish*n*u LIII, 2. But see Gautama XXII, 29.

52. Let him burn a *S*ûdra (who commits adultery with an Âryan) in a straw-fire.

53. Now they quote also (the following verses):

PRASNA II, ADHYÂYA 2, KANDIKÂ 4.

1. 'Anybody but a Brâhma*n*a shall suffer corporal punishment for adultery.'

2. 'The wives (of men) of all castes must be guarded more carefully than wealth.'

3. 'But corporal punishment (shall) not (be inflicted) for (adultery with) the wives of minstrels and with those who appear on the stage. For (the husbands) carry them (to other men), or, lying concealed (at home), permit them to hold culpable intercourse.'

4. 'Women (possess) an unrivalled means of purification; they never become (entirely) foul. For month by month their temporary uncleanness removes their sins.'

5. 'Soma gave them cleanliness, the Gandharva their melodious voice, and Fire purity of all (limbs); therefore women are free from stains.'

---

52. Vasish*th*a XXI, 1, 5.

4. 1. Âpastamba II, 10, 26, 20; 10, 27, 11. Govinda thinks that non-Brâhmanical offenders should be burned, in accordance with Vasish*th*a XXI, 2–3. But mutilation may also be intended. Sa*m*graha*n*a, 'adultery,' probably includes all those acts mentioned Manu VIII, 354–358.

2. Manu VIII, 359.

3. Manu VIII, 362. I read conjecturally, 'sa*m*sar*g*ayanti te hyetâ niguptâ*s* *k*âlayantyapi,' basing my emendations on Manu's text. The MSS. and Govinda have, sa*m*sar*g*ayanti tâ hyetân niguptâ*ms* *k*âlayanty api, which gives no good sense. Govinda explains *k*âra*n*a-dârâ*h*, 'the wives of minstrels,' by devadâsya*h*, 'temple-slaves.'

4. Vasish*th*a XXVIII, 4. 5. Vasish*th*a XXVIII, 6.

6. 'Let him abandon a barren (wife) in the tenth year, one who bears daughters (only) in the twelfth, one whose children (all) die in the fifteenth, but her who is quarrelsome without delay.'

7. A widow shall avoid during a year (the use of) honey, meat, spirituous liquor, and salt, and sleep on the ground.

8. Maudgalya (declares that she shall do so) during six months.

9. After (the expiration of) that (time) she may, with the permission of her Gurus, bear a son to her brother-in-law, in case she has no son.

10. Now they quote also (the following verse): 'One whose appointment can have no result, (viz.) a barren woman, one who has borne sons, one who is past child-bearing, one whose children are (all) dead, and one who is unwilling must not be appointed.'

11. The sister of a maternal uncle and of the father, a sister, a sister's daughter, a daughter-in-law, a maternal uncle's wife, and the wife of a

6. Manu IX, 81.

7-8. Vasish*th*a XVII, 55. The word madya, 'spirituous liquor,' occurs in M. and the I. O. copy of the commentary. The MSS. from the Dekhan and Gu*g*arât, including K., read ma*gg*ana or ma*dd*âna, the compound letter being very indistinct.

9. Vasish*th*a XVII, 56, where the term 'Gurus' is fully explained.

10. Vasish*th*a XVII, 57-59. M. and the two copies of the commentary read pi*s*â*k*otpannaputrâ *k*a instead of vasâ *k*otpannaputrâ *k*a, 'a barren woman and one who has borne sons.' I follow the Dekhan and Gu*g*arât MSS., which undoubtedly give the genuine reading. Perhaps the term ava*s*âm, Vasish*th*a XVII, 57, should be corrected to va*s*âm.

11-12. These two Sûtras are additions to II, 1, 2, 13. See also Nârada XII, 73-74; Vasish*th*a XXI, 16.

friend are females who must never be approached (agamyâ).

12. For intercourse with females who must not be approached (agamyâ), a K*rikkh*ra and an Atik*rikkh*ra (and) a *K*ândrâya*n*a are the penances prescribed for all.

13. Thereby (the rule regarding) intercourse with a female of the *Kand*âla caste has been declared.

14. Now they quote also (the following verses): 'A Brâhma*n*a who unintentionally approaches a female of the *Kand*âla caste, eats (food given by a *Kand*âla) or receives (presents from him), becomes an outcast; but (if he does it) intentionally, he becomes equal (to a *Kand*âla).

15. 'He who approaches his father's, his teacher's, or a king's wife, is guilty of the crime of violating a Guru's bed; the penance ordained for him has been declared above.'

16. (A Brâhma*n*a) who is unable (to subsist) by teaching, sacrificing for others, or the acceptance of gifts, shall maintain himself by following the duties of Kshatriyas, because that is the next following (caste).

---

13. Vasish*th*a XXIII, 41; Vish*n*u LIII, 5-6.

14. Manu XI, 176.

15. Govinda thinks that the penance intended is that mentioned in Sûtra 12. Probably a severer one is meant. The verse is interesting, as it clearly is a quotation from some metrical work on law, not merely of traditional detached *s*lokas.

16. Vasish*th*a II, 22. The Sûtra 'adhyâpanayâganapratigrahair a*s*akta*h* kshatradharme*n*a *g*îvet pratyanantaratvât' occurs in the two copies of the commentary only. The I.O. copy of the commentary has, however, before it the following words: [dharmya] svâdhyâyapravakane evety adhikânâ*m* [kâra*m*] dar*s*ayati pratig*r*ihîtâ tâd*r*ik pratigrahîtâra*m* g*r*idhnuvanti [târa *r*idhnu°] *r*itvigyagamânâ yâginau

17. Gautama (declares that one shall) not (act thus). For the duties of Kshatriyas are too cruel for a Brâhma*n*a.

18. Now they quote also (the following verse): 'Out of regard for the sacred law a Brâhma*n*a and a Vai*s*ya may take up arms for (the protection of) cows or Brâhma*n*as, or when a confusion of the castes (threatens to take place).

19. (Or) the livelihood of a Vai*s*ya should be adopted, because that is the one following (next).

20. (If he lives by agriculture) he shall plough before breakfast,

21. With two bulls whose noses have not been pierced, not striking them with the goad, (but) frequently coaxing them.

22. The (sacred domestic) fire (shall be kindled) at the wedding; the religious ceremonies up to the Agnyâdheya (shall be) performed in that.

[°*g*ane] tada*s*aktau kshatradharmau. M. reads, dharmanasvâdhyâyapravaka*n*a [ne] ityadhikâra*m* dar*s*ayati pratigrahîtâd*ri*k pratigrahîtâra *ri*dhnuvanti *ri*tvigyagamâna yâ*g*anau tada*s*aktau svâdhyâyadhyâ [°yâdhyâ] panayag*ñ*ayâ*g*anapratigrahair a*s*aktama [ta*h*] kshatradharmme*n*a *g*îvet. The Dekhan and Gu*g*arât MSS. read, dhârmye svâdhyâyapravakane ityadhikâra*m* dar*s*ayati । pratigrahe dâtâ pratigrahîtâ[ra] *ri*dhnuvanti । *ri*tvigyagamânâ yâ*g*ane । tada*s*aktau kshatradharme*n*a *g*îvayet, or have corruptions of this passage. I cannot come to any other conclusion than that the passage which precedes the words translated by me are a very ancient interpolation, caused by the embodiment of a portion of an old Bhâshya with the text, and that all our MSS., however much they may differ, go back to one codex archetypus.

17. Gautama Introduction, p. lii.

18. Gautama VII, 25. 19. Vasish*th*a II, 24.

20–21. Vasish*th*a II, 32.

22. Vasish*th*a VIII, 3. The religious ceremonies to be performed with the sacred domestic fire, which, according to Baudhâyana,

23. Now, beginning with the Agnyâdheya, follow these (rites in an) uninterrupted (series), as, for instance, the Agnyâdheya, the Agnihotra, the new and full moon sacrifices, the Âgraya*n*a at the winter and summer solstices, the animal sacrifice, the *K*âturmâsyas at the beginning of each season, the Sha*ddh*ot*ri* in spring, the Agnish*t*oma. Thus the attainment of bliss (is secured).

24. Now they quote also (the following verse): 'Neither he who is accustomed to sleep in the day-time, nor he who eats the food of anybody, nor he who falls from a height to which he has climbed, can reach heaven as he desires.'

25. Let him avoid meanness, hard-heartedness, and crookedness.

26. Now they quote also with reference to this (subject the following) verse in the dialogue between the daughters of U*s*anas and V*ri*shaparvan: 'Thou, forsooth, art the daughter of one who praises (others), who begs and accepts (gifts); but I am the child of one who is praised, who gives gifts and does not accept them.'

---

should be kindled at the wedding, not on the division of the paternal estate (Gautama V, 7), are the so-called G*ri*hya ceremonies (Gautama V, 8–9).

23. Vasish*th*a XI, 46. The sacrifices enumerated in this Sûtra require three fires, and belong to the *s*rauta or vaitânika ya*gñ*as. The Sha*ddh*ot*ri* mentioned here seems to be the animal sacrifice mentioned in the commentary on Kâtyâyana *S*rauta-sûtra VI, 1, 36.

24. An ârû*dh*apatita, 'he who falls from a height to which he has climbed,' is, according to Govinda, an ascetic who slides back into civil life.

25. Vasish*th*a VI, 40; X, 30. Govinda explains *s*â*th*yam, 'hard-heartedness,' by *s*aktau satyâm api paropakârâkara*n*am, 'not doing a kindness to others though one is able to do so.'

26. The dialogue mentioned is that between *S*armish*th*â and

PRASNA II, ADHYÂYA 3, KANDIKÂ 5.

1. Bathing is suitable for (the practice of) austerity.

2. The libation to the manes (is offered) after the gods have been satisfied (with water).

3. They pour out water which gives strength, from one Tîrtha after the other.

4. Now they quote also (the following verses): 'With flowing, unconfined water twice-born men of the three castes shall satisfy the gods, *Ri*shis, and manes, when they have risen in the morning.'

5. 'They shall not offer (libations of water) confined (in tanks and wells). (If they do it), he who made the embankment, will obtain a share (of the merit of their devotion).'

6. 'Therefore let him avoid embankments (around tanks) and wells made by others.'

7. Now they quote also (the following verse): 'Or, in times of distress—not as a rule—he may bathe in (water) confined (in tanks), after taking out three lumps (of earth); from a well (let him take three) lumps of clay and three jars of water.'

Devayânî, which occurs Mahâbhârata I, 78. The verse quoted is the tenth of that Adhyâya, and agrees with ours, except that sutâham is read for athâham in the beginning of the second half verse.

5. 3. As to the Tîrthas, see above, I, 5, 8, 15–16.

5. Manu IV, 201. 6. Vish*n*u LXIV, 1.

7. Vish*n*u LXIV, 2. I read the verse as follows: uddh*ri*tya vâpi trîn pi*nd*ân kuryâd âpatsu no sadâ । niruddhâsu *k*a m*ri*tpi*nd*ân kûpât trîn abgha*t*â*m*statheti ॥ The Dekhan MSS. read at the end of the second half verse, kûpâ*m*strînava*t*â*m*stathâ; M. has kupâtrînabapa*t*ânstathâ; while C. I. gives kûpât trîn gha*t*â*m*stathâ. Nandapa*nd*ita on Vish*n*u, loc. cit., seems to have had the latter

8. If he has accepted presents from one who is able to give presents to many, or from one whose presents ought not to be accepted, or if he has sacrificed for one for whom he ought not to have sacrificed, or if he has eaten food (given by a person) whose food must not be eaten, he shall mutter the Taratsamandîya.

9. Now they quote also (the following verse): 'Those who improperly associate with (an outcast) teacher, those who improperly associate with (outcast) pupils, and those who improperly associate (with outcasts) by (accepting their) food or by (reciting) Mantras (for them), enter into deep darkness.'

10. Now (follow) the duties of a Snâtaka.

11. After offering at the morning and at the evening (meals) with (a portion of) the food which he may have, the Vaisvadeva and the Bali-offerings, he shall honour, according to his ability, Brâhma*n*as, Kshatriyas, Vai*s*yas, and *S*ûdras (who may come to his house as) guests.

12. If he cannot (afford to give food) to many, let him give (something) to one who possesses good qualities,

13. Or to him who has come first.

14. If a *S*ûdra (has come as) a guest, he shall order him (to do some) work, (and feed him afterwards);

---

reading, and to have changed it to 'kûpât tu trîn gha*t*â*m*stathâ,' in order to save the metre. The sense remains the same.

8. Manu XI, 254. The text is found Rig-veda IX, 58. Govinda explains bahupratigrâhya, 'one who is able to give presents to many,' by bahubh*ri*tyabhara*n*akshama, 'one who is able to support many servants.'

10. Vasish*th*a XII, 1. 11. Vasish*th*a XI, 3–9.

14. Âpastamba II, 2, 4, 19.

15. Or (if he cannot spare much), he may give a first portion (agrya) to a *S*rotriya.

16. It is prescribed that the division (of the food) shall be made without detriment to (the interests of) those who daily receive a portion.

17. But he shall never eat without having given away (some small portion of the food).

18. Now they quote also two verses which have been proclaimed by (the goddess of) food: 'Him who, without giving me to the gods, the manes, his servants, his guests and friends, consumes what has been prepared and (thus), in his exceeding folly, swallows poison, I consume, and I am his death. But for him who, offering the Agnihotra, performing the Vaisvadeva, and honouring guests, eats, full of contentment, purity, and faith, what remains after feeding those whom he must support, I become ambrosia, and he (really) enjoys me.'

19. Presents of money must be given, according to one's ability, to good Brâhma*n*as, *S*rotriyas, and Vedapâragas, when they beg outside the Vedi, for the sake of Gurus, in order to defray (the expenses of) their marriages, or of medicine, or when they are distressed for a livelihood, or desirous to offer a sacrifice, or engaged in studying, or on a journey, or have performed a Visva*g*it sacrifice.

---

15. Vasish*th*a XI, 5. Govinda quotes a verse, according to which an agrya, 'first portion,' is equal to sixteen mouthfuls, each of the size of a peahen's egg.

16. Âpastamba II, 4, 9, 10–11. 'Those who daily receive a portion' (nityabhâktika), i.e. sons, wives, and so forth.—Govinda. But see also Âpastamba, loc. cit.

19. Gautama V, 20–21, and notes. 'A good Brâhma*n*a, i.e. one who follows the rule of conduct.'—Govinda.

20. Cooked food (must be given) to other (beggars).

21. Let him eat (seated) in a pure, enclosed place, after having well washed his hands and feet and after having sipped water, respectfully receiving the food which is brought to him, keeping himself free from lust, anger, hatred, greed, and perplexity, (conveying the food into his mouth) with all his fingers and making no noise (during mastication).

Prasna II, Adhyâya 3, Kandikâ 6.

1. Let him not put back into the dish a remnant of food.

2. If he eats (food), containing meat, fish, or sesamum, he shall (afterwards) wash and touch fire,

3. And bathe after sunset.

4. Let him avoid a seat, clogs, sticks for cleaning the teeth, and other (implements) made of Palâsa wood.

---

20. Gautama V, 22.

21. Vasishtha XII, 19–20; Vishnu LXVIII, 46. 'This is the rule for him who makes an offering to Âtman (i. e. performs the Prânâgnihotra at his meal).'—Govinda. See also below, II, 7, 12.

6. 1. 'I. e. he shall take up as much food only as he can swallow at one mouthful.'—Govinda.

2. The Dekhan and Gugarât MSS., including K., add madhu, 'honey,' after sesamum.

3. This and the following six Sûtras are left out in M. and the two copies of the commentary. If they have, nevertheless, been received into the text, the reason is that similar rules occur in all Dharmasûtras, and that Sûtra 3 begins with astamite, while astamaye occurs in Sûtra 10. It seems therefore probable that the writer of the MS. from which M. and Govinda's copies are derived, skipped over a line by mistake.

4–7. Vasishtha XII, 34–38.

5. Let him not eat (food placed) in his lap,

6. Nor on a chair.

7. He shall carry a staff, made of bamboo, and golden earrings.

8. Let him not rub one foot with the other while bathing, nor place the one on the other while standing,

9. Let him not wear a visible garland.

10. Let him not look at the sun when he rises or sets.

11. Let him not announce (the appearance of a rainbow) to another (man, saying), 'There is Indra's bow.'

12. If he points it out, he shall call it 'the jewelled bow.'

13. Let him not pass between the prakîlaka and the beam at the town gate,

14. Nor let him pass between the two posts of a swing.

15. Let him not step over a rope to which a calf is tied.

16. Let him not step on ashes, bones, hair, chaff, potsherds, nor on a bathing-place (moist with) water.

---

8. Vish*n*u LXXI, 40. 9. Vasish*th*a XII, 39.

10. Vasish*th*a XII, 10.

11–12. Vasish*th*a XII, 32–33.

13. Govinda explains prakîlaka by 'a piece of wood fastened at the town gate.' Etymologically it would mean 'a strong bolt.' Possibly the rule may be equivalent to Âpastamba I, 11, 31, 23, and mean that a Snâtaka is not to creep through the small door which is found in all Indian town gates, and left open after the gates have been shut.

14. Âpastamba I, 11, 31, 16. 15. Vasish*th*a XII, 9.

16. Gautama IX, 15; Manu IV, 132.

17. Let him not announce it to another (man if) a cow suckles (her calf).

18. Let him not say of (a cow which is) not a milch-cow, 'She is not a milch-cow.'

19. If he speaks (of such a one), let him say, 'It is one which will become a milch-cow.'

20. Let him not make empty, ill-sounding, or harsh speeches.

21. Let him not go alone on a journey,

22. Nor with outcasts, nor with a woman, nor with a *S*ûdra.

23. Let him not set out (on a journey) towards evening.

24. Let him not bathe (entirely) naked.

25. Let him not bathe at night.

26. Let him not cross a river swimming.

27. Let him not look down into a well.

28. Let him not look down into a pit.

29. Let him not sit down there, where another person may order him to rise.

30. Way must be made for a Brâhma*n*a, a cow, a king, a blind man, an aged man, one who is suffering under a burden, a pregnant woman, and a weak man.

31. A righteous man shall seek to dwell in a village where fuel, water, fodder, sacred fuel, Ku*s*a grass, and garlands are plentiful, access to which is

---

17. Vish*n*u LXXI, 62. 18–19. Gautama IX, 19.

20. Manu IV, 177; Vish*n*u LXXI, 57, 72, 74.

21–23. Manu IV, 140. 24. Gautama IX, 61.

26. Vasish*th*a XII, 45.

29. E. g. in the palace of a king, whence the attendants may drive him.

30. Vasish*th*a XIII, 58. 31. Gautama IX, 65.

R 2

easy, where many rich people dwell, which abounds in industrious people, where Âryans form the majority, and which is not easily entered by robbers.

32. 'A Brâhma*n*a who, having wedded a wife of the *S*ûdra caste and dwells during twelve years in a village where water (is obtainable) from wells only, becomes equal to a *S*ûdra.'

33. (If you say that) he who lives in a town and whose body is covered with the dust, (raised) by others, and whose eyes and mouth are filled with it, will obtain salvation, if he restrains himself, (I declare that) that is impossible.

34. 'The dust raised by carriages, horses, elephants, and cows, and (that which comes) from grain is pure, blamed is (that raised) by a broom, goats, sheep, donkeys, and garments.'

35. Let him honour those who are worthy of honour.

36. 'A *Ri*shi, a learned man, a king, a bridegroom, a maternal uncle, a father-in-law, and an officiating priest are mentioned in the Sm*ri*ti as worthy of the honey-mixture at certain times and occasions.'

37. 'A *Ri*shi, a learned man, and a king must be

---

33. Âpastamba I, 11, 32, 21.

36. Vasish*th*a XI, 1–2. A *Ri*shi is, according to Govinda, a man who knows not only the text of the Mantras, but also their sense. But Baudhâyana, G*ri*hya-sûtra I, 11, 4, says that a man who knows, besides the *S*âkhâ and its Aṅgas, the Kalpa also, is called *Ri*shikalpa, i. e. one almost a *Ri*shi. See also Âpastamba I, 2, 5, 5. A learned man (vidvas) is probably a student who has finished not only his vow, but learned the Veda, a so-called vidyâsnâtaka, Âpastamba I, 11, 30, 3. Regarding the arghya or madhuparka, the honey-mixture, see Âpastamba II, 4, 8, 7–9.

37. Gautama V, 27–30. I read kriyârambhe varartvigau. The

honoured whenever they come, a bridegroom and a priest at the beginning of the religious rites, a maternal uncle and a father-in-law when a year has elapsed since their last visit.'

38. 'Let him raise his right arm on (entering) the place where the sacred fire is kept, in the midst of a herd of cows, in the presence of Brâhma*n*as, at the daily recitation of the Veda, and at dinner.'

39. 'An upper garment must be worn on the following five occasions: during the daily study, during the evacuation (of excrements), when one bestows gifts, at dinner, and while one sips water.'

40. 'While one offers oblations in the fire, while one dines, bestows gifts, offers (food to deities or Gurus), and accepts presents, (the right hand) must be placed between the knees.'

41. 'The revealed texts declare, that the creatures depend on food, food is life; therefore gifts of food must be made. Food is the most excellent of sacrificial viands.'

42. 'Sin is removed by burnt offerings, burnt oblations are surpassed by (gifts of) food, and gifts of food by kind speeches. That (is declared) to us in the revealed texts.'

Pra*s*na II, Adhyâya 4, Ka*nd*ikâ 7.

1. Now, therefore, we will declare the rule for (performing) the twilight devotions.

---

meaning is that a bridegroom is to receive the honey-mixture when he comes to his father-in-law's house for his wedding, and an officiating priest when he comes to perform a sacrifice.

38. Vish*n*u LXXI, 60. Govinda adds that the act is performed as a salutation.

41. See e.g. Taittirîya Âra*n*yaka VIII, 2.

2. Going to a (sacred) bathing-place, he shall bathe, in case he is impure; in case he is pure, he may, optionally, omit the bath. (But in either case) he shall wash his feet and hands. Sipping water and sprinkling himself, while he recites the (*Ri*k-verses) containing the word Surabhi, the Ablingas, those addressed to Varu*n*a, the Hira*n*yavar*n*as, the Pâvamânîs, the (sacred syllables called) Vyâh*ri*tis, and other purificatory (texts), he becomes pure (and fit to perform the twilight devotions).

3. Now they quote also (the following verse): 'Submersion in water (and) bathing are prescribed for all the (four) castes. But sprinkling (water over the body), while Mantras (are being recited), is the particular (duty) of the twice-born.'

4. He who sprinkles himself (with water) at the beginning of any sacred rite,—before the time of the twilight devotions,—while reciting that same collection of purificatory (texts), becomes pure.

5. Now they quote also (the following rules): Seated, with his face to the west, on Darbha grass and holding Darbha blades in his (right) hand, which

---

7. 2. 'A sacred bathing-place, i. e. a river or pond outside the village.'—Govinda. The same author adds that the hands must be washed as far as the wrist, that while sipping water the worshipper is to repeat in the evening, Taittirîya Âra*n*yaka X, 31, and in the morning X, 32, and that if he bathes, Taittirîya Âra*n*yaka X, 1, 12, and other texts must be recited. The *Ri*k containing the word Surabhi is found Taittirîya Sa*m*hitâ I, 5, 11, 4, 7; the three Ablingas, Taittirîya Âra*n*yaka X, 1, 11; the four verses addressed to Varu*n*a, Taittirîya Sa*m*hitâ III, 4, 11, 4, and Taittirîya Âra*n*yaka II, 4, 4. By the term Pâvamânîs the Pavamânânuvâka, Taittirîya Brâhma*n*a I, 4, 8, is meant.

5. The injunction to turn the face to the west refers to the evening prayer; see also below, Sûtra 10.

is filled with water, he shall repeat the Sâvitrî one thousand times;

6. Or (he may recite the verse) one hundred times, suppressing his breath;

7. Or mentally ten times, adding the syllable Om at the beginning and at the end and the seven Vyâh*ri*tis.

8. And if he is tired by three suppressions of his breath (performed) with (the recitation of) the (Anuvâka called) Brahmah*ri*daya (the heart of Brahman, then let him repeat the Sâvitrî).

9. In the evening he worships (the sun) with the two (verses) addressed to Varu*n*a, 'Hear this my call, O Varu*n*a,' and 'Therefore I go to thee.'

10. The same (rules apply to the twilight devotion) in the morning, (but the worshipper) shall face the east and stand upright.

11. In the day-time he worships (the sun) with the two (verses) addressed to Mitra, 'The glory of Mitra, who supports men,' and 'Mitra causes men to join.'

12. Let him begin (the twilight devotion) in the

---

6. Govinda states that prâ*n*âyâma*s*a*h*, 'suppressing his breath,' has in this Sûtra no technical meaning.

7. Govinda says that the order to be observed in this case is as follows: First the syllable Om is to be recited, next the seven Vyâh*ri*tis, beginning with Bhû*h* and ending with Satyam, then the Sâvitrî, and finally again the syllable Om.

8. The Brahmah*ri*daya is Taittirîya Âra*n*yaka X, 28. This Anuvâka may be repeated three times for each Prâ*n*âyâma (see Vasish*th*a XXV, 13), or altogether nine times, and, if the worshipper is then tired, he may go on repeating the Sâvitrî without suppressing his breath.

9. Taittirîya Sa*m*hitâ II, 1, 11, 6. 10. Gautama II, 11.

11. Taittirîya Sa*m*hitâ III, 4, 11, 5.

12. Very early, i.e. when the stars are still visible; see also Gautama II, 11, and note.

morning very early, and finish it when the sun has risen.

13. Let him begin (the twilight devotion) in the evening, when (the sun) has set, (and finish it) very soon after (the appearance of the stars);

14. And the complete observance of the twilight devotions (produces as its reward) an uninterrupted succession of days and nights.

15. Now they quote with reference to this (subject) also the following two verses, which have been proclaimed by the Lord of created beings (Pragâpati): 'How can those twice-born men be called Brâhma*n*as who do not perform their twilight devotions, in the morning and in the evening at the proper time? At his pleasure a righteous king may appoint those Brâhma*n*as who neglect to daily perform the twilight devotions, both at morn and at eve, to do the work of *S*ûdras.'

16. If the time for the (twilight devotion) is allowed to pass in the evening, (the offender shall) fast during the night; and if it is neglected in the morning, he shall fast during the (next) day.

17. He obtains (thereby) the (same) reward as if he had remained standing and sitting (in the twilight).

18. Now they quote also (the following verses): 'Whatever sin (a man) may have committed with his organ, with his feet, with his arms, by thoughts or by speech, from (all) that he is freed by performing the twilight devotion in the evening.'

19. (The worshipper) becomes also connected

14. The day and night will not be cut off from his existence.

16. Vasish*th*a XX, 4–5.

18. Vasish*th*a XXVI, 2.

(thereby) with the (next) night, and Varu*n*a will not seize him.

20. In like manner he becomes free from the sin committed during the night by worshipping in the morning.

21. He is also connected with the (next) day, Mitra protects him and Âditya leads him up to heaven.

22. It is declared in the Veda, 'A Brâhma*n*a who in this same manner daily worships in the twilight, both at morn and at eve and, being sanctified by the Brahman, becoming one with the Brahman, and resplendent through the Brahman, follows the rules of the *S*âstra, gains the heaven of Brahman.'

PRA*S*NA II, ADHYÂYA 5, KA*ND*IKÂ 8.

1. Now, after washing his hands, he shall take his waterpot and a clod of earth, go to a (sacred) bathing-place and thrice clean his feet (with earth and water) and thrice his body.

2. Now some say, 'One must not enter a burial-ground, water, a temple, a cowpen, nor a place where Brâhma*n*as (sit) without having cleaned one's feet.'

---

20. Vasish*th*a XXVI, 3.

22. Brahman means here the Veda, the Sâvitrî, and the universal soul.

8. 1. Vish*n*u LXIV, 18. This Adhyâya contains the rules for bathing, and the subject is introduced, as Govinda observes, because in the preceding chapter II, 4, 7, 2, it has been said that an impure person must bathe before he performs the twilight devotions. Govinda also states that the word *k*a, 'and,' which stands after m*r*itpi*nd*am, 'a clod,' indicates that gomaya, 'cowdung,' must also be employed.

3. Then he enters the water, (reciting the following verse): 'I take refuge with gold-horned Varuna, give me at my request (O Varuna) a purifying bathing-place. May Indra, Varuna, Brihaspati, and Savitri again and again cleanse me from all sin which I have committed by eating the food of unholy men, by receiving gifts from the wicked, and from all evil which I have done by thoughts, speeches, or deeds.'

4. Then he takes up water in his joined hands, (saying), 'May the waters and the herbs be propitious to us.'

5. (Next) he pours (the water) out in that direction in which an enemy of his dwells, (saying), 'May they work woe to him who hates us and whom we hate.'

6. Then he sips water, and thrice makes the water eddy around himself turning from the left to the right (and saying), 'May that which is hurtful, which is impure, and which is inauspicious in the water be removed.'

7. After having submerged himself and having emerged from the water,

8. (Acts of) personal purification, washing the clothes by beating them on a stone and sipping

3. The verse is found Taittirîya Âranyaka X, 1, 12.

4. Taittirîya Âranyaka X, 1, 11.

5. Taittirîya Âranyaka, loc. cit. This and the following Sûtras, down to II, 6, 11, 15, are wanting in the Gugarât and Dekhan MSS. except in K.

6. Taittirîya Âranyaka X, 1, 13.

7. Govinda points out that the completion of this Sûtra is to be found in Sûtra 10. He adds that Baudhâyana inserted Sûtras 8–9 in the middle, because he was afraid to forget the rules contained in them.

8. Vishnu LXIV, 10, 11.

water are not (permitted to the worshipper) as long as he is in the water.

9. If (the water used for bathing) has been (taken from a) confined (place, such as a well), he worships it with the following (Mantra): 'Adoration to Agni, the lord of the waters; adoration to Indra; adoration to Varuna; adoration to Vârunî; adoration to the waters.'

10. After having ascended the bank and having sipped water, let him again sip water, though he has done so before, (and recite the following Mantras): 'May water purify the earth, may the purified earth purify me, may Brahmanaspati (and) Brahman purify, may the purified (earth) purify me. May water purify me, (taking away) all (the guilt which I incurred by eating) remnants of food, and forbidden food, (by committing) evil deeds, (by) receiving gifts from wicked men, Svâhâ!'

11. Making two Pavitras he rubs (his body) with water. Having rubbed himself, (reciting the) three (verses), 'Ye waters are,' &c., the four (verses), 'The golden-coloured, pure, purifying,' &c., (and) the Anuvâka, 'He who purifies,' &c., he performs, stepping back into the water, three Prânâyâmas with the Aghamarshana (hymn); then he ascends the bank, squeezes (the water) out of his dress, puts on garments which have been washed and dried in the air and which are not the worse for wear, sips water,

---

9. Taittirîya Âranyaka X, 1, 12.

10. Taittirîya Âranyaka X, 23. Govinda says that the rule is intended to indicate also that a person who recites sacred texts while sipping water, must do so only after having taken water once before. K. inserts before this Mantra, also Anuvâka 22.

11. Vishnu LXIV, 13–14; 18–19. The Vedic passages intended

sits down on Darbha grass, and, holding Darbha grass (in his hands), recites, facing the east, the Gâyatrî one thousand times, (or) one hundred times, or any number of times, or at least twelve times.

12. Then he worships the sun (reciting the following Mantras): 'Out of darkness we,' &c., 'Up that bright,' &c., 'That eye which is beneficial to the gods,' &c., (and) 'He who rose,' &c.

13. Now they quote also (the following maxim): 'The syllable Om, the Vyâhritis, and the Sâvitrî, these five Veda-offerings daily cleanse the Brâhmana from guilt.'

14. Being purified by the five Veda-offerings, he next satiates the gods (with water, saying),

Prasna II, Adhyâya 5, Kandikâ 9.

1. 'I satiate the deities of the eastern gate, Agni, Pragâpati, Soma, Rudra, Aditi, Brihaspati, together with the lunar mansions, with the planets, with the days and nights, and with the Muhûrtas; Om, I also satiate the Vasus;

are found Taitt. Samhitâ IV, 1, 5, 1; V, 6, 1, 1; and Taitt. Brâhmana I, 4, 8. Pavitras, i.e. blades of Kusa grass. 'He performs three Prânâyâmas with the Aghamarshana hymn (Rig-veda X, 190),' i.e. he thrice suppresses his breath (prânâyâma) and recites during each suppression the Aghamarshana three times, just as on other occasions the Gâyatrî is recited three times.

12. The first Mantra is found Taitt. Samhitâ IV, 1, 7, 4; the third and the fourth Taitt. Âranyaka IV, 42, 32–33.

14. Vishnu XLIV, 24. The ceremony is the so-called Tarpana, which is usually described in the Grihya-sûtras, e.g. Sânkhâyana IV, 9–10, and the quotations in Professor Oldenberg's notes, Indische Studien XV, 152.

9. 1. This and the next Kandikâs are given in full by K. only. M. gives the first and last words of both, the commentary the

2. 'Om, I satiate the deities of the southern gate, the Pitris, Yama, Bhaga, Savitri, Tvashtri, Vâyu, Indrâgnî, together with the lunar mansions, with the planets, with the days and nights, and with the Muhûrtas; Om, I also satiate the Rudras.

3. 'Om, I satiate the deities of the western gate, Mitra, Indra, the Mahâpitris, the Waters, all the gods, Brahman, Vishnu, together with the lunar mansions, with the planets, with the days and nights, and with the Muhûrtas; Om, I also satiate the Âdityas.

4. 'Om, I satiate the deities of the northern gate, the Vasus, Varuna, Aga-ekapâd, Ahibudhnya, Ushas, the two Asvins, Yama, together with . . . . . .

5. 'Om, I satiate all the gods; the Sâdhyas; Brahman; Pragâpati; the four-faced god; Hiranyagarbha; Svayambhû; the male attendants of Brahman; Parameshthin; the female attendants of Brahman; Agni; Vâyu; Varuna; Sûrya; the moon; the lunar mansions; Sadyogâta; Bhûh-purusha; Bhuvah-purusha; Suvah-purusha; Bhûh; Bhuvah; Suvah; Mahah; Ganah; Tapah; Satya.

6. 'Om, I satiate the god Bhava; Sarva; Îsâna; Pasupati; Rudra; Ugra; Bhîmadeva; Mahâdeva; the wife of the god Bhava; of the god Sarva; of the god Îsâna; of the god Pasupati; of the god Rudra; of the god Ugra; of Bhîmadeva; of Mahâdeva; the son of Bhava; of Sarva; of Îsâna; of Pasupati; of

beginning of 9 and the end of 10 only. The text of K. is probably interpolated, as it seems impossible that Baudhâyana could have mentioned his successors, Âpastamba and Satyâshâdha Hiranyakesin, whose names occur below, II, 5, 9, 14. On the other hand, it is not doubtful that the number of Mantras must nevertheless have been very large, as the numeration in M. shows that they filled two entire Kandikâs.

Rudra; of Ugra; of Bhîmadeva; of Mahâdeva; Om, I also satiate the Rudras; the attendants of Rudra.

7. 'Om, I satiate Vighna; Vinâyaka; Vîra; Sthûla; Varada; Hastimukha; Vakratu*nd*a; Ekadanta; Lambodara; the male attendants of Vighna; the female attendants of Vighna.

8. 'Om, I satiate Sanatkumâra; Skanda; Indra; Shash*th*î; Sha*n*mukha; Vi*s*âkha; Mahâsena; Subrahma*n*ya; the male attendants of Skanda; the female attendants of Skanda.

9. 'Om, I satiate Âditya; Soma; Aṅgâraka; Budha; B*ri*haspati; *S*ukra; *S*anai*sk*ara; Râhu; Ketu.

10. 'Om, I satiate Ke*s*ava; Nârâya*n*a; Mâdhava; Govinda; Vish*n*u; Madhusûdana; Trivikrama; Vâmana; *S*rîdhara; H*ri*shîke*s*a; Padmanâbha; Dâmodara; the goddess *S*rî; the goddess Sarasvatî; Push*t*i; Tush*t*i; Vish*n*u; Garutmat; the male attendants of Vish*n*u; the female attendants of Vish*n*u.

11. 'Om, I satiate Yama; Yamarâ*g*a; Dharma; Dharmarâ*g*a; Kâla; Nîla; M*ri*tyu; M*ri*tyuñ*g*aya; Vaivasvata; *K*itragupta; Audumbara; the male attendants of Vaivasvata; the female attendants of Vaivasvata.

12. 'Om, I satiate the gods of the earth; Kâ*s*yapa; Antariksha; Vidyâ; Dhanvantari; the male attendants of Dhanvantari; the female attendants of Dhanvantari.'

13. Next, passing the sacrificial thread round the neck, (he offers the following libations):

14. 'Om, I satiate the *Ri*shis; the great *Ri*shis; the best *Ri*shis; the Brahmarshis; the divine *Ri*shis; the royal *Ri*shis; the *S*rutarshis; the Seven *Ri*shis;

the *Ri*shis of the Kâ*nd*as (of the Ya*g*ur-veda); the *Ri*shikas; the wives of the *Ri*shis; the sons of the *Ri*shis; Ka*n*va Baudhâyana; Âpastamba, the author of the Sûtra; Satyâshâ*dh*a Hira*n*yake*s*in; Vâ*g*a*s*a-neyin Yâ*gñ*avalkya; Â*s*valâyana *S*aunaka; Vyâsa; the syllable Om; the Vyâh*ri*tis; the Sâvitrî; the Gâyatrî; the *Kh*andas; the *Ri*g-veda; the Ya*g*ur-veda; the Sâma-veda; the Atharvâṅgirasa; the Itihâsa and Purâ*n*a; all the Vedas; the servants of all gods; all beings.'

15. Then, passing the sacrificial string over the right shoulder, (he offers the following libations):

PRA*S*NA II, ADHÂYA 5, KA*ND*IKÂ 10.

1. 'Om, I satiate the fathers, Svadhâ, adoration! the grandfathers; the great-grandfathers; the mothers; the grandmothers; the great-grandmothers; the maternal grandfathers; the maternal grandmother; the mother's grandmother; the mother's great-grandmother.

2. 'Om, I satiate the teacher (â*k*ârya), Svadhâ, adoration! the wife of the teacher; the friends; the wives of the friends; the relatives; the wives of the relatives; the inmates of the house (amâtya); the wives of the inmates of the house; all; the wives of all.'

3. He pours the water out from the several Tîrthas (of the hand sacred to the several deities).

4. (He recites at the end of the rite the following

---

3. I. e. the water must be poured out in accordance with the rule given above.

4. Vâ*g*asaneyi Sa*m*hitâ II, 34. The translation of the Mantra follows Govinda's explanation.

Mantra): '(Ye waters), who bring food, ambrosia, clarified butter, milk, and barley-gruel, are food for the manes; satiate my ancestors! May you be satiated, may you be satiated!'

5. Let him not perform ceremonies in honour of the gods while his clothes are wet, or while he is dressed in one garment only;

6. Nor those connected with the manes. That (is the opinion) of some (teachers).

PRASNA II, ADHYÂYA 6, KANDIKÂ 11.

1. Now these five great sacrifices, which are also called the great sacrificial sessions, are the sacrifice to be offered to the gods, the sacrifice to be offered to the manes, the sacrifice to be offered to all beings, the sacrifice to be offered to men, (and) the sacrifice to be offered to Brahman,

2. Let him daily offer (something to the gods with the exclamation) Svâhâ, be it only a piece of fuel. Thereby he performs that sacrifice to the gods.

3. Let him daily offer (something to the manes with the exclamation) Svadhâ, be it only a vessel filled with water. Thereby he performs that sacrifice to the manes.

4. Let him daily pay reverence to (all beings) endowed with life. Thereby he performs that sacrifice to the beings.

---

11. 1. This and the next four Sûtras agree almost literally with *S*atapatha-brâhma*n*a XI, 5, 6, 1. See also Taitt. Âra*n*yaka II, 10; Âpastamba I, 4, 12, 15–13, 1.

4. Govinda says that the Mantra is to be 'bhûtebhyo nama*h*, adoration to all beings,' and adds that some consider the first three

5. Let him daily give food to Brâhma*n*as, be it only roots, fruit, or vegetables. Thereby he performs that sacrifice to men.

6. Let him daily recite the Veda privately, be it only the syllable Om or the Vyâh*ri*tis. Thereby he performs that sacrifice to be offered to Brahman.

7. 'The private recitation of the Veda is, indeed, the sacrifice to Brahman. At that sacrifice to Brahman speech, forsooth, (takes the place of) the *G*uhû, the internal organ (that of) the Upabh*ri*t, the eye (that of) the Dhruvâ, the understanding (that of) the Sruva, truth (that of) the final bath, heaven (is) the conclusion of the sacrifice. He who, knowing this, daily recites the Veda to himself, gains as much heavenly bliss as, and more than, he who gives away this whole earth that is filled with wealth, and imperishable (beatitude), and conquers death. Therefore the Veda should be recited in private. Thus speaks the Brâhma*n*a.'

8. Now they quote also (the following passage): 'If, well anointed, well fed, and lying on a comfortable couch, one recites (the portion of the Veda referring to) any sacrifice, one has offered it thereby.'

Mahâyag*ñ*as to be performed by the Vais*v*adeva and the Bali-offering, while others enjoin their separate performance.

7. *S*atapatha-brâhma*n*a XI, 5, 6, 2. See also Taitt. Âra*n*yaka II, 17. K. reads dh*ri*tir dhruvâ, 'the firm resolve (takes the place of) the Dhruvâ,' which is apparently a correction made according to the Âra*n*yaka. According to the commentary the text of the last portion of the quotation runs thus, 'yâvanta*m* ha vâ imâ*m* vittasya pûr*n*â*m* dadat svarga*m* loka*m* *g*ayati tâvanta*m* loka*m* *g*ayati bhûyâ*m*sa*m* *k*âkshayya*m* *k*âpa m*ri*tyum *g*ayati ya eva*m* vidvân,' &c. M. and K. do not give the whole passage. The published text of the *S*atapatha-brâhma*n*a slightly differs from Govinda's version.

8. *S*atapatha-brâhma*n*a XI, 5, 7, 3-4.

9. Some (teachers) declare (that there is a text) which teaches a fourfold division of these sacred duties. (But) as no (other meaning is) perceptible, (the text) 'Four paths,' &c., refers to sacrificial rites.

10. (Viz.) to Ish*t*is, animal sacrifices, Soma sacrifices, and Darvîhomas.

11. The following (*Rik*) declares that, 'Four paths, leading to the world of the gods, go severally from the earth to heaven. All ye gods, place us on that among them which will gain us undecaying prosperity.'

12. The student, the householder, the hermit in the woods, the ascetic (constitute the four orders).

13. A student (shall) obey his teacher until death.

---

9. I read the text as follows, 'tasya ha vâ etasya dharmasya *k*aturdhâ bhedam eka âhu*h*.' M. has bhedakam, the I. O. copy of the commentary bheda*s*aṅkâm, and K. tasya ha vâ etasya yag*ñ*asyâ*k*aturdhâ bhûtam eka âhu*h*. Below in the commentary on Sûtra 27, Govinda repeats the latter part of this Sûtra in the form which I have adopted. The discussion which begins here is the same as that which occurs Âpastamba II, 9, 23, 3–24, 15.

11. Taittirîya Sa*m*hitâ V, 7, 2, 3.

12. K. omits this Sûtra. After it M. and K. have the following passage: 'brahma*k*âri*n*o 'tyantam âtmânam upasa*m*g*ri*hyâ '*k*âryân bruvate vane *s*râmyantyeke [yâ*m*tyete, K.] savaneshvapa upasp*ri*-*s*anto vanyenânnenaikâgni*m* [nyenânnena naikâgni*m*, K.; vânye-naikâna*ñ*, M.] guhvâna*h* [guhvâs, M.] satyasyaike karmâ*n*i [karma*n*i, M.] anagnayo 'niketanâ*h* [tvâ*h* ka*m*, K.] kaupînâ*kkh*â-danâ varshâsv ekasthâ uddh*ri*taparipûtâbhir adbhi*h* kârya*m* [apa-kârya*m*, M.] kurvâ*n*â*h* [kurvâ*n*âs tatrodâharanti, K.] sannamusale vyaṅgâre niv*ri*tta*s*arâvasampâte bhikshanta*h* sarvata*h* parimoksham [parimeke, M.] apavidhya vaidikâni karmâ*n*y abhayata*h* pari*kkh*innâ madhyamam padam upa*s*lishyâmaha iti vadanto.' The commentary gives a few portions of this passage further on. Irrespective of minor corruptions, it gives no sense in the place where it stands, and it seems probable that we have to deal with a confused and badly corrupted text, which Govinda arranged either as seemed good to him, or on the authority of better MSS.

14. A hermit is he who regulates his conduct entirely according to the Institutes proclaimed by Vikhanas.

15. A Vaikhânasa (shall live) in the forest, subsisting on roots and fruit, practising austerities and bathing at morn, noon, and eve; he shall kindle a fire according to the *S*râma*n*aka (rule); he shall eat wild-growing (vegetables and grain) only; he shall worship gods, manes, Bhûtas, men, and *Ri*shis; he shall receive hospitably (men of) all (castes) except those (with whom intercourse is) forbidden; he may even use the flesh of animals killed by carnivorous beasts; he shall not step on ploughed (land); and he shall not enter a village; he shall wear his hair in braids, and dress in (garments made of) bark or skins; he shall not eat anything that has been hoarded for more than a year.

16. An ascetic shall leave his relatives and, not attended by any one nor procuring any property, depart (from his house performing the customary ceremony) according to the rule.

17. He shall go into the forest (and live there).

18. He shall shave his hair excepting the top-lock.

---

15. This passage, which Govinda gives as one Sûtra, agrees word for word with Gautama III, 26–35, except in the beginning, where Gautama omits 'bathing at morn, noon, and eve.' The MSS. all read bhaiksham, 'begged food,' instead of baishkam, 'the flesh of animals slain by carnivorous beasts.' But Govinda's explanation leaves no doubt as to the correctness of the latter reading. The Dekhan and Gugarât MSS., including K., read agrâmyabhog*î* ॥ agrâmyabhog*î*.

16. I adopt the readings of the Dekhan MSS., aparigraha*h* (for apratigraha*h*) and pravra*g*et (for parivra*g*et). The rule for the ceremony is given below, II, 10, 17.

18. This is Govinda's explanation of *s*ikhâmu*nd*a*h*, the reading of all MSS.

19. He shall wear a cloth to cover his nakedness.

20. He shall reside in one place during the rainy season.

21. He shall wear a dress dyed yellowish-red.

22. He shall go to beg when the pestle lies motionless, when the embers have been extinguished, and when the cleaning of the dishes has been finished.

23. With the three means of punishment, (viz.) words, thoughts, and acts, he shall not injure created beings.

24. He shall carry a cloth for straining water for the sake of purification.

25. He shall perform the necessary purifications with water which has been taken out (of a well or tank) and has been strained.

26. (Ascetics shall) say, 'Renouncing the works taught in the Veda, cut off from both (worlds), we attach ourselves to the central sphere (Brahman).'

27. But the venerable teacher (declares) that there is one order only, because the others do not beget offspring.

28. With reference to this matter they quote also (the following passage): 'There was, forsooth, an Âsura, Kapila by name, the son of Prahlâda.

---

20 and 22. These two Sûtras are omitted in K. and M., which give them in the passage following Sûtra 12, as well as in the Dekhan and Gugarât MSS.

24. See below, II, 10, 17, 11. Govinda explains pavitra, 'a cloth for straining water,' by 'a bunch of Kusa grass for removing insects from the road.'

25. According to Govinda such water is to be used for washing off the stains of urine &c., not for drinking.

26. This Sûtra is again omitted in the MSS. of the text. M. and K. give it in the passage following Sûtra 12.

27. Gautama III, 36.

Striving with the gods, he made these divisions. A wise man should not take heed of them.'

29. Because no (other meaning is) perceptible, (the text) 'Four paths,' &c., refers to sacrificial rites, (viz.) to Ish*t*is, animal sacrifices, Soma sacrifices, Darvîhomas.

30. With respect to this (question the following verse also) is quoted: 'That eternal greatness of the Brâhma*n*a is neither increased by works, nor diminished. The soul knows the nature of that (greatness); knowing that, he is not stained by evil deeds.'

31. If he says that, (let him reflect on the following verse): 'He who knows not the Veda, does not at death think of that great, all-perceiving soul, through which the sun, resplendent with brilliancy, gives warmth, and the father has a father through the son at his birth from the womb.'

32. (Moreover), 'Those who, being neither true Brâhma*n*as nor performers of Soma sacrifices, work not for that which is near, nor for that which is far, take hold of the word and with sinful (speech) ignorantly perform the rites.'

33. There are innumerable (passages in the Veda) which refer to the debts (to be paid by a Brâhma*n*a), such as, 'May I obtain, O Agni, immor-

30-31. Taitt. Brâhma*n*a III, 12, 9, 7.

32. Rig-veda X, 71, 9. My rendering of the difficult verse is merely tentative, and I have left out the word sirî*h*, for which I am as little able as other Sanskritists to offer a safe explanation. The general meaning of the verse, I think, has been rightly understood by Sâya*n*a and Govinda, who both say that it contains a reproach, addressed to those Brâhma*n*as who, contented with the letter of the Veda, do not master its meaning.

33-34. The commentary omits these two Sûtras, which, however, seem necessary for the completion of the discussion. The

tality through offspring;' 'A Brâhma*n*a on being born, (owes) a son to his ancestors,' &c.

34. 'Those dwell with us, who fulfil the following (duties), the study of the three Vedas, the studentship, the procreation of offspring, faith, austerity, sacrificing, and giving gifts; he who praises other (duties) becomes dust and perishes.'

PRA*S*NA II, ADHYÂYA 7, KA*N*D*I*KÂ 12.

1. Now we will explain the oblations (offered) to the vital air (prâ*n*a) by *S*âlînas (householders) and Yâyâvaras (vagrants), who sacrifice to the soul.

2. At the end of all the necessary (daily rites), let him sit down, facing the east, in a place that has been well cleaned and smeared with cowdung; next let him worship that prepared (food) which is being brought, (saying), 'Bhû*h*, Bhuva*h*, Sva*h*, Om,' (and then) remain silent.

3. (Next) he pours water round the food which has been placed (before him), turning his right hand towards it, and reciting the Mahâvyâh*ri*tis; (afterwards), continuing to hold (the dish) with his left hand, he first drinks water, (saying), 'Thou art a substratum for ambrosia,' and (finally) offers five oblations of food to the vital airs, (reciting the

---

second occurs also Âpastamba II, 9, 24, 8. Though Baudhâyana does not express himself as clearly as Âpastamba, he disapproves, as it would seem, like the latter, of the opinion of those who gave an undue preference to asceticism at the expense of married life, the order of the householders.

12. 1. The Prâ*n*âgnihotra is alluded to by Âpastamba II, 7, 17, 16. Regarding the terms *S*âlîna and Yâyâvara, see below, III, 1, 3–4.

3. The Mahâvyâh*ri*tis are the Mantras given Taittirîya Âra*n*yaka X, 2. The second Mantra is found Taittirîya Âra*n*yaka X, 32, and

texts), 'Full of reverence, I offer ambrosia to Prâ*n*a; mayest thou propitiously enter me, not in order to burn me. To Prâ*n*a, Svâhâ!' &c.

4. After offering the five oblations of food to the vital airs, let him finish his meal silently. Meditating in his heart on the lord of created beings, let him not emit speech while (eating).

5. If he emits speech, he shall mutter 'Bhû*h*, Bhuva*h*, Sva*h*, Om,' and afterwards continue to eat.

6. Now they quote also (the following rule): 'If he sees (bits of) skin, hair, nail-(parings), insects, or the dung of rats (in his food), he shall take out a lump, sprinkle that spot with water, scatter ashes on it, again sprinkle it with water, and use (the remainder of the food), after it has been declared fit (for use).'

7. Now they quote also (the following verse): 'He shall eat, seated with his face towards the east, silent, not despising his food, not scattering (fragments on the ground), and solely attend (to his dinner); and, after he has eaten, he shall touch fire.'

8. He shall not cut off with his teeth (pieces from) eatables (that must be swallowed) entire, (such as) cakes, bulbs, roots, fruit, and flesh.

9. (Let him) not (eat) to repletion.

10. After (dinner) he shall drink water, (reciting the text), 'Thou art a covering for ambrosia,' and stroke (the region of) the heart, (saying), 'Thou art the bond that connects the vital airs; (thou art)

---

the third ibid. X, 34. The translation of the Mantras follows Govinda, who somewhat differs from Sâya*n*a.

6. Vasish*th*a XIV, 23. 7. Vish*n*u LXVIII, 40–43.

9. Vish*n*u LXVIII, 47.

10. The first text is found Taittirîya Âra*n*yaka X, 35, and the second ibid. X, 37. I translate the first according to Govinda.

Rudra and Death; enter me; mayest thou grow through this food.'

11. After sipping water a second time, he allows (the drops from) the hand to flow on the big toe of his right foot (and recites the following text): 'May the male be pleased, he who is of the size of a thumb, who occupies (a space of the size of) a thumb, who is the lord of the whole world, masterful, and the enjoyer of the universe.'

12. Let him perform the subsequent consecration (anumantra*n*a) of the (food which has been) offered, with raised arms, (and let him recite) the five (texts beginning), 'With faith, worshipping Prâ*n*a, (I have) offered ambrosia; mayest thou increase Prâ*n*a through this food,'

13. (And let him address the soul with the last text of the Anuvâka), '(May) my soul (gain) immortality in the universal soul.'

14. And let him (meditate on his) soul (as) united with the imperishable (syllable Om).

15. He who sacrifices to the soul, surpasses him who offers all sacrifices.

PRA*S*NA II, ADHYÂYA 7, KA*N*DIKÂ 13.

1. Now they quote also (the following verse): 'As cotton and reeds, thrown into a fire, blaze up, even so all the guilt of him who sacrifices to the soul is consumed;'

---

11. Taittirîya Âra*n*yaka X, 38. The individual soul which resides in the heart is here identified with the universal soul; see also Kâ*th*aka Upanishad IV, 12.

12–13. Taittirîya Âra*n*yaka X, 36.

14. The syllable Om is Brahman, the universal soul.

2. (Moreover), 'He who eats merely (in order to satisfy his own hunger) reaps only guilt. In vain (the fool) takes food.'

3. Let him daily, both in the morning and in the evening, sacrifice in this manner;

4. Or (he may offer) water in the evening.

5. Now they quote also (the following verses): 'Let him first feed his guests, next the pregnant women, then the infants and the aged, thereafter the distressed and particularly the diseased. But he who eats first, without having given (food) to those (persons) according to the rule, does not know that he is being eaten. He does not eat, (but) he is eaten.'

6. 'Let him eat silently what remains, (after he has given their portions) to the manes, the gods, the servants, his parents, and his Gurus; that is declared to be the rule of the sacred law.'

7. Now they quote also (the following verses): 'Eight mouthfuls are the meal of an ascetic, sixteen that of a hermit in the woods, thirty-two that of a householder, and an unlimited (quantity) that of a student.'

8. 'An Agnihotrin, a draught-ox, and a student, those three can do their work only if they eat (much); without eating (much) they cannot do it.'

9. 'A householder, or a student who practises

---

13. 2. Rig-veda X, 117, 6, and Taittirîya Brâhma*n*a II, 8, 8, 3. The words have been transposed.

5. Vasish*th*a XI, 6–8; Manu III, 114–115. I write, with the Dekhan and Gu*g*arât MSS., na sa bhuṅkte, sa bhu*g*yate, instead of the senseless reading of M. and the commentary, na sa bhuṅkte na bhu*g*yate.

6. Vasish*th*a XI, 11. 7–8. Âpastamba II, 4, 9, 13.

9–10. Âpastamba II, 4, 9, 12, and note on II, 1, 1, 2.

austerity by fasting, becomes an Avakîrnin through the omission of the sacrifice to the vital airs;'

10. Except when he performs a penance. In the case of a penance that (fasting) is the rule.

11. Now they quote also (the following verses): 'He who never eats between the morning and the evening meals, (obtains the same reward as he who) constantly fasts.'

12. 'As in case one obtains no materials (for the sacrifice), one must mutter the sacred texts to be recited at the Agnihotra, offered in the three fires, even so one should mutter the texts to be recited at the Prânâgnihotra, when one is prevented from dining.'

13. 'He who acts thus, will become one with Brahman.' Thus spake Pragâpati (the lord of created beings).

PRASNA II, ADHYÂYA 8, KANDIKÂ 14.

1. The offering to the manes secures long life and heaven, is worthy of praise and a rite ensuring prosperity.

2. Persons who sanctify the company are, a Trimadhu, a Trinâkiketa, a Trisuparna, one who keeps five fires, and one who knows the six Aṅgas, one who performs the vow called Siras, one who knows the Gyeshthasâman, (and) a Snâtaka;

3. On failure of these, one who knows the (texts called) Rahasya.

14. 1. Âpastamba II, 7, 16, 1–2.

2. Âpastamba II, 7, 17, 22; Vasishtha III, 19. Govinda states that the Atharvavedins know the vow called Siras; see also Vasishtha XXVI, 12, and note.

3. Govinda says that persons acquainted with the Rahasyas or

4. The *Ri*k-verses, the Ya*g*us-formulas, and the Sâmans (give) lustre to a funeral offering. Therefore he may feed (on that occasion) even a Sapi*nd*a relation who (knows) those (texts).

5. Let him who feeds (Brâhma*n*as at a funeral sacrifice) cause them to hear successively the Rakshoghna Sâmans, the Ya*g*us-formulas (called) Svadhâvat, the *Ri*k-verses (called) Madhu, and the (texts called) Pavitras.

6. Having invited on the day before (the *S*râddha), or just in the morning, virtuous, pure (men), such as Trimadhus, who know the Vedâṅgas and the sacred texts, who are not related by marriage, nor members of the same family, nor connected through the Veda, at least three, (but always) an odd number, the (sacrificer) makes them sit down on prepared seats, covered with Darbha grass, facing the east or the north.

7. Then he offers to them water mixed with sesamum seed, adorns them with scents and garlands (and says), 'I wish to offer oblations in the fire.'

Âra*n*yakas are preferable to those mentioned in the preceding Sûtra, and thus the order must be reversed.

4. Âpastamba II, 7, 17, 5.

5. The texts on which the Rakshoghna Sâmans are based occur Sâma-veda I, 1, 1, 3, 4–6; the Svadhâvat Ya*g*us, Taitt. Brâhma*n*a I, 3, 10, 2; the Madhu *Rik*as, Rig-veda I, 90, 6; and the three Pavitras, Taitt. Brâhma*n*a I, 4, 8, 2.

6. Âpastamba II, 7, 14, 5. All the MSS., including those of the commentary, read yonigotramantrasambandhân instead of yonigotramantrâsambandhân. But the explanation of gotrasambandhâ*h* by asagotrâ*h* shows still a faint trace of the former existence of the reading which I have restored conjecturally and translated. Its correctness is proved by the parallel passage of Âpastamba.

7. Vish*n*u LXXIII, 12–13; Manu III, 208–211. The Agnimukha

When he has received permission (to do so), he heaps fuel on the sacred fire, scatters Kusa grass around it, performs (all the ceremonies) up to the end of the Agnimukha, and offers three burnt oblations of food only, (reciting the following texts): 'To Soma, accompanied by the manes, Svâhâ!' 'To Yama, accompanied by the Aṅgiras and by the manes, Svâhâ!' 'To Agni, who carries the offerings to the manes, who causes sacrifices to be well performed, Svâhâ!'

8. He shall make these three oblations with food only which has been sprinkled with the remainder of the (clarified butter).

9. Let him give a cake of food to the birds.

10. For it is declared in the Veda, 'The manes roam about in the shape of birds.'

11. Next he touches the (other food) with his hand and with the thumb,

12. (And recites the following texts): 'Fire sees thee, who art co-extensive with the earth, the *Ri*k-verses are thy greatness, lest the gift be in vain; the earth is the vessel for thee, the sky the cover; I offer thee in the mouth of Brahman, I offer thee in the Prâ*n*a and the Apâna of learned Brâhma*n*as; thou art imperishable, mayest thou never fail to (the manes of our) fathers yonder, in the other world.' 'Air hears thee, who art co-extensive with the middle sphere,

---

is a term denoting all the preliminaries which precede the Pradhânahoma of a ceremony. The Dekhan and Gugarât MSS. read âgyasya instead of annasyaiva.

8. Clarified butter is necessary for the rites included in the Agnimukha.

12. The Mantras are addressed to the food which is to be offered.

the Ya*g*us-formulas are thy greatness, lest the gift be in vain; the earth is the vessel for thee, the sky the cover; . . . . mayest thou never fail to the (manes of our) grandfathers yonder, in the other world.' 'The sun reveals thee, who art co-extensive with the sky, the Sâmans are thy greatness, lest the gift be in vain; . . . . mayest thou never fail to the (manes of our) great-grandfathers yonder, in the other world.'

PRA*S*NA II, ADHYÂYA 8, KA*N*D*I*KÂ 15.

1. Now indeed (that) happens (also which the following verses teach):

2. 'Let him sprinkle that food with the remainder of the burnt oblations. But what is given without (touching it with) the thumb does not gladden the manes.'

3. 'The malevolent Asuras seek an opportunity (to snatch away) that food intended for the manes, which is not supported with both hands.'

4. 'The Yâtudhânas and Pi*s*â*k*as, who receive no share, steal the food if sesamum grains are not scattered (on the seats of the guests), and the Asuras (take it) if (the host) is under the sway of anger.'

5. 'If a person dressed in reddish clothes mutters prayers, offers burnt oblations, or receives gifts, the sacrificial viands, offered at sacrifices to the gods or to the manes, do not reach the deities.'

---

15. 2. Manu III, 215. See also above, II, 8, 14, 10.

3. Vasish*th*a XI, 25.

4. Vish*n*u LXXIII, 11; Manu III, 229.

5. Govinda states that the rule is intended to teach that the sacrificer and the guests at a *S*râddha must be dressed in white,

6. 'If gifts are given or received without (touching them with) the thumb and, if one sips water standing, (the performer of the act) is not benefited thereby.'

7. At the beginning and at the end (of a *S*râddha) water must be given (to the guests).

8. In every case the muttering (of sacred texts) and the other (necessary acts must be performed) according to the rule.

9. The remaining (rules) have been prescribed (in the section) on the burnt oblations on Ash*t*akâ (days).

10. 'He shall feed two (Brâhma*n*as) at the offering to the gods and three at the offering to the manes, or a single man on either occasion. Even a very wealthy man shall not be anxious (to entertain) a large company.'

11. 'A large company destroys these five (advantages), the respectful treatment (of the invited guests, the propriety of) time and place, purity and (the selection of) virtuous Brâhma*n*a (guests); therefore he shall not invite (a large number).'

12. 'In front (feed) the fathers of the (sacrificer), to the left the grandfathers, to the right the great-grandfathers, and at the back those who pare off (portions) from the cakes.'

---

and that ascetics are not to be invited. But see Vasish*th*a XI, 17, 34.

7. Vish*n*u LXXIII, 12, 27, and above, II, 8, 14, 6.

9. Baudhâyana G*ri*hya-sûtra II, 17, 18.

10–11. Vasish*th*a XI, 27–28.

12. In the beginning of the verse I read with M. and the I. O. copy of the commentary urasta*h* pitaras tasya, and in the end with the Dekhan and Gugarât MSS. pi*nd*atakshakâ*h*. M. reads pi*nd*a-tarkyâ, and the copies of the commentary pi*nd*odakâ*h*. Both these

PRASNA II, ADHYÂYA 9, KANDIKÂ 16.

1. (Now follows some) advice for him who is desirous of offspring.

2. The two Asvins have declared, that fame is gained by the procreation (of sons);

3. 'Performing acts which tend to prolong life and austerities, intent on the performance of the private recitation and of sacrifices, and keeping his organs in subjection, let him carefully beget offspring in his own caste.'

4. 'From his birth a Brâhmana is loaded with three debts; these let him pay. A prudent man is free from doubts regarding the sacred law.'

5. 'If he worships the sages through the study of the Veda, Indra with Soma sacrifices, and the manes of his ancestors through (the procreation of) children, he will rejoice in heaven, free from debt.'

6. 'Through a son he conquers the worlds, through a grandson he obtains immortality, but through his son's grandson he ascends to the (highest) heaven.' (All that) has been declared in the Veda.

7. The Veda shows the existence of the three debts in the following (passage): 'A Brâhmana is born loaded with three debts; (he owes) the studentship to the sages, sacrifices to the gods, and a son to the manes;'

---

readings are clearly corrupt, and so is the var. lect. of the Grihyasamgraha, quoted in the Petersburg Dictionary, pindatarkukâh. Pindatakshakâh, 'the cutters or parers of the cakes,' is appropriate, because the remoter ancestors, who, as Govinda too declares, are meant by the term, obtain the fragments of the funeral cakes.

6. Vasishtha XVII, 5.

7. Vasishtha XI, 48. After this Sûtra the MSS. of the text

8. Through the procreation of a virtuous son he saves himself.

9. He who obtains a virtuous son saves from the fear of sin seven in the descending line and seven in the ascending line, (viz.) six others (in each), himself being the seventh.

10. Therefore he obtains a reward if he begets issue.

11. Therefore he should sedulously beget offspring,

---

insert the following corrupt passage: bandham ri*n*amoksham pragâyâs *k*âyattam pi*tri*nâm *k*ânukarsha*s*abda*s* *k*a pragâyâm dar*s*ayati । anutsanna*h* pragâvân bhavati । yâ vad ena*m* pragânug*ri*h*n*îte tâvad akshaya*m* loka*m* *g*ayati. The commentary does not notice it, and it seems to me that it needlessly interrupts the context.

11. M. and K. add to this Sûtra, âtmana*h* phalalâbhâya, 'in order to gain a reward for himself.' The same two MSS., further, insert the following Sûtras: tasmât putra*m* *k*otpâdyâtmânam evotpâdayatîti । vig*ñ*âyate *k*âtmâ vai putranâmâsîti । eva*m* dvitîya âtmâ *g*îvatâ drash*t*avyo ya*h* putram utpâdayati । sa tathâ bhavati । tasmân nâtmâ kva*k*id akshetra utsrash*t*avya*h* । âtmânam avamanyate hi । yathâtmânam utpâdayati sa tathâ bhavati । tasmâd âdita eva kshetram anvi*kkh*et sarvavar*n*e sa*m*sk*ri*tam upade*s*ena । tasmin dârasa*m*yoge pragâm utpâdayed ॥ 'Therefore (they say) that he who begets a son produces even his own self; and it is declared in the Veda, "Thou art self, called a son." Thus he who begets a son will see, during his lifetime, a second self. He becomes like him. Therefore one's own self must not be begotten on an unworthy female. For (he who does that) despises himself. He becomes even so, as he produces himself. Therefore (every man), each in his own caste, should first look out for a female who has been sanctified according to the injunction (of the sacred texts). Taking her to be his wedded wife, he shall beget a son.' It is possible that this passage really belongs to Baudhâyana, for it is written in the usual style of our Sûtra, and the last word of this passage as well as of Sûtra 11, as given in the Dekhan MSS., is utpâdayet. But it is not absolutely required by the context, and the commentary too omits it.

12. Through the application of medicines and sacred texts.

13. The advice to him (who is intent on the procreation of children) is given in agreement with the revealed texts.

14. For it produces results in the case of all the castes.

Prasna II, Adhyâya 10, Kandikâ 17.

1. Now we will explain the rule for entering the order of ascetics (samnyâsa).

2. Some (teachers say), 'He who has finished his studentship may become an ascetic immediately on (the completion of) that.'

3. But (according to others, asceticism is befitting) for Sâlînas and Yâyâvaras who are childless;

4. Or a widower (may become an ascetic).

5. (In general) they prescribe the profession of asceticism after the completion of the seventieth year and after the children have been firmly settled in (the performance of) their sacred duties.

6. Or a hermit in the woods (may become an

---

13. I read with M., whose reading is confirmed by the explanation given in the commentary, tasyopadesah srutisâmânyenopadisyate. The other MS. reads tasyopadesena, and in the text of the commentary the first word is left out.

17. 2. Gautama III, 1.

3. Regarding the two terms Sâlîna and Yâyâvara, see below, III, 1, 3–4.

4. Vidhura, translated, according to Govinda's explanation, by 'widower,' perhaps includes all persons who have been separated from their families.

6. Regarding the ceremonies to be performed by hermits in the wood, see above, II, 6, 11, 15, and below, III, 3.

ascetic) on finishing the (special) ceremonies (prescribed for him).

7. 'That eternal greatness of the Brâhma*n*a is neither increased nor diminished by works. The soul knows the nature of that (greatness). He who knows that, is not stained by evil deeds.'

8. 'It leads to the cessation of births.'

9. 'The eternal one leads (him) to glory.' The greatness (of asceticism is declared by these passages).

10. After having caused the hair of his head, his beard, the hair on his body, and his nails to be cut, he prepares

11. Sticks, a rope, a cloth for straining water, a water vessel, and an alms-bowl.

12. Taking these (implements, let him go) to the extremity of the village, or to the extremity of the boundary (of the village), or to the house where the sacred fires are kept, partake of a threefold (mixture of) clarified butter, milk, (and) sour milk, and (afterwards) fast;

13. Or (he may partake of) water.

14. (Saying), 'Om, Bhû*h*, I enter the Sâvitrî, tat savitur vare*n*yam; Om, Bhuva*h*, I enter the Sâvitrî, bhargo devasya dhîmahi; Om, I enter the Sâvitrî, dhiyo yo na*h* pra*k*odayât;' (he shall recite the Sâvitrî) foot by foot, half-verse by half-verse, (and finish by repeating) the whole or the parts (of the verse).

---

7. See above, II, 6, 11, 30. 11. Yâ*gñ*avalkya III, 58–60.

14. This part of the ceremony is called Sâvitrîpravesa, 'entering the Sâvitrî.' According to the Dharmasindhu, fol. 84 a, l. 8, the last Mantra is 'Om, Bhû*h*, Bhuva*h*, Sva*h*, I enter the Sâvitrî; we meditate on that adorable light of divine Savit*ri*, who may impel our thoughts.'

15. It is declared in the Veda, 'Entering order after order, (man) becomes (one with) Brahman.'

16. Now they quote also (the following verse): 'He who has passed from order to order, has offered burnt oblations and kept his organs in subjection, becomes afterwards, tired with (giving) alms and (making) offerings, an ascetic.'

17. Such an ascetic (becomes one with) the infinite (Brahman).

18. Before the sun sets, he heaps fuel on the Gârhapatya fire, brings the Anvâhâryapa*k*ana fire (to the spot), takes the flaming Âhavanîya fire out (of the Gârhapatya), melts butter on the Gârhapatya fire, cleanses it (with Ku*s*a grass), takes four times (portions of it) in the sacrificial spoon (called Sru*k*), and offers in the Âhavanîya fire on which sacred fuel has been heaped, (four times) a full oblation, (saying), 'Om, Svâhâ!'

19. It is declared in the Veda that this (offering is) the Brahmânvâdhâna (putting fuel on the sacred fires for the sake of the universal soul).

20. Now in the evening, after the Agnihotra has been offered, he scatters grass to the north of the Gârhapatya fire, places the sacrificial vessels in pairs, the upper part turned downwards, on it, strews Darbha grass to the south of the Âhavanîya fire on the seat destined for the Brahman priest, covers

16. Manu VI, 34.

18. Anvâhâryapa*k*ana is another name of the so-called Dakshi*n*âgni, in which the sacrificial viands are cooked. The cleansing of the butter (utpavana) is performed by taking hold of the ends of blades of Ku*s*a grass and dipping the bent middle part into the melted butter and then drawing it upwards. A full burnt oblation (pûr*n*âhuti) consists of a whole spoonful. As four spoonfuls are to be taken out, it follows that four oblations are to be offered.

it with the skin of a black antelope, and remains awake during that night.

21. A Brâhmana who, knowing this, dies after fasting during the night of Brahman and repositing within himself the sacred fires, conquers all guilt, even (that of) killing a Brâhmana.

22. Then he rises in the muhûrta sacred to Brahman, and offers the early Agnihotra just at the (appointed) time.

23. Next, after covering the (part of the altar called) Prishthyâ and bringing water, he prepares (an offering) to (Agni) Vaisvânara (which is cooked) in twelve potsherds. That (well-)known Ishti is the last (which he performs).

24. Afterwards he throws the sacrificial vessels, which are neither made of earth nor of stone, into the Âhavanîya fire,

25. (And) throwing the two Aranis into the Gârhapatya fire (with the words), 'May ye be of one mind with us,' he reposits the sacred fires in himself.

26. (Reciting the sacred text), 'O Fire, that body of thine, which is fit for the sacrifice,' he inhales the smell of (the smoke of) each fire thrice three times.

27. Then, standing within the sacrificial enclosure, (he says) thrice in a low voice and thrice aloud, 'Om, Bhûh, Bhuvah, Svah, I have entered the order of ascetics, I have entered the order of ascetics, I have entered the order of ascetics.'

---

21. The night during which the ascetic keeps watch near the fires is called 'the night of Brahman.'

25. The Aranis are the two pieces of wood used for producing fire by friction, Taittirîya Samhitâ I, 3, 7, 1–2.

28. It is declared in the Veda, 'The gods are trebly true.'

29. (Finally) he pours out as much water as will fill his joined hands, (saying), 'I promise not to injure any living being.'

30. Now they quote also (the following verse): 'An ascetic who roams about after having given a promise of safety to all living beings, is not threatened with danger by any creature.'

31. (Henceforth) he must restrain his speech.

32. He grasps his staff, (saying), '(Thou art my) friend, protect me.'

33. He takes the rope, (reciting the verse), 'The brilliant light,' &c.

34. He takes the cloth for straining water, (reciting the text), 'With which means of purification the gods,' &c.

35. He takes the waterpot, (reciting the verse), 'Through that light, by which the gods rose on high,' &c.

36. He takes the alms-bowl, (reciting the Vyâh*ri*tis).

37. Taking with him the staves, the rope, the

28. Taittirîya Âra*n*yaka II, 18, 6.

29. All gifts must be confirmed by a libation of water, which in other cases is poured into the hand of the recipient. The ceremony proves more clearly even than the numerous other passages of the Sm*ri*tis, in which ascetics are exhorted to abstain from injuring living beings, that the so-called ahi*m*sâ doctrine is not of Buddhistic, but of Brâhmanical origin.

30. Vasish*th*a X, 1–2. 31. Gautama III, 17.

33. Taittirîya Brâhma*n*a III, 7, 8, 1.

35. Taittirîya Sa*m*hitâ V, 7, 2, 2.

37. The Surabhimatî occurs Taittirîya Brâhma*n*a III, 9, 7, 5. For the other texts named, see above, II, 4, 7, 2. The Tarpa*n*a has been fully described above, II, 5, 9–10.

cloth for straining water, the waterpot, (and) the alms-bowl, he goes where water (is to be obtained), bathes, sips water, (and) washes himself, (reciting the verses called) Surabhimatî, Abliṅgâs, Vâru*n*îs, Hira*n*yavar*n*âs, and Pâvamânîs. Entering the water, he performs sixteen suppressions of the breath, (mentally repeating) the Aghamarsha*n*a hymn, ascends the bank, wrings out his dress, puts on another pure dress, sips water, takes the cloth for straining, (saying), 'Om, Bhû*h*, Bhuva*h*; Sva*h*,' and performs the Tarpa*n*a (with the following texts), 'Om, Bhû*h*, I satiate,' 'Om, Bhuva*h* —, Om, Sva*h* —, Om, Maha*h* —, Om, *G*ana*h* —, Om, Tapa*h* —, Om, Satyam —.'

38. He takes up as much water as his joined hands will hold for the manes, (and satiates them with it) exactly in the same manner as the gods, (saying), 'Om, Bhû*h* Svadhâ, Om, Bhuva*h* Svadhâ,' &c.

39. Then he worships the sun, (reciting) the two verses (which begin), 'Ud u tya*m* *k*itram,' &c.

40. (Saying), 'Om, this (syllable Om), forsooth, is Brahman; this (syllable) which sheds warmth is light; this which gives warmth is the Veda; this must be known as that which sheds warmth;' he thus satiates the soul (and afterwards) worships the soul (with these texts), 'The soul (is) Brahman, (is) light.'

---

38. 'In the same manner as the gods,' i. e. without passing the sacred string over the right shoulder.—Govinda.

40. The Gugarât and Dekhan MSS., including K., place after the first Om two additional Mantras, 'Brahman (is) Om; this universe (is) Om.' The object of the Mantras given in the Madras MSS. is to identify the Pra*n*ava with the Brahman, the sun, and the Veda.

41. Let him repeat the Sâvitrî one thousand times, or one hundred times, or an unlimited number of times.

42. (Saying), 'Bhûh, Bhuvah, Suvah,' he takes up the cloth for straining, (and) fetches water.

43. Let him not, (at any period) after that (moment), sip water which has not been drawn up (from a well and the like), which has not been strained, and which has not been completely cleansed.

44. Let him not wear any longer a white dress.

45. (He may carry) one staff or three staves.

Prasna II, Adhyâya 10, Kandikâ 18.

1. Now the following vows are (to be kept by an ascetic):

2. Abstention from injuring living beings, truthfulness, abstention from appropriating the property of others, continence, (and) liberality.

3. There are five minor vows, (viz.) abstention from anger, obedience towards the Guru, avoidance of rashness, cleanliness and purity in eating.

4. Now (follows the rule for) begging. Let him

---

43. Manu VI, 46. Aparipûtâbhih, 'which has not been completely cleansed,' probably refers to the so-called drishtyâ paripavana, 'carefully looking at it in order to see if any living being remains in it.'

18. 2. The five vows (vratas) named here are the principal ones. As to the vow of 'liberality' Govinda remarks that though the ascetic possesses no 'store' and no property in the ordinary sense of the word, still he can have books and give those away.

3. 'Avoidance of rashness,' i. e. committing any act which might destroy life.

4. 'When the Vaisvadeva offering has been finished,' i. e. when people have had their dinner; see also Vasishtha X, 7.

ask Brâhma*n*as, both those who have houses (*s*âlîna) and those who lead a wandering life (yâyâvara), for alms, when the Vai*s*vadeva offering has been finished.

5. Let him ask (for it), prefacing (his request with the word) Bhavat.

6. Let him stand begging no longer than the time required for milking a cow.

7. When he returns from begging, he lays (the alms) down in a pure place, washes his hands and feet, and announces (what he obtained) to the sun, (reciting the text), 'Ud u tya*m* *k*itram,' &c. He (also) announces it to Brahman (with the text), 'The first-born Brahman,' &c.

8. It is declared in the Veda, 'After the Brahmâdhâna the sacrificer himself (contains) the sacrificial fires. His respiration (prâ*n*a, represents) the Gârhapatya fire, the air that goes downwards (apâna, represents) the Anvâhâryapa*k*ana (or Dakshi*n*a) fire, the circulation in the body (vyâna, represents) the Âhavanîya fire, the cerebral circulation (udâna) and the abdominal circulation (samâna, represent) the Sabhya and Âvasathya fires. These five fires are abiding in the soul. He (therefore) offers (the oblations) in the soul alone.'

9. 'This sacrifice, offered in the soul, which is located in and based on the soul, leads the soul to happiness.'

10. Giving, compassionately, portions (of his food) to the living beings, and sprinkling the re-

7. The second text occurs repeatedly in the Taittirîya-veda, e.g. Taittirîya Âra*n*yaka X, 1, 10.

8. Regarding the Brahmâdhâna, see above, II, 10, 17, 19.

mainder with water, he shall eat it as if it were a medicine.

11. After he has eaten and sipped water, he mutters (the texts), 'Out of darkness we,' &c., (and), 'My speech resides in the mouth,' &c., and worships the sun with the (verse called) *G*yotishmatî.

12. Let him eat food, given without asking, regarding which nothing has been settled beforehand and which has reached him accidentally, so much only as is sufficient to sustain life.

13. Now they quote also (the following verses): 'Eight mouthfuls (make) the meal of an ascetic, sixteen (that) of a hermit in the woods, thirty-two (that) of a householder, an unlimited (quantity that) of a student.'

14. 'Alms (may) either (be obtained) from (men of) the three castes, or the food (given) by a single Brâhma*n*a (may be eaten); or (he may obtain food) from (men of) all castes, and not (eat) that given by a single Brâhma*n*a.'

15. Now they quote (the following special rules) for the case that the teachers explain (the doctrine) of the Upanishads: 'Diligently standing (in the day-time), keeping silence, sitting (at night) with crossed legs, bathing three times a day, and eating

---

11. The first text occurs frequently in the Taittirîya-veda, e.g. Taittirîya Sa*m*hitâ IV, 1, 7, 4; the second, Taittirîya Âra*n*yaka X, 72. The *G*yotishmatî is, according to Govinda, the first of the two Mantras quoted.

12. According to Govinda this verse gives the opinion of 'some' teachers, not the author's. Asa*m*k*l*iptam, 'regarding which nothing has been settled beforehand,' indicates, according to Govinda, that the ascetic must not even mentally determine what he is going to eat.

13. See above, II, 7, 13, 7.

at the fourth, sixth, or eighth (meal-time only), he shall subsist entirely on (rice) grains, oil-cake, food prepared from barley, sour milk, (and) milk.'

16. It is declared in the Veda, 'On that (occasion) he shall rigidly keep silence; pressing the teeth together he may converse, without opening his mouth, as much as is necessary with teachers deeply versed in the three Vedas (and) with ascetics possessing a great knowledge of the scriptures, not with women, nor when he would break (his vow).'

17. (Let him keep) only one of (the rules which enjoin) standing (in the day-time), rigid silence, and sitting (at night) with crossed legs; let him not keep all three together.

18. It is declared in the Veda, 'And he who has gone there may eat, in times of distress, a small quantity of the food prescribed by his vow after (having partaken of other dishes), provided he does not break (his vow).'

19. 'Eight (things) do not cause him who is intent on standing (in the day-time), keeping rigid silence, sitting (at night) with crossed legs, bathing three times a day, and (eating) at the fourth, sixth, or eighth meal-time only, to break his vow, (viz.) water, roots, clarified butter, milk, sacrificial food, the wish of a Brâhma*n*a, an order of his teacher, and medicine.'

20. Let him mutter the (Mantras which must be

18. 'The meaning is, that in times of distress, having partaken at his pleasure (of other food), he may afterwards eat of one (of the substances mentioned above, viz.) rice-grains and the rest.'—Govinda.

19. All the MSS. except M. have snâna, 'bathing,' instead of sthâna, 'standing (in the day-time),' though the reading is clearly wrong.

recited at the) Agnihotra, in the evening and in the morning,

21. After performing his evening devotions by (reciting the verses called) Vâruṇîs, and his morning devotions by (reciting the verses called) Maitrîs.

22. 'An ascetic shall keep no fire, have no house, no home, and no protector. He may enter a village in order to collect alms, and emit speech at the private recitation of the Veda.'

23. It is declared in the Veda, 'Limited in number are the Ṛik-verses, limited in number are the Sâmans, limited is the answer (of the Adhvaryu priest).'

24. 'Thus (an ascetic) shall not give up the Veda, (but live), until he is liberated from the body, at the root of the tree.'

25. 'The tree (is) the Veda; the syllable Om is its root; the syllable Om is the essence of the Veda.'

26. 'Meditating on the syllable Om, he becomes

---

21. The Maitrîs occur Taitt. Saṃhitâ III, 4, 11, 5, and the Vâruṇîs follow them immediately.

22. Âpastamba II, 9, 21, 10.

23. This and the next Sûtras are intended to teach that ascetics may limit their private recitation to the repetition of the praṇava, 'the syllable Om.' According to Govinda the passage of the Veda quoted refers originally to the Katurhotâraḥ, which the Taittirîya Brâhmaṇa II, 2, 1, 4, and III, 12, 5, 1 identifies with the Brahman, and where the pratigara, the answer of the Adhvaryu priest, is 'Oṃ hotaḥ' (Aitareya Brâhmaṇa V, 25).

24. I have taken vṛikshamûlikovedasaṃnyâsî to stand for vṛikshamûliko avedasaṃnyasî. For the vedasaṃnyâsa, 'giving up the Veda,' is not permitted to an ascetic; see e.g. Vasishṭha X, 4. But even without the negative particle vedasaṃnyâsî may convey a sense not opposed to the general teaching of the Smṛitis. For it may be taken to mean 'abandoning (the recitation of other portions of) the Veda.'

fit (to be united with) Brahman.' Thus spake the lord of created beings.

27. Let him cleanse the vessel of Brahman with the seven Vyâh*ri*tis.

Prasna III, Adhyâya 1.

1. Now, therefore, (we will speak) of those who desire (to fulfil) the duties of *S*âlînas (dwellers in houses), Yâyâvaras (wanderers), and *K*akra*k*aras (circle-goers), who subsist by nine (different) means of livelihood.

2. The term 'livelihood' (v*ri*tti) is used because they subsist thereby (tadvartanât).

3. The word *S*âlîna (is used) because they dwell in houses (*s*âlâ).

4. To be a Yâyâvara (means that one) goes on by means of a most excellent livelihood (v*ri*ttyâ varayâ yâti).

5. The term *K*akra*k*ara is derived from going by turns (to the houses of rich men).

6. We will explain those (above-mentioned means of livelihood) in their proper order.

7. They are nine, (viz.) Sha*nn*ivartanî, Kauddâlî, Dhruvâ, Samprakshâlanî, Samûhâ, Pâlanî, *S*ilo*ñkh*â, Kapotâ, and Siddho*ñkh*â.

---

27. Govinda is uncertain if the term brahmabhâ*g*ana, 'the vessel of Brahman,' refers to the alms-bowl or to the body of the ascetic. Probably both are meant, and the Sûtra is intended to prescribe the frequent recitation of the Vyâh*ri*tis in addition to the syllable Om.

1. 5. Govinda says that *K*akra*k*ara is another name for Yâyâvara, and that anukrama*k*ara*n*a, 'going by turns,' means going successively to the houses of Brâhma*n*as, Kshatriyas, and Vai*s*yas.

7. The terms left untranslated are fully explained in the next

8. (In addition) to these there is a tenth way of living, viz. forest-life.

9. (If he desires to adopt) any of the nine ways of living,

10. He causes the hair of his head, his beard, the hair on his body, and his nails to be cut, and besides gets ready (the following objects),

11. (Viz.) the skin of a black antelope, a water-pot, a staff, a yoke for carrying burdens, (and) a sickle.

12. He desires to go forth, after having offered a Traidhâtavîya (offering) or a Vaisvânarî (ish*t*i).

13. Now on the (following) morning, after the sun has risen, he makes the sacred fires burn brightly, melts butter on the Gârhapatya fire, cleanses it (with Kusa grass), heats the (spoons called) Sru*k* and Sruva, cleans (them), takes out four (spoonfuls of butter) in the Sru*k*, and offers the Vâstoshpatîya (oblation) in the Âhavanîya fire according to (the rules of his) Sûtra.

---

chapter. All the MSS. read kauntâlî for kauddâlî, which occurs in the commentary alone.

11. The vîvadha, 'a yoke for carrying burdens,' consists usually of a bamboo pole, to the ends of which two ropes are attached for fastening the loads. Kuthahârî, 'a sickle,' seems to be the name of a particular kind of sickle, since Govinda explains it by vâsavasâsanadâtram. He adds that the term includes 'a spade' (kuddâla) and other implements.

12. The meaning is that on the evening before his departure from the old home he is to offer the Traidhâtavîya-homa. According to the *S*rauta-sûtras (see the Petersb. Dict. s. v. traidhâtavî) the latter offering always occurs at the end of a great sacrifice. Hence it is appropriate for a person who wishes to begin a new mode of life.

13. This is the leave-taking from the old dwelling.

14. Having recited the Puronuvâkyâ (verse), 'O lord of the dwelling, permit us,' &c., he offers (the oblation) with the Yâgyâ verse, 'O lord of the dwelling, with thy kind company,' &c.

15. Some (declare that) every person who has kindled the sacred fires (shall offer these Homas).

16. Others (say that) a Yâyâvara alone (shall do it).

17. After departing (from his house), he stops at the extremity of the village, or at the extremity of the boundary of the village, builds there a hut or a cottage, and enters that.

18. Let him use the skin of the black antelope and the other (objects) which he has prepared for the several purposes which they are intended to serve.

19. Known (is) the (duty of) serving the fires; known (is) the (duty of) offering the new and full moon sacrifices; known (is) the successive performance of the five Mahâyagñas; it is seen that the vegetables, which have been produced, are offered.

20. He hallows those (vegetables), either (reciting the text),' I offer what is agreeable to all the gods,' or silently, and cooks (them).

---

14. The two verses occur Taittirîya Samhitâ III, 4, 10, 1. It is specially mentioned by Sâyana that the two verses have to be recited by an Agnihotrin on departing from his home.

17. Matha, 'a cottage,' is, according to Govinda, a house resting on many posts or pillars, while kutî is the simple shed with four posts and a roof of leaves.

19. The last clause, probably, is meant to prescribe a simpler form of the Vaisvadeva.

20. Govinda adds that the meaning is that the sacrificer shall eat the boiled rice in silence.

21. For such (a man the duty of) teaching, sacrificing for others, accepting gifts, and (performing) other sacrifices (than those mentioned) ceases.

22. (The use of) sacrificial food fit to be eaten during the performance of a vow is seen;

23. That is as follows: (his food may be) mixed with clarified butter or sour milk, (it must) not (contain) pungent condiments or salt, nor meat, nor (be) stale.

24. (He shall remain) chaste, or approach (his wife) in season.

25. (It is necessary) to have the hair of his head, his beard, the hair on his body, and his nails cut on each Parva day, and the rules of purification (are obligatory on him).

26. Now they quote also (the following verses): 'Two kinds of purification, which the *S*ish*t*as reverentially practise, are mentioned in the Veda,—external (purification), which consists in the removal of impure stains and foul smells, and internal (purification), which consists in the abstention from injuring live creatures.'

27. 'The body is purified by water, the understanding by knowledge, the soul of beings by abstention from injuring, (and) the internal organ by truth.'

PRA*S*NA III, ADHYÂYA 2.

1. As regards (the mode of subsistence called) Sha*nn*ivartanî, (that) is (as follows):

---

21. Govinda adds that the obligation of performing other meritorious deeds, such as digging wells and tanks (pûrta), also ceases.

27. Vasish*th*a III, 60.

2. He cultivates six Nivartanas (of) fallow (land); he gives a share to the owner (of the soil), or solicits his permission (to keep the whole produce).

3. Let him plough before breakfast with two bulls whose noses have not been pierced, not striking (them) with the goad, (but) frequently coaxing (them).

4. If he cultivates six Nivartanas in this manner (and subsists thereby), that is (the mode of living called) Sha*nn*ivartanî (subsistence on six Nivartanas).

5. (As regards the mode of subsistence called) Kauddâlî, he digs up (the soil) near a water(-course or tank) with a spade, a ploughshare, or a pointed piece of wood, sows seed, (and) grows bulbs, roots, fruit, pot-herbs, and vegetables.

6. (If he thus) cultivates (land) with a spade (and lives on its produce), that is the (mode of life called) Kauddâlî (subsistence by the spade).

7. He who lives by the (mode of subsistence called) Dhruvâ, wraps up his head in a white dress (saying), 'For the sake of welfare I wrap thee up, O head,' (and) takes the skin of a black antelope (with the words), '(Thou art) spiritual pre-eminence, (I take thee) for the sake of spiritual pre-eminence;' the Pavitra (reciting) the Abliṅga texts; the water-pot (saying), 'Thou art strength, (I take) thee for

2. 2. A Nivartana is a measure of 4000 square hastas, the ancient equivalent of the modern Bîghâ.

3. Identical with II, 2, 4, 21.

6. Govinda says that according to some the following ceremonies need only be performed when one goes out begging for the first time, while others insist on their being performed daily.

7. The Mânastokîya, i. e. the text beginning 'mâ nas toke,'

the sake of strength;' the yoke for carrying burdens (saying), 'Thou art grain, (I take) thee for the sake of prosperity;' the staff (saying), '(Thou art) a friend, protect me.'

8. On leaving (his hut), he mutters the Vyâh*ri*tis, and (afterwards the verse used for) hallowing the quarters of the horizon, 'May the earth, the middle sphere, the sky, the constellations, and all the quarters of the horizon, fire, air, and sun, (may all these) deities protect me on my road.'

9. Because, after muttering the Mânastokîya (text) and entering the village, he shows himself with the yoke (on his shoulder) at the door of each house, they call it 'showing oneself.'

10. Because, if every (other) livelihood fails, he persistently (dhruvam) supports himself by this (mode of living), it is called Dhruvâ (the unchangeable).

11. (As regards the mode of life called) Samprakshâlanî, (if, in order to show that) there is no waste of the vegetable (substances) obtained nor

occurs repeatedly in the Taittirîya-veda, e.g. Taitt. Sa*m*hitâ III, 4, 11, 2. Govinda adds that the beggar must remain silent, and not stop longer at each door than the time required for milking a cow.

10. Both the text and the scanty commentary on this Sûtra are corrupt. K. reads, v*ri*tter v*ri*ttair avârtâyâ*m* tayaiva tasya dhruva*m* varttayatîti dhruveti parikîrtitâ; D. v*ri*tte v*ri*ttair avârttâthâ, &c.; M. v*ri*tte v*ri*tter av*ri*ttâyâm av*ri*ttâyâ*m* tathaiva tasyâ*h* ddh*ri*va*m* varttamânâd iti, &c.; C. I. v*ri*tter v*ri*tter âvartâyâm âvartâyâm tathaiva tasyâ*m* dhruva*m* vartanâd iti, &c. The Telugu copy omits the text. From the commentary it is clear that Govinda read at the beginning of the Sûtra 'v*ri*tter v*ri*tter,' and the Telugu copy proves that 'tayaiva' is the correct reading. I restore the Sûtra conjecturally, as follows, v*ri*tter v*ri*tter avârttâyâ*m* tayaiva tasya dhruva*m* vartanâd iti dhruveti parikîrtitâ.

11. I read, samprakshâlanîti | utpannânâm oshadhînâm prakshe-

any hoarding, he turns the dishes, after washing them, upside down, (that is the livelihood called) Sampraksh*â*lan*î* (living by washing).

12. As to the (mode of subsistence called) Samûhâ, (if) he sweeps up (grain) with a broom in permitted places where (grain-bearing) plants are found, either on a road or in fields the access to which is not obstructed (by hedges), and lives on (what he has thus obtained), that (livelihood is called) Samûhâ (living by sweeping).

13. As to the (mode of life called) Pâlanî, it is also named Ahi*m*sakâ (not hurting), and the following (definition) is given. (If) he tries to obtain from virtuous men husked rice or seeds, and maintains (himself) thereby, that (is the mode of subsistence called) Pâlanî.

14. As to the (mode of life called) *S*ilo*ñkh*â, (if) he gleans single ears in permitted places where (grain-bearing) plants grow, on a road or in fields the access to which is not obstructed, and supports himself by (these) gleanings, (collected) from time

pa*n*am nâstîti ni*k*ayo vâ bhâ*g*anâni sa*m*prakshâlya nyub*g*ayatîti samprakshâlanî || M. has nâsti ni*k*ayo vâ, and C. I. reads also ni*k*ayo and omits 'vâ.' The Dekhan MSS. have nâstîti *k*ayo vâ. The description is not very clear; but it seems that a person who lives by the Samprakshâlanî v*ri*tti must obtain grain and vegetables by begging in such quantities as will suffice for one meal, and prove by the way in which he treats his dishes that he has neither wasted his food nor any store remaining.

13. The translation of this Sûtra is merely tentative, as the two MSS. of the commentary omit the text, and contain only a fragment of Govinda's explanation. The latter seems to have differed from my interpretation. The text, as given by the other MSS., runs as follows: pâlanîty [pâli°, MSS.] ahi*m*sakety evedam uktam bhavati [°tîti, M.] tushavihînâ*m*s ta*nd*ulân i*kkh*ati sa*gg*anebhyo bî*g*âni vâ [*k*â, D.] pâlayatîti pâlanî [phâla°, phâlani, M.; pâlinô, K. D.]

to time, that (is the mode of subsistence called) *S*ilo*ñkh*â (gleaning).

15. As to the (livelihood called) Kapotâ, (if) he picks up with two fingers single grains in permitted places, where (grain-bearing) plants grow, either on the road or in fields the access to which is not obstructed, that (is called), because he acts like a pigeon, Kapotâ (pigeon-life).

16. As to (the mode of life called) Siddho*ñkh*â, (if) tired with the (other) ways of subsistence, he asks, because he has become old or diseased, virtuous men for cooked food, that (is the livelihood called) Siddho*ñkh*â (gleaning cooked food).

17. If (he adopts) the latter, he must reposit (the sacred fires) in his soul and behave like an ascetic, except (in using) the cloth for straining water and (wearing) a reddish-brown dress.

18. If he subsists on the produce of the forest, (the fruits) of trees, creepers, and lianas, and of grasses, such as wild millet (*s*yâmâka) and wild sesamum, that (is called) forest-life.

19. Now they quote also (the following verse): 'Moving about with the beasts, dwelling together with them, and maintaining oneself in a manner similar to theirs, that is clearly the road to heaven.'

Pra*s*na III, Adhyâya 3.

1. Now the hermits in the wood belong to two classes,

15. Govinda mentions a varia lectio not found in our MSS., kapotavatsa*m*da*ms*inî, 'because he pecks like a pigeon.'

16. Here as well as above, III, 1, 7, the Dekhan MSS. read siddhe*kkh*â, 'begging cooked food,' instead of siddho*ñkh*â.

3. 1. Compare for the whole Adhyâya, Âpastamba II, 9, 21, 20–23, 2.

2. Those who cook (their food), and those who do not cook it.

3. Among them, those who cook (their food are divided) into five subdivisions, (viz.) those who eat everything which the forest contains, those who live on unhusked (wild-growing grain), those who eat bulbs and roots, those who eat fruit, and those who eat pot-herbs.

4. Those who eat everything which the forest produces are, again, of two kinds: they either subsist on forest-produce generated by Indra, or on that which has been generated from semen.

5. Among these, that which has been generated by Indra (is the produce) of lianas, shrubs, creepers, and trees. Fetching (that) and cooking it, they offer the Agnihotra in the evening and in the morning, give (food) to ascetics, guests, and students, and eat the remainder.

6. That which is generated from semen is the flesh (of animals) slain by tigers, wolves, falcons, and other (carnivorous beasts), or by one of them. Fetching (that) and cooking it, they offer the Agnihotra in the evening and in the morning, give (shares) to ascetics, guests, and students, and eat the remainder.

7. Those who eat unhusked grain only, fetch rice, avoiding (husked) corn, boil it, offer the Agnihotra both in the evening and in the morning, give (food) to ascetics, guests, and students, and eat the remainder.

8. Those who eat bulbs and roots, or fruit, or pot-herbs, (act) exactly in the same manner.

9. Those (hermits) who do not cook (their food are divided into) five (classes), Unmaggakas, Pra-

v*ri*ttâ*s*ins, Mukhenâdâyins, Toyâhâras, and Vâyubhakshas.

10. Among these, the Unma*gg*akas (collect and prepare their food), avoiding (the use of) iron and stone implements,

11. The Prav*ri*ttâ*s*ins take it with the hand,

12. The Mukhenâdâyins take it with the mouth (only, like beasts),

13. The Toyâhâras subsist on water only,

14. And the Vâyubhakshas (air-eaters) eat nothing.

15. In this manner ten (different) initiations are prescribed for hermits who follow the rule of Vikhanas (vaikhânasa).

16. He who has agreed (to obey) the Institutes of his (order, shall wear) a staff, (shall keep) rigid silence, and (shall) abstain from rash acts.

17. Hermits following the rule of Vikhanas (vaikhânasa) are purified (from sin), and (especially) those who abstain from food.

18. The sum of the rules applicable to all Brahma-Vaikhânasas (is as follows):

19. 'Let him not injure (even) gadflies or gnats; let him bear cold and perform austerities; let him constantly reside in the forest, be contented, and

---

11. Prav*ri*ttâ*s*in, i.e. he who eats food only which comes to him accidentally.

15–17. These three Sûtras are omitted in the commentary, but found in all the MSS. of the text.

18. Govinda proposes two explanations for the term brahmavaikhânasa; he thinks that it may mean either brahma*n*â d*ri*sh*t*â vaikhânasâ*h*, 'hermits seen by Brahman,' i.e. whose duties have been revealed by Brahman, or 'hermits who are Brâhma*n*as by caste.' The true sense, however, is probably 'a hermit (who strives) to (become one with) Brahman' (brahmârtha*m* vaikhânasa).

delight in (dresses made of) bark and skins, (and in carrying) water (in his pot).'

20. 'A devotee shall first honour the guests who have come to his hermitage at (dinner) time; he shall be sedulous in (worshipping) gods and Brâhma*n*as, in (offering) the Agnihotra, and in practising austerities.'

21. 'A Brâhma*n*a who has taken to forest-life, and who has adopted this difficult (but) pure mode of existence, which keeps him apart from wicked men, which must never be given up, which is similar to (that of the) beasts and birds, which allows the collection of the necessaries of life for one day only, and which necessitates the consumption of astringent and bitter (food), never sinks low.'

22. 'Moving about with the beasts, dwelling together with them, and maintaining oneself in a manner similar to theirs, that is clearly the road to heaven.'

PRA*S*NA III, ADHYÂYA 4.

1. Now if a student commits any act against his vow, eats meat, or approaches a woman, whenever any evil befals him,

2. He heaps fuel on the fire in the interior of the house, scatters (Ku*s*a grass) around it, and performs the ceremonies up to the end of the Agnimukha; then he offers oblations of clarified butter, (reciting the following texts): 'It was done by lust, lust does

22. See above, III, 2, 19.

4. 1. The clause striya*m* vopeyât, 'or approaches a woman,' is omitted by Govinda. The whole chapter is a supplement to the rules given above, II, 1, 1, 30–35, where some of the Vedic passages mentioned here have already been given.

it, to lust (belongs) all this, to him who draws me on, Svâhâ;' 'It was done by the internal organ, the internal organ does it, to the internal organ (belongs) all this, to him who draws me on, Svâhâ;' 'It was done by passion, passion does it, to passion (belongs) all this, to him who draws me on, Svâhâ;' 'It was done by ignorance, ignorance does it, to ignorance (belongs) all this, to him who draws me on, Svâhâ;' 'It was done by sin, sin does it, to sin (belongs) all this, to him who draws me on, Svâhâ;' 'It was done by wrath, wrath does it, to wrath (belongs) all this, to him who draws me on, Svâhâ.'

3. That which begins with the muttering (of the Vedic texts) and ends with the gift of a fee (consisting of) a cow is known,

4. (Afterwards) he stays (during the night) behind (i. e. to the west of) the fire, wrapping himself in the skin of a black antelope, the neck of which is turned towards the east and the hair of which is turned outside.

5. When the day dawns, he drags himself away from the hinder part (of the skin), goes to a bathing-place, bathes (there) in the manner which is known, (but) performs, while in the water, sixteen suppressions of breath with the Aghamarsha*n*a hymn; next he performs the known (ceremonies) up to the worship of the sun, and afterwards goes to the house of his teacher.

6. Let him know for certain that that is equally (effective) as bathing (with the priests) at the end of a horse-sacrifice.

---

5. Govinda says that this manner of crawling out of the skin is symbolical of a new birth.

PRASNA III, ADHYÂYA 5.

1. Now we will explain the rule of the most holy Aghamarshana.

2. He goes to a bathing-place and bathes (there). Dressed in a pure dress let him raise, close to the water, an altar, and moistening his clothes by one (application of water), and filling his hand once (with water), let him recite the Aghamarshana hymn (in the manner of his daily) private recitation.

3. (Let him repeat it) one hundred times in the morning, one hundred times at midday, and one hundred times or an unlimited number of times in the afternoon.

4. When the stars have risen, let him partake of gruel prepared of one handful of barley.

5. After seven (days and) nights he is freed from all minor sins (upapâtaka), whether they have been committed intentionally or unintentionally, after twelve (days and) nights (from all other sins) excepting the murder of a learned Brâhmana, the violation of a Guru's bed, stealing gold, and drinking Surâ.

6. After twenty-one (days and) nights he overcomes even those (crimes) and conquers them.

---

5. 1. Vasishtha XXVI, 8.

2. Sthandila, 'an altar,' is a slightly raised mound of earth, which, according to Govinda, in this case must have the shape of the sun's disc. According to the same authority the hand of the performer must remain filled with water as long as the recitation lasts, and the performer stands behind the altar facing the east.

5. Regarding the prasritiyâvaka, '(subsisting on) gruel prepared from a handful of barley,' see below, III, 6.

7. He overcomes everything, he conquers all, he obtains the reward of all sacrifices, he has bathed at all sacred bathing-places, he has performed the vows required for (the study of) all the Vedas, he becomes known to all the gods, he sanctifies a company (of Brâhmanas) by merely looking (at them), and his undertakings are successful. Thus speaks Baudhâyana.

PRASNA III, ADHYÂYA 6.

1. Now if a man feels his conscience charged with (evil) actions committed by himself, let him boil for himself (alone), when the stars have risen, a handful of barley, (and prepare) gruel (with that).

2. Let him not perform the Vaisvadeva oblation with (a portion of) that,

3. Nor (shall) a Bali offering (be performed) on that (occasion).

4. Let him consecrate the barley before it is boiled, while it is being boiled, and after it has been boiled, with the (following) Mantras:

5. 'Thou art barley, thou art the king of grains, thou art sacred to Varuna and mixed with honey, the sages have proclaimed thee an expeller of all guilt and a means of purification.'

---

7. Govinda is of opinion that the words, 'thus speaks Baudhâyana,' indicate that this part of the work has been composed by a pupil or some other person.

6. 1. For the whole Adhyâya compare Vishnu XLVIII.

5. According to Govinda, Vâmadeva is the Rishi of these Mantras. The phrase, 'Thou art sacred to Varuna,' is to be explained, according to Govinda, by the fact that offerings presented to Varuna frequently consist of barley. 'Honey' means, according to some, 'sweet butter,' with which the dish is seasoned.

'Ye barley-grains are clarified butter and honey, ye barley-grains are water and ambrosia. May you remove my guilt and all my sins:'

'Those committed by words, by acts, and by evil thoughts; ill-fortune and the night of all-destroying time,—all that avert from me, ye barley-grains.'

'(From the sin of eating) food which had been worried by dogs or pigs, or which had been defiled by crows and impure men, from the sin of disobedience towards mother and father,—from all that purify me, ye barley-grains.'

'From the dreadful (guilt of) mortal sins and of the crime (of serving) a king, from the wrong done to infants or aged men, from (the guilt) of stealing gold, of breaking my vows, of sacrificing for an unworthy man, of speaking evil of Brâhma*n*as,—from all that purify me, ye barley-grains.'

'From (the sin of eating) the food of many men, of harlots and of *S*ûdras, of (partaking of) funeral dinners and of (the food given by) persons who are unclean on account of a death or a birth, of that given by thieves, or at a funeral sacrifice offered to one who lately died,—from all that purify me, ye barley-grains.'

6. (While the barley) is being boiled, he must protect it (and recite the text), 'Adoration to Rudra, the lord of created beings; pacified is the sky;' the Anuvâka (beginning), 'Give strength;' the five sentences (beginning), 'The gods who are seated in front, led by Agni;' the two (texts), 'Do not hurt

6. The Anuvâka meant is Taitt. Sa*m*hitâ I, 2, 14. The five sentences are found, ibid. I, 8, 7, 1. Regarding the text mâ nastoke, 'do not hurt our offspring,' see above, III, 2, 9. The last

our offspring,' (and) 'The Brahman-priest among the gods.'

7. Having purified himself (by sipping water, &c.), he shall eat a little of the boiled (mess), after pouring it into (another) vessel.

8. Let him offer it as a sacrifice to the soul, (reciting the text), 'May the gods, who are born from the internal organ and joined to the internal organ, who are very strong, whose father is Daksha, protect us (and) guard us; adoration to them, to them Svâhâ.'

9. Let him who desires intelligence (subsist on such food) during three (days and) nights.

10. A sinner who drinks it during six (days and) nights becomes pure.

11. He who drinks it during seven (days and) nights is purified from (the guilt of) the murder of a learned Brâhmana, of violating a Guru's bed, of stealing gold, and of drinking Surâ.

12. He who drinks it during eleven (days and) nights, removes even the sins committed by his ancestors.

13. 'But he who during twenty-one days (drinks gruel made) of barley-grains which have passed through a cow, sees the Ganas and the lord of the Ganas, sees the goddess of learning and the lord of learning.' Thus speaks the venerable Baudhâyana.

Mantra occurs Taitt. Samhitâ III, 4, 11, 1. Govinda says that material protection, too, in the shape of an iron platter or cover is to be given to the boiling barley.

8. The text occurs Taitt. Samhitâ I, 2, 3, 1. It consists of five sentences, and is addressed to the five vital airs, to each of which the eater offers one oblation.

PRASNA III, ADHYÂYA 7.

1. 'Let him who considers himself impure offer (burnt oblations), reciting the Kûshmâ*nd*as.'

2. 'He who has had forbidden intercourse, or has committed a crime against nature, becomes even like a thief, even like the slayer of a learned Brâhma*n*a.'

3. 'He is freed from any sin which is less than the crime of slaying a learned Brâhma*n*a.'

4. If, after wasting his strength except in his sleep, he desires to become free from the stain and holy,

5. He causes the hair of his head, his beard, the hair on his body, and his nails to be cut on the day of the new moon or of the full moon, and takes upon himself a vow according to the rule prescribed for students,

6. (To be kept) during a year, or a month, or twenty-four days, or twelve nights, or six or three nights.

7. Let him not eat meat, nor approach a woman, not sit on (a couch or seat, and) beware of (speaking an) untruth.

8. To subsist on milk (alone is) the most excellent mode of living; or, using barley-gruel (as his food), he may perform a K*rikkh*ra (penance) of twelve days, or he may (maintain himself by) begging.

---

7. 1–3. Taittirîya Âra*n*yaka II, 8, 1–3.

6. Taitt. Âra*n*yaka II, 8, 5–6. 7. Taitt. Âra*n*yaka II, 8, 7.

8. Taitt. Âra*n*yaka II, 8, 8. As the next Sûtra shows, these rules refer to Brâhma*n*as. Regarding the K*rikkh*ra, see below, IV, 57.

9. On such (occasions) a Kshatriya (shall subsist on) barley-gruel, a Vaisya on curds of two-milk whey.

10. Having kindled the sacred fire in the morning according to the rule for Pâkayagñas, having scattered (Kusa grass) around it, and having performed (the preliminary ceremonies) up to the end of the Agnimukha, he next offers in addition burnt oblations, reciting the three Anuvâkas (beginning), 'What cause of anger to the gods, ye gods,' 'The debts which I contracted,' (and) 'May worshipful Agni give thee by every means long life.'

11. Let him offer with each Rik-verse a portion of clarified butter.

12. After having offered four oblations with (the spoon called) Sruva, reciting (the texts), 'That strength which lies in the lion, in the tiger, and in the panther,' &c., and the four Abhyâvartinîs (i.e. the texts), 'Thou, O fire, who turnest back,' &c., 'O Aṅgiras,' &c., 'Again with strength,' &c., (and) 'With wealth,' &c., after having taken his position, with sacred fuel in his hands, in the place allotted to the sacrificer, he worships (the fire) with the hymn which contains twelve verses (and begins), 'To Vaisvânara we announce.'

13. Having placed the piece of sacred fuel (on the fire with the text), 'Whatever sin I ever com-

10. For the rule, see Taitt. Âranyaka II, 7, 4. The three Anuvâkas mentioned are Taitt. Âranyaka II, 3–5.

12. Taitt. Âranyaka II, 7, 4. The first four texts occur Taitt. Brâhmana II, 7, 7, 1–2, the next four Taitt. Samhitâ IV, 2, 1, 2–3, and the hymn Taitt. Âranyaka II, 6. The place of the sacrificer to the south of the fire.

13. Taitt. Âranyaka II, 6, 2 (13).

mitted by thoughts or words, from all that free me (O fire, being duly) praised, for thou knowest the truth, Svâhâ,' he gives a fee.

14. (The ceremonies) which begin with the muttering (of the texts) and end with the gift of a cow as a fee are known.

15. One (person) only (shall) perform the service of the fire.

16. Now (let him offer) at the Agnyâdheya full oblations (pûrnâhuti, with the texts), 'Whatever cause of anger to the gods, ye gods;' 'The debts which I contracted;' 'May worshipful Agni give thee by every means long life.'

17. Having offered (it), he who is about to perform the Agnihotra, (worships) with the Dasahotri (texts); having offered (it), he who is about to perform the new and full moon sacrifices (worships) with the Katurhotri (texts); having offered (it), he who is about to offer the Kâturmâsya sacrifices (worships) with the Pañkahotri (texts); having offered it, (he worships) at an animal sacrifice with the Shaddhotri (texts), at a Soma-sacrifice with the Saptahotri (texts).

18. And it is declared in the Veda, 'Let him sacrifice (with the Kûshmânda texts) at the beginning of the rites; purified (thereby) he gains the world of the gods.' Thus (speaks) the Brâhmana.

---

16. From this and the next Sûtras it must be understood that the Kûshmândahoma is not only to be used as a penance, but may be offered at the beginning of the great Srauta sacrifices, in order to sanctify the performer and to secure special benefits.

17. The Saptahotri and the other texts mentioned occur Taitt. Âranyaka III, 1–5. I understand the verb 'worship' on account of Lâtyâyana X, 12, 10.

18. Taitt. Âranyaka II, 7, 5.

Prasna III, Adhyâya 8.

1. Now, therefore, we will explain the rule of the *K*ândrâya*n*a (lunar penance).

2. Let him fast on the fourteenth day of the bright half of the month.

3. Having had the hair on his head, his beard, the hair on his body, and his nails, or his beard alone, cut, let him enter, dressed in new clothes and speaking the truth, the place where the sacrificial fire is preserved.

4. There a (common) fire, (which may be) fetched once (only, shall serve) him; or (the fire) must be produced by friction with the Ara*n*is.

5. Let a student, who is a friend (of the performer), be ready at hand to (carry out his) directions;

6. And sacrificial viands (shall be his) food during the performance of the vow.

7. Having heaped fuel on the fire, scattered (Kusa grass) around it, and performed (the ceremonies) up to the end of the Agnimukha, he offers burnt oblations, (cutting off portions) from the cooked food,

8. (The first) to Agni, (the second) to the lunar day whichever it may be, (the third and the fourth)

---

8. 1. For this chapter compare Gautama XXVII.

4. The meaning of the Sûtra is that the fire which has been carried into the âvasatha must be kept burning during the whole month which the *K*ândrâya*n*a lasts. For a burnt oblation has to be performed at the end of the penance. Should it be extinguished, it must be rekindled by friction.

8. The text quoted occurs Taitt. Brâhma*n*a I, 5, 8, 1.

to the lunar mansion together with its guardian deity, the fifth to the moon (with the verse), 'Atrâha gor amanvata,' the sixth to the sky and the earth, the seventh to day and night, the eighth to Rudra, the ninth to the sun, the tenth to Varu*n*a, the eleventh to Indra, and the twelfth to all the gods.

9. Now they mention (the following) other (oblations which are to be offered) to the points of the horizon and to their (guardian) deities, to the wide middle sphere and to its (guardian) deity.

10. Having offered (the oblation) to Agni Svish*t*akr*i*t (with the verse), 'Ever new,' &c., he then places the remainder of the sacrificial viands into a goblet (ka*m*sa) or a cup (*k*amasa), pours seasoning, that is fit for sacrifices, over them, and eats fifteen morsels of ordinary size,

11. The first (saying, 'I offer) thee to Prâ*n*a,' the second (saying, 'I offer) thee to Apâna,' the third (saying, 'I offer) thee to Vyâna,' the fourth (saying, I offer) thee to Udâna,' the fifth (saying, 'I offer) thee to Samâna.' If there are only four (mouthfuls, he eats) the first reciting two (texts); if there are three, (he eats) the first two reciting two (texts) with each; if there are two, (he eats) the first reciting two (texts and) the second reciting three texts; (if there is only) one, (he recites) all (the five texts) together.

12. Having drunk water (with the text), 'Thou

---

10. Taitt. Sa*m*hitâ II, 3, 5, 3.

11. This is an imitation of the Prâ*n*âgnihotra described above, II, 7, 12.

12. Taitt. Sa*m*hitâ III, 1, 8, 1. The seven Anuvâkas are Taitt. Âra*n*yaka X, 51–57. One oblation is to be offered with each Anuvâka.

art water used for moistening Soma,' &c., he then offers the (following) additional oblations of clarified butter, with the seven Anuvâkas (beginning), 'May my Prâ*n*a, Apâna, Vyâna, Udâna, and Samâna be purified;' 'May my voice, mind, eye, ear,' &c.; 'May my head, hands, feet;' 'May my skin;' 'May the sense of hearing, touch;' 'May earth, water;' 'May that which consists of food.'

13. (The ceremonies) beginning with the muttering (of sacred texts) and ending with the gift of a cow as a fee are known.

14. He worships the sun with (three verses) addressed to Sûrya and the moon with (three verses) addressed to *K*andramas.

15. When he goes to rest, he mutters (the verse), 'O fire, keep thou good watch,'

16. When he awakes (in the morning, the verse), 'O fire, thou art the protector of vows.'

17. Let him not talk with women and *S*ûdras addressing them first; let him not look at urine and ordure.

18. If he has seen any impure substance, he mutters (the text), 'Unrestrained (was) the internal organ, wretched my eye; the sun is the most

---

13. Govinda here mentions that the whole of the ceremonies alluded to are the uttara*m* dârvihomika*m* tantram.

14. As Govinda states, the former verses are 'ud vaya*m* tamasas pari,' Taitt. Sa*m*hitâ IV, 1, 7, 4; 'ud u tya*m* *g*âtavedasa*m*,' ibid. I, 1, 8, 4; '*k*itram devânâm,' ibid. I, 4, 43, 1; while the verses addressed to the moon are 'navo navo,' ibid. II, 4, 14, 1; 'sa *k*itra*k*itram,' Rig-veda VI, 6, 7; and 'atrâha gor,' Taitt. Brâhma*n*a I, 5, 8, 1.

15. Taitt. Sa*m*hitâ I, 2, 3, 1. 16. Taitt. Sa*m*hitâ, loc. cit.

18. Taitt. Sa*m*hitâ III, 1, 1, 2.

excellent among the lights of heaven; O initiation, mayest thou not forsake me.'

19. On the first day of the latter half (of the month he eats) fourteen mouthfuls.

20. Thus (he takes every day) one (mouthful) less up to the day of the new moon.

21. On the day of the new moon there is not (even) one mouthful (left to take).

22. On the first day of the first half (of the month) one (mouthful may be eaten), on the second two.

23. Thus he daily increases (his meal) by one (mouthful) up to the day of the full moon.

24. On the day of the full moon he offers a Sthâlîpâka to Agni, to the lunar day whichever it may be, and to the lunar mansions as well as to their (guardian) deities.

25. Having offered a burnt oblation to (the lunar mansion) Abhi*g*it (which stands) before *S*ro*n*â, and to its (guardian) deity, he must give a cow to the Brâhma*n*as.

26. That is the ant-shaped lunar penance; (that which is performed in the) inverted (order is called) the barleycorn-shaped (lunar penance).

27. A sinner who has performed either of these two (penances) becomes free from all mortal sins (pâtaka).

28. They declare that the (*K*ândrâya*n*a) shall be performed for the sake of the fulfilment of wishes of all kinds.

29. 'Thereby man obtains every wish which he may conceive.'

---

26. Vish*n*u XLVII, 3-5.

30. 'Thereby the sages formerly purified themselves and accomplished their objects. That (rite) procures wealth, spiritual merit, sons, cattle, long life, heavenly bliss, and fame; it secures the fulfilment of all desires.'

31. 'He who studies this, becomes the companion of the lunar constellations, of sun and moon, and dwells in their world.'

Prasna III, Adhyâya 9.

1. Now, therefore, we will explain the rule of the Anasnatpârâyana (recitation of the whole Veda during a fast).

2. Let him wear a clean garment or a dress made of bark (or grass).

3. Let him desire food, fit for a sacrifice, or water and fruit.

4. Going forth from the village in an easterly or northerly direction, smearing a quadrangular sthandila, 'a bull's hide' in size, with cowdung, sprinkling it, drawing the marks on it, sprinkling it with water, heaping fuel on the fire and scattering (Kusa grass) around it, he offers burnt oblations to the following deities, to Agni Svâhâ, to Pragâpati

---

9. 2. M. and the MSS. of the commentary read kiravâsâh instead of kîravâsâh, 'clad with a garment of bark or grass,' and Govinda explains the var. lect. by 'dressed in old clothes.'

3. This rule refers to the case only where the performer of the vow is unable to bear the prolonged fasting.

4. A sthandila is the raised mound, four fingers high, which is used as the altar for the Grihya ceremonies. Regarding the term, 'a bull's hide,' see Vishnu XCII, 2. The marks (lakshana) are the lines which must be drawn on the altar; see e.g. Âsvalâyana Grihya-sûtra I, 3, 1.

Svâhâ, to Soma Svâhâ, to all the gods Svâhâ, to Svayambhu, to the *Rik*as, to the Yagus, to the Sâmans, to the Atharvans, to faith, to right knowledge, to wisdom, to fortune, to modesty, to Savit*ri*, to the Sâvitrî (verse), to Sadasaspati, and to Anumati.

5. Having offered (these oblations), he must begin with the beginning of the Veda and continuously recite (it).

6. Let him not interrupt (the recitation) by talking, nor by stopping.

7. Now if he converses in between or stops, let him thrice suppress his breath, and begin just there where he left off.

8. If he has forgotten (a passage), he shall recite for as long a time as he does not recollect it, what (he may know, *Ri*k-verses) for *Ri*k-verses, (Yagus-formulas) for Yagus-formulas, (Sâmans) for Sâmans.

9. He may (also) recite the Brâhma*n*a of that (forgotten passage) or (the passage from the Anukrama*n*î regarding) its metre and its deities.

10. Let him recite the Sa*m*hitâ of (his) Veda twelve (times). He thereby removes (faults committed by) studying on forbidden (days, by) angering his teacher, (and through) improper acts. His (knowledge of the) Veda is sanctified, is purified.

11. (If he reads) more than that, a cumulation (of rewards will be the result).

12. If he recites the Sa*m*hitâ of the Veda another twelve (times), he gains thereby the world of U*s*anas.

13. If he recites the Sa*m*hitâ of the Veda another

6. 'By talking, i. e. by uttering words not connected with the Veda.'—Govinda.

twelve (times), he gains thereby the world of B*ri*haspati.

14. If he recites the Sa*m*hitâ of the Veda another twelve (times), he gains thereby the world of Pra*g*âpati.

15. If, fasting, he recites the Sa*m*hitâ one thousand (times), he becomes one with Brahman, resplendent like Brahman (and) Brahman (itself).

16. If he subsists during a year on food obtained by begging, he gains (the power of) supernatural vision.

17. If during six months he subsists on barley-gruel, during four months on water and barley-flour, during two months on fruit, (and) during one month on water, or performs K*rikkh*ra penances of twelve days, he (obtains the power of) suddenly disappearing, and sanctifies seven descendants, seven ancestors, and himself as the fifteenth, and (any) company (of Brâhma*n*as) which he may enter.

18. They call that the ladder of the gods.

19. By means of that the gods reached their divine station and the sages the position of *Ri*shis.

20. The periods for beginning this sacrifice, forsooth, are three, the time of the morning libation, the time of the midday libation, and the last part of the night, (the Muhûrta) sacred to Brahman.

21. Pra*g*âpati, forsooth, proclaimed this (rite) to the seven *Ri*shis, the seven *Ri*shis to Mahâ*g*a*gñ*u, and Mahâ*g*a*gñ*u to the Brâhma*n*as.

---

18. Govinda explains ni*h*sre*n*îm, 'the ladder,' by ni*h*sreyasahetum, 'a cause of supreme bliss.'

21. The name of the *Ri*shi who proclaimed it to the Brâhmans is not certain. The Dekhan MSS. read Mahâ*g*agru and Mahâ*g*agnu, M. Mahâ*g*a*gñ*u, the I. O. copy of the commentary Mahâya*gñ*u and Mahâ*g*a*gñ*u, and the Telugu copy Mahâ*g*a*gñ*u.

Prasna III, Adhyâya 10.

1. The law of castes and of orders has been declared.

2. Now, indeed, man (in) this (world is polluted) by a vile action or acts wrongly, (e. g.) sacrifices for men unworthy to offer a sacrifice, accepts presents from those whose gifts ought not to be accepted, eats the food of those whose food ought not to be eaten, (and) practises what is forbidden.

3. They are in doubt if he shall perform a penance for such (a deed) or if he shall not do it.

4. (They declare that he shall not do it) because the deed does not perish.

5. (The correct opinion is) that he shall perform (a penance).

6. It is declared in the Veda, 'Let him offer a Punastoma; (those who offer it, may) again come to (partake of) the libations of Soma.'

7. 'He who offers a horse-sacrifice conquers all sin, he effaces the guilt of the murder of a Brâhma*n*a.'

---

10. 1. As stated formerly, Sacred Books of the East, vol. ii, p. li, this chapter is borrowed from Gautama XIX. I have therefore adopted the same division of the Sûtras as in the translation of the latter work.

2. I read, with the MSS. of the commentary, atha khalvaya*m* purusho yâpyena karma*n*â mithyâ vâ*k*araty ayâ*g*ya*m* vâ yâ*g*ayaty apratigrâhyasya vâ pratig*ri*h*n*âty anâ*s*yânnasya vânnam a*s*nâty a*k*ara*n*îyena vâ*k*arati. M. reads yâ*g*ayitvâ, and the Dekhan MSS. yâ*g*ayitvâ and pratig*ri*hya.

5. The Dekhan MSS. read kûryâd ity eva, M. kûryâd eva, and Govinda kuryât tv eva.

6. All the MSS. of the text omit the word vig*ñ*âyate, 'it is declared in the Veda,' which is given by Govinda.

7. All the MSS. of the text give at the beginning of this Sûtra

8. Moreover, 'He who is being accused (of a heinous crime) shall perform an Agnish*t*ut sacrifice.'

9. Reciting the Veda, austerity, a sacrifice, fasting, giving gifts are the means for expiating such (a blamable act).

10. The purificatory (texts are), the Upanishads, the initial (verses) of the Vedas, the ends of the Vedas (vedântas), the Sa*m*hitâs of all the Vedas, (the Anuvâkas called) Madhu, (the hymn of) Aghamarsha*n*a, the Atharva*s*iras, (the Anuvâkas called the) Rudras, the Purusha hymn, the two Sâmans (called) Râ*g*ina and Rauhi*n*eya, the B*ri*hat (Sâman) and the Rathantara, the Purushagati (Sâman), the Mahânâmnîs, the Mahâvairâ*g*a (Sâman), the Mahâdivâkîrtya (Sâman), any of the *G*yesh*th*a Sâmans, the Bahishpavamâna Sâman, the Kûshmâ*nd*îs, the Pâvamânîs, and the Sâvitrî.

11. To live on milk alone, as if one were fasting, to eat vegetables only, to eat fruit only, (to live on) gruel prepared of a handful of barley-grains, to eat gold, to eat clarified butter (are the modes of subsistence) which purify.

12. All mountains, all rivers, holy lakes, bathing-places, the dwellings of *Ri*shis, cowpens, (holy) plains and temples of the gods (are) places (which destroy sin).

---

athâpy udâharanti, 'now they quote also,' which Govinda omits, and which is inappropriate, because the following passages are taken from the Veda.

10. The word vedâdaya*h*, which occurs also in some MSS. of Vasish*th*a (XXII, 9), must be explained, according to the analogy of karmâdi, 'the beginning of the sacrifices' (Sâya*n*a on Taitt. Âr. II, 7, 5), by 'the initial verses of the Vedas.' The Pâvamânîs are added on the authority of Govinda alone.

12. 'Kshetra, (holy) plains, e.g. the Kurukshetra.'—Govinda.

13. Abstention from injuring living beings, truthfulness, abstention from theft (or unrighteously appropriating anything), bathing in the morning, at noon, and in the evening, obedience towards Gurus, continence, sleeping on the ground, dressing in one garment only, and abstaining from food (are the various kinds of) austerity.

14. Gold, a cow, a dress, a horse, land, sesamum, clarified butter, and food (are) the gifts.

15. A year, six months, four (months), three (months), two (months), one (month), twenty-four days, twelve days, six days, three days, a day and a night, (and) one day are the periods (for penances).

16. These (acts) may be optionally performed if no (particular penance) has been prescribed,

17. (Viz.) for great crimes difficult (penances) and for trivial faults easy ones.

18. The K*rikkh*ra and the Atik*rikkh*ra, as well as the *K*ândrâya*n*a, are penances for all (offences).

PRA*S*NA IV, ADHYÂYA 1.

1. We will separately explain the various penances for the several offences, both heavier and lighter ones.

2. Let him prescribe whatever may be befitting for each (case),—heavier (penances) for great (crimes) and easier ones for trivial (faults).

3. Let him perform the penances according to the rule given in the Institutes (of the Sacred Law in cases) where an offence has been committed with the organ or with the feet (and) the arms, through

3. The construction is certainly elliptical. I understand tatra with the first half-verse. Govinda separates the two half-verses, yad upasthak*ri*tam papa*m*, &c., from the first, and reads at the end

thoughts or speech, through the ear, the skin, the nose or the eye.

4. Or, in (the case of) transgressions committed through the organ of vision, of hearing, of sensation, of smelling, and through thoughts, he also becomes pure by three suppressions of the breath.

5. In case (he commits the offences) of eating the food of a *S*ûdra or of cohabiting with a *S*ûdra female, severally, he must perform, during seven days, seven suppressions of the breath on each day.

6. For partaking of food unfit for eating or drinking, and for selling forbidden merchandise, excepting honey, meat, clarified butter, oil, pungent condiments and bad food, and for similar (offences), he must perform, during twelve days, twelve suppressions of the breath on each day.

7. For other transgressions excepting mortal sins (pâtaka), crimes causing loss of caste (patanîya), and the minor faults (called upapâtaka), he must perform, during half a month, twelve suppressions of the breath on each day.

8. For other transgressions excepting mortal sins

---

of the half-verse prâ*n*âyâmân samâ*k*aret, 'one should perform suppressions of the breath (in even or equal numbers).'

5. Govinda tries to reconcile this rule with the one given above, I, 1, 2, 7, by assuming that the word *S*ûdra denotes here a Brâhma*n*a who lives like a *S*ûdra and neglects his sacred duties.

6. I read, conjecturally, dvâda*s*âham, 'twelve days.' The MSS. of the text have dvâda*s*a dvâda*s*âham, or corruptions pointing to this reading, and C. I. reads ardhamâsam. Regarding avarânna, 'bad food,' see note on Âpastamba II, 6, 15, 16.

7. I read, conjecturally, ardhamâsa*m*, 'half a month;' D. has ardhamâsân; K. dvâda*s*âha*m*; M. dvâda*s*ârdhamâsam; C. I. dvâda*s*ârdhamâsân, which is explained by sha*n*mâsân.

8. I read with M. dvâda*s*a dvâda*s*âhân. D. K. have dvâda*s*âham. The commentary omits the Sûtra altogether.

and crimes causing loss of caste, he must perform, during twelve periods of twelve days, twelve suppressions of the breath on each day.

9. For other transgressions excepting mortal sins he must perform, during twelve half-months, twelve suppressions of the breath on each day.

10. But for mortal sins he must perform, during a year, twelve suppressions of the breath on each day.

11. Let him give his daughter, while she still goes naked, to a man who has not broken the vow of chastity and who possesses good qualities, or even to one destitute of good qualities; let him not keep (the maiden) in (his house) after she has reached the age of puberty.

12. He who does not give away a marriageable daughter during three years doubtlessly contracts a guilt equal to (that of) destroying an embryo.

13. Such will be the case if anybody asks her in marriage, and also if nobody demands her. Manu has declared that at each appearance of the menses (the father incurs the guilt of) a mortal sin.

14. Three years let a marriageable damsel wait for the order of her father. But after (that) time let her choose for herself in the fourth year a husband (of) equal (rank). If no man (of) equal (rank) be found, she may take even one destitute of good qualities.

15. If a damsel has been abducted by force, and has not been wedded with sacred texts, she may lawfully be given to another man; she is even like a maiden.

---

9. I read with D., K., and M., dvâdasârdhamâsân. The commentary omits also this Sûtra.

11. Vasish*th*a XVII, 67-71, and above.

15. Vasish*th*a XVII, 73.

16. If, after (a damsel) has been given away, or even after (the nuptial sacrifices) have been offered, the husband dies, she who (thus) has left (her father's house) and has returned, may be again wedded according to the rule applicable to second weddings, provided the marriage had not been consummated.

17. He who does not approach, during three years, a wife who is marriageable, incurs, without doubt, a guilt equal to that of destroying an embryo.

18. But the ancestors of that man who does not approach his wife who bathed after her temporary uncleanness, though he dwells near her, lie during that month in the menstrual excretions (of the wife).

19. They declare that the guilt of the husband who does not approach his wife in due season, of him who approaches her during her temporary uncleanness, and of him who commits an unnatural crime (with her), is equally (great).

20. Let him proclaim in the village a wife who, being obdurate against her husband, makes herself sterile, as one who destroys embryos, and drive her from his house.

21. But for the transgression of that husband who does not approach a wife who bathed after temporary uncleanness, (the performance of) one hundred suppressions of the breath is prescribed (as a penance).

16. Vasish*th*a XVII, 74.

21. The MSS. of the text read, *ri*tusnâtâ*m* tu yo bhâryâ*m* niyatâ*m* brahma*k*âri*n*îm | niyamâtikrame tasya prâ*n*âyâma*s*ata*m* sm*ri*tam. The commentary omits the first half of the verse altogether. The latter, as read in the MSS., gives no sense. It seems to me that

22. Seated with Kusa grass in his hands, let him repeatedly suppress his breath, and again and again recite purificatory texts, the Vyâh*ri*tis, the syllable Om, and the daily portion of the Veda.

23. Always intent on the practice of Yoga, let him again and again suppress his breath. (Thus) he performs the highest austerity up to the ends of his hair and up to the ends of his nails.

24. Through the obstruction (of the respiration) air is generated, through air fire is produced, then through heat water is formed; hence he is internally purified by (those) three.

25. Through the practice of Yoga (true) knowledge is obtained, Yoga is the sum of the sacred law, all good qualities are gained through Yoga; therefore let him always be absorbed in the practice of Yoga.

26. The Vedas likewise begin with the syllable Om, and they end with the syllable Om. The syllable Om and the Vyâh*ri*tis are the eternal, everlasting Brahman.

27. For him who is constantly engaged in (reciting) the syllable Om, the seven Vyâh*ri*tis, and the three-footed Gâyatrî, no danger exists anywhere.

28. If, restraining his breath, he thrice recites the Gâyatrî together with the syllable Om and with the (text called) *S*iras, that is called one suppression of breath.

29. But sixteen suppressions of breath, accom-

either its end must have been sa*m*nidhau nopaga*kkh*ati (as in Sûtra 17), or that a whole half-verse has been lost.

22-24. Vasish*th*a XXV, 4-6. 25. Vasish*th*a XXV, 8.
26. Vasish*th*a XXV, 10. 27. Vasish*th*a XXV, 9.
28. Vasish*th*a XXV, 13. 29. Vasish*th*a XXVI, 4.

panied by (the recitation of) the Vyâhr*i*tis and of the syllable Om, repeated daily, purify after a month even the slayer of a learned Brâhma*n*a.

30. That is the highest austerity, that is the best description of the sacred law. That, indeed, is the best means of removing all sin.

Prasna IV, Adhyâya 2.

1. We will separately explain the various penances for the several offences, both heavier and lighter ones.

2. Let him prescribe whatever may be befitting for each (case),—heavier penances for great (crimes), and lighter ones for trivial (faults).

3. Let him perform the penances according to the rule given in the Institutes of the Sacred Law.

4. He who is about to accept gifts, or he who has accepted gifts, must repeatedly recite the four *Ri*k-verses (called) Taratsamandîs.

5. But in case one has eaten any kind of forbidden food, or that given by a person whose food must not be eaten, the means of removing the guilt is to sprinkle water (over one's head) while one recites the Taratsamandî *Ri*kas.

6. But we will, hereafter, declare another rule for (the expiation of) the murder of a learned Brâhma*n*a, whereby (men) are freed also from mortal sins of all (kinds).

7. Let him (perform), during twelve nights, sup-

4. Gautama XXIV, 2. The gift is, of course, one which ought not to be accepted.

5. Rig-veda IX, 58. Mârganam, literally 'rubbing,' means sprinkling the head with a handful of water.—Govinda.

pressions of the breath (and) mutter purificatory texts, the Vyâhritis, the syllable Om, (and) the Aghamarshana hymn, (living) on milk;

8. Or (he becomes) pure if he bathes, and during three (days and) nights subsists on air and (remains dressed) in wet clothes.

9. But if he has repeatedly committed forbidden acts of all kinds, and has (afterwards) worshipped reciting the Vârunî (texts), he is freed from all sin.

10. Now a student who has broken his vow (avakîrnin) shall heap fuel on the fire on the night of the new moon, perform the preparatory ceremonies required for a Darvîhoma, and offer two oblations of clarified butter (reciting the following texts): 'O Lust, I have broken my vow, my vow I have broken, O Lust, to Lust Svâhâ;' 'O Lust, I have done evil, I have done evil, O Lust, to Lust Svâhâ.'

11. After he has made the offering, he shall address the fire, closely joining his hands and turning sideways, (with the following texts): 'May the Maruts grant me, may Indra, may Brihaspati, may this fire grant me long life and strength, make me long-lived.' The Maruts, forsooth, give back to him the vital airs, Indra gives back to him strength, Brihaspati the lustre of Brahman, Fire all the remainder. (Thus) his body is made whole, and he attains the full length of life. Let him next address (the gods) with three (repetitions of the texts).

9. 'Upasthâna, "worshipping," i.e. sprinkling one's head with a handful of water.'—Govinda.

10. A repetition of the rule given above, II, 1, 1, 34; see also III, 4.

For the gods are trebly true. (All that) has been declared in the Veda.

12. He who considers himself defiled by minor offences (upapâtaka), will be freed from all guilt if he offers burnt oblations according to this same rule;

13. Or if he has partaken of food unfit to be eaten or to be drunk or of forbidden food, and if he has committed sinful acts or performed sinful rites either unintentionally or intentionally, and if he has had connexion with a female of the *S*ûdra caste or committed an unnatural crime, he becomes pure by bathing (and reciting) the Abliṅga (verses) and (those called) Vâru*n*îs.

14. Now they quote also (the following verse): 'If he has partaken of food unfit to be eaten or to be drunk, or of forbidden food, and if he has committed forbidden acts or performed forbidden rites, he will, nevertheless, be freed from (crimes) committed intentionally which are similar to mortal sins, nay, even from mortal sins (pâtaka).'

15. Or let him fast during three (days and) nights, bathe thrice a day, and, suppressing his breath, thrice recite the Aghamarsha*n*a. Manu has declared that that is equal (in efficacy) to the final bath at a horse-sacrifice.

---

12. Gautama XXV, 6.

13. Govinda gives, like Haradatta on Gautama XXV, 7, as an instance of a doshavat karma, 'a sinful rite,' the abhi*k*âra or 'magic rite in order to harm enemies.' The expression has, however, in our Sûtra, a wider sense.

14. I. e. if he performs the penance prescribed in the preceding Sûtra.

15. Vasish*th*a XXVI, 8; Gautama XXIV, 10.

16. And it is declared in the Veda, '(That is) the ancient purificatory rite, which is widely known (in the Institutes of the Sacred Law); purified thereby man conquers sin. May we, sanctified by this holy means of purification, conquer our enemy, sin.'

PRASNA IV, ADHYÂYA 3.

1. We will explain the (secret) penances which are not prescribed (by others, but by the offender himself, and) particularly what shall be done in (case) faults (have been committed) by men who, with concentrated minds, (are) intent (on the performance of their duties).

2. (Such a man) may sip water, (in order to atone) for all mortal sins, reciting the syllable Om and all the Vyâh*ri*tis.

3. When he sips water the first time, he gladdens the *Ri*g-veda, the second time the Ya*g*ur-veda, the third time the Sâma-veda.

4. When he wipes (his lips) the first time, he gladdens the Atharva-veda, the second time the Itihâsas and Purâ*n*as.

5. When he sprinkles water on the right hand, the feet, the head, the heart, the nostrils, the eyes, the ears, and the navel, he gladdens the trees and herbs and all deities. Therefore he is freed from all sin by sipping water.

---

3. 1. Vasish*th*a XXV, 1–2. The whole Adhyâya is left out in the Dekhan MSS., including K. The omission may have been caused by the circumstance that the initial verses of Adhyâyas 3 and 4 are identical.

2. Gautama XXV, 9; Vasish*th*a XXV, 4.

3–5. See the rules for sipping water, given above, I, 5, 8, 19–26.

6. Or let him offer in the fire eight pieces of sacred fuel, reciting (the following) eight (texts): 'Thou art the expiation of sin committed by the gods, Svâhâ;' 'Thou art the expiation of sin committed by men, Svâhâ;' 'Thou art the expiation of sin committed by the manes, Svâhâ;' 'Thou art the expiation of sin committed by myself, Svâhâ;' 'Thou art the expiation of the sin which we have committed either by day or by night, Svâhâ;' 'Thou art the expiation of the sin which we have committed either sleeping or waking, Svâhâ;' 'Thou art the expiation of the sin which we have committed either intentionally or unintentionally, Svâhâ;' 'Thou art the expiation of every sin, Svâhâ.'

7. When he has offered (these eight oblations) he will be freed from all guilt.

8. Now they quote also (the following verse): 'The Aghamarsha*n*a, the Devak*ri*ta, the Suddhavatîs, the Taratsamâs, the Kûshmâ*nd*îs, the Pâvamânîs, the Virâ*g*âs, the M*ri*tyulâṅgala, the Durgâ (Sâvitrî), the Vyâh*ri*tis, and the Rudras (are texts) which are very efficacious for effacing sin.'

Prasna IV, Adhyâya 4.

1. We will explain the (secret) penances which are not prescribed (by others, but by the offender himself, and) particularly what shall be done in (case) faults (have been committed) by men who, with concentrated minds, (are) intent (on the performance of their duties).

6. Gautama XXV, 10. The Mantras occur Taitt. Âra*n*yaka X, 59.

8. Vish*n*u LVI, 3, and note; Vasish*th*a XXVIII, 10–15.

2. He who, standing in water, thrice recites that (hymn of) Aghamarshana (which begins), 'Both right and truth,' will be freed from all guilt.

3. He who, standing in water, thrice recites the verse, 'This spotted bull,' &c., will be freed from all guilt;

4. He who, standing in water, thrice recites the verse, 'Freed from the post as it were,' will be freed from all guilt.

5. He who, standing in water, thrice recites the verse, 'A swan dwelling in purity,' will be freed from all guilt;

6. Or, he who, standing in water, thrice recites the Sâvitrî, foot by foot, half verse by half verse, and afterwards entire, will be freed from all guilt;

7. Or, he who, standing in water, thrice recites the Vyâhritis, both separately and altogether, will be freed from all guilt;

8. Or, he who, standing in water, thrice recites the syllable Om alone, will be freed from all guilt.

9. Let him not teach these Institutes of the Sacred Law to one who is neither his son nor his pupil, nor has resided (in his house) less than a year.

10. The fee (for teaching it) is one thousand (panas, or) ten cows and a bull, or the worship of the teacher.

Prasna IV, Adhyâya 5.

1. Now, therefore, I will proclaim by what rites, connected with the Sâman, *Ri*k, Yagus, and Atharva-

4. 2. Taitt. Âranyaka X, 1, 13. 3. Taitt. Âranyaka I, 5, 3, 1.
4. Taitt. Brâhmana II, 4, 4, 9.
5. Taitt. Samhitâ I, 8, 15, 2. 9. Vasishtha XXIV, 6–7.
5. 1. All the Dekhan MSS., including K., have been copied from

vedas, (man) quickly attains the wishes of his heart.

2. Having purified his body by muttered prayers, burnt oblations, Ish*t*is, restraints, and the like, he will accomplish all his objects. He will not attain success in any other way.

3. A Brâhma*n*a, who is going to mutter prayers, to offer burnt oblations or Ish*t*is, or to practise restraints, shall, first, during the bright half of the month, on a lucky day and under a lucky constellation, cause his hair and beard to be cut.

4. Let him bathe in the morning, at noon, and in the evening; let him beware of anger and untruth; let him not address women and *S*ûdras; let him be continent, and subsist solely on food fit for offerings.

5. Avoiding to sleep in the day-time, let him worship cows, Brâhma*n*as, manes, and gods. As long as he is engaged in muttering prayers, offering Homas and Ish*t*is, and practising restraints, let him stand during the day and sit during the night.

6. The K*rikkh*ra (penance) revealed by Pra*g*âpati lasts twelve days, (which are divided into four separate) periods of three days; (during the first period of three days he eats) in the day-time (only, during the second) at night (only, during the third he subsists on) food given without asking, (and during the fourth) finally (he lives on) air.

---

a MS. the leaves of which were out of order. After the first words of ver. 1, they have kshîra*m* dadhisarpi*h* ku*s*odakam, which belongs to ver. 26, and they go on with the text down to IV, 7, 7, after which the end of IV, 5, 1 and 2–25 are given.—'Yantra, "restraints," i.e. K*rikkh*ras and the like, (which are called so) on account of the restraint of the senses (required for them).'—Govinda.

3–5. Vasish*th*a XXIV, 5.

6. Vasish*th*a XXI, 20. Repeated, see above, II, 1, 2, 38.

Y 2

7. (If one eats on) one (day in) the morning (only), and (on the following day) at night (only, on the next day food) given without asking, (and on the fourth day) subsists on air, and repeats this three times, that is called the K*rikkh*ra (penance) of children.

8. (If) one eats one mouthful only at each (meal), following, during (three) periods of three days, the rules given above, and subsists during another period of three days on air, that is called the Atik*rikkh*ra penance.

9. (If) during those (first) three periods of three days one partakes of water only, and subsists afterwards (during three days) on air, that third (variety) must be known to be the most efficacious K*rikkh*râtik*rikkh*ra penance.

10. If one drinks hot milk, (hot) clarified butter, (and a hot) decoction of Ku*s*a grass, each during three days, and fasts during another three days, that is called the Taptak*rikkh*ra.

11. (If one lives during one day) on cow's urine, (during one day) on cowdung, (during one day) on milk, (during one day) on sour milk, (during one day) on clarified butter, (during one day) on a decoction of Ku*s*a grass, and during one (day and) night on air, that is called the Sâ*m*tâpana K*rikkh*ra.

12. Let him take the çow's urine, reciting the Gâyatrî; the cowdung, (reciting the text), 'Gandha-

---

7. Vasish*th*a XXIII, 43; see above, II, 1, 2, 39.
8. Vasish*th*a XXIV, 2-3; see above, II, 1, 2, 40.
9. See above, II, 1, 2, 41.
10. See above, II, 1, 2, 37.
11. Vasish*th*a XXVII, 13; Vish*n*u XLVI, 19.
12. The texts quoted are found, Taitt. Âra*n*yaka X, 1, 10; III, 17; Taitt. Sa*m*hitâ I, 5, 11, 4, 7; I, 1, 10, 3; VII, 1, 11, 1.

dvârâm;' the milk, (reciting the verse), 'Âpyâyasva;' the sour milk, reciting (the verse), 'Dadhikrâv*n*â;' the clarified butter, (saying), '*S*ukram asi;' the decoction of Ku*s*a grass (with the text), 'Devasya tvâ;'

13. (And mix together) one part of cow's urine, half as much cowdung, three parts of milk, two of sour milk, one part of clarified butter, and one part of water boiled with Ku*s*a grass; a Sâ*m*tâpana K*rikkh*ra (performed) in this manner will purify even a *S*vapâka.

14. He who subsists during five (days and) nights on cow's urine, cowdung, milk, sour milk, and clarified butter will be purified by (that) Pa*ñk*agavya (the five products of the cow).

15. If, self-restrained and attentive, he fasts during twelve days, that is called a Parâka K*rikkh*ra, which destroys all sin.

16. If he subsists on cow's urine and the other (substances named above), one day on each, and continues (this mode of life) during thrice seven days, the theologians call that a Mahâsâ*m*tâpana K*rikkh*ra.

17. If he daily adds to his food one mouthful during the bright (half of the month) and diminishes it daily by one mouthful during the dark (half of the month), and keeps two fasts in the two halves of the month, that is called a *K*ândrâya*n*a.

18. If, with concentrated mind, a Brâhma*n*a eats four mouthfuls in the morning and four mouthfuls when the sun has set, he will perform the *K*ândrâya*n*a of children.

13. Vasish*th*a XXVII, 13. 14. Vasish*th*a XXVII, 14.
15. Vish*n*u XLVI, 18. 16. Vish*n*u XLVI, 20.
17. Vasish*th*a XXVII, 21; see above, III, 8.
18. Vish*n*u XLVII, 8.

19. If, self-restrained, he daily eats, during a month, at midday eight mouthfuls of food, fit for a sacrifice, he will perform the *K*ândrâya*n*a of ascetics.

20. But a Brâhma*n*a who eats anyhow, during a month, thrice eighty mouthfuls of food, fit for a sacrifice, goes to the world of the moon.

21. As the rising moon frees the world from the fear of darkness, even so a Brâhma*n*a who performs a *K*ândrâya*n*a removes the fear of sin.

22. He who lives one day on (rice)-grains, three days on oil-cakes, five days on buttermilk mixed with water, seven days on water, and (one day) on air, (performs) the guilt-destroying Tulâpurusha.

23. Living on barley-gruel (yâvaka) removes the guilt of corporeal beings after seven days, and so does a fast of seven days; that has been recognised by wise men.

24. By dressing in wet clothes, by living in the open air, and by exposing himself to the sun during the light halves of the months Pausha (December–January), Bhâdrapada (August–September), and *G*yesh*th*a (May–June), a Brâhma*n*a is freed from (all) sin excepting crimes causing loss of caste (patanîya).

25. (If one swallows) cows' urine, cowdung, milk,

---

19. Vish*n*u XLVII, 7.

20. Vish*n*u XLVII, 9. Govinda places this verse before Sûtra 19.

22. Vish*n*u XLVII, 22.

24. The meaning is that the performer is to stand in wet clothes during the first half of the month Pausha, in the cold season; to live in the open air during the first half of Bhâdrapada, in the rainy season; and to allow himself to be broiled by the sun in *G*yesh*th*a, the hottest time of the hot season.

25. I doubt if the reading of Govinda, yavâ*k*âmena (explained

sour milk, clarified butter, and a decoction of Ku*s*a grass, mixed with barley gruel, that is the most sanctifying Brahmakûr*k*a.

26. He who fasts on the new moon day and eats sesamum grains on the full moon day, will be freed in the course of a year from the sins which he committed in the bright and the dark halves of the month.

27. He who lives on alms obtained from Agnihotrins is purified in one month; (he who obtains his food) from a Yâyâvara, in ten days; he who receives it from a hermit in the forest, in five days;

28. (He who lives) on food given by a person who has a store sufficient for one day only, will be purified in one day; he who drinks water given by a person subsisting by the Kapota-v*r*itti (pigeon-life), is purified in three (days).

29. If one recites the whole *Ri*g-veda, Ya*g*ur-veda, and Sâma-veda, or thrice reads one of these Vedas and fasts, (that is) a most efficient means of purification.

30. Now if one is in haste to finish, one may live on air during a day, and pass the night standing in water, that is equal (in efficacy) to a Prâ*g*âpatya (K*rikkh*ra).

31. He who at sunrise mutters the Gâyatrî one thousand and eight times, is free from all sin, provided he has not slain a learned Brâhma*n*a.

---

by yavâgû*h*) sa*m*yuktam, 'mixed with barley-gruel,' is correct. All the MSS. of the text have yavânâm ekasa*m*yukto, which I do not understand. Govinda has Brahmak*rikkh*ra*h* instead of Brahmakûr*kah*. But see the Petersb. Dict. s. v. brahmakûr*k*a.

28. Regarding the Kapota-v*r*itti, see above, III, 2, 15.

30. Vasish*th*a XXVII, 17. Govinda adds after kartum, 'to finish,' 'the rites connected with the Vedas' (Sûtra 1).

32. He who distributes food, speaks the truth, and has compassion on all living beings, is more (holy) than all those who have been purified by the restraints mentioned above.

PRASNA IV, ADHYÂYA 6.

1. The (eleven Anuvâkas called) Rudras together with (the ten hymns) seen by Madhu*kkh*andas, the Gâyatrî with the syllable Om, and likewise the seven Vyâh*ri*tis (are the texts) which should be muttered (and) which remove guilt.

2. The M*ri*gâresh*t*i, the Pavitresh*t*i, the Trihavis, the Pâvamânî are the Ish*t*is which efface sin, if they are (each) combined with the Vai*s*vânara (Dvâda*s*a-kapâla).

3-4. Learn, also, the following most excellent secret; he will be freed from all sins of all kinds who sprinkles himself with water, reciting the Pavitras, who mutters the eleven (Anuvâkas called) Rudras, who offers burnt oblations of butter, reciting the Pavitras, and gives gold, a cow, and sesamum (to Brâhma*n*as).

5. He who partakes of boiled barley-gruel, mixed with cow's urine, liquid cowdung, sour milk, milk, and butter, is quickly freed from sin.

6. Both he who has begotten a child on a *S*ûdra woman and he who has had connexion with a female,

---

6. 1. The hymns are Rig-veda I, 1-10.

2. Regarding the M*ri*gâresh*t*i, see Taitt. Sa*m*hitâ IV, 7, 15. In explanation of the term Trihavis, Govinda adds the word Savanesh*t*i.

5. Yâvaka, translated, as usually, by barley-gruel, can also denote, as Govinda points out, other dishes made of barley.

6. See above, II, 1, 2, 7, 10, 13-14.

intercourse with whom is forbidden (agamyâ), are purified (if they live) according to this rule during seven days.

7. (That is likewise) the remedy when one has swallowed semen, ordure, and urine, or eaten the food of persons whose food must not be eaten, (and also) when a younger brother has kindled the sacred fire, has offered a *S*rauta sacrifice, or taken a wife before the elder.

8. He who has committed even a great number of (wicked) actions, excepting mortal sins, will be freed (by that rule) from all guilt. That is the statement of the virtuous.

9. But (this) ordinance, which is based on the authority of the sacred texts, is stated (to be that) through which Bharadvâ*g*a and others became equal to Brahman.

10. Through the performance of these rites a Brâhma*n*a, whose heart is full of peace, obtains whatever desires he may have in his heart.

PRA*S*NA IV, ADHYÂYA 7.

1. The wishes of a Brâhma*n*a who has left off evil deeds and is (ever) engaged in holy works are fulfilled even without (the practice of) restraints.

2. Upright Brâhma*n*as quickly accomplish what-

7. See above, II, 1, 1, 21, 39–40. I follow the reading of M. and of the commentary, paryâdhâne*g*yayor etat parivitte *k*a bheshagam. The reading of the Dekhan MSS. is etat patite *k*aiva bho*g*anam, 'that food must be eaten . . . ., and when one has become an outcast.'

7. 1. Yantrâ*n*i, 'restraints,' i.e. K*rikkh*ras, the fasts, and other practices described in the preceding chapters.

ever they wish in their hearts, if they are purified by honest actions.

3. Thus a wise man should practise those restraints until he has purified his bodily frame.

4. He who has been purified by those restraints should, after fasting three (days and) nights, begin the performance of that sacred rite through which he wishes to gain the fulfilment of his desires,—

5. (Reciting) the Kshâpavitra, the Sahasrâksha, the M*ri*gâra, the two Ga*n*as (called) A*m*homu*k*, the Pâvamanîs, the Kûshmâ*nd*îs, and the *Rik*as, addressed to Vai*s*vânara,

6. (And) offering with (each of) these (Mantras) boiled rice and clarified butter during seven days, in the morning, at midday, and in the evening, keeping a rigid silence, living on food fit for a sacrifice, restraining his senses and his actions,

7. He is freed from all crimes, even mortal sins, after looking on a cross-road at a pot filled with water, (and reciting the text), 'Si*m*he me manyu*h*.'

8. He is freed from the multitude of sins, committed unintentionally in old age, in youth, and in infancy, and even from those belonging to former births;

9. After feeding at the end (of the seven days) Brâhma*n*as with milk and rice, well mixed with

5. According to Govinda the Kshâpavitra, or as the Dekhan MSS. read, Kshmâpavitra, occurs in the Sûtrapâ*th*a of the Taittirîyas, consists of six verses, and begins 'Agne naya.' The text meant must be similar to Taitt. Sa*m*hitâ I, 1, 14, 3. The Sahasrâksha is the Purushasûkta. The M*ri*gâra consists of the Yâgyânuvâkyâs of the M*ri*gâreshfi, Taitt. Sa*m*hitâ IV, 7, 15. The two Ga*n*as called A*m*homu*k* are found Taitt. Sa*m*hitâ II, 3, 13, 1, 'yâ vâm indrâvaru*n*au' and 'yo vâm indrâvaru*n*au.' The verses addressed to Agni Vai*s*vânara are the first eight of Taitt. Sa*m*hitâ I, 5, 11.

butter, and distributing to them after their dinner cows, land, sesamum, and gold,

10. A Brâhma*n*a becomes internally pure, his guilt being consumed like fuel, and fit for the performance of rites which secure the fulfilment of wishes and of rites like the kindling of the sacred fire.

Prasna IV, Adhyâya 8.

1. He who, through excessive greed or carelessness, performs this rite for others, is tainted by sin, and perishes like one who has swallowed poison.

2. A Brâhma*n*a who performs this rite for his teacher, his father, his mother, or for himself is resplendent like the sun. Therefore this rite may be performed for those (persons).

3. Ka (Pra*g*âpati) purified by means of this rite the god with a thousand eyes (Sahasrâksha), Fire, Wind, the Sun, Soma, Yama, and other lords of the gods.

4. Whatever there is in these three worlds, famed as possessing a holy name, Brâhma*n*as and the rest, (all) that was produced by Ka through this rite of sanctification.

5. This sin-destroying secret of Pra*g*âpati was first produced; thereafter thousands of purificatory rites came into existence.

6. He who performs those eight Ga*n*ahomas on the (first) day of the year, of a half-year, of a season, or of a fortnight, sanctifies ten ancestors and ten descendants of his line;

7. And, while still on earth, he is known to the

8. 5. I. e. those mentioned V, 7, 5.

gods in heaven as a holy man, and (after death) that virtuous man rejoices for a very long time in heaven like a god.

8. If a Brâhma*n*a is unable to offer those eight Ga*n*ahomas, let him offer one; thereby his guilt is effaced.

9. He, also, whose sons or pupils offer those eight Ga*n*ahomas, is freed from his sin which is bought off by his having instructed (them).

10. Through a desire of removing one's guilt one even may cause (these oblations) to be offered by men who have been engaged for money, in case oneself is unable (to do it); a man need not torment himself.

11. Even among the virtuous a distribution of wealth is made (for the success) of holy rites; sometimes a man who is free from debt is (thereby) freed from guilt.

12. Liberated according to this rule from the ocean of guilt and debt, he considers himself pure and able to successfully perform the sacred rites.

13. But in the case of that pure mortal who, freed from all sin and debts, begins the sacred rites, they will succeed without any effort.

14. Let him daily (study and) teach this holy (rule) of Pra*g*âpati, which the sage has proclaimed, let him remember it or hear it. (By doing that) he is freed from all guilt and will be exalted in Brahman's world.

---

10. The meaning is that in case a wealthy man is unable to bear 'the restraints,' he may hire others to perform the Homas. Though the hired performer will be guilty of a serious offence (Sûtra 1), the person who causes them to be performed will derive benefit from them.

15. Let him mutter during twelve days those sacred texts through which he wishes to accomplish (his desires), eating once (a day) at night boiled rice with clarified butter, with milk, or with sour milk.

16. (Let him offer) ten times a burnt oblation and sprinkle clarified butter. (That is) the preliminary worship (which must be performed) when one desires to accomplish one's objects through those sacred texts.

PARI*S*ISH*T*A.

Pra*s*na VII, Adhyâya 5.

1. We will explain the rule for the adoption of a son.

2. Man, formed of virile seed and uterine blood, proceeds from his mother and father (as an effect) from its cause.

3. (Therefore) the father and the mother have power to give, to abandon, or to sell their (son).

4. But let him not give nor receive (in adoption) an only son;

5. For he (must remain) to continue the line of the ancestors.

6. Let a woman neither give nor receive a son except with the permission of her husband.

7. He who is desirous of adopting (a son) procures two garments, two earrings, and a finger-ring; a spiritual guide who has studied the whole Veda; a layer of Ku*s*a grass and fuel of Pâlâ*s*a wood and so forth.

---

5. 1. This chapter has been translated by Mr. Sutherland, Dattaka Mîmâ*m*sâ V, 42, and Dattaka *K*andrikâ II, 16, and by myself, Journal Bengal Br. Roy. As. Soc., vol. XXXV, p. 162.

2–6. Identical with Vasish*th*a XV, 1–5. The best MS. omits the particle tu, 'but,' in Sûtra 6, while others have it.

7–8. Vasish*th*a XV, 7. The translation of madhye by 'in their presence' rests on the authority of the Sa*m*skârakaustubha 47 b, 11, where it is explained madhye [a] iti bandhusamaksham. The other explanation 'in the middle (of his dwelling),' to which the interpolated text of the Dattaka Mîmâ*m*sâ and Dattaka *K*andrikâ refers, is, however, also possible.

8. Then he convenes his relations, informs the king (of his intention to adopt) in (their) presence, feeds the (invited) Brâhma*n*as in the assembly or in (his) dwelling, and makes them wish him 'an auspicious day,' 'hail,' (and) 'prosperity.'

9. Then he performs the ceremonies which begin with the drawing of the lines on the altar and end with the placing of the water-vessels, goes to the giver (of the child) and should address (this) request (to him), 'Give me (thy) son.'

10. The other answers, 'I give (him).'

11. He receives (the child with these words), 'I take thee for the fulfilment of (my) religious duties; I take thee to continue the line (of my ancestors).'

12. Then he adorns him with the (above-mentioned) two garments, the two earrings, and the finger-ring, performs the rites which begin with the placing of the (pieces of wood called) paridhis (fences round the altar) and end with the Agnimukha, and offers (a portion) of the cooked (food) in the fire.

13. Having recited the Puronuvâkyâ (verse), 'He who thinking of thee with a discerning mind,' &c., he offers an oblation, reciting the Yâ*g*yâ (verse), 'To which performer of good deeds, thou, O *G*âtavedas,' &c.

14. Then he offers (oblations, reciting) the Vyâh*ri*tis;—(the ceremonies) which begin the oblation to Agni Svish*t*ak*ri*t and end with the presentation

---

8. The ceremony alluded to is the so-called pu*n*yâhavâ*k*anam.

12. The correct reading is pakvâ*g* *g*uhoti.

13. The two texts are found Taittirîya Sa*m*hitâ I, 4, 46, 1.

14. Vasish*th*a XV, 7. The parenthetical phrase occurs frequently in the Dharma-sûtra; see e.g. III, 4, 3.

of a cow as a fee (to the officiating priest are) known;—

15. And presents (to the spiritual guide) as a sacrificial fee those two dresses, those two earrings, and that finger-ring (with which he had adorned the child).

16. If after the performance of these (rites) a legitimate son of his own body is born (to the adopter, then the adopted son) receives a fourth (of the legitimate son's) share. Thus says Baudhâyana.

16. Vasishtha XV, 9.

INDEX

TO

VOLS. II AND XIV.

INDEX TO VOLS. II AND XIV.

Ap. = Âpastamba; Ga. = Gautama; Va. = Vasish*th*a; Ba. = Baudhâyana.

Z 2

ADDITIONS AND CORRECTIONS

TO VOLS. II AND XIV.

Vol. II.

Page xxxii, note 1. Maitrâya*n*îyas still exist in Gu*g*arât, see Report on Sanskrit MSS. for 1879–80; Schröder, Maitrâya*n*î Sa*m*hitâ, pp. xxii–xxiii.

P. xxxii, l. 1. Râo Sâheb V. N. Mâ*nd*lik, Vyavahâra Mayûkha and Yâ*gñ*avalkya, p. 300, has challenged the accuracy of my statement regarding the prevalence of the Âpastamba *S*âkhâ in Bombay. He, however, admits that some De*s*asthas and Drâvi*d*as actually follow the *S*âkhâ. His dissent really refers to the Koṅka*n*asthas, the division to which he himself belongs. Among the latter those who originally were Âpastambîyas have partly gone over to the Haira*n*yake*s*as. But in the old list of the Koṅkanastha families (see Elph. Coll. collection of 1867–68, Cl. xii, no. 5) which I procured from Mr. Limaye of Ash*t*e, the families which really are Âpastambîyas are carefully enumerated. Both in Pu*n*a and Bombay I have met with a number of Brâhmans, who called themselves sometimes De*s*asthas and sometimes Koṅka*n*asthas, and were able and willing to recite portions of the Âpastamba Sûtras for a small consideration.

P. xxxvii, note 1. The date of the Kâ*s*ikâ v*ri*tti has been shown by Professor Max Müller to be about 650 A. D.

P. xlix, l. 10, *for* Baudhâyana I, 1, 21, *read* Baudhâyana I, 1, 2–6.

P. xlix, l. 28, *for* Baudhâyana I, 1, 17–24, *read* Baudhâyana I, 1, 2, 1–8.

P. li, note 1, l. 5 seqq., *for* Baudhâyana III, 5, *read* Baudhâyana III, 10.

P. 78, l. 32 (Ap. I, 9, 23, 28, note), *for* Baudhâyana, Pr. I, Adhy. 10, *read* Baudhâyana I, 10, 19, 1.

P. 90, l. 33 (Ap. I, 10, 29, 9, note), *for* Baudhâyana Pr. I, Adhy. 12, *read* Baudhâyana II, 1, 2, 18.

P. 176, l. 20 (Ga. I, 28, note), *read* Vasish*th*a III, 43.

P. 206, l. 33 (Ga. VI, 5, note), *for* Manu III, 123, *read* Manu II, 123.

P. 210, l. 18 (Ga. VII, 17), *for* others *read* for another.

P. 222, l. 13 (Ga. IX, 61), *read* Nor shall he bathe, &c.

P. 254, l. 9 (Ga. XV, 17), *read* Whosoever lives, &c.

P. 291, l. 2–3, *for* Defiled by, &c., *read* Oh lust, I have been incontinent, incontinent, &c.; oh lust, I have committed evil, I have committed evil, oh lust, &c.

Vol. XIV.

P. 24, l. 25 (Va. III, 56, note), *for* Baudhâyana I, 5, 52, *read* Baudhâyana I, 5, 9, 11.

P. 50, l. 9 (Va. XI, 7). Govindasvâmin on Baudhâyana II, 7, 13, 3 gives

Aa 2

for pradâtâh the reading pragâtâh, '(newly)-confined women,' which seems to be the correct one. Owing to the peculiar Indian pronunciation of ga as a d mouillé, da sometimes occurs by mistake for ga in Sanskrit MSS. In Prakrit words da is also sometimes the representative of ga.

P. 99, l. 3 (Va. XIX, 23), *for* pradâtâh *read* pragâtâh, '(newly)-confined women.'

P. 102, l. 12 (Va. XIX, 48), *read* for a sacrificial session.

P. 111, l. 27 (Va. XXI, 6, note). The *S*iras text occurs Taitt. Âr. X, 35.

P. 122, l. 19 (Va. XXIII, 39), *dele* which does not cause loss of caste.

P. 127, l. 31 (Va. XXVI, 8), *for* Manu LI, 251, *read* Manu XI, 251.

P. 206, l. 19 (Ba. I, 11, 20, 12), *for* the sixth *read* the fifth.

P. 207, l. 1 (Ba. I, 11, 20, 13), *for* the fifth *read* the sixth.

P. 223, l. 33 (Ba. II, 1, 2, 41, note), *add at end:* But the word refers to the numeration of the K*rikkh*ra penances, given Gautama XXVI, 20, and its occurrence shows that Baudhâyana simply copied Gautama.

P. 267–268 (Ba. II, 8, 14, 7, note), *dele note and substitute:* 'The Agnimukha is a term denoting the last of the offerings which precede the Pradhânahoma. See Baudhâyana G*ri*hya-sûtra I, 4, end, and 5.'

TRANSLITERATION OF ORIENTAL ALPHABETS ADOPTED FOR THE TRANSLATIONS OF THE SACRED BOOKS OF THE EAST.

CONSONANTS.	MISSIONARY ALPHABET. I Class.	II Class.	III Class.	Sanskrit.	Zend.	Pehlevi.	Persian.	Arabic.	Hebrew.	Chinese.
Gutturales.										
1 Tenuis	k	...	....	क	𐬐	𐭪	ک	ك	כּ	k
2 „ aspirata	kh	...	....	ख	𐬑	𐭧	...	...	כ	kh
3 Media	g	...	....	ग	𐬔	𐭢	گ	...	גּ	...
4 „ aspirata	gh	...	....	घ	𐬖	𐭢	...	...	ג	...
5 Gutturo-labialis	q	...	....	...	....	...	ق	ق	ק	...
6 Nasalis	ṅ (ng)	...	....	ङ	{𐬣 (ng) / 𐬧 (N)}	...	...	...	...	...
7 Spiritus asper	h	...	....	ह	𐬵 (𐬓 *hv*)	𐭧	ه	ه	ה	h, hs
8 „ lenis	'	...	....	...	....	...	ا	ا	א	...
9 „ asper faucalis	ʻh	...	....	...	....	...	ح	ح	ח	...
10 „ lenis faucalis	ʼh	...	....	...	....	...	ع	ع	ע	...
11 „ asper fricatus	...	ʻ*h*	....	...	....	...	خ	خ	ח	...
12 „ lenis fricatus	...	ʼ*h*	....	...	....	...	...	...	...	...
Gutturales modificatae (palatales, &c.)										
13 Tenuis	...	*k*	....	च	𐬗	𐭰	چ	...	...	*k*
14 „ aspirata	...	*kh*	....	छ	....	...	...	...	...	*kh*
15 Media	...	*g*	....	ज	𐬘	𐭰	ج	ج	...	...
16 „ aspirata	...	*gh*	....	झ	....	...	ژ	...	...	...
17 „ Nasalis	...	*ñ*	....	ञ	....	...	...	...	...	...

CONSONANTS (*continued*).	MISSIONARY ALPHABET. I Class.	II Class.	III Class.	Sanskrit.	Zend.	Pehlevi.	Persian.	Arabic.	Hebrew.	Chinese.
18 Semivocalis	y	. . .	. . . .	य	𐬌𐬌, 𐬫 init.	𐭥	ي	ي	י	y
19 Spiritus asper	. . .	(ẏ)	. . . .	. . .	. . . .	. . .	. . .	. . .	. . .	. . .
20 „ lenis	. . .	(ẏ)	. . . .	. . .	. . . .	. . .	. . .	. . .	. . .	. . .
21 „ asper assibilatus	. . .	*s*	. . . .	श	𐬱	𐭱	ش	ش	. . .	. . .
22 „ lenis assibilatus	. . .	*z*	. . . .	. . .	𐬲	𐭦	ژ	. . .	. . .	*z*
Dentales.										
23 Tenuis	t	. . .	. . . .	त	𐬙	𐭲	ت	ت	תּ	t
24 „ aspirata	th	. . .	. . . .	थ	𐬚	. . .	. . .	. . .	ת	th
25 „ assibilata	. . .	. . .	TH	. . .	. . . .	. . .	ث	ث	. . .	. . .
26 Media	d	. . .	. . . .	द	𐬛	𐭣	د	د	דּ	. . .
27 „ aspirata	dh	. . .	. . . .	ध	𐬜	. . .	. . .	. . .	ד	. . .
28 „ assibilata	. . .	. . .	DH	. . .	. . . .	. . .	ذ	ذ	. . .	. . .
29 Nasalis	n	. . .	. . . .	न	𐬥	𐭭	ن	ن	נ	n
30 Semivocalis	l	. . .	. . . .	ल	. . . .	𐭫	ل	ل	ל	l
31 „ mollis 1	. . .	*l*	. . . .	ळ	. . . .	. . .	. . .	. . .	. . .	. . .
32 „ mollis 2	. . .	. . .	L	. . .	. . . .	. . .	. . .	. . .	. . .	. . .
33 Spiritus asper 1	s	. . .	. . . .	स	𐬯	𐭮	س (ث)	س	שׂ	s
34 „ asper 2	. . .	. . .	s (ʃ)	. . .	. . . .	. . .	. . .	. . .	ס	. . .
35 „ lenis	z	. . .	. . . .	. . .	𐬰	𐭦	ز (ذ)	ز	ז	z
36 „ asperrimus 1	. . .	. . .	z (ʒ)	. . .	. . . .	. . .	ص	ص	צ	ʒ, ʒh
37 „ asperrimus 2	. . .	. . .	ẓ (ʒ)	. . .	. . . .	. . .	ض	. . .	. . .	. . .

	I	II	III	Sanskrit	Zend	Pehlevi	Persian	Arabic	Hebrew	Chinese
Dentales modificatae (linguales, &c.)										
38 Tenuis	...	*t*	...	ट	...	...	ط	ط	ט	...
39 „ aspirata	...	*th*	...	ठ	...	...	ظ	ظ	...	...
40 Media	...	*d*	...	ड	𐬜	[illegible]	...	...	...	...
41 „ aspirata	...	*dh*	...	ढ	...	...	...	ض	...	...
42 Nasalis	...	*n*	...	ण	𐬣	...	...	...	...	...
43 Semivocalis	r	...	...	र	𐬭	[illegible]	ر	ر	ר	...
44 „ fricata	...	*r*	...	...	...	...	...	...	...	r
45 „ diacritica	...	...	R	...	...	...	...	...	...	...
46 Spiritus asper	sh	...	...	ष	𐬴	[illegible]	...	...	...	sh
47 „ lenis	zh	...	...	...	...	...	...	...	...	...
Labiales.										
48 Tenuis	p	...	...	प	𐬞	[illegible]	پ	...	פּ	p
49 „ aspirata	ph	...	...	फ	...	...	...	...	פ	ph
50 Media	b	...	...	ब	𐬠	[illegible]	ب	ب	בּ	...
51 „ aspirata	bh	...	...	भ	...	...	...	...	ב	...
52 Tenuissima	...	*p*	...	...	...	...	...	...	...	...
53 Nasalis	m	...	...	म	𐬨	[illegible]	م	م	מ	m
54 Semivocalis	w	...	...	...	𐬬	...	...	...	...	w
55 „ aspirata	hw	...	...	...	...	...	...	...	...	...
56 Spiritus asper	f	...	...	...	𐬟	[illegible]	ف	ف	...	f
57 „ lenis	v	...	...	व	𐬎	[illegible]	و	و	ו	...
58 Anusvâra	...	*m*	...	अं	𐬄 ã	...	...	...	...	...
59 Visarga	...	*h*	...	अः	...	...	...	...	...	...

VOWELS.	MISSIONARY ALPHABET. I Class.	II Class.	III Class.	Sanskrit.	Zend.	Pehlevi.	Persian.	Arabic.	Hebrew.	Chinese.
1 Neutralis	0	. . .	. . . .	. . .	. . . .	. . .	. . .	. . .	ְ	ă
2 Laryngo-palatalis	ĕ	. . .	. . . .	. . .	. . . .	. . .	. . .	. . .	. . .	. . .
3 „ labialis	ŏ	. . .	. . . .	. . .	. . . .	𐮅 fin.	. . .	. . .	. . .	. . .
4 Gutturalis brevis	a	. . .	. . . .	अ	𐬀	𐮀 init.	ـَ	ـَ	ַ	a
5 „ longa	â	(*a*)	. . . .	आ	𐬁	𐮀	ـَا	ـَا	ָ	â
6 Palatalis brevis	i	. . .	. . . .	इ	𐬌	. . .	ـِ	ـِ	ִ	i
7 „ longa	î	(*i*)	. . . .	ई	𐬍	𐮊	ـِي	ـِي	ִי	î
8 Dentalis brevis	*li*	. . .	. . . .	ऌ	. . . .	. . .	. . .	. . .	. . .	. . .
9 „ longa	*lî*	. . .	. . . .	ॡ	. . . .	. . .	. . .	. . .	. . .	. . .
10 Lingualis brevis	*ri*	. . .	. . . .	ऋ	. . . .	. . .	. . .	. . .	. . .	. . .
11 „ longa	*rî*	. . .	. . . .	ॠ	. . . .	. . .	. . .	. . .	. . .	. . .
12 Labialis brevis	u	. . .	. . . .	उ	𐬎	. . .	ـُ	ـُ	ֻ	u
13 „ longa	û	(*u*)	. . . .	ऊ	𐬏	𐮅	ـُو	ـُو	וּ	û
14 Gutturo-palatalis brevis . . .	e	. . .	. . . .	. . .	𐬈 (e) 𐬉 (*e*)	. . .	. . .	. . .	ֶ	e
15 „ longa . . .	ê (ai)	(*e*)	. . . .	ए	𐬀𐬉, 𐬀𐬉	𐮊	. . .	. . .	ֵ	ê
16 Diphthongus gutturo-palatalis	âi	(*ai*)	. . . .	ऐ	. . . .	. . .	ـَيْ	ـَيْ	. . .	âi
17 „ „	ei (ĕi)	. . .	. . . .	. . .	. . . .	. . .	. . .	. . .	. . .	ei, êi
18 „ „	oi (ŏu)	. . .	. . . .	. . .	. . . .	. . .	. . .	. . .	. . .	. . .
19 Gutturo-labialis brevis	o	. . .	. . . .	. . .	𐬊	. . .	. . .	. . .	ָ	o
20 „ longa	ô (au)	(*o*)	. . . .	ओ	𐬋	𐮅	. . .	. . .	וֹ	. . .
21 Diphthongus gutturo-labialis	âu	(*au*)	. . . .	औ	𐬀𐬊 (*au*)	. . .	ـَوْ	ـَوْ	. . .	âu
22 „ „	eu (ĕu)	. . .	. . . .	. . .	. . . .	. . .	. . .	. . .	. . .	. . .
23 „ „	ou (ŏu)	. . .	. . . .	. . .	. . . .	. . .	. . .	. . .	. . .	. . .
24 Gutturalis fracta	ä	. . .	. . . .	. . .	. . . .	. . .	. . .	. . .	. . .	. . .
25 Palatalis fracta	ï	. . .	. . . .	. . .	. . . .	. . .	. . .	. . .	. . .	ü
26 Labialis fracta	ü	. . .	. . . .	. . .	. . . .	. . .	. . .	. . .	. . .	. . .
27 Gutturo-labialis fracta	ö	. . .	. . . .	. . .	. . . .	. . .	. . .	. . .	. . .	. . .

October, 1882.

Clarendon Press, Oxford.

A SELECTION OF

BOOKS

PUBLISHED FOR THE UNIVERSITY BY

HENRY FROWDE,

AT THE OXFORD UNIVERSITY PRESS WAREHOUSE,

7 PATERNOSTER ROW, LONDON.

ALSO TO BE HAD AT THE

CLARENDON PRESS DEPOSITORY, OXFORD.

LEXICONS, GRAMMARS, &c.

(See also Clarendon Press Series, pp. 21, 24.)

A Greek-English Lexicon, by Henry George Liddell, D.D., and Robert Scott, D.D. Sixth Edition, Revised and Augmented. 1870. 4to. cloth, 1*l*. 16*s*.

A copious Greek-English Vocabulary, compiled from the best authorities. 1850. 24mo. bound, 3*s*.

A Practical Introduction to Greek Accentuation, by H. W. Chandler, M.A. Second Edition. 1881. 8vo. cloth, 10*s*. 6*d*.

A Latin Dictionary, founded on Andrews' edition of Freund's Latin Dictionary, revised, enlarged, and in great part rewritten by Charlton T. Lewis, Ph.D., and Charles Short, LL.D., Professor of Latin in Columbia College, New York. 1879. 4to. cloth, 1*l*. 5*s*.

The Book of Hebrew Roots, by Abu 'l-Walîd Marwân ibn Janâh, otherwise called Rabbî Yônâh. Now first edited, with an Appendix, by Ad. Neubauer. 1875. 4to. cloth, 2*l*. 7*s*. 6*d*.

A Treatise on the use of the Tenses in Hebrew. By S. R. Driver, M.A. Second Edition, Revised and Enlarged. 1881. Extra fcap. 8vo. cloth, 7*s.* 6*d.*

Hebrew Accentuation of Psalms, Proverbs, and Job. By William Wickes, D.D. 1881. Demy 8vo. stiff cover, 5*s.*

Thesaurus Syriacus: collegerunt Quatremère, Bernstein, Lorsbach, Arnoldi, Field: edidit R. Payne Smith, S.T.P.R.

Fasc. I–V. 1868–79. sm. fol. each, 1*l.* 1*s.*
Vol. I, containing Fasc. I–V. sm. fol. cloth, 5*l.* 5*s.*

A Practical Grammar of the Sanskrit Language, arranged with reference to the Classical Languages of Europe, for the use of English Students, by Monier Williams, M.A., Boden Professor of Sanskrit. Fourth Edition, 1877. 8vo. cloth, 15*s.*

A Sanskrit-English Dictionary, Etymologically and Philologically arranged, with special reference to Greek, Latin, German, Anglo-Saxon, English, and other cognate Indo-European Languages. By Monier Williams, M.A., Boden Professor of Sanskrit. 1872. 4to. cloth, 4*l.* 14*s.* 6*d.*

Nalopákhyánam. Story of Nala, an Episode of the Mahá-Bhárata: the Sanskrit text, with a copious Vocabulary, and an improved version of Dean Milman's Translation, by Monier Williams, M.A. Second Edition, Revised and Improved. 1879. 8vo. cloth, 15*s.*

Sakuntalā. A Sanskrit Drama, in seven Acts. Edited by Monier Williams, M.A. Second Edition, 1876. 8vo. cloth, 21*s.*

An Anglo-Saxon Dictionary, based on the MS. Collections of the late Joseph Bosworth, D.D., Professor of Anglo-Saxon, Oxford. Edited and enlarged by Prof. T. N. Toller, M.A., Owens College, Manchester. (To be completed in four parts). Parts I and II. 4to. 15*s.* each. *Just Published.*

An Icelandic-English Dictionary, based on the MS. collections of the late Richard Cleasby. Enlarged and completed by G. Vigfússon. With an Introduction, and Life of Richard Cleasby, by G. Webbe Dasent, D.C.L. 1874. 4to. cloth, 3*l.* 7*s.*

A List of English Words the Etymology of which is illustrated by comparison with Icelandic. Prepared in the form of an APPENDIX to the above. By W. W. Skeat, M.A., stitched, 2*s.*

A Handbook of the Chinese Language. Parts I and II, Grammar and Chrestomathy. By James Summers. 1863. 8vo. half bound, 1*l.* 8*s.*

An Etymological Dictionary of the English Language, arranged on an Historical Basis. By W. W. Skeat, M.A., Elrington and Bosworth Professor of Anglo-Saxon in the University of Cambridge. 1882. 4to. cloth, 2*l.* 4*s.*

Part IV., completing the Work, 10*s.* 6*d.*

A Concise Etymological Dictionary of the English Language. By W. W. Skeat, M.A. 1882. Crown 8vo. cloth, 5*s.* 6*d.*

GREEK CLASSICS, &c.

Heracliti Ephesii Reliquiae. Recensuit I. Bywater, M.A. Appendicis loco additae sunt Diogenis Laertii Vita Heracliti, Particulae Hippocratei De Diaeta Libri Primi, Epistolae Heracliteae. 1877. 8vo. cloth, price 6*s.*

Homer: A Complete Concordance to the Odyssey and Hymns of Homer; to which is added a Concordance to the Parallel Passages in the Iliad, Odyssey, and Hymns. By Henry Dunbar, M.D., Member of the General Council, University of Edinburgh. 1880. 4to. cloth, 1*l.* 1*s.*

Plato: The Apology, with a revised Text and English Notes, and a Digest of Platonic Idioms, by James Riddell, M.A. 1878. 8vo. cloth, 8*s.* 6*d.*

Plato: Philebus, with a revised Text and English Notes, by Edward Poste, M.A. 1860. 8vo. cloth, 7*s.* 6*d.*

Plato: Sophistes and Politicus, with a revised Text and English Notes, by L. Campbell, M.A. 1866. 8vo. cloth, 18*s.*

Plato: Theaetetus, with a revised Text and English Notes, by L. Campbell, M.A. New Edition in the Press.

Plato: The Dialogues, translated into English, with Analyses and Introductions, by B. Jowett, M.A., Regius Professor of Greek. A new Edition in 5 volumes, medium 8vo. 1875. cloth, 3*l.* 10*s.*

Plato: The Republic, translated into English, with an Analysis and Introduction, by B. Jowett, M.A. Medium 8vo. cloth, 12*s.* 6*d.*

Plato: Index to. Compiled for the Second Edition of Professor Jowett's Translation of the Dialogues. By Evelyn Abbott, M.A. 1875. 8vo. paper covers, 2*s.* 6*d.*

Thucydides: Translated into English, with Introduction, Marginal Analysis, Notes, and Indices. By B. Jowett, M.A., Regius Professor of Greek. 2 vols. 1881. Medium 8vo. cloth, 1*l.* 12*s.*

THE HOLY SCRIPTURES, &c.

The Holy Bible in the earliest English Versions, made from the Latin Vulgate by John Wycliffe and his followers: edited by the Rev. J. Forshall and Sir F. Madden. 4 vols. 1850. Royal 4to. cloth, 3*l.* 3*s.*

Also reprinted from the above, with Introduction and Glossary by W. W. Skeat, M.A.

The New Testament in English, according to the Version by John Wycliffe, about A.D. 1380, and Revised by John Purvey, about A.D. 1388. Extra fcap. 8vo. cloth, 6*s.*

The Books of Job, Psalms, Proverbs, Ecclesiastes, and the Song of Solomon: according to the Wycliffite Version made by Nicholas de Hereford, about A.D. 1381, and Revised by John Purvey, about A.D. 1388. Extra fcap. 8vo. cloth, 3*s.* 6*d.*

The Holy Bible: an exact reprint, page for page, of the Authorized Version published in the year 1611. Demy 4to. half bound, 1*l.* 1*s.*

Vetus Testamentum ex Versione Septuaginta Interpretum secundum exemplar Vaticanum Romae editum. Accedit potior varietas Codicis Alexandrini. Tomi III. Editio Altera. 18mo. cloth, 18*s.*

Origenis Hexaplorum quae supersunt; sive, Veterum Interpretum Graecorum in totum Vetus Testamentum Fragmenta. Edidit Fridericus Field, A.M. 2 vols. 1867–1874. 4to. cloth, 5*l.* 5*s.*

Libri Psalmorum Versio antiqua Latina, cum Paraphrasi Anglo-Saxonica. Edidit B. Thorpe, F.A.S. 1835. 8vo. cloth, 10*s.* 6*d.*

Libri Psalmorum Versio antiqua Gallica e Cod. MS. in Bibl. Bodleiana adservato, una cum Versione Metrica aliisque Monumentis pervetustis. Nunc primum descripsit et edidit Franciscus Michel, Phil. Doct. 1860. 8vo. cloth, 10*s.* 6*d.*

The Psalms in Hebrew without points. 1879. Crown 8vo. cloth, 3*s.* 6*d.*

The Book of Wisdom: the Greek Text, the Latin Vulgate, and the Authorised English Version; with an Introduction, Critical Apparatus, and a Commentary. By William J. Deane, M.A., Oriel College, Oxford; Rector of Ashen, Essex. Small 4to. cloth, 12*s.* 6*d.*

The Book of Tobit. A Chaldee Text, from a unique MS. in the Bodleian Library; with other Rabbinical Texts, English Translations, and the Itala. Edited by Ad. Neubauer, M.A. 1878. Crown 8vo. cloth, 6*s.*

A Commentary on the Book of Proverbs. Attributed to Abraham Ibn Ezra. Edited from a Manuscript in the Bodleian Library by S. R. Driver, M.A. Crown 8vo. paper cover, 3*s.* 6*d.*

Horae Hebraicae et Talmudicae, a J. Lightfoot. A new Edition, by R. Gandell, M.A. 4 vols. 1859. 8vo. cloth, 1*l.* 1*s.*

Novum Testamentum Graece. Antiquissimorum Codicum Textus in ordine parallelo dispositi. Accedit collatio Codicis Sinaitici. Edidit E. H. Hansell, S.T.B. Tomi III. 1864. 8vo. half morocco, 2*l.* 12*s.* 6*d.*

Novum Testamentum Graece. Accedunt parallela S. Scripturae loca, necnon vetus capitulorum notatio et canones Eusebii. Edidit Carolus Lloyd, S.T.P.R., necnon Episcopus Oxoniensis. 18mo. cloth, 3*s.*

The same on writing paper, with large margin, cloth, 10*s.*

Novum Testamentum Graece juxta Exemplar Millianum. 18mo. cloth, 2s. 6d.

The same on writing paper, with large margin, cloth, 9s.

Evangelia Sacra Graece. fcap. 8vo. limp, 1s. 6d.

The Greek Testament, with the Readings adopted by the Revisers of the Authorised Version:—

(1) Pica type. Second Edition, with Marginal References. Demy 8vo. cloth, 10s. 6d.

(2) Long Primer type. Fcap. 8vo. cloth, 4s. 6d.

(3) The same, on writing paper, with wide margin, cloth, 15s.

Canon Muratorianus: the earliest Catalogue of the Books of the New Testament. Edited with Notes and a Facsimile of the MS. in the Ambrosian Library at Milan, by S. P. Tregelles, LL.D. 1868. 4to. cloth, 10s. 6d.

FATHERS OF THE CHURCH, &c.

St. Athanasius: Orations against the Arians. With an Account of his Life by William Bright, D.D. 1873. Crown 8vo. cloth, 9s.

St. Athanasius: Historical Writings, according to the Benedictine Text. With an Introduction by William Bright, D.D. 1881. Crown 8vo. cloth, 10s. 6d.

St. Augustine: Select Anti-Pelagian Treatises, and the Acts of the Second Council of Orange. With an Introduction by William Bright, D.D. Crown 8vo. cloth, 9s.

The Canons of the First Four General Councils of Nicaea, Constantinople, Ephesus, and Chalcedon. 1877. Crown 8vo. cloth, 2s. 6d.

Notes on the Canons of the First Four General Councils. By William Bright, D.D. 1882. Crown 8vo. cloth, 5s. 6d.

Cyrilli Archiepiscopi Alexandrini in XII Prophetas. Edidit P. E. Pusey, A.M. Tomi II. 1868. 8vo. cloth, 2*l.* 2*s.*

Cyrilli Archiepiscopi Alexandrini in D. Joannis Evangelium. Accedunt Fragmenta Varia necnon Tractatus ad Tiberium Diaconum Duo. Edidit post Aubertum P. E. Pusey, A.M. Tomi III. 1872. 8vo. 2*l.* 5*s.*

Cyrilli Archiepiscopi Alexandrini Commentarii in Lucae Evangelium quae supersunt Syriace. E MSS. apud Mus. Britan. edidit R. Payne Smith, A.M. 1858. 4to. cloth, 1*l.* 2*s.*

The same, translated by R. Payne Smith, M.A. 2 vols. 1859. 8vo. cloth, 14*s.*

Ephraemi Syri, Rabulae Episcopi Edesseni, Balaei, aliorumque Opera Selecta. E Codd. Syriacis MSS. in Museo Britannico et Bibliotheca Bodleiana asservatis primus edidit J. J. Overbeck. 1865. 8vo. cloth, 1*l.* 1*s.*

Eusebius' Ecclesiastical History, according to the text of Burton, with an Introduction by William Bright, D.D. 1881. Crown 8vo. cloth, 8*s.* 6*d.*

Irenaeus: The Third Book of St. Irenaeus, Bishop of Lyons, against Heresies. With short Notes and a Glossary by H. Deane, B.D., Fellow of St. John's College, Oxford. 1874. Crown 8vo. cloth, 5*s.* 6*d.*

Patrum Apostolicorum, S. Clementis Romani, S. Ignatii, S. Polycarpi, quae supersunt. Edidit Guil. Jacobson, S.T.P.R. Tomi II. Fourth Edition, 1863. 8vo. cloth, 1*l.* 1*s.*

Socrates' Ecclesiastical History, according to the Text of Hussey, with an Introduction by William Bright, D.D. 1878. Crown 8vo. cloth, 7*s.* 6*d.*

ECCLESIASTICAL HISTORY, BIOGRAPHY, &c.

Baedae Historia Ecclesiastica. Edited, with English Notes, by G. H. Moberly, M.A. 1881. Crown 8vo. cloth, 10*s.* 6*d.*

Bright (W., D.D.). Chapters of Early English Church History. 1878. 8vo. cloth, 12*s.*

Burnet's History of the Reformation of the Church of England. A new Edition. Carefully revised, and the Records collated with the originals, by N. Pocock, M.A. 7 vols. 1865. 8vo. *Price reduced to* 1*l.* 10*s.*

Councils and Ecclesiastical Documents relating to Great Britain and Ireland. Edited, after Spelman and Wilkins, by A. W. Haddan, B.D., and W. Stubbs, M.A., Regius Professor of Modern History, Oxford. Vols. I. and III. 1869–71. Medium 8vo. cloth, each 1*l.* 1*s.*

Vol. II. Part I. 1873. Medium 8vo. cloth, 10*s.* 6*d.*

Vol. II. Part II. 1878. Church of Ireland; Memorials of St. Patrick. Stiff covers, 3*s.* 6*d.*

Hammond (C. E.). Liturgies, Eastern and Western. Edited, with Introduction, Notes, and a Liturgical Glossary. 1878. Crown 8vo. cloth, 10*s.* 6*d.*

An Appendix to the above. 1879. Crown 8vo. paper covers, 1*s.* 6*d.*

John, Bishop of Ephesus. The Third Part of his Ecclesiastical History. [In Syriac.] Now first edited by William Cureton, M.A. 1853. 4to. cloth, 1*l.* 12*s.*

The same, translated by R. Payne Smith, M.A. 1860. 8vo. cloth, 10*s.*

Monumenta Ritualia Ecclesiae Anglicanae. The occasional Offices of the Church of England according to the old use of Salisbury the Prymer in English, and other prayers and forms, with dissertations and notes. By William Maskell, M.A. Second Edition. 1882. 3 vols. 8vo. cloth, 2*l.* 10*s.*

The Ancient Liturgy of the Church of England, according to the uses of Sarum, York, Hereford, and Bangor, and the Roman Liturgy arranged in parallel columns, with preface and notes. By William Maskell, M.A. Third Edition. 1882. 8vo. cloth, 15*s.*

The Liturgy and Ritual of the Celtic Church. By F. E. Warren, B.D., Fellow of St. John's College, Oxford. 1881. 8vo. cloth, 14*s.*

The Leofric Missal. By the same Editor. In the Press.

Records of the Reformation. The Divorce, 1527-1533. Mostly now for the first time printed from MSS. in the British Museum and other libraries. Collected and arranged by N. Pocock, M.A. 1870. 2 vols. 8vo. cloth, 1*l.* 16*s.*

Shirley (*W. W.*). *Some Account of the Church in the Apostolic Age.* Second Edition, 1874. fcap. 8vo. cloth, 3*s.* 6*d.*

Stubbs (*W.*). *Registrum Sacrum Anglicanum.* An attempt to exhibit the course of Episcopal Succession in England. 1858. small 4to. cloth, 8*s.* 6*d.*

ENGLISH THEOLOGY.

Butler's Works, with an Index to the Analogy. 2 vols. 1874. 8vo. cloth, 11*s.*

Butler's Sermons. 8vo. cloth, 5*s.* 6*d.*

Butler's Analogy of Religion. 8vo. cloth, 5*s.* 6*d.*

Heurtley's Collection of Creeds. 1858. 8vo. cloth, 6*s.* 6*d.*

Homilies appointed to be read in Churches. Edited by J. Griffiths, M.A. 1859. 8vo. cloth, 7*s.* 6*d.*

Hooker's Works, with his Life by Walton, arranged by John Keble, M.A. Sixth Edition, 1874. 3 vols. 8vo. cloth, 1*l.* 11*s.* 6*d.*

Hooker's Works; the text as arranged by John Keble, M.A. 2 vols. 1875. 8vo. cloth, 11*s.*

Pearson's Exposition of the Creed. Revised and corrected by E. Burton, D.D. Sixth Edition, 1877. 8vo. cloth, 10*s.* 6*d.*

Waterland's Review of the Doctrine of the Eucharist, with a Preface by the present Bishop of London. 1880. Crown 8vo. cloth, 6*s.* 6*d.*

Wheatly's Illustration of the Book of Common Prayer. A new Edition, 1846. 8vo. cloth, 5*s.*

Wyclif. A Catalogue of the Original Works of John Wyclif, by W. W. Shirley, D.D. 1865. 8vo. cloth, 3*s.* 6*d.*

Wyclif. Select English Works. By T. Arnold, M.A. 3 vols. 1871. 8vo. cloth. *Price reduced to* 1*l.* 1*s.*

Wyclif. Trialogus. With the Supplement now first edited. By Gotthard Lechler. 1869. 8vo. cloth. *Price reduced to* 7*s.*

HISTORICAL AND DOCUMENTARY WORKS.

British Barrows, a Record of the Examination of Sepulchral Mounds in various parts of England. By William Greenwell, M.A., F.S.A. Together with Description of Figures of Skulls, General Remarks on Prehistoric Crania, and an Appendix by George Rolleston, M.D., F.R.S. 1877. Medium 8vo. cloth, 25*s.*

Britton. A Treatise upon the Common Law of England, composed by order of King Edward I. The French Text carefully revised, with an English Translation, Introduction, and Notes, by F. M. Nichols, M.A. 2 vols. 1865. Royal 8vo. cloth, 1*l.* 16*s.*

Clarendon's (Edw. Earl of) History of the Rebellion and Civil Wars in England. 7 vols. 1839. 18mo. cloth, 1*l.* 1*s.*

Clarendon's (Edw. Earl of) History of the Rebellion and Civil Wars in England. Also his Life, written by himself, in which is included a Continuation of his History of the Grand Rebellion. With copious Indexes. In one volume, royal 8vo. 1842. cloth, 1*l.* 2*s.*

Clinton's Epitome of the Fasti Hellenici. 1851. 8vo. cloth, 6*s.* 6*d.*

Clinton's Epitome of the Fasti Romani. 1854. 8vo. cloth, 7*s.*

Freeman's (E. A.) History of the Norman Conquest of England; its Causes and Results. In Six Volumes. 8vo. cloth, 5*l.* 9*s.* 6*d.*

Vols. I–II together, 3rd edition, 1877. 1*l.* 16*s.*
Vol. III, 2nd edition, 1874. 1*l.* 1*s.*
Vol. IV, 2nd edition, 1875. 1*l.* 1*s.*
Vol. V, 1876. 1*l.* 1*s.*
Vol. VI. Index. 1879. 8vo. cloth, 10*s.* 6*d.*

Freeman (E. A.). The Reign of William Rufus and the Accession of Henry the First. 2 vols. 8vo. cloth, 1*l.* 16*s.*

Gascoigne's Theological Dictionary ("Liber Veritatum"): Selected Passages, illustrating the condition of Church and State, 1403–1458. With an Introduction by James E. Thorold Rogers, M.P. Small 4to. cloth, 10*s.* 6*d.*

Magna Carta, a careful Reprint. Edited by W. Stubbs, M.A., Regius Professor of Modern History. 1879. 4to. stitched, 1*s.*

Olaf. Passio et Miracula Beati Olavi. Edited from a Twelfth-Century MS. in the Library of Corpus Christi College, Oxford, with an Introduction and Notes, by Frederick Metcalfe, M.A. Small 4to. stiff cover, 6*s.*

Protests of the Lords, including those which have been expunged, from 1624 to 1874; with Historical Introductions. Edited by James E. Thorold Rogers, M.A. 1875. 3 vols. 8vo. cloth, 2*l.* 2*s.*

Rogers's History of Agriculture and Prices in England, A.D. 1259–1793.

Vols. I and II (1259–1400). 1866. 8vo. cloth, 2*l.* 2*s.*
Vols. III and IV (1401–1582). 1882. 8vo. cloth, 2*l.* 10*s.*

Sturlunga Saga, including the Islendinga Saga of Lawman Sturla Thordsson and other works. Edited by Dr. Gudbrand Vigfússon. In 2 vols. 1878. 8vo. cloth, 2*l.* 2*s.*

Two of the Saxon Chronicles parallel, with Supplementary Extracts from the Others. Edited, with Introduction, Notes, and a Glossarial Index, by J. Earle, M.A. 1865. 8vo. cloth, 16*s.*

Statuta Universitatis Oxoniensis. 1882. 8vo. cloth, 5*s*.

The Student's Handbook to the University and Colleges of Oxford. Sixth Edition. 1881. Extra fcap. 8vo. cloth, 2*s*. 6*d*.

MATHEMATICS, PHYSICAL SCIENCE, &c.

Astronomical Observations made at the University Observatory, Oxford, under the direction of C. Pritchard, M.A., Savilian Professor of Astronomy. No. 1. 1878. Royal 8vo. paper covers, 3*s*. 6*d*.

Treatise on Infinitesimal Calculus. By Bartholomew Price, M.A., F.R.S., Professor of Natural Philosophy, Oxford.

Vol. I. Differential Calculus. Second Edition, 8vo. cloth, 14*s*. 6*d*.

Vol. II. Integral Calculus, Calculus of Variations, and Differential Equations. Second Edition, 1865. 8vo. cloth, 18*s*.

Vol. III. Statics, including Attractions; Dynamics of a Material Particle. Second Edition, 1868. 8vo. cloth, 16*s*.

Vol. IV. Dynamics of Material Systems; together with a chapter on Theoretical Dynamics, by W. F. Donkin, M.A., F.R.S. 1862. 8vo. cloth, 16*s*.

Rigaud's Correspondence of Scientific Men of the 17th Century, with Table of Contents by A. de Morgan, and Index by the Rev. J. Rigaud, M.A., Fellow of Magdalen College, Oxford. 2 vols. 1841–1862. 8vo. cloth, 18*s*. 6*d*.

Vesuvius. By John Phillips, M.A., F.R.S., Professor of Geology, Oxford. 1869. Crown 8vo. cloth, 10*s*. 6*d*.

Geology of Oxford and the Valley of the Thames. By the same Author. 1871. 8vo. cloth, 21*s*.

Synopsis of the Pathological Series in the Oxford Museum. By H. W. Acland, M.D., F.R.S., 1867. 8vo. cloth, 2*s*. 6*d*.

Thesaurus Entomologicus Hopeianus, or a Description of the rarest Insects in the Collection given to the University by the Rev. William Hope. By J. O. Westwood, M.A., F.L.S. With 40 Plates. 1874. Small folio, half morocco, 7*l*. 10*s*.

Text-Book of Botany, Morphological and Physiological. By Dr. Julius Sachs, Professor of Botany in the University of Würzburg. *A New Edition.* Translated by S. H. Vines, M.A. Royal 8vo. 1*l*. 11*s*. 6*d*. *Just Published.*

Johannes Müller on Certain Variations in the Vocal Organs of the Passeres that have hitherto escaped notice. Translated by F. J. Bell, B.A., and edited with an Appendix, by A. H. Garrod, M.A., F.R.S. With Plates. 1878. 4to. paper covers, 7*s*. 6*d*.

MISCELLANEOUS.

Bacon's Novum Organum. Edited, with English notes, by G. W. Kitchin, M.A. 1855. 8vo. cloth, 9*s*. 6*d*.

Bacon's Novum Organum. Translated by G. W. Kitchin, M.A. 1855. 8vo. cloth, 9*s*. 6*d*. (See also p. 37.)

The Works of George Berkeley, D.D., formerly Bishop of Cloyne; including many of his writings hitherto unpublished. With Prefaces, Annotations, and an Account of his Life and Philosophy, by Alexander Campbell Fraser, M.A. 4 vols. 1871. 8vo. cloth, 2*l*. 18*s*.

The Life, Letters, &c. 1 vol. cloth, 16*s*. See also p. 37.

The Logic of Hegel; translated from the Encyclopaedia of the Philosophical Sciences. With Prolegomena by William Wallace, M.A. 1874. 8vo. cloth, 14*s*.

Smith's Wealth of Nations. A new Edition, with Notes, by J. E. Thorold Rogers, M.A. 2 vols. 1880. cloth, 21*s*.

A Course of Lectures on Art, delivered before the University of Oxford in Hilary Term, 1870, by John Ruskin, M.A., Slade Professor of Fine Art. 8vo. cloth, 6*s*.

Aspects of Poetry; being Lectures delivered at Oxford by John Campbell Shairp, LL.D., Professor of Poetry, Oxford. Crown 8vo. cloth, 10*s*. 6*d*.

A Critical Account of the Drawings by Michel Angelo and Raffaello in the University Galleries, Oxford. By J. C. Robinson, F.S.A. 1870. Crown 8vo. cloth, 4*s*.

Catalogue of the Castellani Collection of Antiquities in the University Galleries, Oxford. By W. S. W. Vaux, M.A., F.R.S. Crown 8vo. stiff cover, 1*s*.

The Sacred Books of the East.

TRANSLATED BY VARIOUS ORIENTAL SCHOLARS, AND EDITED BY F. MAX MÜLLER.

Vol. I. *The Upanishads.* [Translated by F. Max Müller.] Part I. The *Kh*ândogya-upanishad, The Talavakâra-upanishad, The Aitareya-âra*n*yaka, The Kaushîtaki-brâhma*n*a-upanishad, and The V*â*gasaneyi-sa*m*hitâ-upanishad. 8vo. cloth, 10*s*. 6*d*.

Vol. II. *The Sacred Laws of the Âryas*, as taught in the Schools of Âpastamba, Gautama, Vâsish*th*a, and Baudhâyana. [Translated by Prof. Georg Bühler.] Part I, Âpastamba and Gautama. 8vo. cloth, 10*s*. 6*d*.

Vol. III. *The Sacred Books of China.* The Texts of Confucianism. [Translated by James Legge.] Part I. The Shû King, The Religious portions of the Shih King, and The Hsiâo King. 8vo. cloth, 12*s*. 6*d*.

Vol. IV. *The Vendîdâd.* Translated by James Darmesteter. 8vo. cloth, 10*s*. 6*d*.

Vol. V. *The Bundahis, Bahman Yast, and Shâyast-lâ-Shâyast.* Pahlavi Texts, Part I. Translated by E. W. West. 8vo. cloth, 12*s*. 6*d*.

Vols. VI and IX. *The Qur'ân.* Parts I and II. Translated by Professor E. H. Palmer. 8vo. cloth, 21*s*.

Vol. VII. *The Institutes of Vishnu.* Translated by Professor Julius Jolly. 8vo. cloth, 10*s*. 6*d*.

Vol. VIII. *The Bhagavadgîtâ, Sanatsugâtîya, and Anugîtâ.* Translated by Kâshinâth Trimbak Telang. 8vo. cloth, 10*s*. 6*d*.

Vol. X. *The Dhammapada*, translated by Professor F. Max Müller; and *The Sutta Nipâta*, translated by Professor Fausböll; being Canonical Books of the Buddhists. 8vo. cloth, 10*s*. 6*d*.

Vol. XI. *The Mahâparinibbâna Sutta, The Tevigga Sutta, The Mahâsudassana Sutta, The Dhamma-Kakkappavattana Sutta.* Translated by T. W. Rhys Davids. 8vo. cloth, 10*s*. 6*d*.

Vol. XII. *The Satapatha-Brâhmana.* Translated by Professor Eggeling. Vol. I. 8vo. cloth, 12*s*. 6*d*.

Vol. XIII. *The Pâtimokkha.* Translated by T. W. Rhys Davids. *The Mahâvagga*, Part I. Translated by Dr. H. Oldenberg.

Vol. XVI. *The Yî King*, with an Appendix on the Philosophy of the Scholars of the Sung dynasty, professedly derived from the Yî. Translated by James Legge.

The following Volumes are in the Press:—

Vol. XIV. *The Sacred Laws of the Âryas*, as taught in the Schools of Vâsish*th*a and Baudhâyana. Translated by Professor Georg Bühler.

Vol. XV. *The Upanishads.* Part II. Translated by F. Max Müller.

Vol. XVII. *The Mahâvagga, and Kullavagga.* Part II. Translated by T. W. Rhys Davids and Dr. H. Oldenberg.

Vol. XVIII. *The Dâdistân-î Dînîk, and Epistles of Mânûskihar.* Pahlavi exts, Part II. Translated by E. W. West.

Vol. XIX. *The Fo-sho-hing-tsan-king.* Translated by Samuel Beal.

Vol. XX. *The Vâyu-Purâna.* Translated by Professor Bhandarkar, of Elphinstone College, Bombay.

Vol. XXI. *The Saddharma-pundarîka.* Translated by Professor Kern.

Vol. XXII. *The Âkârâṅga-Sûtra.* Translated by Professor Jacobi.

Anecdota Oxoniensia:

Classical Series. Vol. I. Part I. *The English Manuscripts of the Nicomachean Ethics,* described in relation to Bekker's Manuscripts and other Sources. By J. A. Stewart, M.A., Classical Lecturer, Christ Church. Small 4to. 3*s*. 6*d*.

Classical Series. Vol. I. Part II. *Nonius Marcellus,* de Compendiosa Doctrina, Harleian MS. 2719. Collated by J. H. Onions, M.A., Senior Student of Christ Church. Small 4to. 3*s*. 6*d*.

Semitic Series. Vol. I. Part I. *Commentary on Ezra and Nehemiah.* By Rabbi Saadiah. Edited by H. J. Matthews, M.A., Exeter College, Oxford. Small 4to. 3*s*. 6*d*.

Aryan Series. Vol. I. Part I. *Buddhist Texts from Japan.* Edited by F. Max Müller. Small 4to. 3*s*. 6*d*.

Mediaeval and Modern Series. Vol. I. Part I. *Sinonoma Bartholomei;* A Glossary from a Fourteenth-Century MS. in the Library of Pembroke College, Oxford. Edited by J. L. G. Mowat, M.A., Fellow of Pembroke College. Small 4to. 3*s*. 6*d*.

Clarendon Press Series

The Delegates of the Clarendon Press having undertaken the publication of a series of works, chiefly educational, and entitled the **Clarendon Press Series**, have published, or have in preparation, the following.

Those to which prices are attached are already published; the others are in preparation.

I. ENGLISH.

A First Reading Book. By Marie Eichens of Berlin; and edited by Anne J. Clough. Extra fcap. 8vo. stiff covers, *4d.*

Oxford Reading Book, Part I. For Little Children. Extra fcap. 8vo. stiff covers, *6d.*

Oxford Reading Book, Part II. For Junior Classes. Extra fcap. 8vo. stiff covers, *6d.*

An Elementary English Grammar and Exercise Book. By O. W. Tancock, M.A., Head Master of Norwich School. Second Edition. Extra fcap. 8vo. cloth, 1*s.* *6d.*

An English Grammar and Reading Bobk, for Lower Forms in Classical Schools. By O. W. Tancock, M.A., Head Master of Norwich School. Third Edition. Extra fcap. 8vo. cloth, 3*s.* *6d.*

Typical Selections from the best English Writers, with Introductory Notices. Second Edition. In Two Volumes. Extra fcap. 8vo. cloth, 3*s.* *6d.* each.

Vol. I. Latimer to Berkeley. Vol. II. Pope to Macaulay.

The Philology of the English Tongue. By J. Earle, M.A., formerly Fellow of Oriel College, and Professor of Anglo-Saxon, Oxford. Third Edition. Extra fcap. 8vo. cloth, 7*s.* *6d.*

A Book for the Beginner in Anglo-Saxon. By John Earle, M.A., Professor of Anglo-Saxon, Oxford. Second Edition. Extra fcap. 8vo. cloth, 2s. 6d.

An Anglo-Saxon Reader. In Prose and Verse. With Grammatical Introduction, Notes, and Glossary. By Henry Sweet, M.A. Third Edition. Extra fcap. 8vo. cloth, 8s. 6d.

An Anglo-Saxon Primer, with Grammar, Notes, and Glossary. By the same Author. Extra fcap. 8vo. cloth, 2s. 6d.

The Ormulum; with the Notes and Glossary of Dr. R. M. White. Edited by Rev. R. Holt, M.A. 1878. 2 vols. Extra fcap. 8vo. cloth, 21s.

Specimens of Early English. A New and Revised Edition. With Introduction, Notes, and Glossarial Index. By R. Morris, LL.D., and W. W. Skeat, M.A.

Part I. From Old English Homilies to King Horn (A.D. 1150 to A.D. 1300). Extra fcap. 8vo. cloth, 9s.

Part II. From Robert of Gloucester to Gower (A.D. 1298 to A.D. 1393). Second Edition. Extra fcap. 8vo. cloth, 7s. 6d.

Specimens of English Literature, from the 'Ploughmans Crede' to the 'Shepheardes Calender' (A.D. 1394 to A.D. 1579). With Introduction, Notes, and Glossarial Index. By W. W. Skeat, M.A. Extra fcap. 8vo. cloth, 7s. 6d.

The Vision of William concerning Piers the Plowman, by William Langland. Edited, with Notes, by W. W. Skeat, M.A. Third Edition. Extra fcap. 8vo. cloth, 4s. 6d.

Chaucer. The Prioresses Tale; Sir Thopas; The Monkes Tale; The Clerkes Tale; The Squieres Tale, &c. Edited by W. W. Skeat, M.A. Second Edition. Extra fcap. 8vo. cloth, 4s. 6d.

Chaucer. The Tale of the Man of Lawe; The Pardoneres Tale; The Second Nonnes Tale; The Chanouns Yemannes Tale. By the same Editor. Extra fcap. 8vo. cloth, 4s. 6d. (See also p. 19.)

C

Old English Drama. *Marlowe's Tragical History of Dr. Faustus*, and Greene's Honourable History of Friar Bacon and Friar Bungay. Edited by A. W. Ward, M.A., Professor of History and English Literature in Owens College, Manchester. 1878. Extra fcap. 8vo. cloth, 5*s*. 6*d*.

Marlowe. Edward II. With Introduction, Notes, &c. By O. W. Tancock, M.A., Head Master of Norwich School. Extra fcap. 8vo. cloth, 3*s*.

Shakespeare. Hamlet. Edited by W. G. Clark, M.A., and W. Aldis Wright, M.A. Extra fcap. 8vo. stiff covers, 2*s*.

Shakespeare. Select Plays. Edited by W. Aldis Wright, M.A. Extra fcap. 8vo. stiff covers.

The Tempest, 1*s*. 6*d*.	King Lear, 1*s*. 6*d*.
As You Like It, 1*s*. 6*d*.	A Midsummer Night's Dream, 1*s*. 6*d*.
Julius Cæsar, 2*s*.	Coriolanus, 2*s*. 6*d*.
Richard the Third, 2*s*. 6*d*.	Henry the Fifth, 2*s*.

Twelfth Night. *In the Press.* (For other Plays, see p. 19.)

Milton. Areopagitica. With Introduction and Notes. By J. W. Hales, M.A., late Fellow of Christ's College, Cambridge. Second Edition. Extra fcap. 8vo. cloth, 3*s*.

Bunyan. Holy War. Edited by E. Venables, M.A. In the Press. (See also p. 20.)

Locke's Conduct of the Understanding. Edited, with Introduction, Notes, &c., by T. Fowler, M.A., Professor of Logic in the University of Oxford. Extra fcap. 8vo. cloth, 2*s*.

Addison. Selections from Papers in the Spectator. With Notes. By T. Arnold, M.A., University College. Second Edition. Extra fcap. 8vo. cloth, 4*s*. 6*d*.

Burke. Four Letters on the Proposals for Peace with the Regicide Directory of France. Edited, with Introduction and Notes, by E. J. Payne, M.A. Extra fcap. 8vo. cloth, 5*s*. (See also p. 20.)

Also the following in paper covers:—

Goldsmith. The Deserted Village. 2*d.*

Gray. Elegy and Ode on Eton College. 2*d.*

Johnson. Vanity of Human Wishes. With Notes by E. J. Payne, M.A. 4*d.*

Keats. Hyperion, Book I. With Notes by W. T. Arnold, B.A. 4*d.*

Milton. With Notes by R. C. Browne, M.A.

Lycidas, 3*d.* L'Allegro, 3*d.* Il Penseroso, 4*d.* Comus, 6*d.* Samson Agonistes, 6*d.*

Parnell. The Hermit. 2*d.*

Scott. Lay of the Last Minstrel. Introduction and Canto I, with Preface and Notes by W. Minto, M.A. 6*d.*

A SERIES OF ENGLISH CLASSICS,

Designed to meet the wants of Students in English Literature, by the late Rev. J. S. BREWER, M.A., of Queen's College, Oxford, and Professor of English Literature at King's College, London.

1. *Chaucer. The Prologue to the Canterbury* Tales; The Knightes Tale; The Nonne Prestes Tale. Edited by R. Morris, Editor of Specimens of Early English, &c., &c. Sixth Edition. Extra fcap. 8vo. cloth, 2*s.* 6*d.* (See also p. 17.)

2. *Spenser's Faery Queene.* Books I and II. Designed chiefly for the use of Schools. With Introduction, Notes, and Glossary. By G. W. Kitchin, M.A.

   Book I. Eighth Edition. Extra fcap. 8vo. cloth, 2*s.* 6*d.*

   Book II. Sixth Edition. Extra fcap. 8vo. cloth, 2*s.* 6*d.*

3. *Hooker. Ecclesiastical Polity, Book I.* Edited by R. W. Church, M.A., Dean of St. Paul's; formerly Fellow of Oriel College, Oxford. Second Edition. Extra fcap. 8vo. cloth, 2*s.*

4. *Shakespeare.* Select Plays. Edited by W. G. Clark, M.A., Fellow of Trinity College, Cambridge; and W. Aldis Wright, M.A., Trinity College, Cambridge. Extra fcap. 8vo. stiff covers.

   I. The Merchant of Venice. 1*s.*

   II. Richard the Second. 1*s.* 6*d.*

   III. Macbeth. 1*s.* 6*d.* (For other Plays, see p. 18.)

C 2

5. *Bacon.*

I. Advancement of Learning. Edited by W. Aldis Wright, M.A. Second Edition. Extra fcap. 8vo. cloth, 4*s*. 6*d*.

II. The Essays. With Introduction and Notes. By J. R. Thursfield, M.A., Fellow and formerly Tutor of Jesus College, Oxford.

6. *Milton.* Poems. Edited by R. C. Browne, M.A. 2 vols. Fourth Edition. Extra fcap. 8vo. cloth, 6*s*. 6*d*.

Sold separately, Vol. I. 4*s*.; Vol. II. 3*s*. (See also p. 19.)

7. *Dryden.* Select Poems. Stanzas on the Death of Oliver Cromwell; Astræa Redux; Annus Mirabilis; Absalom and Achitophel; Religio Laici; The Hind and the Panther. Edited by W. D. Christie, M.A. Second Edition. Extra fcap. 8vo. cloth, 3*s*. 6*d*.

8. *Bunyan. The Pilgrim's Progress, Grace* Abounding, Relation of the Imprisonment of Mr. John Bunyan. Edited, with Biographical Introduction and Notes, by E. Venables, M.A. 1879. Extra fcap. 8vo. cloth, 5*s*.

9. *Pope.* With Introduction and Notes. By Mark Pattison, B.D., Rector of Lincoln College, Oxford.

I. Essay on Man. Sixth Edition. Extra fcap. 8vo. 1*s*. 6*d*.
II. Satires and Epistles. Third Edition. Extra fcap. 8vo. 2*s*.

10. *Johnson. Rasselas; Lives of Pope and* Dryden. Edited by Alfred Milnes, B.A. (London), late Scholar of Lincoln College, Oxford. Extra fcap. 8vo. cloth, 4*s*. 6*d*.

11. *Burke.* Select Works. Edited, with Introduction and Notes, by E. J. Payne, M.A., of Lincoln's Inn, Barrister-at-Law, and Fellow of University College, Oxford.

I. Thoughts on the Present Discontents; the two Speeches on America. Second Edition. Extra fcap. 8vo. cloth, 4*s*. 6*d*.

II. Reflections on the French Revolution. Second Edition. Extra fcap. 8vo. cloth, 5*s*. (See also p. 18.)

12. *Cowper.* Edited, with Life, Introductions, and Notes, by H. T. Griffith, B.A., formerly Scholar of Pembroke College, Oxford.

I. The Didactic Poems of 1782, with Selections from the Minor Pieces, A.D. 1779–1783. Extra fcap. 8vo. cloth, 3*s*.

II. The Task, with Tirocinium, and Selections from the Minor Poems, A.D. 1784–1799. Extra fcap. 8vo. cloth, 3*s*.

II. LATIN.

An Elementary Latin Grammar. By John B. Allen, M.A., Head Master of Perse Grammar School, Cambridge. Third Edition, Revised and Corrected. Extra fcap. 8vo. cloth, 2*s*. 6*d*.

A First Latin Exercise Book. By the same Author. Third Edition. Extra fcap. 8vo. cloth, 2*s*. 6*d*.

A Second Latin Exercise Book. By the same Author. *Preparing.*

Anglice Reddenda, or Easy Extracts, Latin and Greek, for Unseen Translation. By C. S. Jerram, M.A. Second Edition, Revised and Enlarged. Extra fcap. 8vo. cloth, 2*s*. 6*d*.

Passages for Translation into Latin. For the use of Passmen and others. Selected by J. Y. Sargent, M.A., Fellow and Tutor of Magdalen College, Oxford. Fifth Edition. Extra fcap. 8vo. cloth, 2*s*. 6*d*.

First Latin Reader. By T. J. Nunns, M.A. Third Edition. Extra fcap. 8vo. cloth, 2*s*.

Second Latin Reader. In Preparation.

Caesar. The Commentaries (for Schools). With Notes and Maps. By Charles E. Moberly, M.A.

Part I. *The Gallic War.* Third Edition. Extra fcap. 8vo. cloth, 4*s*. 6*d*.

Part II. *The Civil War.* Extra fcap. 8vo. cloth, 3*s*. 6*d*.

The Civil War. Book I. Extra fcap. 8vo. cloth, 2*s*.

Cicero. Selection of interesting and descriptive passages. With Notes. By Henry Walford, M.A. In three Parts. Second Edition. Extra fcap. 8vo. cloth, 4*s*. 6*d*. Each Part separately, limp, 1*s*. 6*d*.

Part I. Anecdotes from Grecian and Roman History.

Part II. Omens and Dreams: Beauties of Nature.

Part III. Rome's Rule of her Provinces.

Cicero. Selected Letters (for Schools). With Notes. By the late C. E. Prichard, M.A., and E. R. Bernard, M.A. Second Edition. Extra fcap. 8vo. cloth, 3*s*.

Cicero. Select Orations (for Schools). With Notes. By J. R. King, M.A. Extra fcap. 8vo. cloth, 2*s*. 6*d*.

Cornelius Nepos. With Notes. By Oscar Browning, M.A. Second Edition. Extra fcap. 8vo. cloth, 2*s*. 6*d*.

Livy. Selections (for Schools). With Notes and Maps. By H. Lee-Warner, M.A. Extra fcap. 8vo. In Parts, limp, each 1*s*. 6*d*.

Part I. The Caudine Disaster.
Part II. Hannibal's Campaign in Italy.
Part III. The Macedonian War.

Livy. Books V–VII. With Introduction and Notes. By A. R. Cluer, B.A. Extra fcap. 8vo. cloth, 3*s*. 6*d*.

Ovid. Selections for the use of Schools. With Introductions and Notes, and an Appendix on the Roman Calendar. By W. Ramsay, M.A. Edited by G. G. Ramsay, M.A., Professor of Humanity, Glasgow. Second Edition. Extra fcap. 8vo. cloth, 5*s*. 6*d*.

Pliny. Selected Letters (for Schools). With Notes. By the late C. E. Prichard, M.A., and E. R. Bernard, M.A. Second Edition. Extra fcap. 8vo. cloth, 3*s*.

Catulli Veronensis Liber. Iterum recognovit, apparatum criticum prolegomena appendices addidit, Robinson Ellis, A.M. 1878. Demy 8vo. cloth, 16*s*.

A Commentary on Catullus. By Robinson Ellis, M.A. 1876. Demy 8vo. cloth, 16*s*.

Catulli Veronensis Carmina Selecta, secundum recognitionem Robinson Ellis, A.M. Extra fcap. 8vo. cloth, 3*s*. 6*d*.

Cicero de Oratore. With Introduction and Notes, by A. S. Wilkins, M.A., Professor of Latin, Owens College, Manchester.

Book I. 1879. 8vo. cloth, 6*s*. Book II. 1881. 8vo. cloth, 5*s*.

Cicero's Philippic Orations. With Notes. By J. R. King, M.A. Second Edition. 1879. 8vo. cloth, 10s. 6d.

Cicero. Select Letters. With English Introductions, Notes, and Appendices. By Albert Watson, M.A. Third Edition. 1881. Demy 8vo. cloth, 18s.

Cicero. Select Letters. Text. By the same Editor. Extra fcap. 8vo. cloth, 4s.

Cicero pro Cluentio. With Introduction and Notes. By W. Ramsay, M.A. Edited by G. G. Ramsay, M.A. Extra fcap. 8vo. cloth, 3s. 6d.

Horace. With a Commentary. Volume I. The Odes, Carmen Seculare, and Epodes. By Edward C. Wickham, M.A., Head Master of Wellington College. Second Edition. 1877. Demy 8vo. cloth, 12s.

Horace. A reprint of the above, in a size suitable for the use of Schools. Extra fcap. 8vo. cloth, 5s. 6d.

Livy, Book I. With Introduction, Historical Examination, and Notes. By J. R. Seeley, M.A., Regius Professor of Modern History, Cambridge. Third Edition. 1881. 8vo. cloth, 6s.

Ovid. P. Ovidii Nasonis Ibis. Ex Novis Codicibus Edidit. Scholia Vetera Commentarium cum Prolegomenis Appendice Indice addidit, R. Ellis, A.M. Demy 8vo. cloth, 10s. 6d.

Persius. The Satires. With a Translation and Commentary. By John Conington, M.A. Edited by Henry Nettleship, M.A. Second Edition. 1874. 8vo. cloth, 7s. 6d.

Virgil. With Introduction and Notes, by T. L. Papillon, M.A., Fellow of New College, Oxford. Two vols. crown 8vo. cloth, 10s. 6d.

Selections from the less known Latin Poets. By North Pinder, M.A. 1869. Demy 8vo. cloth, 15s.

Fragments and Specimens of Early Latin. With Introductions and Notes. 1874. By John Wordsworth, M.A. 8vo. cloth, 18s.

Tacitus. The Annals. With Essays and Notes. Preparing.

Vergil: Suggestions Introductory to a Study of the Aeneid. By H. Nettleship, M.A. 8vo. sewed, 1s. 6d.

Ancient Lives of Vergil; with an Essay on the Poems of Vergil, in connection with his Life and Times. By H. Nettleship, M.A. 8vo. sewed, 2s.

The Roman Satura: its original form in connection with its literary development. By H. Nettleship, M.A. 8vo. sewed, 1s.

A Manual of Comparative Philology. By T. L. Papillon, M.A., Fellow and Lecturer of New College. Second Edition. Crown 8vo. cloth, 6s.

The Roman Poets of the Augustan Age. By William Young Sellar, M.A., Professor of Humanity in the University of Edinburgh. Virgil. 1877. 8vo. cloth, 14s.

The Roman Poets of the Republic. By the same Author. New Edition, Revised and Enlarged. 1881. 8vo. cloth, 14s.

III. GREEK.

A Greek Primer, for the use of beginners in that Language. By the Right Rev. Charles Wordsworth, D.C.L. Bishop of St. Andrews. Sixth Edition, Revised and Enlarged Extra fcap. 8vo. cloth, 1s. 6d.

Graecae Grammaticae Rudimenta in usum Scholarum. Auctore Carolo Wordsworth, D.C.L. Twentieth Edition 1882. 12mo. cloth, 4s.

A Greek-English Lexicon, abridged from Liddell and Scott's 4to. edition, chiefly for the use of Schools. Nineteenth Edition. Carefully Revised throughout. 1880. Square 12mo. cloth, 7*s*. 6*d*.

Greek Verbs, Irregular and Defective; their forms, meaning, and quantity; embracing all the Tenses used by Greek writers, with references to the passages in which they are found. By W. Veitch. Fourth Edition. Crown 8vo. cloth, 10*s*. 6*d*.

The Elements of Greek Accentuation (for Schools): abridged from his larger work by H. W. Chandler, M.A., Waynflete Professor of Moral and Metaphysical Philosophy, Oxford. Extra fcap. 8vo. cloth. 2*s*. 6*d*.

A Series of Graduated Greek Readers:—

First Greek Reader. By W. G. Rushbrooke, M.L., formerly Fellow of St. John's College, Cambridge, Second Classical Master at the City of London School. Extra fcap. 8vo. cloth, 2*s*. 6*d*.

Second Greek Reader. By A. M. Bell, M.A. Extra fcap. 8vo. cloth, 3*s*. 6*d*.

Third Greek Reader. In Preparation.

Fourth Greek Reader; being Specimens of Greek Dialects. With Introductions and Notes. By W. W. Merry, M.A., Fellow and Lecturer of Lincoln College. Extra fcap. 8vo. cloth, 4*s*. 6*d*.

Fifth Greek Reader. Part I. Selections from Greek Epic and Dramatic Poetry, with Introductions and Notes. By Evelyn Abbott, M.A., Fellow of Balliol College. Extra fcap. 8vo. cloth, 4*s*. 6*d*.

Part II. By the same Editor. In Preparation.

The Golden Treasury of Ancient Greek Poetry; being a Collection of the finest passages in the Greek Classic Poets, with Introductory Notices and Notes. By R. S. Wright, M.A., Fellow of Oriel College, Oxford. Extra fcap. 8vo. cloth, 8*s*. 6*d*.

A Golden Treasury of Greek Prose, being a collection of the finest passages in the principal Greek Prose Writers, with Introductory Notices and Notes. By R. S. Wright, M.A., and J. E. L. Shadwell, M.A. Extra fcap. 8vo. cloth, 4*s*. 6*d*.

Aeschylus. Prometheus Bound (for Schools). With Introduction and Notes, by A. O. Prickard, M.A., Fellow of New College. Extra fcap. 8vo. cloth, 2*s.*

Aeschylus. Agamemnon. With Introduction and Notes by Arthur Sidgwick, M.A., Tutor of Corpus Christi College, Oxford; late Fellow of Trinity College, Cambridge, and Assistant Master of Rugby School. Extra fcap. 8vo. cloth, 3*s.*

Aeschylus. The Choephoroe. With Introduction and Notes by the same Editor. Preparing.

Aristophanes. In Single Plays, edited, with English Notes, Introductions, &c., by W. W. Merry, M.A. Extra fcap. 8vo.

The Clouds, 2*s.* The Acharnians, 2*s.*

Other Plays will follow.

Arrian. Selections (for Schools). With Notes. By J. S. Phillpotts, B.C.L., Head Master of Bedford School.

Cebes. Tabula. With Introduction and Notes by C. S. Jerram, M.A. Extra fcap. 8vo. cloth, 2*s.* 6*d.*

Euripides. Alcestis (for Schools). By C. S. Jerram, M.A. Extra fcap. 8vo. cloth, 2*s.* 6*d.*

Euripides. Helena. Edited with Introduction, Notes, and Critical Appendix, for Upper and Middle Forms. By C. S. Jerram, M.A. Extra fcap. 8vo. cloth, 3*s.*

Herodotus. Selections from. Edited, with Introduction, Notes, and a Map, by W. W. Merry, M.A., Fellow and Lecturer of Lincoln College. Extra fcap. 8vo. cloth, 2*s.* 6*d.*

Homer. Odyssey, Books I–XII (for Schools). By W. W. Merry, M.A. Twenty-fourth Thousand. Extra fcap. 8vo. cloth, 4*s.* 6*d.*

Book II, separately, 1*s.* 6*d.*

Homer. Odyssey, Books XIII–XXIV (for Schools). By the same Editor. Extra fcap. 8vo. cloth, 5*s.*

Homer. Iliad, Book I (for Schools). By D. B. Monro, M.A. Extra fcap. 8vo. cloth, 2*s.*

Homer. Iliad, Books VI and XXI. With Introduction and Notes. By Herbert Hailstone, M.A., late Scholar of St. Peter's College, Cambridge. Extra fcap. 8vo. cloth, 1*s.* 6*d.* each.

Lucian. Vera Historia (for Schools). By C. S. Jerram, M.A. Extra fcap. 8vo. cloth, 1*s.* 6*d.*

Plato. Selections (for Schools). With Notes. By B. Jowett, M.A., Regius Professor of Greek; and J. Purves, M.A., Fellow and late Lecturer of Balliol College, Oxford. In the Press.

Sophocles. In Single Plays, with English Notes, &c. By Lewis Campbell, M.A., Professor of Greek in the University of St. Andrew's, and Evelyn Abbott, M.A., Balliol College, Oxford. Extra fcap. 8vo. limp.

Oedipus Tyrannus. New and Revised Edition. 2*s.*
Oedipus Coloneus, Antigone, 1*s.* 9*d.* each.
Ajax, Electra, Trachiniae, Philoctetes, 2*s.* each.

Sophocles. Oedipus Rex: Dindorf's Text, with Notes by the present Bishop of St. David's. Ext. fcap. 8vo. limp, 1*s.* 6*d.*

Theocritus (for Schools). With Notes. By H. Kynaston, M.A. (late Snow), Head Master of Cheltenham College. Third Edition. Extra fcap. 8vo. cloth, 4*s.* 6*d.*

Xenophon. Easy Selections (for Junior Classes). With a Vocabulary, Notes, and Map. By J. S. Phillpotts, B.C.L., and C. S. Jerram, M.A. Third Edition. Extra fcap. 8vo. cloth, 3*s.* 6*d.*

Xenophon. Selections (for Schools). With Notes and Maps. By J. S. Phillpotts, B C.L., Head Master of Bedford School. Fourth Edition. Extra fcap. 8vo. cloth, 3*s.* 6*d.*

Xenophon. Anabasis, Book II. With Notes and Map. By C. S. Jerram, M.A. Extra fcap. 8vo. cloth, 2*s.*

Aristotle's Politics. By W. L. Newman, M.A., Fellow of Balliol College, Oxford.

Aristotelian Studies. I. On the Structure of the Seventh Book of the Nicomachean Ethics. By. J. C. Wilson, M.A., Fellow of Oriel College, Oxford. 1879. Medium 8vo. stiff, 5*s.*

Demosthenes and Aeschines. The Orations of Demosthenes and Æschines on the Crown. With Introductory Essays and Notes. By G. A. Simcox, M.A., and W. H. Simcox, M.A. 1872. 8vo. cloth, 12*s.*

Homer. Odyssey, Books I–XII. Edited with English Notes, Appendices, etc. By W. W. Merry, M.A., and the late James Riddell, M.A. 1876. Demy 8vo. cloth, 16*s.*

Homer. Iliad. With Introduction and Notes. By D. B. Monro, M.A., Vice-Provost of Oriel College, Oxford. Preparing.

A Grammar of the Homeric Dialect. By D. B. Monro, M.A., Fellow of Oriel College. Demy 8vo. cloth, 10*s.* 6*d.* *Just Published.*

Sophocles. The Plays and Fragments. With English Notes and Introductions, by Lewis Campbell, M.A., Professor of Greek, St. Andrews, formerly Fellow of Queen's College, Oxford. 2 vols.

Vol. I. Oedipus Tyrannus. Oedipus Coloneus. Antigone. Second Edition. 1879. 8vo. cloth, 16*s.*

Vol. II. Ajax. Electra. Trachiniae. Philoctetes. Fragments 1881. 8vo. cloth, 16*s.*

Sophocles. The Text of the Seven Plays. By the same Editor. Extra fcap. 8vo. cloth, 4*s.* 6*d.*

A Manual of Greek Historical Inscriptions. By E. L. Hicks, M.A., formerly Fellow and Tutor of Corpus Christi College, Oxford. Demy 8vo. cloth, 10*s.* 6*d.*

IV. FRENCH.

An Etymological Dictionary of the French Language, with a Preface on the Principles of French Etymology. By A. Brachet. Translated into English by G. W. Kitchin, M.A. Second Edition. Crown 8vo. cloth, 7*s*. 6*d*.

Brachet's Historical Grammar of the French Language. Translated into English by G. W. Kitchin, M.A. Fourth Edition. Extra fcap. 8vo. cloth, 3*s*. 6*d*.

A Short History of French Literature. By George Saintsbury, M.A. Crown 8vo. cloth, 10*s*. 6*d*.

Specimens of French Literature, from Villon to Hugo. Selected and arranged by the same Editor. *Preparing.*

A Primer of French Literature. By the same Author. Extra fcap. 8vo. cloth, 2*s*.

French Classics, Edited by GUSTAVE MASSON, B.A.

Corneille's Cinna, and Molière's Les Femmes Savantes. With Introduction and Notes. Extra fcap. 8vo. cloth, 2*s*. 6*d*.

Racine's Andromaque, and Corneille's Le Menteur. With Louis Racine's Life of his Father. Extra fcap. 8vo. cloth, 2*s*. 6*d*.

Molière's Les Fourberies de Scapin, and Racine's Athalie. With Voltaire's Life of Molière. Extra fcap. 8vo. cloth, 2*s*. 6*d*.

Selections from the Correspondence of Madame de Sévigné and her chief Contemporaries. Intended more especially for Girls' Schools. Extra fcap. 8vo. cloth, 3*s*.

Voyage autour de ma Chambre, by Xavier de Maistre; Ourika, by *Madame de Duras;* La Dot de Suzette, by *Fievée;* Les Jumeaux de l'Hôtel Corneille, by *Edmond About;* Mésaventures d'un Écolier, by *Rodolphe Töpffer*. Extra fcap. 8vo. cloth, 2*s*. 6*d*.

Regnard's Le Joueur and Brueys and Palaprat's Le Grondeur. Extra fcap. 8vo. cloth, 2*s*. 6*d*.

Louis XIV and his Contemporaries; as described in Extracts from the best Memoirs of the Seventeenth Century. With English Notes, Genealogical Tables, &c. Extra fcap. 8vo. cloth, 2*s.* 6*d.*

V. GERMAN.

LANGE'S German Course. By HERMANN LANGE, Teacher of Modern Languages, Manchester:

The Germans at Home; a Practical Introduction to German Conversation, with an Appendix containing the Essentials of German Grammar. Second Edition. 8vo. cloth, 2*s.* 6*d.*

The German Manual; a German Grammar, a Reading Book, and a Handbook of German Conversation. 8vo. cloth, 7*s.* 6*d.*

A Grammar of the German Language. 8vo. cloth, 3*s.* 6*d.*

This 'Grammar' is a reprint of the Grammar contained in 'The German Manual,' and, in this separate form, is intended for the use of Students who wish to make themselves acquainted with German Grammar chiefly for the purpose of being able to read German books.

German Composition; Extracts from English and American writers for Translation into German, with Hints for Translation in footnotes. In the Press.

Lessing's Laokoon. With Introduction, English Notes, etc. By A. Hamann, Phil. Doc., M.A. Extra fcap. 8vo. cloth, 4*s.* 6*d.*

Wilhelm Tell. A Drama. By Schiller. Translated into English Verse by E. Massie, M.A. Extra fcap. 8vo. cloth, 5*s.*

Also, Edited by C. A. BUCHHEIM, Phil. Doc., Professor in King's College, London:

Goethe's Egmont. With a Life of Goethe, &c. Third Edition. Extra fcap. 8vo. cloth, 3*s*.

Schiller's Wilhelm Tell. With a Life of Schiller; an historical and critical Introduction, Arguments, and a complete Commentary. Fourth Edition. Extra fcap. 8vo. cloth, 3*s*. 6*d*.

Lessing's Minna von Barnhelm. A Comedy. With a Life of Lessing, Critical Analysis, Complete Commentary, &c. Fourth Edition. Extra fcap. 8vo. cloth, 3*s*. 6*d*.

Schiller's Historische Skizzen; Egmonts Leben und Tod, and Belagerung von Antwerpen. Second Edition. Extra fcap. 8vo. cloth, 2*s*. 6*d*.

Goethe's Iphigenie auf Tauris. A Drama. With a Critical Introduction and Notes. Extra fcap. 8vo. cloth, 3*s*.

Modern German Reader. A Graduated Collection of Prose Extracts from Modern German writers:—

Part I. With English Notes, a Grammatical Appendix, and a complete Vocabulary. Second Edition. Extra fcap. 8vo. cloth, 2*s*. 6*d*.

Parts II and III in Preparation.

Lessing's Nathan der Weise. With Introduction, Notes, etc. Extra fcap. 8vo. cloth, 4*s*. 6*d*. *Just Published.*

In Preparation.

Becker's (K. F.) Friedrich der Grosse.

Schiller's Maria Stuart. With Notes, Introduction, &c.

Schiller's Jungfrau von Orleans. With Notes, Introduction, &c.

Selections from the Poems of *Schiller* and *Goethe*.

VI. MATHEMATICS, &c.

Figures Made Easy: a first Arithmetic Book. (Introductory to 'The Scholar's Arithmetic.') By Lewis Hensley, M.A., formerly Fellow and Assistant Tutor of Trinity College, Cambridge. Crown 8vo. cloth, 6*d.*

Answers to the Examples in Figures made Easy, together with two thousand additional Examples formed from the Tables in the same, with Answers. By the same Author. Crown 8vo. cloth, 1*s.*

The Scholar's Arithmetic; with Answers to the Examples. By the same Author. Crown 8vo. cloth, 4*s.* 6*d.*

The Scholar's Algebra. An Introductory work on Algebra. By the same Author. Crown 8vo. cloth, 4*s.* 6*d.*

Book-keeping. By R. G. C. Hamilton, Financial Assistant Secretary to the Board of Trade, and John Ball (of the Firm of Quilter, Ball, and Co.), Co-Examiners in Book-keeping for the Society of Arts. New and enlarged Edition. Extra fcap. 8vo. limp cloth, 2*s.*

A Course of Lectures on Pure Geometry. By Henry J. Stephen Smith, M.A., F.R.S., Fellow of Corpus Christi College, and Savilian Professor of Geometry in the University of Oxford.

Acoustics. By W. F. Donkin, M.A., F.R.S., Savilian Professor of Astronomy, Oxford. 1870. Crown 8vo. cloth, 7*s.* 6*d.*

A Treatise on Electricity and Magnetism. By J. Clerk Maxwell, M.A., F.R.S., Professor of Experimental Physics in the University of Cambridge. Second Edition. 2 vols. Demy 8vo. cloth, 1*l.* 11*s.* 6*d.*

An Elementary Treatise on Electricity. By the same Author. Edited by William Garnett, M.A. Demy 8vo. cloth, 7*s.* 6*d.*

A Treatise on Statics. By G. M. Minchin, M.A., Professor of Applied Mathematics in the Indian Engineering College, Cooper's Hill. Second Edition, Revised and Enlarged. 1879. 8vo. cloth, 14*s.*

A Treatise on the Kinetic Theory of Gases. By Henry William Watson, M.A., formerly Fellow of Trinity College, Cambridge. 1876. 8vo. cloth, 3*s*. 6*d*.

A Treatise on the Application of Generalised Coordinates to the Kinetics of a Material System. By H. W. Watson, M.A., and S. H. Burbury, M.A. 1879. 8vo. cloth, 6*s*.

Geodesy. By Colonel Alexander Ross Clarke, C.B., R.E. 1880. 8vo. cloth, 12*s*. 6*d*.

VII. PHYSICAL SCIENCE.

A Handbook of Descriptive Astronomy. By G. F. Chambers, F.R.A.S. Third Edition. 1877. Demy 8vo. cloth, 28*s*.

A Cycle of Celestial Objects. Observed, Reduced, and Discussed by Admiral W. H. Smyth, R.N. Revised, condensed, and greatly enlarged by G. F. Chambers, F.R.A.S. 1881. 8vo. cloth, 21*s*.

Chemistry for Students. By A. W. Williamson, Phil. Doc., F.R.S., Professor of Chemistry, University College, London. A new Edition, with Solutions. 1873. Extra fcap. 8vo. cloth, 8*s*. 6*d*.

A Treatise on Heat, with numerous Woodcuts and Diagrams. By Balfour Stewart, LL.D., F.R.S., Professor of Natural Philosophy in Owens College, Manchester. Fourth Edition. 1881. Extra fcap. 8vo. cloth, 7*s*. 6*d*.

Lessons on Thermodynamics. By R. E. Baynes, M.A., Senior Student of Christ Church, Oxford, and Lee's Reader in Physics. 1878. Crown 8vo. cloth, 7*s*. 6*d*.

Forms of Animal Life. By G. Rolleston, M.D., F.R.S., Linacre Professor of Physiology, Oxford. Illustrated by Descriptions and Drawings of Dissections. A New Edition in the Press.

D

Exercises in Practical Chemistry. Vol. I. Elementary Exercises. By A. G. Vernon Harcourt, M.A.; and H. G. Madan, M.A. Third Edition. Revised by H. G. Madan, M.A. Crown 8vo. cloth, 9*s*.

Tables of Qualitative Analysis. Arranged by H. G. Madan, M.A. Large 4to. paper covers, 4*s*. 6*d*.

Crystallography. By M. H. N. Story-Maskelyne, M.A., Professor of Mineralogy, Oxford; and Deputy Keeper in the Department of Minerals, British Museum. In the Press.

VIII. HISTORY.

The Constitutional History of England, in its Origin and Development. By William Stubbs, D.D., Regius Professor of Modern History. Library Edition. Three vols. demy 8vo. cloth, 2*l*. 8*s*.

Also in 3 vols. crown 8vo. price 12*s*. each.

Select Charters and other Illustrations of English Constitutional History, from the Earliest Times to the Reign of Edward I. Arranged and Edited by W. Stubbs, M.A. Fourth Edition. 1881. Crown 8vo. cloth, 8*s*. 6*d*.

A History of England, principally in the Seventeenth Century. By Leopold Von Ranke. Translated by Resident Members of the University of Oxford, under the superintendence of G. W. Kitchin, M.A., and C. W. Boase, M.A. 1875. 6 vols. 8vo. cloth, 3*l*. 3*s*.

A Short History of the Norman Conquest of England. By E. A. Freeman, M.A. Extra fcap. 8vo. cloth, 2*s*. 6*d*.

Genealogical Tables illustrative of Modern History. By H. B. George, M.A. Second Edition. Small 4to. cloth, 12*s*.

A History of France. With numerous Maps, Plans, and Tables. By G. W. Kitchin, M.A. In Three Volumes. 1873–77. Crown 8vo. cloth, each 10*s*. 6*d*.

Vol. 1. Second Edition. Down to the Year 1453.

Vol. 2. From 1453–1624.

Vol. 3. From 1624–1793.

A History of Germany and of the Empire, down to the close of the Middle Ages. By J. Bryce, D.C.L., Regius Professor of Civil Law in the University of Oxford.

A History of British India. By S. J. Owen, M.A., Reader in Indian History in the University of Oxford.

A Selection from the Despatches, Treaties, and other Papers of the Marquess Wellesley, K.G., during his Government of India. Edited by S. J. Owen, M.A., formerly Professor of History in the Elphinstone College, Bombay. 1877. 8vo. cloth, 1*l*. 4*s*.

A Selection from the Despatches, Treaties, and other Papers relating to India of Field-Marshal the Duke of Wellington, K.G. By the same Editor. 1880. 8vo. cloth, 24*s*.

A History of the United States of America. By E. J. Payne, M.A., Barrister-at-Law, and Fellow of University College, Oxford. In the Press.

A History of Greece from its Conquest by the Romans to the present time, B.C. 146 to A.D. 1864. By George Finlay, LL.D. A new Edition, revised throughout, and in part re-written, with considerable additions, by the Author, and Edited by H. F. Tozer, M.A., Tutor and late Fellow of Exeter College, Oxford. 1877. 7 vols. 8vo. cloth, 3*l*. 10*s*.

A Manual of Ancient History. By George Rawlinson, M.A., Camden Professor of Ancient History, formerly Fellow of Exeter College, Oxford. Second Edition. Demy 8vo. cloth, 14*s*.

A History of Greece. By E. A. Freeman, M.A., formerly Fellow of Trinity College, Oxford.

Italy and her Invaders, A.D. 376–476. By T. Hodgkin, Fellow of University College, London. Illustrated with Plates and Maps. 2 vols. 8vo. cloth, 1*l*. 12*s*.

IX. LAW.

The Elements of Jurisprudence. By Thomas Erskine Holland, D.C.L., Chichele Professor of International Law and Diplomacy, and Fellow of All Souls College, Oxford. Second Edition. Demy 8vo. cloth, 10*s*. 6*d*.

D 2

The Institutes of Justinian, edited as a recension of the Institutes of Gaius. By the same Editor. Second Edition, 1881. Extra fcap. 8vo. cloth, 5s.

Gaii Institutionum Juris Civilis Commentarii Quatuor; or, Elements of Roman Law by Gaius. With a Translation and Commentary by Edward Poste, M.A., Barrister-at-Law, and Fellow of Oriel College, Oxford. Second Edition. 1875. 8vo. cloth, 18s.

Select Titles from the Digest of Justinian. By T. E. Holland, D.C.L., Chichele Professor of International Law and Diplomacy, and Fellow of All Souls' College, Oxford, and C. L. Shadwell, B.C.L., Fellow of Oriel College, Oxford. 8vo. cloth, 14s.

Also sold in Parts, in paper covers, as follows:—

Part I. Introductory Titles. 2s. *6d.*
Part II. Family Law. 1s.
Part III. Property Law. 2s. *6d.*
Part IV. Law of Obligations (No. 1). 3s. *6d.*
Part IV. Law of Obligations (No. 2). 4s. *6d.*

An Introduction to the Principles of Morals and Legislation. By Jeremy Bentham. Crown 8vo. cloth, 6s. *6d.*

Elements of Law considered with reference to Principles of General Jurisprudence. By William Markby, M.A., Judge of the High Court of Judicature, Calcutta. Second Edition, with Supplement. 1874. Crown 8vo. cloth, 7s. *6d.* Supplement separately, 2s.

Alberici Gentilis, I.C.D., I.C. Professoris Regii, De Iure Belli Libri Tres. Edidit Thomas Erskine Holland I.C.D., Iuris Gentium Professor Chicheleianus, Coll. Omn. Anim. Socius. necnon in Univ. Perusin. Iuris Professor Honorarius. 1877. Small 4to. half morocco, 21s.

International Law. By William Edward Hall, M.A., Barrister-at-Law. Demy 8vo. cloth, 21s.

An Introduction to the History of the Law of Real Property, with original Authorities. By Kenelm E. Digby, M.A., of Lincoln's Inn, Barrister-at-Law. Second Edition. 1876. Crown 8vo. cloth, 7s. *6d.*

Principles of the English Law of Contract, and of Agency in its Relation to Contract. By Sir William R. Anson, Bart., D.C.L., Warden of All Souls College, Oxford Second Edition. Demy 8vo. cloth, 10s. 6d. *Just Published.*

X. MENTAL AND MORAL PHILOSOPHY.

Bacon. Novum Organum. Edited, with Introduction, Notes, &c., by T. Fowler, M.A., Professor of Logic in the University of Oxford. 1878. 8vo. cloth, 14s.

Locke's Conduct of the Understanding. Edited, with Introduction, Notes, &c., by T. Fowler, M.A., Professor of Logic in the University of Oxford. Extra fcap. 8vo. cloth, 2s.

Selections from Berkeley, with an Introduction and Notes. For the use of Students in the Universities. By Alexander Campbell Fraser, LL.D. Second Edition. Crown 8vo. cloth, 7s. 6d. (See also p. 13.)

The Elements of Deductive Logic, designed mainly for the use of Junior Students in the Universities. By T. Fowler, M.A., Professor of Logic in the University of Oxford. Seventh Edition, with a Collection of Examples. Extra fcap. 8vo. cloth, 3s. 6d.

The Elements of Inductive Logic, designed mainly for the use of Students in the Universities. By the same Author. Third Edition. Extra fcap. 8vo. cloth, 6s.

A Manual of Political Economy, for the use of Schools. By J. E. Thorold Rogers, M.A., formerly Professor of Political Economy, Oxford. Third Edition. Extra fcap. 8vo. cloth, 4s. 6d.

XI. ART, &c.

A Handbook of Pictorial Art. By R. St. J. Tyrwhitt, M.A., formerly Student and Tutor of Christ Church, Oxford. With coloured Illustrations, Photographs, and a chapter on Perspective by A. Macdonald. Second Edition. 1875. 8vo. half morocco, 18s.

A Music Primer for Schools. By J. Troutbeck, M.A., Music Master in Westminster School, and R. F. Dale, M.A., B. Mus., Assistant Master in Westminster School. Crown 8vo. cloth, 1s. 6d.

A Treatise on Harmony. By Sir F. A. Gore Ouseley, Bart., Professor of Music in the University of Oxford. Second Edition. 4to. cloth, 10s.

A Treatise on Counterpoint, Canon, and Fugue, based upon that of Cherubini. By the same Author. Second Edition. 4to. cloth, 16s.

A Treatise on Musical Form and General Composition. By the same Author. 4to. cloth, 10s.

The Cultivation of the Speaking Voice. By John Hullah. Second Edition. Extra fcap. 8vo. cloth, 2s. 6d.

XII. MISCELLANEOUS.

The Construction of Healthy Dwellings; namely Houses, Hospitals, Barracks, Asylums, &c. By Douglas Galton, late Royal Engineers, C.B., F.R.S., &c. Demy 8vo. cloth, 10s. 6d.

A Treatise on Rivers and Canals, relating to the Control and Improvement of Rivers, and the Design, Construction, and Development of Canals. By Leveson Francis Vernon-Harcourt, M.A., Balliol College, Oxford, Member of the Institution of Civil Engineers. 2 vols. (Vol. I, Text. Vol. II, Plates.) 8vo. cloth, 21s.

A System of Physical Education: Theoretical and Practical. By Archibald Maclaren. Extra fcap. 8vo. cloth, 7s. 6d.

Specimens of Lowland Scotch and Northern English. By Dr. J. A. H. Murray. Preparing.

English Plant Names from the Tenth to the Fifteenth Century. By J. Earle, M.A. Small fcap. 8vo. cloth, 5s.

An Icelandic Prose Reader, with Notes, Grammar, and Glossary by Dr. Gudbrand Vigfússon and F. York Powell, M.A. 1879. Extra fcap. 8vo. cloth, 10s. 6d.

Dante. Selections from the Inferno. With Introduction and Notes. By H. B. Cotterill, B.A. Extra fcap. 8vo. cloth, 4*s.* 6*d.*

Tasso. La Gerusalemme Liberata. Cantos i, ii. With Introduction and Notes. By the same Editor. Extra fcap. 8vo. cloth, 2*s.* 6*d.*

The Modern Greek Language in its relation to Ancient Greek. By E. M. Geldart, B.A. Extra fcap. 8vo. cloth, 4*s.* 6*d.*

Outlines of Textual Criticism applied to the New Testament. By C. E. Hammond, M.A., Fellow and Tutor of Exeter College, Oxford. Third Edition. Extra fcap. 8vo. cloth, 3*s.* 6*d.*

A Handbook of Phonetics, including a Popular Exposition of the Principles of Spelling Reform. By Henry Sweet, M.A. Extra fcap. 8vo. cloth, 4*s.* 6*d.*